Mastering macOS Programming

Combine macOS programming with Cocoa and Swift 3 to build powerful applications

Stuart Grimshaw

BIRMINGHAM - MUMBAI

Mastering macOS Programming

First published: May 2017

Production reference: 1300517

Published by Packt Publishing Ltd.
Livery Place
35 Livery Street
Birmingham
B3 2PB, UK.
ISBN 978-1-78646-169-8

www.packtpub.com

Credits

Author
Stuart Grimshaw

Reviewer
Fernando Rodríguez

Commissioning Editor
Ashwin Nair

Acquisition Editor
Divya Poojari

Content Development Editor
Arun Nadar

Technical Editors
Akansha Bathija
Shivani Mistry

Copy Editor
Dhanya Baburaj

Project Coordinator
Ritika Manoj

Proofreader
Safis Editing

Indexer
Aishwarya Gangawane

Graphics
Jason Monteiro

Production Coordinator
Shantanu Zagade

About the Author

Stuart Grimshaw has programmed for Apple computers since the days before OS X and has been involved with developing for the Apple Watch since its release. Born in the UK and having lived in Germany and the Netherlands, he is currently a freelance iOS/tvOS/macOS developer in Auckland, New Zealand, where he works on some of Australia-New Zealand's largest video and TV delivery apps and leads the research and development of both watchOS and tvOS applications. He is passionate about the potential of the Apple Watch and Apple TV, as well as Apple's Swift programming language, and is a keen proponent of beach coding.

About the Reviewer

Fernando Rodríguez has more than 20 years of experience in developing and teaching other developers. Although he currently specializes in the Apple stack of tools, he's a nerd of all trades with a strong interest in big data and automated trading.

He has taught iOS development at the Big Nerd Ranch, Udacity, and Keepcoding, ranging from Facebook developers to indie devs.

He was awarded as an "Outstanding instructor" at Udemy for his introductory course to iOS development. This course was mentioned in the Financial Times, Venture beat, and InformationWeek.

Code long and prosper!

www.PacktPub.com

For support files and downloads related to your book, please visit `www.PacktPub.com`.

Did you know that Packt offers eBook versions of every book published, with PDF and ePub files available? You can upgrade to the eBook version at `www.PacktPub.com` and as a print book customer, you are entitled to a discount on the eBook copy. Get in touch with us at `service@packtpub.com` for more details.

At `www.PacktPub.com`, you can also read a collection of free technical articles, sign up for a range of free newsletters and receive exclusive discounts and offers on Packt books and eBooks.

`https://www.packtpub.com/mapt`

Get the most in-demand software skills with Mapt. Mapt gives you full access to all Packt books and video courses, as well as industry-leading tools to help you plan your personal development and advance your career.

Why subscribe?

- Fully searchable across every book published by Packt
- Copy and paste, print, and bookmark content
- On demand and accessible via a web browser

Customer Feedback

Thanks for purchasing this Packt book. At Packt, quality is at the heart of our editorial process. To help us improve, please leave us an honest review on this book's Amazon page at https://www.amazon.com/dp/1786461692.

If you'd like to join our team of regular reviewers, you can e-mail us at customerreviews@packtpub.com. We award our regular reviewers with free eBooks and videos in exchange for their valuable feedback. Help us be relentless in improving our products!

For Jane.
And because this book is twice as thick as the last one, for my mum too.

Table of Contents

Preface

This book will take your Swift programming skills to a level at which you can work as a professional software engineer, using a step-by-step approach, ensuring that the introduction of each new concept is preceded by a thorough understanding of those preceding it.

The book covers a range of technologies, particularly those that you'll typically need, if not on day one of a new project (or a new job), then at least pretty soon after. These include not just Apple's Xcode, but also the Terminal app, Git version control, package management, the Swift REPL, and the LLDB debugger, all of which are essential skills.

Each chapter focuses on a particular topic or technology, giving you a deep dive into the skills and know-how that will take your work to a professional standard, in terms of code quality, maintainability, and robustness. This entails general topics, such as programming paradigms and design patterns, a general look at the Cocoa frameworks and their place in the macOS ecosystem, and of course specific technologies around networking, storage, and advanced graphics and animation.

Furthermore, a significant portion of the text is devoted to such thorny issues as concurrency, asynchronous programming, and error handling.

By the end of this book, you will be able to confidently approach projects of much greater size and complexity, and be well placed to comfortably deal with the various issues that all programming inevitably brings with it.

Coding is a never-ending journey. This book aims to get you on the right track, and a fair way along it.

What this book covers

Chapter 1, *Hello macOS*, explores the context in which the rest of the book is set and takes a look at developing for Apple platforms in general, and the direction that development is heading in.

Chapter 2, *Basic Swift*, takes a broad, high-level view of the Swift programming language.

Chapter 3, *Checking out the Power of Xcode*, introduces some pro-orientated aspects of this powerful, integrated Development Environment created by Apple.

Chapter 4, *MVC and Other Design Patterns*, covers a number of ways to help you plan your projects, from high-level conceptual down to the benefits offered by different styles of programming at the code level.

Chapter 5, *Advanced Swift*, investigates some of Swift's more powerful language features and idioms.

Chapter 6, *Cocoa Frameworks - The Backbone of Your Apps*, covers the large palette of ready-written framework code that relieve many of the burdens of low-level coding and boilerplate.

Chapter 7, *Creating Views Programmatically*, is concerned with giving you total control of your user interface, by moving beyond the constraints of visual UI editing.

Chapter 8, *Strings and Text*, looks at how to master the all-important textual features that are part of nearly every app you'll write for macOS.

Chapter 9, *Getting More from Interface Builder*, gets you through the maze of functionality offered by Apple's user interface creation tool.

Chapter 10, *Drawing on the Strength of Core Graphics*, drops us down to some low-level drawing routines, when the preconfigured UI offerings just aren't enough.

Chapter 11, *Core Animation*, takes you to the heart of what makes macOS such a polished and visually engaging platform.

Chapter 12, *Handling Errors Gracefully*, deals with the various tools you have at your disposal to handle all eventualities in your app, to produce a smooth and frustration-free user experience.

Chapter 13, *Persistent Storage*, introduces some of the most commonly used scenarios for storing data on disk.

Chapter 14, *The Benefits of Core Data*, takes you deeper into structured data persistence, keeping that critical user data organized and quickly accessible.

Chapter 15, *Connect to the World - Networking*, looks at connecting your code to the Internet, using the web session frameworks that Cocoa provides.

Chapter 16, *Concurrency and Asynchronous Programming*, aims to set some best practices, as well as investigate the appropriate tools, for dealing with time-sensitive data flows.

Chapter 17, *Understanding Xcode's Debugging Tools*, helps you master some of the most important tools at our disposal--Xcode's debugging features--for those moments when it doesn't go *quite* like your plan.

Chapter 18, *LLDB and the Command Line*, takes you into, and demystifies, working in the terminal, where all the really good stuff lives.

Chapter 19, *Deploying Third - Party Code*, helps you understand the role of third-party frameworks and libraries, and how to productively integrate them into your codebase.

Chapter 20, *Wrapping It Up*, gets your code from your hard drive to the App Store, avoiding the most common pitfalls along the way.

What you need for this book

To create and build the code presented here, you will need nothing more than Apple's Xcode software package, which you can download for free in the App Store, and a Mac to run it on. A number of other tools are introduced, such as the OS X Terminal app, which are already installed on your Mac.

Testing the code can be done on any installation of macOS.

Who this book is for

If you have intermediate knowledge of programming in Swift and are looking for the best way to take your development skills to a professional level, this book is just the right one for you.

Conventions

In this book, you will find a number of text styles that distinguish between different kinds of information. Here are some examples of these styles and an explanation of their meaning.

Code words in text, database table names, folder names, filenames, file extensions, pathnames, dummy URLs, user input, and Twitter handles are shown as follows: "But what if we want to make changes to, say, the app's Build Settings, or even its `Info.plist` file? Can we do that too?"

A block of code is set as follows:

```
cosmicDoor.shadowColor = .gold
cosmicDoor.shadowOffset = CGSize(width: 5.0, height: -5.0)
cosmicDoor.shadowRadius = 15.0
cosmicDoor.shadowOpacity = 1.0
```

When we wish to draw your attention to a particular part of a code block, the relevant lines or items are set in bold:

```
override func viewDidLoad()
{
  super.viewDidLoad()
  customView.wantsLayer = true
  setUpButton()
}
```

New terms and **important words** are shown in bold. Words that you see on the screen, for example, in menus or dialog boxes, appear in the text like this: "Click **Options**, and ensure that **Copy Items if Needed** is ticked."

Warnings or important notes appear in a box like this.

Tips and tricks appear like this.

Reader feedback

Feedback from our readers is always welcome. Let us know what you think about this book-what you liked or disliked. Reader feedback is important for us as it helps us develop titles that you will really get the most out of.

To send us general feedback, simply e-mail feedback@packtpub.com, and mention the book's title in the subject of your message.

If there is a topic that you have expertise in and you are interested in either writing or contributing to a book, see our author guide at www.packtpub.com/authors.

Customer support

Now that you are the proud owner of a Packt book, we have a number of things to help you to get the most from your purchase.

Downloading the example code

You can download the example code files for this book from your account at http://www.packtpub.com. If you purchased this book elsewhere, you can visit http://www.packtpub.com/support and register to have the files e-mailed directly to you.

You can download the code files by following these steps:

1. Log in or register to our website using your e-mail address and password.
2. Hover the mouse pointer on the **SUPPORT** tab at the top.
3. Click on **Code Downloads & Errata**.
4. Enter the name of the book in the **Search** box.
5. Select the book for which you're looking to download the code files.
6. Choose from the drop-down menu where you purchased this book from.
7. Click on **Code Download**.

Once the file is downloaded, please make sure that you unzip or extract the folder using the latest version of:

- WinRAR / 7-Zip for Windows
- Zipeg / iZip / UnRarX for Mac
- 7-Zip / PeaZip for Linux

The code bundle for the book is also hosted on GitHub at https://github.com/PacktPublishing/Mastering-macOS-Programming. We also have other code bundles from our rich catalog of books and videos available at https://github.com/PacktPublishing/. Check them out!

Downloading the color images of this book

We also provide you with a PDF file that has color images of the screenshots/diagrams used in this book. The color images will help you better understand the changes in the output. You can download this file from `https://www.packtpub.com/sites/default/files/down loads/MasteringmacOSProgramming_ColorImages.pdf`.

Errata

Although we have taken every care to ensure the accuracy of our content, mistakes do happen. If you find a mistake in one of our books-maybe a mistake in the text or the code-we would be grateful if you could report this to us. By doing so, you can save other readers from frustration and help us improve subsequent versions of this book. If you find any errata, please report them by visiting `http://www.packtpub.com/submit-errata`, selecting your book, clicking on the **Errata Submission Form** link, and entering the details of your errata. Once your errata are verified, your submission will be accepted and the errata will be uploaded to our website or added to any list of existing errata under the Errata section of that title.

To view the previously submitted errata, go to `https://www.packtpub.com/books/conten t/support` and enter the name of the book in the search field. The required information will appear under the **Errata** section.

Piracy

Piracy of copyrighted material on the Internet is an ongoing problem across all media. At Packt, we take the protection of our copyright and licenses very seriously. If you come across any illegal copies of our works in any form on the Internet, please provide us with the location address or website name immediately so that we can pursue a remedy.

Please contact us at `copyright@packtpub.com` with a link to the suspected pirated material.

We appreciate your help in protecting our authors and our ability to bring you valuable content.

Questions

If you have a problem with any aspect of this book, you can contact us at `questions@packtpub.com`, and we will do our best to address the problem.

1
Hello macOS

Goodbye and thank you OS X, hello and welcome macOS!

Sierra is here, also known as macOS 10.12. Apple's latest OS release, announced at the 2016 World Wide Developers Conference, offers the modern app developer more tools than ever with which to create engaging, productive, and entertaining apps for what an ever-increasing number of people deem the world's most advanced operating system.

Now that it's here, it seems it was a long time coming. Apple has renamed its desktop operating system to reflect its integral part in the Apple ecosystem, which comprises iOS, tvOS, watchOS, and finally macOS. This makes a lot of sense, since so much of what we know both as users and as developers from one platform is reflected in the others, sometimes very closely, sometimes adapted to differences in the hardware with which these platforms are used.

The cross-fertilization of Apple's platforms is rapidly increasing, giving new impetus to the desktop operating system that has in many ways taken a back seat to the mobile juggernaut that the iPhone and iPad represent. The massive adoption of mobile technologies has provided a spurt of innovation that Apple has begun to integrate seriously into what has become macOS. At the same time, decades of experience with macOS, then OS X, and now macOS have flowed into the mobile space as the processors in phones and other devices grow more powerful.

But although the name has changed, the OS is in every sense the next version of OS X, as the 10.12 version number makes clear. Visually, nothing has changed either; **About This Mac** still shows the same small info window--only the mountain has changed:

This is really a great time to be an app developer. It is no exaggeration to describe what is happening across the globe as the digital revolution, and whether we're interested in productivity, entertainment, dissemination of information, or any one of scores of other development genres, we find ourselves on extremely fertile ground. It seems there are as many opportunities out there as there are souls ready to take on the challenges of creating the software that continues to drive progress at a breathtaking pace.

When approaching macOS as a developer, you will be able to make use of any and all experience you may have with programming for OS X, and if your background is in iOS and/or one of the other platforms, you will also discover the great extent to which you can leverage the knowledge and skills you have developed on those platforms. Indeed, much of the code you write for one platform will be directly usable in another, with little or no adaptation necessary.

If you are coming from a non-Apple background, I think it is safe to say you will find developing in **Swift** for macOS a rewarding expansion of your skills. Swift is a rich, flexible and expressive language, but not one that is hard to learn. It has, to some extent, a syntactic similarity to many modern object-oriented programming languages such as Python and Java (okay, modern in comparison to earlier popular successes such as Lisp and Fortran).

In this first chapter, we will look at the following topics:

- The Swift programming language
- Xcode and other development tools
- How this book is structured
- Some prerequisites for getting the most from this book
- What this book will do for you once you have read it

So, let's look at where this book is going to take you, and how it will get you there.

It's going to be Swift

In just a little over two years, Swift has become one of the software development world's most talked-about programming languages, and is even the most forked repository on GitHub (but then, how many new languages have the power of a multinational like Apple behind them?). The language has undergone (and is still undergoing) incredibly rapid evolution, guided principally by Chris Lattner and the team at Apple, but also by the wider community, since it was open-sourced in December 2015, with proposals for language changes by non-Apple developers being included in the release of version 3.0. This radical departure from Apple's usually secretive product development strategy has meant that Swift has already benefitted from the experience and perspective of a great number of developers of mixed backgrounds (in every sense), with Apple itself saying that release 3.0 contains work by a total of three hundred and sixty-odd contributors.

If you are coming to Swift from Objective C for the first time, you will find it a much more succinct and clear language, one that needs fewer lines of boilerplate code, not to mention fewer semicolons, than its predecessor. If your background is in Python, JavaScript, or Java (to name the obvious ones), you'll find the code much easier to understand at first glance than would have been the case with Objective C--this is a good time to add Apple's platforms to your portfolio.

The code in this book will be in Swift version 3. Readers familiar with Swift 2.2 or earlier will notice that much has changed in the new version. We will not go into the details of those changes explicitly here, although they will be apparent from the next chapter onwards.

And more than Swift

But whether you refer to yourself as a software engineer, app developer, or hacker, there is substantially more to the job than writing Swift code inside Xcode. We will also be looking at interacting with bash shells in Terminal, dealing with files in XML format, data returned from the Web in JSON format, a little HTML, and the odd sprinkling of other languages, which may be used outside Xcode to good advantage.

We won't be going into a great amount of depth in these peripheral topics (if they can even be considered peripheral), but we will present what is essentially needed to get the job done, and give the reader an idea of the role they play in the larger picture. The interested reader will find no shortage of books and web resources with which to expand on the information presented here. There are also a number of articles available on the website that accompanies this book: `http://grimshaw.de/macOS-book`.

It's going to be Xcode and more

Much of this book, particularly the later chapters, will look at leveraging the considerable power of the Xcode-integrated development environment, in order to familiarize the reader with many aspects of development that go beyond code writing, to include debugging, performance measurement and improvement, working with source control within a team, and many others.

Software development is rarely a matter of using one single program, and we will be utilizing several tools other than Xcode to get the most out of the time we spend coding, compiling, and testing our work. You might be pleased to learn that none of these tools are going to cost you any money (although like any other tool, they come at the cost of a certain amount of time to be invested in order to reach a moderate level of proficiency). You might be even more pleased to learn that we will be covering this ground step by step, and no previous knowledge is assumed.

Prerequisites

Despite the varied backgrounds that readers of this book are likely to have, we will make some broad assumptions about the level of skill and experience you bring with you. There are also some hardware requirements, though nothing you're unlikely to have already.

To be able to comfortably follow this book, you will need to have the following:

- A reasonably high level of familiarity with the macOS/OS X operating system and its day-to-day use, including trackpad gestures (in addition to mouse clicks, obviously), the file system as accessed through the Finder, and the general features of both Apple and third-party software.
- Some basic experience of programming using an object-oriented programming language such as Swift, Objective C, or Java.
- An Apple computer running at least macOS Sierra, with Xcode 8.0 or above already installed.
- Some chapters will require an Internet connection.

There are also a number of areas in which some experience will prove useful, though not necessarily essential, before we start, which are as follows:

- Using the Terminal app, and some knowledge of basic **bash** operation
- An understanding of the general principles of **HTTP** requests and responses, including **JSON** data
- Some knowledge of XML and HTML will also help

If any of those are completely new to you, you might want to find a little time to familiarize yourself with them. The website that accompanies this book contains introductions to all of the topics listed here, as well as several others is `http://www.grimshaw.de/macOS-book`.

The book's overall structure

Broadly speaking, the book can be thought of as consisting of three parts:

1. The first few chapters will make sure that the basics have been covered, albeit very concisely. Less experienced readers may find it advisable to take these chapters slowly and possibly that some extra work is necessary to get up to speed.

2. The second part concerns topics that are very much tied to programming for Apple devices in general, and macOS in particular, making use of native code provided by Apple through the **Cocoa** application programming interface. The chapters don't necessarily need to be read sequentially.
3. The third part of the book moves beyond writing the code, to look at how to handle some of the challenges involved in producing robust and maintainable code in an up-to-date and practice-oriented context, and the tools that are available to make that easier.

How Unix, macOS, Cocoa, and AppKit fit together

In the beginning, there was Unix, developed by AT&T in the 1970s and initially intended for use inside the Bell system. Toward the end of that decade, the University of California, Berkeley, released a modified--and free--version of it, called **Berkeley Software Distribution (BSD)**.

Darwin

Apple released the Darwin operating system in 2000. It was derived from BSD and a number of other sources, including NextStep (which is why the Cocoa class names are generally prefixed with the letters NS), and contains the I/O Kit device driver API that saves you ever having to worry about getting keyboard or mouse input into the computer, and a million other things.

Info about Darwin is available at `puredarwin.org`, and if device drivers are your thing, Apple's I/O Kit documentation starts here:
`https://developer.apple.com/library/mac/documentation/DeviceDrivers/Conceptual/`
`IOKitFundamentals/Introduction/Introduction.html.`

macOS

Strictly speaking, macOS, like OS X before it, is a platform built on the Darwin operating system, although we generally think of it as being the OS itself (hardly surprising given the name), and it provides a collection of frameworks, a large group of which comprise Cocoa, which turn what is basically Unix into something that is basically much more than Unix.

Cocoa

All the shiny stuff, all those browser windows, sliders and buttons, movies, animations, sounds, file access (this list could get very long), what Cocoa does. Cocoa is what you use to create apps, mixed in with some logical organization and design. If devs were portrait painters, then Cocoa would be a cupboard full of brushes and tubes of paint.

Cocoa itself breaks down into different layers, including what Apple refers to as the Cocoa umbrella framework, made up of the AppKit, Foundation, and Core Data frameworks.

AppKit is part of the Cocoa application layer, and is made up of 125 classes and protocols, providing macOS with its user interface; event handling, drawing, menus, views, tables, text and fonts, printing, file system access, and so on are all to be found in AppKit.

Foundation provides us with the lower-level stuff such as data storage, arrays, dates, notifications and such, as well as abstract data classes that are not used directly, but from which many other classes are derived.

Core Data, as we will see in `Chapter 9`, *Getting More from Interface Builder*, provides us with a powerful framework for the management of persistent data.

The term Cocoa is very fluid; even at Apple it gets used in a more general sense to mean the whole range of frameworks, at many levels, available to you, the developer. And does it matter? I would argue that it does not. Whether a framework belongs to AppKit or Foundation, or some other layer, is going to make very little difference to your ability to craft engaging and useful software.

Harnessing that power

Cocoa is basically many, many lines of code, written by Apple's own developers, for use on its own platforms. How many lines? I'd love to know, too, but I don't see Cupertino releasing that kind of information anytime soon. Suffice to say, drawing a window on a screen starting with nothing but 1s and 0s is far from trivial, and you should be glad you don't need to do it yourself. Apple has done it for you, millions of times. Despite the fact that drawing such a window involves as much logic as a small Xcode project itself, all you need to do is write a couple of lines of code and there it is, ready for you to add the sexy stuff. All the detail, all that boilerplate, has been abstracted away for you. And the same goes for countless other blocks of repetitive but superbly tweaked code that you will likely never see (and quite possibly never think about again).

All you need to do to make use of this mountain of tested, optimized, and field-hardened code is issue the correct instructions to the libraries, which means knowing the Cocoa API. It's a very large API, to be sure. And nobody--nobody at all, not even at Apple--knows all of it. Some parts you may have learned inside and out already; others you certainly will learn. But for as long as you write Cocoa apps, you will be looking things up in Apple's documentation, or searching Stack Overflow and other developer forums for help and advice.

 In case you don't know it (yet), Stack Overflow frequently abbreviated to SO, is one of the most valuable resources on the Web. You can search and read the site without membership, but once you're signed up, you can post questions and, indeed, answer them. The rules are quite strict, and the levels of discipline and respect are very high. Seriously, if you're into development, you'll love SO. It can be found here: http://stackoverflow.com.

The various Cocoa frameworks presented in the second section of this book are those that are likely to be of relevance to a majority of readers. A firm grounding in these topics will provide you with a solid fundament on which to mold Apple's huge repository of code into apps of a professional standard, and with experience of one set of frameworks, you'll find it ever easier to get to grips with new ones, even to the extent that you will often be able to make an educated guess rather than consulting the docs. The Cocoa APIs have been updated to work more expressively with Swift, which in turn means it becomes easier to recognize the patterns being used in the frameworks you use, as the interface between Cocoa and the Swift language itself become more consistent.

The serious developer's toolkit

The third part of the book will cover topics that concern any desktop application developer, but here they are dealt with in the context of programming Cocoa apps for macOS.

Some of these will seem more appealing than others. There are many topics in the early stages of learning to program that are (or perhaps just seem to be) less important and/or exciting, such as just writing a few pages full of code and hitting the **Run** button; but these things later become an essential and rewarding part of what we do as developers. As one moves from working on relatively small and simple projects, usually as a sole coder, to working on larger, more complex, and longer-term projects, frequently as part of a team of both devs and management staff, there is a profound change in priorities, as code clarity, code re-use, integration, documentation, and communication become major aspects of our work.

There are also fascinating challenges around dealing with some of the unpredictable aspects of software that needs to integrate itself successfully with a digital universe lying outside our app and beyond our control, particularly with regard to the Internet, as our code will need to deal robustly, efficiently, and gracefully with whatever comes back at it across the network.

Producing high-quality code, while working quickly and communicating effectively, is partly a matter of experience and partly a matter of knowing what tools are available to make the best use of the hours you spend coding, and which techniques to choose when designing the internal workings of your app.

These chapters will look at the challenges posed by asynchronous programming, error handling, debugging, and many other areas that are an indispensable part of producing software in a professional environment: on time, on budget, maintainable code. Which is basically what the industry needs from you.

And for which you will be handsomely paid. Just saying.

What you'll get from this book

This brings us quite nicely to the goals of this book.

Well, in a general sense, its goal is to help you reach yours, of course. But how exactly are we going to do that?

The focus of this book is very much on real-world programming skills and best practices, with a clear preference for techniques that provide solid, maintainable code over a long app lifetime, as opposed to the latest Thing from the developer conferences. Similarly, we will concentrate more on the functional interior of the code rather than short-lived user-interface design trends that will be of little interest a year from now.

There is also a strong emphasis on developing the skills that a developer will need when working in the industry, within a team that may include other developers, including those working on different platforms, as well as graphic artists, technical leads, project and product managers, system administrators and back-end developers, and any number of other roles with which it is necessary to communicate with clarity and accuracy. These people will have their own corners of the business to attend to, to which you will frequently have to adapt your work, making it all the more important that you have a number of tools at your disposal to deal with rapidly changing requirements and priorities.

Frequently, it is necessary to include third-party frameworks and libraries, often ones that you would not choose yourself: maybe because the team has been using them within a project already; maybe because a client has requested the addition of an analytics engine to an app, or to add functionality to an app not available natively. These are perhaps the most common reasons, but they are not the only ones, and an ability to integrate these resources into your work is an essential part of modern app development, and one that is only likely to increase with time.

Professional coding means writing clear code, adhering where appropriate (which means most of the time) to established practices. We will prefer simplicity over cleverness every time, and hopefully this is a habit you will develop yourself.

 Write every line of code for somebody else. That may mean someone else in your team, or it might mean your successor when you move on. It will frequently mean yourself in a year's time--which is when you'll be most glad you wrote logical, well-structured code.

A huge part of coding wisely means knowing which techniques to deploy, and which are better left out, in any given situation. It means learning to strike the right balance between clarity and the inevitable complexity that results from the growth of a project over time.

You will also learn to deal with version control safely, an essential part of working on larger projects, even as a sole developer.

Debugging your code is an essential part of programming, and we will look at the tools available to you in Xcode to make these tasks easier, faster, and safer. Fixing bugs can become a major part of your work, and your skills in this area will contribute greatly to your ability to deliver reliable code.

Finally, we will not shy away from references to resources beyond this book. The time is long gone when a developer can be expected to know every detail of a language or platform, and knowing where to search for documentation and help is an indispensable part of our work as developers. It has been said that a good developer spends two thirds of the time reading and one third coding. Although that should perhaps be taken with a pinch of salt, if only because it overlooks writing documentation, testing, and talking to clients, managers, and team members, it nevertheless makes clear that writing code is not only not everything, it's not even most of it.

Our highest priority is to impart knowledge that will be immediately and enduringly useful to you as a developer. That may seem like stating the obvious, but you will notice that the content of this book does not necessarily reflect the buzz and hype around the blogosphere's latest shiny new toys. It is true that even the oldest, best-tested tools were new once, but it is not our intention here to get lost in the esoteric delights of functional programming, protocol-oriented programming, reactive programming, or whatever else is the subject of heated debate at the time of writing.

That is not to say that such topics are somehow not thrilling, valuable, and thought-provoking. They most definitely are, but they are not within the scope of this book. However, the website is not limited in size, so we'll see what we can do.

Also not covered here is the migration and adaptation of Swift 2 code to Swift 3. There will doubtless be any number of articles out there covering this, but for the purposes of this book, we will treat Swift 3 as the only version of interest. And although it's an important topic, moving from Objective C to Swift is beyond the scope of this book.

Finally, we will not cover unit tests and integration testing. This field is a wide one, space here is limited, and the reader is encouraged to find resources that can do justice to both the topic itself, and the wide range of opinions surrounding it.

Summary

None of this is going to involve quantum leaps of comprehension. Assuming you understand the concepts summarized in the first few chapters (and we *will* make that assumption), this book will guide you, step by step, from a position of being able to code adequately to a position of being able to code well.

You will not only write better code, you'll write faster; you will be able to get across new frameworks more quickly; you'll soak up more of what you read on the Web and elsewhere; you'll be able to communicate your thoughts clearly to work colleagues and clients.

And I hope, very much, that you'll continue to feel that feeling of accomplishment you felt the first time you coded up `Hello World` in whatever language it was at the time. It's that spark that will enable you to code not only well, but brilliantly, if you stick with it.

The next chapter will provide a rapid-but-thorough review of the basics of the language's core features and syntax, assuming a basic familiarity with object-oriented programming, but no advanced knowledge of Swift's previous incarnations. So, without further ado, let us take a rapid tour of the basics of Swift 3.0.

2
Basic Swift

So, let's get going with a rapid rundown of Swift's basic types and syntax. As befits a book aimed at developers with some experience of programming under their belts, this chapter will not be about the basics of programming, but simply an overview of what we will assume you know as we move through the following chapters. Think of it as a kind of Swift comments cheat-sheet, if you like.

You already understand something of variable declaration, control flow, arrays and dictionaries, and functions. Make sure you fully understand everything that is presented in this chapter, and if there are any concepts you don't understand by the end of it, it's probably a good idea to delve into them somewhat before moving on to `Chapter 5`, *Advanced Swift*.

I have tried in this chapter to flag a few typical *gotchas* that occur when coming from other languages or earlier versions of Swift. Some of the terms used in Swift are used in other languages with a different meaning, and some concepts behave differently.

If Swift is the only language you have used, and you have used it often, you might want to skip this chapter. But you'll miss all of the wit and enlightening commentary if you do.

 This chapter, and indeed the whole book, does not try to provide an exhaustive documentation of the Swift language. It's a good idea (sooner or later) to have read Apple's eBook, *The Swift Programming Language*. This is available for free in *iBooks*.

By the time we reach the end of this chapter, you should have a basic but solid understanding of the following topics:

- Swift's simple data types
- Array, dictionaries, and sets
- Value and reference types
- Operators
- Structs, classes, and other data structures
- Optionals, and why they are important
- Control-flow statements
- Defining and calling functions

Variables and types

We can declare variables as follows:

```
var a: Int = 1
```

In the preceding line of code, a is declared to be of type Int, with a value of 1. Since only an Int can be assigned the value 1, Swift can automatically infer the type of a, and it is not necessary to explicitly include the type information in the variable declaration:

```
var a = 1
```

In the preceding code, it is equally clear to both Swift and the reader what type a belongs to.

What, no semicolons?

You can add them if you want to, and you'll have to if you want to put two statements on the same line (why would you do that?). But no, semicolons belong to C and its descendants, and despite its many similarities to that particular family of languages, Swift has left the nest.

The value of a var can be changed by simply assigning to it a new value:

```
var a = 1
a = 2
```

However, in Swift, we can also declare a *constant*, which is *immutable*, using the `let` keyword:

```
let b = 2
```

The value of `b` is now set permanently. The following attempt to change it will produce a compiler error:

```
b = 3
```

The error is shown in the following screenshot:

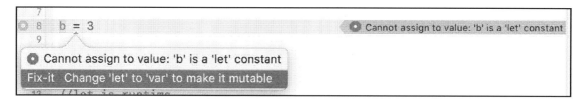

As can be seen here, Xcode also suggests how to fix it, by offering to change the `let` declaration to a `var`.

If you do not need to change a variable, use `let`. Indeed, if you never change the value of a `var` once you have declared it, Xcode will suggest that you change it to `let`:

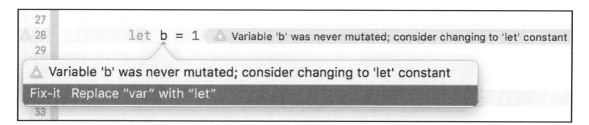

The `let` keyword is a little different to using the `const` keyword in C (or its equivalent in many other languages), because the value of the declaration is evaluated at runtime, not compile time, enabling it to be set dynamically, according to values not available at compile time.

Number types

Swift offers a range of number types typical of modern programming languages.

Integers

Most of the time, you will use `Int` for all integers. Apple's advice is to use `Int` for all cases except where you need to work with a specific size of integer. Similarly, `Int` should be preferred to `UInt` even for values that cannot be negative, unless you need an unsigned integer type of the same size as the platform's native word size.

If you're not sure what that means, don't worry about it; just use `Int`.

The following table shows all the integer types available in Swift, along with their maximum and minimum values (unsigned minima are, of course, 0):

Integer Type	Value
Int.min	-9223372036854775808
Int.max	9223372036854775807
Int8.min	-128
Int8.max	127
Int16.min	-32768
Int16.max	32767
Int32.min	-2147483648
Int32.max	2147483647
Int64.max	-9223372036854775808
Int64.min	9223372036854775807
UInt.max	18446744073709551615
UInt8.max	255
Int16.max	32767
UInt32.max	4294967295
UInt64.max	18446744073709551615

You have a number of options when using `Int`. Very handy is a feature that lets you add underscores in any way that helps you to present the number more clearly (from a human perspective), which the compiler simply ignores:

```
let million = 1_000_000
```

Can anyone here claim they have never been out by a factor of ten due to a 0 typo?

Integers can also be expressed in binary, octal, and hexadecimal form:

```
let myBinary = 0b101010
let myOctal = 0o52
let myHexadecimal = 0x2a
```

All three of the numbers are of the type `Int` with a value of 42. Thus, they can be used together in calculations:

```
let c = myBinary + myOctal
```

No complaints from the compiler here.

To declare a non-whole number, you have two native options. You can declare a decimal number with the `Double` type:

```
let myDouble = 42.0
```

In this case, Swift will infer `myDouble` to be of type `Double` (whatever you care to name it, it's not understanding `myDouble`).

So, if you need a `Float`, you'll need to make the type explicit, as follows:

```
let myFloat: Float = 42.0
```

Number types are not automatically cast to compatible types as they are in many languages, so conversion from one number type to another needs to be done explicitly. The following code will produce a type error:

```
let myResult: myFloat * myDouble
```

But each number type has an initialization method that will take a value of another number type as its argument:

```
let a = Double(42)
let b = Int(4.9)
let c = Int("42")
```

Note that the value of b will be 4, as one would expect of conversion from a decimal type to an integer type. To round a double to the nearest integer, you'll need to use round:

```
let d = round(4.9)
let e = Int(d)
```

The following line is a little more succinct:

```
let e = Int(round(4.9))
```

Booleans

In Swift, Booleans are capitalized:

```
let myBool: Bool = true
```

It will not surprise you to learn that Boolean values come in two flavors: true and false.

However, that really is all you get; true doesn't equal 1, and false doesn't mean nil, or 0, or anything else but false:

```
let myBool = false
myBool == nil // no it doesn't
myBool == 0   // error
```

The second line evaluates to false, because myBool *does* have a value and so will not be equivalent to nil (whether its value is true or false). You'll see shortly that Swift is very choosy about how it handles the concept of nil (see the *Optionals* section of this chapter).

The third line will not even compile--you'll get an error informing you that you can't compare a Bool with an Int. In Swift, you can have 0 teeth, but you can't have false teeth.

Strings

In Swift, the syntax around using Strings is very much simpler than in Objective C, and the basics are similar to many modern languages.

We can create a string literal by using double quotes, as follows:

```
let salutation = "Hi Sally"
```

Single quotes won't do it:

```
let salutation = 'Hi Bob' // error
```

We can declare the empty string as an empty literal:

```
var emptyString1 = ""
```

We can also declare it by using the `String` initializer:

```
var emptyString2 = String()
```

The empty `String` object is not `nil`. To declare a `String` with no initialization, producing a `nil` `String` object, we do the following:

```
var nilString: String
```

To check for an empty (but non-nil) string, we can use the `.isEmpty` method of String:

```
emptyString1.isEmpty //returns true
```

A `String` comparison is simpler than comparing `NSString` objects:

```
emptyString1 == emptyString2
emptyString1 != emptyString2
"a" < "b"
```

As you can see, the < and > operators behave as one would wish them to, with the preceding code evaluating to `true`.

`String` objects are like any other objects in Swift; they can be declared to be mutable or immutable with `var` and `let`, respectively.

String concatenation is similarly intuitive:

```
let greeting = "Hello " + "World"
```

(There we are, we have got *Hello World* out of the way.)

`String` has methods for changing the case of a `String` object:

```
let upper = greeting.uppercased()
let lower = greeting.lowercased()
```

String representations of other objects in Swift are mercifully simple, by including the object in \(...) within the quotes:

```
let count = 11
let average = 1.2
let message = "\( count) tasks, average grade \( average)"
```

This prints to the console:

```
11 tasks, average grade 1.2
```

Unlike NSString objects in Objective C, String objects are passed by value, not reference (see the *Passed by value* section of this chapter).

Much was made of the fact that Swift will accept any Unicode characters, including emojis, making the following a perfectly legal String:

```
let s2 = "Anyone fancy    ?"
```

But this also means that a lot of Unicode goodness is available to us with no extra work, and we'll be looking at this in more depth later on.

A String is not an array; you cannot subscript it with myString[0] or similar. To access individual Characters, use the .characters property of String, which is a CharacterView Struct, similar to an Array, more of which in Chapter 5, *Advanced Swift*:

```
let name = "Babbage"
let charlesChars = name.characters
```

Declaring a Character literal requires explicit typing (since it would otherwise produce a String of length 1):

```
let dollarCharacter: Character = "$"
```

However, once the type is set, reassignment looks the same as String reassignment:

```
var currencyCharacter: Character = "$"
currencyCharacter = "£"
```

It might be a good idea to name the variable appropriately, to avoid confusion.

Use the `append` method of String to append a `Character` to a `String`:

```
var region = "NZ"
region.append(dollarCharacter)
```

The `region` variable is now `"NZ$"`.

We will take a closer look at the `String` and `Character` types in `Chapter 5`, *Advanced Swift* (and there is much to look at), but it's worth mentioning here, for readers familiar with Objective C, that `String` objects can be cast to `NSString` objects in order to access the full functionality of the latter.

Printing to the console

Swift's `print()` command automatically calls an object's String representation, so these last two lines of code are equivalent:

```
let age = 6
print("\(age)")
print(age)
```

Comments

Swift has adopted C-style comments of both forms:

```
// We have used this one already
// in previous sections of this chapter
```

When it starts to get messy, with `//` at the beginning of each commented line, we have the following multiline comments:

```
/*
This is a multiline
comment, for those times when
you just can't say it
in a few words
*/
```

Unlike some languages, you can nest these comments, which is handy if you need to comment out a large section of code that itself contains comments:

```
/*
Comments can be nested,
/*
like this one
*/
which can be helpful.
*/
```

Arrays, dictionaries, and sets

Swift offers a comprehensive set of collection types, as one would expect. In common with many other languages, each of these collection types will only hold values of the same type. Thus, the type of an Array of Int values is distinct from the type of an Array of Float values, for example. If you're coming from Objective C, you may quickly come to appreciate the type safety and simplicity of Swift Array objects over NSArray.

There are no separate mutable and immutable collection types, as such, since all objects in Swift can be declared with either var or let.

Arrays

Arrays are zero-based, and look like this:

```
let myArr = [21, 22, 23]
```

They are equipped with a pretty standard set of methods, such as count and accessor methods:

```
let count = myArr.count // 3
let secondElmt = myArr[1] // 22
let firstElmt = myArr.first // 21
let lastElmt = myArr.last // 23
```

Elements are set, logically enough, as follows:

```
myArr[1] = 100
```

They are a lot more convenient to work with than `NSArray`:

```
let arr1 = [1,2]
let arr2 = [3,4]
let arr3 = arr1 + arr2 // [1,2,3,4]
```

So, concatenating arrays is nice and simple, and this approach is reflected across the methods available on Swift's collection objects.

We can declare an `Array` object without initializing it, as follows:

```
var emptyArr1: [Int]
var emptyArr2: Array<Int>
```

These two methods are equivalent.

We can declare and initialize an empty array at the same time with one of the following methods, which here, too, are all equivalent:

```
var emptyArr3 = [Int]()
var emptyArr4: [Int] = []
var emptyArr5: Array<Int> = []
```

Once the type of `Array` is clear:

```
var myArr = [1,2,3]
```

Here, `myArr` is initialized as an `Array` of `Int` type; we can set it to the empty array with just the empty brackets:

```
myArr = []
```

If we declare an `Array` object with `let`, we cannot change its values:

```
let constArr = [1,2,3]
constArr[0] = 5
```

The second line will produce a compiler error.

If you are familiar with Swift's collection types, you'll know there's a lot more than this; but more of that later.

Dictionaries

`Dictionary` objects look like this:

```
let myDict = ["One":"Eins", "Two":"Zwei", "Three":"Drei"]
```

They are how Swift stores key-value pairs. A value is set and retrieved by using its key instead of an index, as one would with an array. Each key can occur only once in any particular `Dictionary`.

 They're called `Dictionary` in Swift, but they're called `map` in Clojure, and `object` in JavaScript. That's not helped by the fact that both `map` and `object` are used in Swift, but have rather different meanings. Elsewhere, you may find dictionaries referred to as `associative arrays` or `symbol tables`. And yes, the first time I worked closely with a JavaScript programmer on a project, the conversation became a lot easier after we'd cleared that up.

`Dictionary` keys must be objects that conform to the `Hashable` protocol; these include `String` and `Int` objects.

Like the `Array`, `Dictionary` objects also come equipped with a pretty standard set of methods:

```
let count2 = myDict.count
let uno = myDict["One"] // "Eins"
```

If the `Dictionary` does not contain a key-value pair with the required key, it returns `nil`:

```
let quattro = myDict["Four"]
```

So, `quattro` will be `nil`.

We declare a mutable `Dictionary` with `var`:

```
var varDict = ["One": "Eins", "Two": "Zwei"]
```

A key-value pair is added to and removed from a mutable `Dictionary` as follows:

```
varDict["Three"] = "Drei"
varDict.removeValue(forKey: "One")
```

No prizes for guessing that values for existing keys are changed as follows:

```
varDict["One"] = "Een"
```

We can declare a `Dictionary` object without initializing it, as follows:

```
var emptyDict1: [String: String]
var emptyDict2: Dictionary<String, String>
```

These two methods are equivalent (the parallels with `Array` declarations are obvious). We declare and initialize an empty `Dictionary` with one of the following methods:

```
var emptyDict3 = [String: String]()
var emptyDict4: [String: String] = [:]
var emptyDict5: Dictionary<String, String> = [:]
```

Once the type of `Dictionary` is clear:

```
var myDict = ["One": "Eins", "Two": "Zwei", "Three": "Drei"]
```

(here, `myDict` is initialized as a `Dictionary` of type `<String: String>`), we can set it to the empty array with just the empty brackets:

```
myDict = [:]
```

Don't forget the colon, though; it's not an `Array`.

If we declare a `Dictionary` object with `let`, we cannot change its values:

```
let constDict = ["One": "Eins", "Two": "Zwei"]
constDict["One"] = "Un"
```

The second line will produce a compiler error.

You may find that it is frequently helpful to use a `typealias` to name a particular `Dictionary` type:

```
typealias memberRank = [String: Int]
```

Sets

`Set` objects are like an unordered `Array` in which any given value can only be present once.

Their declaration looks as follows:

```
let set1: Set = [1, 2]
```

Note that the `Set` literal looks like an `Array`, and so the type must be set explicitly.

The most common `Set` methods are probably the following:

```
var set1: Set = ["a", "b"]
let elementPresent = set1.contains("a")      // true
let (added1, element1) = set1.insert("c")    // (true, "c")
let (added2, element2) = set1.insert("c")    // (false, "c")
let removedElement1 = set1.remove("a")       // "a"
let removedElement2 = set1.remove("x")       // nil
```

Inserting an object that is already in the set leaves the set unaltered, but note that the `insert` method also returns a `tuple` containing a `Bool` of whether the element was added, as well as the element itself.

The `remove` method returns the object--removed if it was present, or `nil` if it was not.

Naming of types and variables

By now, you'll probably have spotted the pattern, but here it is anyway:

`TypeNames` are written in `CapitalizedCamelCase`.

We use `uncapitalizedCamelCase` for `variableNames` and `constantNames`.

Swift is pretty relaxed about what characters you use for naming, but there are a few rules:

- Names may not contain whitespace characters
- Names may not contain math symbols, line-drawing characters, or arrows
- Names may not begin with a number (but numbers are fine anywhere else in the name)
- Names may not be the same as Swift keywords (actually, there is a way to do this, but just don't)

Type aliases

As previously noted, you may use a `typealias` to make your code more readable. A simple example would be as follows:

```
typealias score = Int
```

This might not make much sense for a lowly integer, but this feature will become more valuable later as we look at types beyond the primitives offered by Swift.

Value and reference types

The basic data types of Swift, such as `Int`, `Double`, and `Bool`, are said to be value types. This means that, when passing a value to a function (including assignment of variables and constants), it is copied into its new location:

```
var x1 = 1
var y1 = x1
y1 = 2
x1 == 1 // true
```

However, this concept extends to `String`, `Array`, `Dictionary`, and many other objects that, in some languages, notably Objective C, are passed by reference. Passing by reference means that we pass a pointer to the actual object itself, as an argument, rather than just copy its value:

```
var referenceObject1 = someValue
var referenceObject2 = referenceObject1
referenceObject2 = someNewValue
```

These two variables now point to the same instance.

While this pattern is frequently desirable, it does leave a lot of variables sharing the same data--if you change one, you change the others. And that's a great source of bugs.

So, in Swift, we have many more value types than reference types. This even extends to data structures and classes, which come in two flavors; `struct` and `class` (see *Structs, classes, and other data structures* in this chapter). This is part of a widespread trend in programming toward copying immutable objects rather than sharing mutable ones.

Swift is pretty smart about managing all this copying. An object of value type is not, in fact, copied until the copy is changed, for example, and there are a lot of other tricks going on under the hood, none of which you need to take care of yourself.

So remember, structs, Strings, and Arrays are passed by value, just the same as `Int`, `Double`, and `Bool`.

Operators

We will take a quick tour of the most common operators in Swift, leaving such esoteric topics as custom operators for `Chapter 5`, *Advanced Swift*.

Mathematical operators

The five basic math operators will need no explanation here:

```
–
+
*
/
%
```

They are so-called infix operators, meaning that they are placed between their two operands:

```
let x = (a * a) + (b * b)
```

The usual rules of precedence apply.

Augmented assignment

As in many other C-derived languages, we can replace:

```
x = x + 1
```

With:

```
x += 1
```

There are versions of this for the other mathematical operators:

```
-= *= /= %=
```

Readers should already be familiar with all these operators.

 There is no ++ or -- operator in Swift 3. Older versions of the language did, in fact, retain these from the C family of languages, so don't be too surprised if you come across it in older posts on the Web. If you do need to do an i++ or i-- (although `for` loops make these operators largely unnecessary), use i += 1 or i -= 1.

Comparison operators

Swift's comparison operators are also derived from C; the reader will doubtless recognize them immediately:

```
if x == 0 {print("x is equal to zero")}
if x != 0 {print("x is not equal to zero")}
if x < 0  {print("x is less than zero")}
if x > 0  {print("x is more than zero")}
if x <= 0 {print("x is less than or equal to zero")}
if x >= 0 {print("x is more than or equal to zero")}
```

Logical operators

Swift's logical NOT, AND, and OR operators are the same as most C-based languages:

```
let saturday = true
let raining = false
let christmas = true

let b1 = !saturday // false
let b2 = saturday && raining // false
let b3 = saturday || raining // true
```

Multiple operators are allowed, and are **left-associative**, that is, sub-expressions are evaluated from left to right:

```
let b4 = (saturday || raining) && !christmas
```

In the preceding code, (saturday || raining) is evaluated first, and the result of that evaluation goes on to be evaluated with && !christmas. The parentheses as added are permissible, which can add clarity to your code, although they make no difference here to the code's outcome.

Other standard operators

In addition to the mathematical, comparison, and logical operators available in most languages, there are two further operators.

Ternary operator

The ternary operator is a shorter alternative to an if...else block:

```
let signString = a > 0 ? "positive" : "negative or zero"
```

Be sure to leave a space before the ?, otherwise the compiler will complain.

Nil-coalescing operator

The nil-coalescing operator assigns a value if it is not nil, or an alternative if it is:

```
let title = possibleString ?? "Untitled"
```

We check whether possibleString is nil; if it is, we assign "Untitled" to the title constant.

Structs, classes, and other data structures

Ways of defining and handling structured data are an important part of any programming language that supports object-oriented programming. Swift has extended the patterns typical of Objective C, Java, and the like, to include structures that are passed by value, called **structs**, and those that are passed by reference, called **classes** (see *Value and reference types* in this chapter). There is also the much lighter-weight **tuple**, which offers a kind of bridge between data structures and collection types such as dictionaries.

As well as the fact that `structs` are value types and `classes` are reference types, there are a few other points of departure, but the two structures have a lot more similarities than they do differences.

Structs

A Swift `struct` is basically a group of data, organized into properties, as well as methods that do something to or with those properties. There is more to come, but we'll start there for the sake of simplicity.

Let's set up a `struct` called `Locomotive` (note the capitalized name):

```
struct Locomotive
{
    var name: String?
    var built: Int?
    var museum: String?

    func infoString() -> String
    {
        var infoString = "Name: \(name). Built: \(built)."
        if let museum = museum
        {
            infoString += " Museum: \(museum)."
        }
        return infoString
    }
}
```

So, we have defined a `struct` that has three variable properties (with lowercase names), all of which are declared as optionals. Because those properties are permitted to be `nil`, we can initiate a `Locomotive` object without actually passing it any value for its properties:

```
let loco1 = Locomotive()
```

However, we are more likely to use the automatically defined initializer, with values for each of its properties:

```
let loco2 = Locomotive(name: "E111", built: 1964, museum: nil)
```

The `Locomotive struct` has one method, `infoString`, which returns a simple summary of its properties. You might have noticed that we did not need to refer to `self` to use the `museum` property in the body of the method (although you can, for clarity's sake, and it is sometimes necessary to do so, which we'll see later).

Method or function?

As far as Swift is concerned, a **function** that belongs to a data structure such as `class` or `struct` is called a **method** of that structure. This book will stick to that convention, which is widely adopted in the context of object-oriented programming.

Let's define a `struct` that has non-optional properties:

```
struct Driver
{
    var name: String
    var yearOfBirth: Int
}
```

All non-optional properties need to be initialized to some value, and so calling the initializer with no arguments will not compile. We need to supply a complete set of arguments to the initializer:

```
let driver = Driver(name: "Jones", yearOfBirth: 1964)
```

Once again, we see the emphasis placed on safety by the Swift design team: you can't create a broken `struct`.

Note that we didn't need to write these initializers ourselves (although we can if there is reason to); they are created for us by Swift. Apple calls this **memberwise initialization**.

We haven't mutated any of our `struct` properties after it has been created yet, nor have we used many other powerful features available to us. There is a lot more to be said about the `struct`, and I promise it will be, but for the moment we will put `struct` to one side in order to take a look at `class`, a `struct` reference-value sibling (or at least a close cousin).

Classes

If we take a `struct` instance and copy it, we have two completely separate entities; changing one will have no effect on the other. This behavior of `struct` data types can be a real boon to code safety-unexpected values in shared data structures (or the complete lack of a value) are possibly the most common source of bugs in object-oriented programming. Using `struct`, each function in your code gets its own copy, to deal with as it sees fit, without needing to take into account what some other function somewhere might do to it, or need from it.

But as you probably know already, we very often *need* to pass a reference to one particular unique instance of structured data. Most languages call this a **class**, and Swift is no different.

Let's take a look at a very basic `class`:

```
class SteamTrain
{
    let locName: String?
    var drivers: [String]
    var numberOfCarriages: Int

    init(locName: String,
         drivers: [String],
         numberOfCarriages: Int,
         currentStation: String?)
    {
        self.locName = locName
        self.drivers = drivers
        self.numberOfCarriages = numberOfCarriages
    }

    func add(newCarriages: Int)
    {
        numberOfCarriages += newCarriages
    }
}
```

The similarities to `struct` are clear enough, so what of the differences? Firstly, we notice that there is no automatic memberwise initializer provided, we have had to write one explicitly. Within this initializer, we need to refer to `self` to set the class's properties from the arguments supplied to the initializer.

In contrast to Objective C and many other languages, the `class` need not declare a superclass (or base class), although we will look at subclassing and inheritance in `Chapter 5`, *Advanced Swift*, in which we do provide a superclass.

The method `add(newCarriages: Int)` is used to increase the number of carriages by modifying a class variable property.

Creating an instance of the `class` is similar to doing so with a `struct`:

```
let oldLoc = SteamTrain(locName: "Puffing Billy",
                        drivers: ["Harpo", "Groucho"],
                        numberOfCarriages: 1,
                        currentStation: nil)
```

We access the properties in the same way as those of a `struct`:

```
print(oldLoc.locName)
```

But, we declared `oldLoc` to be constant with `let`. Can we then change its variable properties? Because it is a `class` type, we can:

```
oldLoc.drivers.append("Marco")
```

That is, as long as the property is declared to be variable. We have made the `SteamTrainname` property immutable, and so the following line of code would produce an error:

```
oldLoc locName = "Rocket"
```

If we decided that a `SteamTrain` name might change, we'd have to make it mutable. But who renames a steam locomotive?

Since `class` objects are passed by reference, it is possible to have two variables or constants that point to the same instance:

```
let mysteryLoc = oldLoc
```

We can test for this with the `===` operator, or its negation, `!==`:

```
mysteryLoc === oldLoc
```

This operator means *is the same instance as*. This is different to the equality `==` operator, which you have to define yourself for any given class (see `Chapter 5`, *Advanced Swift*), according to whichever criteria are appropriate for the `class` in question.

Optional instances

Both struct and class objects may be declared as optionals, as follows:

```
let secondDriver: Driver? = Driver(name: "Fred",
                                   yearOfBirth: 1904)
```

An optional instance's properties can be assigned to an optional variable as follows:

```
var nameOnSchedule:String?
nameOnSchedule = secondDriver?.name
```

Note that, by making `nameOnSchedule` an optional, we can assign it to be the name of `secondDriver`, if there is one, or `nil` if there is not, without having to test explicitly.

Tuples

We have seen already that the `Set` object's insert method returns a `tuple` (see *Sets* in this chapter); a `tuple` is a great way to pass around a lightweight, ad hoc data structure, one that may consist of mixed types, since you are not limited by the variety or number of different types:

```
let t1 = (1, 1.1, "1")
let t2 = (9, 9, 9)
let t3 = (t1, t2)
```

Tuples can contain any combination of types, including nested `tuple`. Like `struct`, `tuple` are passed by value.

Decomposition means accessing the individual values of a `tuple`, using its `.index` notation:

```
let i1 = t1.0
let f1 = t1.1
```

If it is convenient to name the elements of a tuple for improved clarity, we can do so:

```
let complex = (r: 11.5, i: 20.0, label: "startPoint")
let real = complex.r
let imaginary = complex.i
let label = complex.label
```

The preceding example may suggest the use of a `typealias`:

```
typealias complexNumber = (Double, Double, String)
var anotherComplex: complexNumber
```

Swift's type safety will now prevent us from creating a `complexNumber` object (or initializing our `anotherComplex` variable) with the wrong value types.

We can't do much more with `tuple` objects than this, so they are no substitute for full-fledged `class` and `struct` structures, but they are a very useful quick-and-easy way to, for example, create a function that returns more than one value, and are an essential part of our data-structure toolkit.

Enumerations

Swift offers another valuable structure, the `Enum`. While enumerations are a common feature of programming languages, Swift's `Enum` offers very much more than a simple mapping of integer values to labels.

Firstly, in cases where there is no logical mapping of `Enum` values to integers (or values of any other type), we can declare an `Enum` to be a type in its own right:

```
enum Color
{
    case red
    case amber
    case green
}
```

So, here we have a case in which it would be nonsensical to map colors to integers. Swift will not allow us to try to derive some integer value from `Color.red`, either.

Note that the `Enum` name is capitalized, whereas a `case` is written in lowercase.

This was not the case (no pun intended) in previous versions of Swift-- another thing to be wary of when reading older posts, tutorials, and documentation.

There are, however, frequent uses for an Enum that do correspond to some underlying value, and Swift lets us do this, too:

```
enum Medal: Int
{
    case gold = 1
    case silver
    case bronze
}
```

Clearly, there is a correspondence between medals and positions, and so it makes absolute sense to map each Medal case to an Int. Note that, after we have set the Int value of the first case, the subsequent cases are assigned incremental values automatically (although there is nothing to stop you overriding this behavior with different values).

To access the underlying value of an Enum case, we use its rawValue property:

```
let position = Medal.bronze.rawValue
```

In the preceding code, the position constant is set to be equal to 3.

We can also use raw values to create a Medal as follows:

```
let myMedal = Medal(rawValue: 2)
```

myMedal, as you would expect, has the value Medal.silver. Using raw values like this makes comparison of Enum cases very simple:

```
Medal.gold.rawValue > Medal.silver.rawValue
```

The preceding line of code evaluates to false (did it catch you out?).

When the type of a variable or constant is already set, we can use an abbreviated syntax without the Enum name:

```
var nextMedal: Medal
nextMedal = .gold
```

Enums have also established themselves as a convenient way to express compile-time constants:

```
enum APIUrlStr: String
{
    case uat = "http.www.theFirm.com/api/uat"
    case prod = "http.www.theFirm.com/api"
}
```

By the way, Swift will turn Enum case names into Strings when the Enum itself is declared to map to Strings:

```
enum Eggs: String
{
    case fried, scrambled, poached
}
let bestWayToEatEggs: String = Eggs.poached.rawValue
```

We'll leave Enums there for the time being; in Chapter 5, *Advanced Swift*, we will see that we have only just scratched the surface of Swift's Enum.

Optionals

Swift is, above all, a language for writing safe code, and its method of dealing with values that may or may not be nil is arguably its most important feature.

Why use optionals?

Let's look at two lines of code:

```
var squareOfTwo = Int("4")
var squareOfThree = Int("Yellow")
```

The Int initializer can take a String as its argument, and will return a valid Int if it can. If it cannot, it will return nil. The return value of that initializer is an optional Int. Thus, the two variables declared above evaluate as follows:

```
squareOfTwo // 4
squareOfThree // nil
```

In Swift, an optional is a special type that holds either a value or `nil`, and is marked by a question mark appended to the type of value it will hold:

```
var optVal1: Int?
```

We can also initialize an optional directly with a literal:

```
var optVal2: Int? = 2
```

It is important to note that `nil` is not the same as zero: 0 is a valid integer, `nil` is no value at all. So, the following two lines of code do not produce the same result:

```
optVal1 = 0
optVal1 = nil
```

The great thing about Swift is that it will not let you pass an optional value, which may or may not be `nil`, to a function that is expecting a non-nil value. This is a massive safety boost; no longer will there be crashes by your program attempting to access a value that does not exist. Or at least, Swift makes you work harder to make these crashes possible. If a function is not equipped to deal with a `nil` value, set its argument type to non-optional.

Be sure to be clear about the fact that an `Int` and an `Int?` are *not* the same type. An attempt to assign an optional value to a non-optional type will produce a type error, so trying this:

```
let x: Int = squareOfTwo
```

Will result in Xcode showing you a warning like this:

Unwrapping an optional

When we need to test an optional value for `nil`, we can do so with a simple `if` statement:

```
if squareOfTwo != nil
{
    //
}
```

 Don't forget, `if squareOfTwo {...}` is not valid code in Swift.

Within the braces of the preceding code, we might need to use the value of `squareOfTwo`, which we can **forceunwrap** as follows:

```
if squareOfTwo != nil
{
    var x = squareOfTwo!
}
```

Note the exclamation mark.

 We could also use `squareOfTwo!` without first checking whether it is `nil`. While there are good reasons to do this, don't do it unless your code guarantees that the value will not be `nil`. Certainly, don't do it just to save yourself the bother of checking.

We also can test the optional and assign its value to a constant with an `if let` statement, as follows:

```
if let answer = squareOfTwo
{
    var x: Int
    x = answer
}
```

The constant `answer` is not an optional; it has been **unwrapped**, and so its value can be assigned to `x`, which is not an optional.

There is nothing to stop us assigning an unwrapped optional to a constant or variable with the same name:

```
if let squareOfTwo = squareOfTwo
{
    var x: Int
    x = squareOfTwo
}
```

After the `if let` statement, the new `squareOfTwo` is not an optional. However, this way of unwrapping may make your code a little confusing, since the `squareOfTwo` inside the braces and the `squareOfTwo` outside are different types! But this is a common pattern, and it has its uses.

We will learn more about optionals when we get to Chapter 5, *Advanced Swift*. In the meantime, here are the main points to remember about optionals:

- Optional and non-optional versions of a data type are not the same data type
- Always use optional data types where a variable's value can be `nil`
- Don't force unwrap an optional unless you're *sure* it cannot be `nil`

Using an optional will let Swift save you from any number of programming errors and needlessly risky programming practices. They do take a little getting used to, to be sure, but once you have been using them for a while, you are likely to value them as highly as most developers using Swift do.

Control flow

Swift's branching features are in some cases more restrictive than the equivalents in other languages, and in other cases are considerably more powerful.

if else

The `if`, `else`, and `if else` statements work as they do in most C-based languages:

```
let x = getxFromSomewhere()

if x == 0
{
    print("x is zero")
}
```

```
    else if x < 0
    {
        print ("x is negative")
    }
    else
    {
        print ("x is positive")
    }
```

The syntax is slightly different in that the condition to be tested does not need to be put in brackets. However, an important point to note is that the test must return a `Bool` type value of `true` or `false`. Attempting to test an object for `nil` as follows will raise a compiler error:

```
    if possibleNil
    {
        // ...
    }
```

The error is shown in the following screenshot:

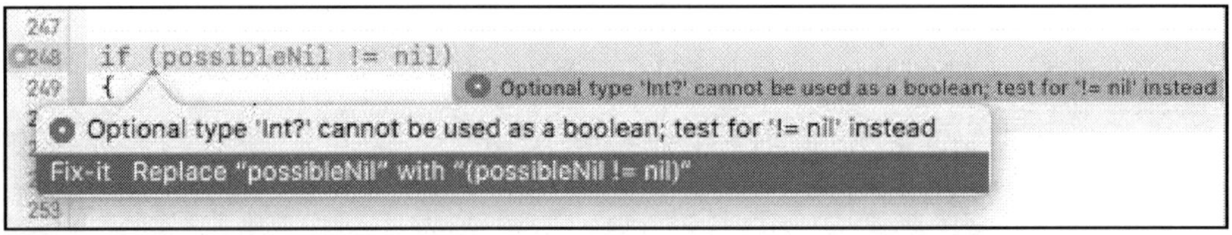

One final thing before we leave `if`: the following will not compile:

```
    if a = b
    {
        //...
    }
```

The assignment operator `=` does not return a `Bool`, and so using that instead of the intended `==` won't make it past the compiler. That's one typo we'll all be glad to see the end of.

switch

Swift's `switch` statement (try saying that three times in quick succession) is a lot more flexible than Objective C's, and indeed most other languages'. We'll look briefly at the basics here, leaving the more advanced stuff for `Chapter 5`, *Advanced Swift*.

Firstly, `switch` will test any kind of value; it doesn't need to be an `Int`. We might have a `String` value called `color`:

```
switch color
{
case "red":
    print("The color is red")
case "yellow":
    print("The color is yellow")
case "green":
    print("The color is green")
default:
    print("You are not at a traffic light")
}
```

Also, a `case` can be quite flexible. Let's assume we have an integer, `luckyNumber`:

```
switch luckyNumber
{
case 0:
    print()
case 1,2:
    print()
case 3..<10:
    print()
case 10...20:
    print()
default:
    print()
}
```

As you can see here, we can test against several cases at once, as in `case1,2:`

We can also test whether x falls within the range 3..<10 (which does not include 10) or 10...20 (which does include 20; note the dots).

 Be careful of ranges in Swift, since they are subtly different to those of some other languages.

- 0..<10 produces the range 0 to 9
- 0...10 produces the range 0 to 10

Finally, the `default` case covers all other integers.

A `switch` block must be exhaustive, so we must add the `default` case to cover all the integers we haven't dealt with explicitly. Xcode will remind us if we don't.

If the value to be tested is a `Bool` or an `Enum` (see *Enums* in this chapter), then we will possibly provide a case for each possible value, and will not, therefore, need a `default` case.

You may have noticed there are no `break` statements. That's because the behavior of `switch` in Swift has no implicit fall-through; once a match has been found, no further cases are tested.

Loops

Swift's looping statements are a pretty advanced set of features, producing code more elegant than the somewhat clunky `for (int i=0: i < aLimit: i++) {...}` of most C-based syntaxes.

That `(int i=0: i < aLimit: i++)` loop syntax, by the way, is no longer available in Swift; but it once was, so once again, beware of older posts on the Web.

Saying goodbye to i++

So, how do we execute loops in an expressive and concise way without our trusted old `i++` syntax? Well, Swift has a few options here, depending on exactly what you want to accomplish:

- `for` loops iterate over ranges and collections
- `while` loops run until a condition is no longer met

Iterating with for loops

Firstly, if we need to perform a loop a specific number of times, we can simply iterate over a range:

```
for i in 1...10
{
    print(i)
}
```

This loop will then print the numbers 1 up to and including 10.

If we don't explicitly care about how many times a loop takes place, but need to iterate over an entire `Array`, we can iterate directly over it, using the following syntax:

```
let arr = [1, 1, 2, 3, 5]
for i in arr
{
    print(i)
}
```

If we need to know the index of each object in the array, we can apply its `enumerated` method, which returns to us a sequence of `(index, value)` tuples:

```
for (index, i) in arr.enumerated()
{
    print("The value at index \(index) is \(i)")
}
```

A similar syntax exists for `Dictionary` objects:

```
let dict = ["a": 1, "b": 2, "c": 3]
for (letter, position) in dict
{
    print(letter, position)
}
```

We can also iterate over `Set` objects:

```
let set:Set = [2,3,5]
for n in set
{
    print(n)
}
```

If one of those doesn't fulfil your needs, you can always roll your own using `while` and `repeat`.

while

Swift's `while` loop functions much the same as it does in any language:

```
while limit > 0
{
    // doSomething()
    limit -= 1
}
```

If you want the code to run first once, and then test a condition, use `repeat`:

```
repeat
{
    doSomethingRepetitive()
    limit -= 1
}
while limit > 0
```

Between them, these two statements will cover the (usually infrequent) cases that are not covered by the enumeration loop statements.

Functions

In this chapter, we will look at the basics of function declaration in Swift, and we'll leave the more advanced features until Chapter 5, *Advanced Swift*.

To define a function in Swift, we use the following syntax:

```
func functionName(argument: argumentType) -> returnType
{
    // code
}
```

We can define a function that takes no arguments and returns no value as follows:

```
func printDate()
{
    print(Date())
}
```

Note that it is not necessary to declare a `Void` return value, though we may do so if we choose.

We would call that function as follows:

```
printDate()
```

Arguments to the function are supplied in the parentheses following the function name, in the form `argName: argType`; if there are more than one, they are separated by commas:

```
func printPoint(x: Int, y:Int)
{
    print(x, y)
}
```

We would call that function as follows:

```
printPoint(x: 11, y: 59)
```

The argument value(s) must be preceded by the argument name(s), as can be seen previously.

 Here we go again: This is new in Swift 3, so you might come across older variations of the calling syntax, in which the first argument name may be left out.

This is how we define a return value:

```
func increment(x: Int) -> Int
{
    return x + 1
}
```

Calling this function looks as follows:

```
let y = increment(x: 0)
```

A function can have one (and only one) **variadic** argument, an arbitrary number of arguments of the same type, as well as other "normal" arguments:

```
func printMyInts(args: Int..., label: String)
{
    print(label)
    for x in args
    {
        print(x)
    }
}
```

The variadic arguments are separated by commas in the call to the function:

```
printMyInts(args: 1, 1, 2, 3, 5, 0, label: "Fibonnacci Five-0")
```

It is quite simple to return any number of values, without having to resort to arrays, or dictionaries, or some other complex data structure, by using a `tuple` to enclose the return values:

```
func sumAndDifference(x: Int, y: Int) -> (sum: Int, diff: Int)
{
    let sum = x + y
    let difference = abs(x - y)
    return (sum, difference)
}
```

We can access the results together as a `tuple`:

```
let results = sumAndDifference(x: 3, y: 5)
```

These can then be decomposed by index or argument name, as with any tuple:

```
print(results.0)
print(results.1)
print(results.sum)
print(results.diff)
```

But we can also do that in one step:

```
let (sum, difference) = sumAndDifference(x: 5, y: 8)
```

So far, so good; we have covered the basics of functions in Swift. But most of the good stuff is yet to come.

Summary

This was quite a whirlwind tour of the basics of Swift, and as stated in the introduction to this chapter, you really do want to be on familiar terms with all the material up till now. In Chapter 5, *Advanced Swift*, we will begin to cover both more advanced features of the language, and those that deviate significantly from what you may already know from other languages, and that's the point at which the book will really take off.

The next chapter will look in depth at some of the features of Xcode that are an invaluable aid to expanding your repertoire of development techniques.

3
Checking Out the Power of Xcode

The longer you work with Xcode, the more adept you become at using it and the greater the range of its capabilities you learn to use effectively. This chapter will be a leg up in that direction.

We'll make a really simple app, and then look at several ways to increase our efficiency while coding by a significant margin. Speed of coding is not everything, that's very true, but saving time gives you more room to plan, to think, and to experiment, and those are the things it is sometimes hardest to find time for when that deadline or go-live is looming over you.

It's time to take your Xcode skills up a few notches.

In this chapter, you will do the following:

- Create a sketch app to try out these new ideas on
- Learn how to use code snippets to code more quickly and reliably
- See how special literals enable your logs to give you clearer and more tailored information
- Learn some advanced breakpoint techniques
- Implement so-called behaviors to streamline working with Xcode
- Use schemes to quickly change between app flavors
- Create and use custom build configurations and compiler flags

A quick and simple sketch app

Just to give us something to type our experiments into, we will create an extremely simplistic app, one that will present a window into which the user can type a rate of sales tax and a pre-tax price, and will present the resulting price inclusive of sales tax.

It shall be called **Sales Tax Calc**. I know, it's not a brilliant name.

 It is assumed the reader is able to create a new Xcode project from scratch, using Xcode 8 or later. If you are new to Xcode, this would be a good moment to consult one of the many excellent resources out there on getting started with Xcode. We'll wait here for you.

Create a new Xcode project called **SalesTaxCalc**, setting it to use Storyboards.

Drag four labels and two standard text fields onto the default View Controller's View object:

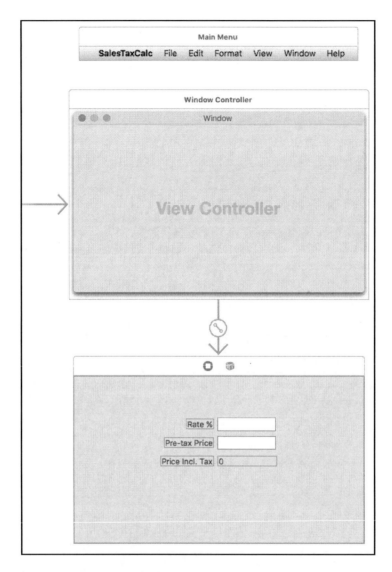

The two text fields and the label in the right-hand column will need to be connected to these outlets in the ViewController.swift file:

```
@IBOutlet weak var rateTextField: NSTextField!
@IBOutlet weak var preTaxTextField: NSTextField!
@IBOutlet weak var resultLabel: NSTextField!
```

The two text fields need to be connected to these two `IBAction` methods:

```swift
@IBAction func rateDidChange(_ sender: AnyObject){
}
@IBAction func preTaxDidChange(_ sender: AnyObject){
}
```

The whole code for the `ViewController.swift` file should look as follows:

```swift
import Cocoa
class ViewController: NSViewController
{
    @IBOutlet weak var rateTextField: NSTextField!
    @IBOutlet weak var preTaxTextField: NSTextField!
    @IBOutlet weak var resultLabel: NSTextField!

    override func viewDidLoad() {
        super.viewDidLoad()
    }

    override var representedObject: Any? {
        didSet {
        }
    }

    @IBAction func rateDidChange(_ sender: AnyObject)
    {
        calculateFullPrice()
    }

    @IBAction func preTaxDidChange(_ sender: AnyObject)
    {
        calculateFullPrice()
    }

    func calculateFullPrice()
    {
        let currencyString = "$"
        let rate = rateTextField.doubleValue / 100.0 + 1.0
        let fullPrice = preTaxTextField.doubleValue * rate
        resultLabel.stringValue = currencyString
        + String(format: "%.2f", fullPrice)
    }
}
```

Hit **Run** to test that the app builds and runs without problems.

Speeding it up with code snippets

One of the best and simplest aids to working quickly in Xcode is the **code snippets** feature. To see the list of both Xcode's default snippets and user code snippets, type *command + option + control + 2* to bring them up in the Utilities pane:

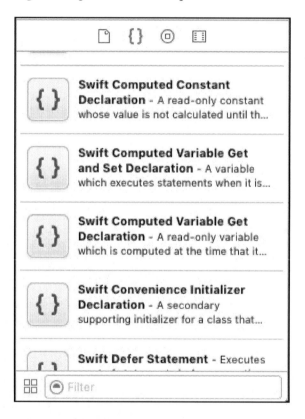

The preceding screenshot shows just a few of the dozens of snippets that come supplied with Xcode. Despite this generous supply, it's probably fair to say that most of them are hardly worth remembering, given that Xcode's code completion has come such a long way. Whether we really need a snippet that is no more than the following example is debatable:

```
deinit {
    <#statements#>
}
```

This is particularly true when one considers that the default set of snippets is not editable, and thus cannot be assigned keyboard shortcuts.

Checking out the supplied snippets

Double-click on a snippet to see its contents. If it's what you're after, you're in luck. Don't worry, we'll be making our own very soon.

Usage

If you do need to use one of the supplied snippets, it's very easy to do; just drag and drop the snippet from the Utilities pane into the appropriate place in your code. In order to save yourself some scrolling, assuming you know (or can guess) the name of the snippet, use the **Filter** bar at the bottom of the snippet list (see the previous screenshot).

Xcode's own snippets do not have a keyboard shortcut, but you can add them to your own (see the following section).

Now, if you've never used a factory-supplied snippet, you're in good company, because I don't think I have either, but if you've never created your own, it's about time you did. I promise you, you'll be glad of it.

Rolling your own snippets

So, now it gets much more interesting. You can (and most definitely should) create your own snippets of any code that you use frequently and which involves more than a trivial amount of typing. You can then also assign a keyboard shortcut to your user snippet, which is a lot faster than calling up the Utilities pane and searching and scrolling your way through the whole list.

It's kind of ironic that Xcode's method to create user snippets is to select the code you want to store as a snippet, and then drag the text into the snippets list. Are we not coders? Can we not do this with our keyboards? It would seem the people in Cupertino think not:

1. So, go ahead: drag some code into the snippets list, and you'll see a new snippet appear. It will be where you dragged it to, although it will be alphabetically sorted along with the rest as soon as you close and reopen the Utilities pane.
2. Double-click on the new snippet to open up a pane in which you can see the snippet's contents, as in the following screenshot:

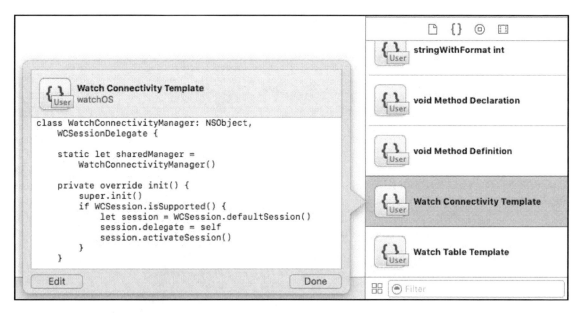

3. So now, as you can see in the preceding screenshot, we have an **Edit** button. Clicking that will take you to the snippet-editing window:

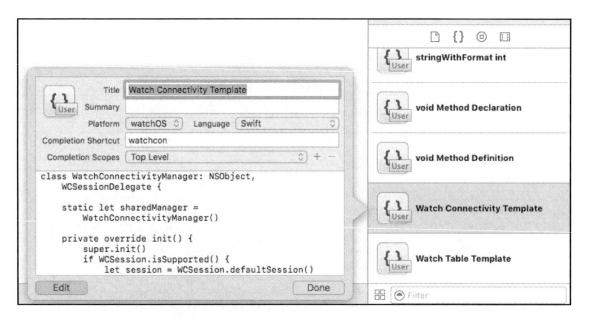

Here you can tailor the snippet in a number of ways:

1. The **Title** is what appears in the snippets list in the Utilities window.
2. The **Summary** is, well, a summary, if you need one.
3. You can restrict a shortcut to a particular **Platform** or programming **Language**, which enables you to use one shortcut for different versions of the code snippet, the most obvious ones being Swift and Objective C.
4. The **Completion Shortcut** is text only, no modifiers. When you type the shortcut into your code, it will be included in the code-completion list (assuming you have not deactivated it).
5. You can also restrict the snippet to one or more particular scopes:

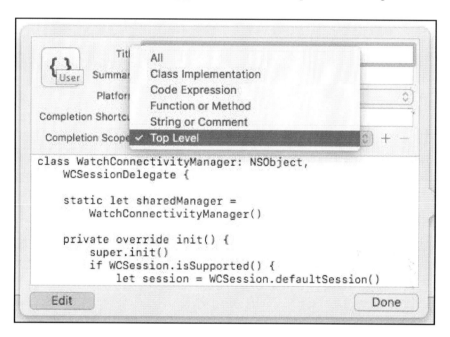

Again, this allows you to use one shortcut for several snippets, according to the context, as well as restricting the degree to which code completion is cluttered by shortcuts you will not use in a given context.

If you wish to restrict a snippet's scope, but have it available to more than one scope, use the + button beside the **Completion Scope** menu.

Your snippets collection will become more valuable to you than your favorite slippers or your Apple Watch. If you need to take them with you, when you're working on someone else's machine, for example, you can find them on your hard drive at the following path: `/Users/.../Library/Developer/Xcode/UserData/CodeSnippets`

Each snippet is simply an XML property-list file (more about them later) You might even like to store them on GitHub for those spontaneous coding sessions away from home.

It really is worth getting into the habit of creating your own code snippets--there is no limit to the number you can have (at least, I'm not aware of anyone discovering one) and they offer the biggest bang for your buck in terms of increased coding speed.

Logging with special literals

Among the reserved keywords of Swift are a small number of what Apple calls **special literals**. These are keywords that are substituted at compile time, and four of them are very useful for debugging purposes. They are as follows:

- `#function`, which is converted into a `String` of the name of the function in which the literal is used
- `#file`, which is converted into a `String` containing the path to the file in which the literal is used, starting with:

  `/Users/...`

- `#line` and `#column` are converted to an `Int` of the line and column number at which they appear

For any kind of ad-hoc debugging, or custom debugging classes, these are an essential tool. Add the following code to the `AppDelegate.swift` file's `applicationDidFinishLaunching` method (or anywhere else, for that matter):

```
print("Function: \(#function)")
print("File: \(#file)")
print("Line: \(#line)")
print("Column: \(#column)")
```

The output from this code will look something like the following:

```
Function: applicationDidFinishLaunching
File: /Users/.../Documents/Books/myBooks/Packt/macOS
Programming/Content/ch03/myApp/myApp/AppDelegate.swift
Line: 41
Column: 26
```

The special literals are useful not only in your code, but also in **breakpoints**, which we'll look at now.

Getting the most out of breakpoints

It's very likely you're using breakpoints already; any debugging you have done will have been very difficult without them. To add a breakpoint to your code, you can do one of the following:

- Click the romantically named **gutter** to the left of the code editor
- Create a breakpoint at the line the cursor is on with the shortcut *command* + \
- The same *command* + \ will also delete an existing breakpoint

And while on the subject, you can disable (though not delete) all breakpoints with the shortcut *command* + *Y*. If you're new to Xcode, that may be new to you. So now you know.

A breakpoint does exactly what you expect it to do: it halts the code immediately at the line it is located at. But it doesn't stop there (well, I suppose it does... no pun intended).

Editing breakpoint options

Right-click on the breakpoint to edit it:

We'll get to **Edit Breakpoint...** in a moment, but for now, note that you can disable and delete the breakpoint from here, or you can show it in the **Breakpoint Navigator**, which is very convenient when you have that huge number of breakpoints that you get when you've totally lost the plot. And who doesn't do that?

Okay, now select **Edit Breakpoint...**.

You have a number of options that can help you make your debugging several orders of magnitude more focused:

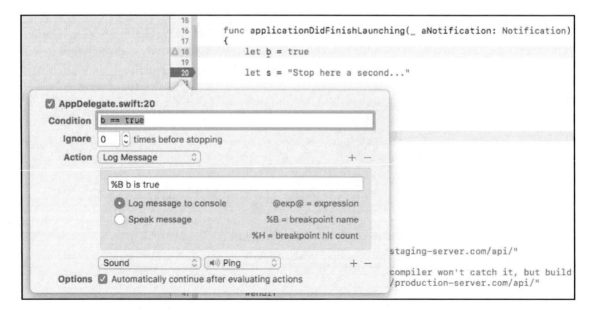

In the preceding screenshot, you can see that we have added a few caveats to the breakpoint:

- A **Condition** is set with a simple Boolean expression (Objective C veterans will appreciate the simplicity here). If the condition is not met, the breakpoint is ignored.
- We have left the **Ignore** value at 0, although it often makes sense to restrict the breakpoint to be active after a line of code has been executed one or more times already. Need to know whether that line is executing more often than you expect it to? This is where to go.
- For the **Action** parameter, we have selected **Log Message** (more of the other actions in a moment). A message can be any string you want, and note the **%B** we have added, which will print the name of the breakpoint's location in the code. The **%H** that prints the hit count can also be a great help in tracking down bugs.
- You can even add an expression here, in the form `@thisInt * thatInt@`, which can be very useful indeed during debug sessions.

By clicking the + sign next to the **Action** menu, we have added a second action, this time choosing to play a sound. Now, this is a feature for those times when you're working alone, or at least have headphones to hand, but don't dismiss it as a gimmick; particularly when you have the option **Automatically continue after evaluating actions** selected, this can be a really practical tool. It allows you to monitor what is going on without having to stop, or even look away from, the code, and a few of these audible breakpoints in quick succession will convey a lot of information without interrupting the flow of the program (or the programmer). I use this a lot. Yes, you'll get caught by your colleagues occasionally and they'll think you're crazy.

Other actions

We can use the other actions as shown in the following sections.

Adding a debugger command

The debugger command will accept anything that would be valid input to the debugger console. This could include informational stuff such as the following:

```
po someObject
```

It could also include expressions to change the internal state of the program, as follows:

```
expr i = 12
```

After that expression has been run by the breakpoint, we have a new value of i. No need to stop, change the code, and run again.

Triggering an AppleScript or shell script

The **AppleScript** option provides you with a field in which to add any text that will run as AppleScript, and the **Shell Command** option will enable you to run any Unix script and specify its arguments (there is an option to pause the code until the shell script has finished, or it can be fired off and left to execute while the program continues to run). In order to run a shell script, you'll have to set permissions on it first, with the following input to Terminal:

```
chmod 755 myScript
```

 There's much more on working with Terminal in Chapter 19: *Deploying Third - Party Code.*

Don't stop me now

This makes breakpoints much more than just a way to stop and inspect the code (although they are, of course, eminently suited to that as well). They are a way to dynamically monitor the program's progress, log the values that are being passed around, and even change those values on the fly, all without a reboot of the app. Enabling the code to continue after breakpoint execution opens up a whole range of possibilities.

Behaviors

There's one little corner of Xcode that has huge potential to make your work with it significantly faster, smoother, and presumably more satisfying: Xcode **Behaviors**.

To get there, complete the following steps:

1. Open up Xcode's Preferences window with *command + ,*(that is to say, *command + comma*).
2. Select the **Behaviors** tab.

This is where you get to tell Xcode how you want things to be when it builds, tests, runs, searches, or engages in several other activities.

As an example, we're going to get Xcode to use a separate window for debug logging (it will create one if it doesn't exist yet), which will keep the code editor window that we are working in free of debug-clutter. The following screenshot shows the settings needed to make our new, non-disruptive, debug window:

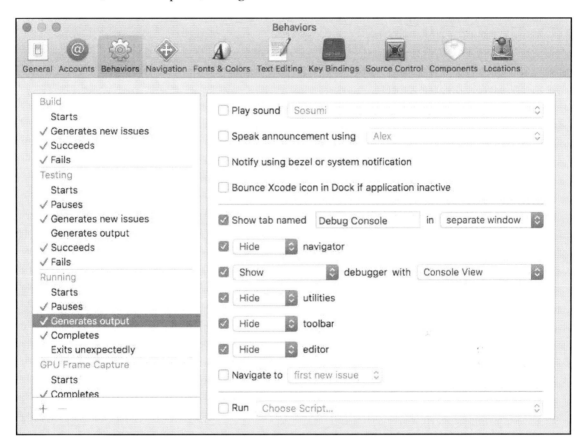

This is especially useful when you are working with more than one monitor, or if you have a crazy-big screen with a corner free for a console.

You're not limited to setting Xcode's behavior while running the processes listed; you can also add custom behaviors which are triggered by keyboard shortcuts.

Have you ever wanted a button that made everything except your code just go away? The navigators, debugger, Utilities panes, all of it? Well this is where you can do just that:

1. Click on the little button to the right of your custom behavior name, and enter the key combination that will be the shortcut.
2. Give the new behavior a name more descriptive than **New Behavior**. I used **Big Reset**, but whatever floats your boat is good. There is now a new **Custom** category in the behaviors list, with your new behavior in it.
3. At the bottom of the behaviors list on the left of the **Behaviors** tab, click the **+** button.

You might find it quite difficult to find one that doesn't clash with something else I use *command + Option + '* (single quote), since it was free and is easy to type with one hand.

4. Set the following values:

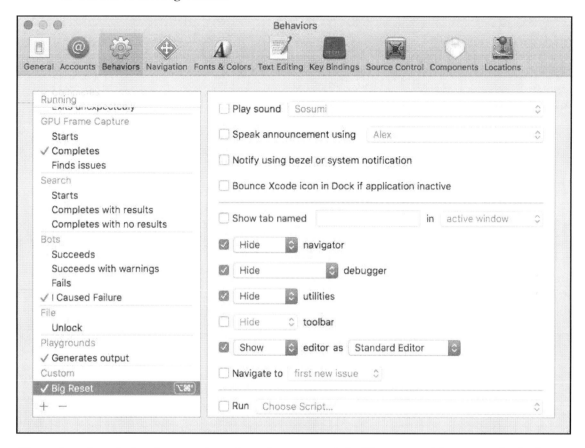

Given that these behaviors can launch scripts, you might like to use this as a method of running scripts via keyboard shortcuts.

Understanding schemes

Imagine a tool that, with a couple of mouse clicks, or even a keyboard shortcut, will change the display name of an app from Flappy Mushroom Test to Flappy Mushroom, change the app's Bundle ID, swap one set of server endpoints for another, and to cap it off, change your application region from system region to Iceland.

That tool, in Xcode, is **scheme selection**. If you haven't used schemes before, we're talking about this thing:

It's the **SalesTaxCalc** bit, in this example. If you click on it with a new project, you'll see this:

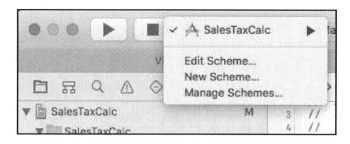

But before we accept the invitation to create a **New Scheme...**, or edit the one we have already, let's see why they're of interest to us.

What schemes actually do

Basically, schemes are way to control many of the things that happen when you hit the **Run** button. There are a whole host of options that we may wish to change when running an app under different circumstances (whether real or simulated), and Xcode exposes to us dozens of settings that are brought together as schemes. Each scheme we create will have something set differently, which in turn will be picked up during the build and applied to the app.

Many of the changes are achieved through the choice of build configurations, which we will get to shortly, but before we go there, let's take a look at some of the simplest ways to feed different information into our apps, without continually commenting and uncommenting sections of code, which is both risky and irritating.

Creating a new scheme

Let's add a scheme to our **SaleTaxCalc** app:

1. From the schemes menu, select **New Scheme...**, and call the new scheme **SalesTaxCalc Dev**. Click **OK**.
2. The scheme is now selected automatically in the schemes menu.

Changing between schemes without reaching for the mouse is easy: type *command* + *control* + [and *command* + *control* +] (square brackets) to move backwards and forwards through the list (which are kind of the same thing when there are only two schemes, of course).

So, now that we have two schemes, let's add some changes to our new **SalesTaxCalc Dev** scheme. From the schemes menu, select **Edit Scheme...**.

If you are using a US keyboard layout, or one very similar to it, there is a keyboard shortcut to open the currently selected scheme in the scheme editor window, *command* + <. However, many keyboards, including all the UK, German, and Australian ones lying around here, have the < character as a shifted key, so you'll have to define a custom shortcut.

Using scheme environment variables

In the scheme editing window, select the **Arguments** tab.

The **Arguments** tab shows two empty lists, **Arguments Passed On Launch** and **Environment Variables**. The former we will leave for a later chapter; for now, we will concentrate on the environment variables.

The environment variables listed here are basically a dictionary of key-value pairs that are available to the app's code via the `ProcessInfo.processInfo.environment` dictionary, which we'll add to the app shortly:

1. Click the **+** button to add an environment variable.
2. **Name** the new environment variable **Currency Symbol**.
3. Set its **Value** to £ or some currency symbol of your choice (New Zealand gave up its £s for $s many years ago). You must include the double quotes.
4. **Close** the window.

If you run the app again, you'll see that the currency has changed:

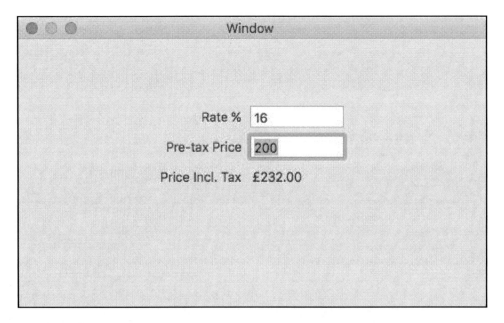

This change is baked into the code in by the compiler. By testing the value of any environment variable key, we can make appropriate adjustments in the content of our code. There are various ways we could have done this, but adjusting a scheme's environment variables has got to be the simplest.

You might like to take the time now to browse through the scheme editor window's other tabs, **Options**, **Diagnostics**, and **Info** (the last of which we are about to use).

 If you collaborate with other developers using a source control repository, you'll need to add the scheme to version control by ticking the **Shared** box in either the scheme editor window, or the manage schemes window, both reachable from the schemes list.

Any changes you want to make within the code can be covered using environment variables. The test is trivial to write and takes place at compile time. But what if we want to make changes to, say, the app's Build Settings, or even its `Info.plist` file? Can we do that too?

We can indeed, but not by using the scheme's environment variables. We now need to enlist the help of another one of Xcode's palette of development-sweetening goodies: **build configurations**.

Why build configs are so cool

Build configurations are at the heart of Xcode's organizational apparatus. All of those hundreds of files that make up a project would be nothing without a clever set of files somewhere that know how to stitch it all together. But of course, we say building, rather than stitching. *Stitch configurations* sounded pretty good to me, but never caught on.

There are many changes that may be desirable according to the circumstances for which an app is being compiled. In this chapter, we're going to imagine the client has asked for two different versions of an app; one might be used to access a staging server to obtain dynamic data, while the other would use the client's actual production server (the one that nobody is going to want to perform experiments on because it's being used by a million users a day).

These two versions will need to reside side by side on a single machine, so they will also need different bundle IDs.

Build configurations allow us to make adjustments both within the code itself, and in the app's build settings and `Info.plist` file, and this is just what we need for the scenario described above--a scenario that is almost universal when building enterprise apps.

These are by no means the only uses of build configurations, but it's an excellent place to start.

The steps we will follow, very broadly, are as follows:

1. Create a new build configuration.
2. Set one of our schemes to use it.
3. Create custom **User-Defined** Build Settings.
4. Set some of the *Info.plist* properties to reference those user-defined build settings.

5. Make some of the app's build settings dependent on which build configuration is being used.
6. Use those settings in our code.

Creating a new build configuration

The default Xcode project template already creates two build configurations for you, **Debug** and **Release**, but we're going to leave those alone and create a new one:

1. Select the project file in the project navigator to go to the project settings screen, and select the **Info** tab:

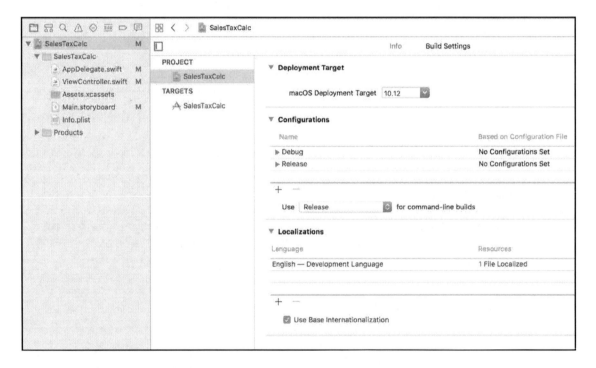

2. Click the + button underneath the configurations list in the **Configurations** section.
3. From the contextual menu that appears, select **Duplicate Debug Configuration** and name it **Dev**.

4. From the schemes menu, select our **SalesTaxCalc Dev** scheme if you haven't already, and then select **Edit Scheme...** from the same menu.

5. In the scheme editor window, select **Run** from the list on the left-hand side of the window (it should be preselected), and choose the **Dev** configuration from the **Build Configuration** menu, as follows:

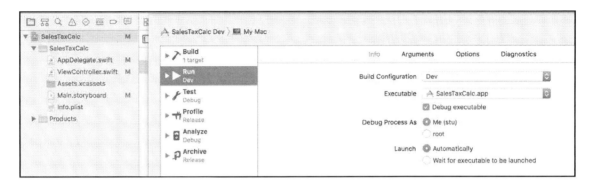

6. Do the same for **Archive**. No need to change the others (**Test**, **Profile**, and so on) at the moment, so click **Close**.

Now, when we hit **Run**, the app will build according to the specifications of the **Dev** build configuration. But of course, we haven't done anything yet to make our configuration any different from the default **Debug** configuration, so running the app again now isn't going to be the most thrilling of experiences. However, when we go to the **Build Settings** tab, we will discover that many of the settings there allow us to specify different values according to which build configuration is used in the active build scheme. That's where the fun starts, and that's our next task.

Creating user-defined build settings

Select the project's **Build Settings** tab, as in the following screenshot (so not the target's settings):

1. Click on the **+** button to the right of the **Level** button and select **Add User-Defined Setting** from the contextual menu.
2. Name the new setting BUNDLE_ID_SETTING. In the **User-Defined** section (at the very bottom) of the **Build Settings** tab, you now have your new setting.
3. Make a short detour to the target's **General** tab, and copy the **Bundle Identifier** field's text:

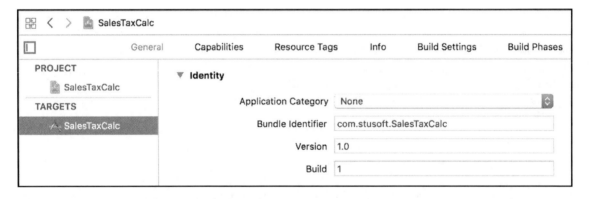

4. Back in the project's **Build Settings** tab, click on the disclosure triangle to the left of the BUNDLE_ID_SETTING name, and paste in the bundle identifier you have just copied.

5. Add the suffix `.dev` to the bundle identifier in the **Dev** configuration's field, so that the three user settings look as follows:

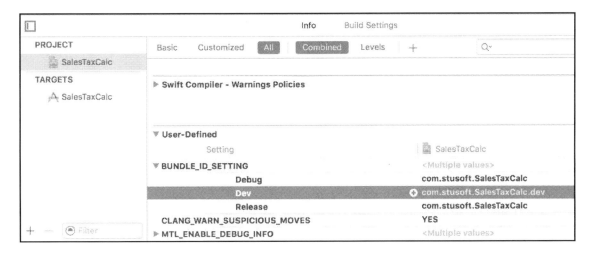

So far, so good. The only thing we need to do now is to modify the `Info.plist` to adopt the new setting.

Adapting the Info.plist file

When the app is built, the compiler consults the `Info.plist` properties list for several pieces of information, including the one that interests us at the moment, the bundle identifier.

Navigate to the project's `Info.plist` file, and change the name of the **Bundle identifier** field from the default setting, `$(PRODUCT_BUNDLE_IDENTIFIER)`, to `$(BUNDLE_ID_SETTING)`, not forgetting the dollar sign and parentheses.

Now we have instructed the compiler to use whatever argument is returned from the build settings `BUNDLE_ID_SETTING` value, with respect to the current build configuration.

Technically speaking, you now have two different apps as far as macOS is concerned, and they will coexist quite happily on the same machine.

Using Swift compiler custom flags

We can instruct the compiler to include or exclude sections of code according to which build configuration is being used. This is used for a range of purposes, some of the more common being setting differing server addresses for production and test versions of the app and third-party API keys, which can also differ according to build config.

This is important for the solo developer, and absolutely essential for work with enterprise clients. Fortunately, it's very simple to do; there are only two steps involved:

- Create a Swift compiler custom flag in the build settings
- Test for this flag in code, and respond appropriately

The compiler will handle the rest.

Creating the custom flag

To create a custom flag, we need to be in the project's **Build Settings** tab:

1. Search for **Other Swift Flags** (you are using the search box for this stuff, aren't you?) in the build settings.
2. Click on the disclosure triangle next to **Other Swift Flags** to see the build configurations.
3. Open the **Dev** build-configuration text field by double-clicking on the right-hand side of that row.
4. Click in the + in the bottom-left corner of the window that opens.

5. Enter –DDEV (including the - character) into the text field and hit *return*:

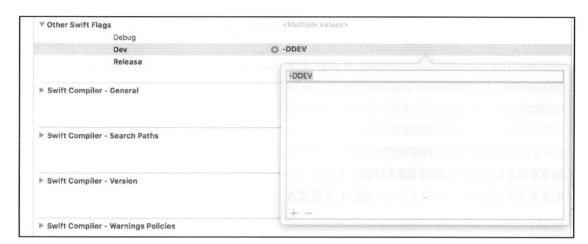

6. Click outside the window to close it.

The **-D** tells the compiler that this is a flag it needs to know about. As for **DEV**, it's just a string; it can be anything you want. Tradition dictates that preprocessor strings (and that's what this is; see the information box in the further section) are written in uppercase.

That's it; we're done with the **Build Settings** tab for the time being, let's move on to some code.

Using custom flags in code

Once upon a time, in the Days Before Swift, there was a language called C, and it had something called preprocessor directives, and they were used and abused for all sorts of things. In Objective C, these directives could test for a value present in the build settings, and Swift does the same thing, except that the preprocessor directives have been renamed **compiler control statements**.

 They even look the same as they did before Swift, preceded by the #, so when you come across the old name and the new name in books and on the Web, don't worry too much about the difference between them.

During development, we're going to save ourselves some typing by prepopulating the app's **Rate** and **Pre-Tax Price** text fields with some arbitrary values.

Navigate to `ViewController.swift`, and add the following code to its `viewDidLoad` method:

```
#if DEV
    rateTextField.stringValue = "16"
    preTaxTextField.stringValue = "144"
#else
    // possibly something else
#endif
```

Here we see Swift's compiler control statements in action (we included the empty `#else` statement for the sake of completeness).

And that's all you need to do. If the compiler can't find `Dev` defined in the build settings, it will ignore the code in the `#if` block and the app will build as if it didn't exist. So, when you select the **Release** scheme for external testing, App Store, or enterprise distribution, the text fields will be empty, as they should be. But when we're in the `Dev` scheme, we won't need to repeatedly enter text into those fields.

Finding the build settings on disk

It's sometimes helpful, or just plain interesting, to locate the build settings on our hard drive. In Xcode 8, they are located in your project's `project` file; right-click and select **Show Package Contents**, then open the `project.pbxproj` file with any text editor (or Xcode itself).

> If you want to see your new custom build configuration, search for this:
> **/* Begin XCBuildConfiguration section */**

Reading through this file is an educational experience, but editing it directly, while possible, should be approached with caution. The **Build Settings** tab won't let you really stuff things up, but your text editor most certainly will.

Now you can ignore that advice and start hacking it. Make a copy first, though, eh?

Summary

I hope that, after this chapter, your project-oriented Xcode skills (as opposed to coding) are significantly sharper than they were at the beginning. In this chapter, you have learned how to create code snippets to make small sections of code instantly available. You have also learned how to turn breakpoints from mere freeze buttons into powerful logging and troubleshooting tools.

You should now be able to tailor Xcode's behavior to your taste, as well as create custom behaviors that are applicable via keyboard shortcuts. Finally, you have learned how to combine build schemes with custom build configurations, user-defined build settings, and compiler flags, to customize each build for the appropriate circumstances.

The next chapter will introduce you to some considerations about how to design the data structure and data flow of an app, at an architectural level, introducing some well-established design patterns.

4

MVC and Other Design Patterns

There are many ways to write a program. At every level, from the overarching architecture of a program's design, through the separation of functionality into distinct layers and the implementation of individual classes, right down to the ways in which functions engage with each other, there is a wide range of strategies to choose from. These are accompanied by innumerable zealots of one style to the detriment of all others, *silver bullet* blog posts, and the dreaded Latest Thing that allegedly only aged, bearded Fortran developers can afford to ignore.

This is made all the more exciting by the fact that there are so many *right* ways of performing so many programming tasks. And it's your privilege as a developer to select the best method for any given task under the given circumstances.

And so, this chapter is dedicated to covering some of the most common programming and design concepts that are potentially applicable to macOS development using Swift. Because macOS is our target platform, we should acknowledge up front that the depth of coverage - or lack of it - of any particular topic is not an indication of its importance, but much more a reflection of its relevance to programming with the Cocoa frameworks.

The material presented here is very far from complete; these are topics worthy of decades of postgrad research, and our intention here is to break the ice, so to speak, and start the process of deepening our understanding of issues above and beyond the code itself.

The aims of this chapter are as follows:

- To give you an idea of the overall landscape of relevant programming paradigms and design patterns
- To provide you with a number of concepts to be aware of while planning and writing your code
- To provide you with some pointers to further reading (sooner or later) and research
- Provide a strong rationale for the strategies followed throughout this book

It is not necessary to memorize every word of this chapter. The concepts covered here come up constantly in our discussions of programming for macOS in the rest of the book. At the moment, we're simply setting a context in which everything that comes later can be comprehended more easily, and many of the ideas here will take a little while to settle down, make sense, and finally, become part of your day-to-day programming.

The topics covered in this chapter include the following:

- The meaning of programming paradigms
- Imperative and object-oriented programming
- Declarative and functional programming
- Encapsulation and isolation

Programming paradigms

It's sometimes hard to imagine that there are ways other than object-oriented programming to write software. It all seems such a no-brainer; variables can be changed, objects are instances of classes and those classes have methods and properties, sub-classing saves a lot of duplicate code, and functions can do whatever they want as long as they return the right type. How could it be otherwise?

It is certainly true that Xcode and Cocoa together encourage an extremely object-oriented view of the world, and for very good reason. But in this section, we will take a look at some alternatives, and the reasons why we may want to employ them, either in whole or in part.

Swift is a multi-paradigm language in that it has strong support for programming in different styles; the content of this chapter is driven by that variety.

So, what is meant by paradigm?

Programming paradigms are ways, or styles, of programming. They are not specific languages; they are not coding templates; they are alternative approaches to dealing with the task of turning ideas into code. The borders between one paradigm and another are often blurred, and many languages support or enable programming in more than one paradigm. Even the programming-theory experts can't always agree on which paradigms are a subset of some other.

We're not going to get too pedantic here, but we will divide programming into two broad categories, **imperative** and **declarative**, both of which are directly relevant to programming in Swift.

Imperative

Let's start with what you know already, assuming that you have some background in Swift, Objective C, Java, or one of the many other C-based object-oriented languages.

The word *imperative* comes from the Latin word for *command*. And that is exactly what imperative programming does; it defines code step by step, with an explicit order of execution. Imperative programming means taking responsibility for everything that needs to be done; imagine sitting next to the driver of a taxi, giving instructions to get to some destination:

```
turn left
drive two hundred meters
stop if the traffic light is red
turn right if it is green
...etc.
```

Imperative programming often uses subroutines, so in the preceding example, `turn left` would represent a block of instructions somewhere else that would read as follows:

```
move the steering wheel anticlockwise
when the car is moving parallel to the pavement, return the steering wheel
to its default position
```

And so on.

Another characteristic of imperative programming is the use of iteration:

```
Put a suitcase into the trunk of the car
If there's still room in the trunk, go back one line.
```

The use of such loops is a mainstay of imperative programming.

Object-oriented programming

It makes perfect sense to put all that car-driving and car-loading code together some place, along with some variables to track the gas in the tank, the number of passengers, and so on.

Thus, we extend the concept of imperative programming to **object-oriented programming**. The lines of code are grouped together into **methods** of each object, the variables are now **properties** of an object, and we can write blueprints for each type of object, called **classes**.

Object-oriented programming, often abbreviated to OOP, is strongly associated with the concepts of mutable data, classes inheriting code from other classes, and message passing between objects. There is also a strong preference for **encapsulation**, the idea that an object is responsible for its own state (its property values) and internal functionality, and provides an interface to the outside world through which properties and methods can be accessed.

When considering the most modern practices around programming with Cocoa, we need to look briefly at two sub-paradigms (if such a word exists) of OOP:

- Class-based programming
- Protocol-oriented programming

Class-based programming

This is what you've probably been using most. Classes are written to include a set of properties and methods, and extending a class is achieved by sub-classing it, and adding to or overriding the properties and behavior of the superclass. A common pattern is to write a class that is not intended for use at all, except to be sub-classed (called an **abstract** class).

Protocol-oriented programming

An alternative to creating a class from which subclasses are derived is to define a **protocol** which any class can adopt. The protocol defines a set of behaviors to which a class, once it has declared itself to be compliant to that protocol, must implement. Thus, a `Car` object that adopts the `Steering` protocol will be required to implement a `turnLeft` method, which can be called by another object that has no need to know what that method involves. A `Steering`-protocol-compliant `Motorbike` object will have a different implementation of `turnLeft`, which again, the calling object need know nothing of.

We will be seeing much more of protocols later on, but for an entertaining and enlightening take on protocol-oriented programming, here is a video of a brilliant session from the 2015 *World Wide Developers Conference*:

`https://developer.apple.com/videos/play/wwdc2015/408/`.

It's possibly the most amusing Apple video you'll ever see (you'll need to use Safari).

The drawbacks of OOP

OOP serves us extremely well, but it has its downsides.

Imperative programming allows, indeed relies on, functions having so-called **side effects**. This means they can have effects on the state of the program beyond simply returning a value. Here is an extreme case:

```
func tripleThisInt(i: Int) -> Int
{
  let result = i * 3
  eraseTheInternet()

  return result
}
```

Side effects represent several challenges.

For a start, you have to just know they're there; you can't see that they happen in the name of the method; there is no indication of them in the arguments to the function, nor does the return statement give any clue (these three together make the method **signature**).

Furthermore, we have the matter of **mutable state** and the problems that go with that. Object A expects object C to be in a certain state, but object B has just used object C's properties, changing its state in the process, and the whole program falls over.

Another thing to beware of with OOP is that programs become very complex very quickly, and software reusability and maintainability (which is the whole point of OOP) soon get lost in the heat of delivery and release deadlines.

Remember we said it's easy to imagine there is no other way? Well there are alternatives, and one that we will look at closely, to see what it can offer us in terms of expanding our repertoire of techniques, is declarative programming.

Declarative programming

Let's go back to our conversation with the taxi driver. Wouldn't it be better to say "Take me to the station"? Someone has already taught the taxi driver to turn left and stop at a red traffic light (although the latter is debatable in many cities). We just need to state our destination.

In declarative programming, the emphasis is more on telling the program *what* to do, as opposed to *how* to do it. Languages that support (or use exclusively) declarative programming are in some sense at a higher level still than OOP, and they include database query languages such as SQL, and even HTML. The HTML we load into our browser doesn't tell it how to render text to a screen, or how to calculate the width of a table that should occupy half of the window width, it simply lists the page elements it wants to see and the content that goes inside those elements.

That doesn't mean, of course, that the rest happens by magic. Either a lot of code is provided (and hidden) by the environment in which the language is deployed (the browser, in the case of HTML), or the code relies on a lot of other code that has been written previously, and built up to the point where the developer is no longer explicitly writing the low-level implementation details of an app, but is instead specifying what needs to be done.

A sub-genre of declarative programming that does exactly that is **functional programming**.

Understanding functional programming

Functional programming has a long history, and it is interesting to note the extent to which its fundamental principles are exerting an increasingly large influence on other, much younger programming styles. As programs become more complex, with increased use of multiple processing cores (and therefore parallel processing), concepts that were originally reserved for the likes of **Haskell** and **Lisp** are making an impact across a wide range of programming scenarios and languages.

We could have a lively and entertaining debate about the one true meaning of the *functional* in functional programming (which we shall henceforth abbreviate to FP), but space is limited, and a debate in a book tends to get a bit one-sided, so instead we'll need to settle for a somewhat fuzzy definition of what FP actually means.

The following aspects of FP are absolutely core to its nature, however:

- A **pure function** always returns a value, and will always return the same value for any given input.
- That's all a pure function does. It has no side effects; the return value is its only way to contribute to the program.
- A function may be passed to another function among its arguments, and a function may also be returned by another function. Functions are said to be **first-class** entities in this case, and functions that either require a function argument or return a function are called **higher-order functions**.
- A function's arguments and return value define its **type**. Functions are typed just like `Int`, `String`, or `[String: Float]` types.

Having listed the defining characteristics of FP, there are other aspects that are so strongly associated with it, we can't possibly leave them unmentioned.

Functional programs allow only **single assignment**. Once we have declared a to be 3, it stays that way forever, and is said to be **immutable**. We've seen this already with Swift's `let` statement. The passing of arguments to other functions is always by value; that means a copy is made and passed to a function that only has access to that copy.

Purely functional programs are stateless; each function deals only with the data it is given, and returns a value.

Rather than iterative loops, FP tends to encourage (or enforce) the use of recursive algorithms. Similarly, the process of applying a function to a list of objects, called the `map` function, is an alternative to the iterative `for myObject in myObjectsArray {...}` approach of OOP, and this feature is now also a part of the Swift language. In the next chapter, we will see what map, and its sibling, **reduce**, can do for us.

FP makes use of **anonymous functions**, which are blocks of code that can be passed around without being defined as a named function first. This is an important part of using higher-order functions. Anonymous functions are called **closures** in Swift, and in the next chapter, we will look at them in some depth. They're seriously cool.

Sometimes it's hard not to burst with enthusiasm for certain concepts and start gushing about the amazing benefits of exploring and absorbing them. I don't know about you, but I tend to stop reading when things get like that.

So here is a calm, sober, subjective-but-sincerely-held opinion:

Time spent getting through the rather alien-seeming ideas around FP will dramatically increase your ability to leverage many of the features available in Swift that are not available in most languages used for writing desktop and mobile applications. Building up an understanding of how FP works, and what advantages it brings, is one of the single most important ways you can improve your skills in programming with Swift. It's also huge fun.

However, we cannot write purely functional code for macOS, or at least not throughout an entire app.

Using functional concepts within OOP

An introduction to FP worthy of the topic is way beyond the scope of this book, but we will make numerous references to the concepts described above throughout the rest of the book, and we'll look at the advantages of those concepts as we progress. That said, here is a quick summary of what FP can offer us, even though programming for macOS is primarily an object-oriented endeavor.

FP's behavior, in passing and returning values rather than accessing properties, leads to much safer code. We don't have a lot of functions accessing the same data, and this avoids many of the nasty surprises thrown up by complex state-dependent structures.

When functions are only working with their own unique copies of values, and can only change the state of a program through their returned values, they are completely thread-safe. There is no need for flags and locks, and the whole rest of the concurrent programming machinery, which leads to simpler, faster, and safer code.

For the same reasons, FP is an appropriate strategy to adopt around parallel processing. Given that we've pretty much reached many of the physical limits of shunting bits around integrated chips, it is a safe bet that parallel cores are going to continue to become an increasingly important part of development.

Functional programming tends to lead to fewer lines of code. Less code means fewer mistakes and better maintainability.

Pure functions are predictable. We can reason about the code much more easily, and because they always return the same value for a given input, we can drastically reduce the extent to which our code needs to be tested as an application increases in size and complexity. From the point of view of a pure function, the world always looks the same; it is entirely ignorant of its context.

However, we will not attempt to fit square pegs into round holes and make unnecessary work for ourselves by trying to write functionally as much as we can (see the Web for where that goes; functional evangelists write some seriously esoteric code at times). But we will help ourselves to FP concepts wherever they prove to be advantageous in an otherwise object-oriented environment.

Learning functional programming the fast way

This might seem like a strange piece of advice in a book about using Swift to develop for macOS, but here goes anyway.

Find yourself a free weekend, and spend it learning the basics of Haskell. I'm not joking; it's so simple and logical that you can get a grip on its simpler concepts, which are the ones that will most benefit your Swift skills, in just a couple of days. If you've never dealt with FP before, I promise you, it will expand your programming horizons forever. This is an excellent site: `http://www.learnyouahaskell.com`.

It's not often that the fastest way of doing something is also the best way, but this is one of those rare occasions. So much of what is available in Swift will make sense much sooner, and more deeply, after a couple of days of looking into a pure functional language such as Haskell.

It's fun, it's logical, and it's totally different to the C family of languages. And there are good reasons why Swift has adopted so many of its patterns.

Encapsulation

The very reason for the existence of object-oriented programming is to make programming more manageable by grouping properties and methods together in objects that are self-contained, re-usable units of code. Objects can communicate with other objects without needing to know the implementation details of those objects. Objects can contain other objects, they can be grouped together and addressed by other objects, and in an ideal world, that hierarchical relationship is straightforward and constant.

It all sounds so simple, and yet the greatest source of errors in any but the smallest of programs is **complexity**. This complexity is partly the result of not applying some of programming's simplest principles, or at least only applying them inconsistently.

The simplest principles of all are those that concern encapsulation. It's just *so* easy to forget.

Separation of concerns

Separation of concerns is important enough to be awarded its own abbreviation, **SoC**. It is a principle that applies to all levels of granularity. It means not only that objects administer their own internal state (and so on), but that entire functional layers of a program are themselves encapsulated and communicate with other layers via strict, well-defined interfaces.

And yet, how often it is that we forget to apply those principles. Take another look at the `ViewController.swift` file of our `SalesTaxCalc` project. Did it jar with you that a view-controller object was being required to perform tax calculations? I hope that, if it didn't, it will by the end of this book. A View Controller's responsibilities are many, but certainly don't include tax calculations. Such code belongs not only in a different class, but to an altogether different area of the program. The View Controller needs to send user input to that layer, and convey to the view the result of the calculation, but the calculation belongs somewhere else.

Not only do we reduce the complexity of the `ViewController` class itself, we also gain the option of changing how the calculation is performed without altering the `ViewController` class's code. Furthermore, if we have some `TaxCalculator` class, we can use it in other parts of the program, or even in a different program.

"But it's only a tiny program!" I hear you think. It would be foolish to suggest that such a small amount of code really needs that separation, but the fact is, all programs start off small, and where do you draw the line? It is hard to say where such a line is drawn, but safe to say that many, if not most, developers draw that line too late, too often.

Simplification

Part of the power of encapsulation (if you'll forgive such a dramatic turn of phrase) is that it offers a perfect opportunity for simplifying the processes of communication between objects, program layers, and everything in between.

The interface of any encapsulated entity should be as small and as simple as possible, rigidly applying a need-to-know approach. If your View Controller needs data from the Web, it shouldn't be creating HTTP requests, and it shouldn't even be telling the HTTP layer to make a request. It should probably not even be talking directly to any web-service layer at all. It should ask for information only, and leave all aspects of where that information comes from, and how it is obtained, to other layers of the program.

So, when you're stubbing data because the server-side software is still being written, or when you change which web service is being used, or when Google's API is changed to French, the View Controller should remain blissfully unaware that anything is different.

Similarly, the web-service layer should be completely user-agnostic, not knowing or needing to know where the HTTP responses are going. It should simply put the response into the closure it has been passed along with the request (a very simple mechanism in Swift, by the way) and call it.

While on the subject of the web-service layer, we should mention the **facade pattern**. The web service layer will probably contain a mish-mash of request types, HTTP methods, requests with headers and requests without, and all sorts of other stuff that can be hidden behind the facade. This facade offers a simple, limited channel through which other layers interact with the complex machinery behind it; a large and complicated set of structures is replaced, to all intents and purposes, by a single, smaller, and much simpler interface.

Here again, we can retain the specifications of the interface even when the whole thing behind it is tweaked, overhauled, or even swapped for something else.

A path through the forest

There's a lot of material to keep in mind as we plan each program layer, specify each class, and write each line of code. So how does all this translate into a concrete set of strategies for our code? And especially all that functional stuff--how does that fit in?

Here are some guidelines that we will follow in this book. It's not everything, of course, but a summary of the takeaways, as they say in the corporate world, representing the most important points presented here and how we intend to apply them.

Functions

As far as possible, we will avoid undeclared side effects in our functions. If a function is there to update a table, that's all it will do; it will have no effect on the rest of the program's data. If the data needs updating before we can use it in the table, then we will create and call a separate `updateData` function before updating the table itself.

Related to this, it should be possible to tell from a function's name, its arguments list, and its return statements, exactly what effects that a function will have. If our function destroys the Death Star and returns a random float between one and zero, we won't call it `randomFloat()`, but `randomFloatWithDeathStarDestruction()`.

Data flow

We will maintain as little state as possible. We will have properties only for values that must persist beyond function calls, so we will try to replace something like this:

```
someProperty = propertyValue
functionThatUsesSomeProperty()
```

With this, wherever possible:

```
functionThatUses(someProperty: propertyValue)
```

In the same vein, we will prefer to replace functions that access a property like this:

```
let customerName = "Sally"
let customerID = 101

func customerDetails() -> String
{
  return customerName
```

---

[94]

```
    + "\n\(customerID)"
}
let customerDetailsString = customerDetails()
```

With functions that take arguments explicitly, like this:

```
func betterCustomerDetails(
customerName: String,
customerID: Int) -> String
{
    return customerName
    + "\n\(customerID)"
}
let betterCustomerDetailsString = betterCustomerDetails(
customerName: "Sally",
customerID: 101)
```

This way, we gain clarity in two places. Firstly, the function's signature shows explicitly that something is to be done with a `customerName` and `customerID` value. Secondly, we can see at the call site what data is required by the function.

 Yes, there's a little more typing to do. This is a tiny price to pay for increased clarity, especially five months from now, when your app is being bought for a zillion dollars by Facebook, and they want *you* to refactor it.

This is the sort of stuff you'll pick up as you develop functional programming habits. Or read this book. Or best of all, both.

Objects

Generally, the internal state of an object will be hidden from the outside world, and any access to that state, or changes to it, will be done by that object's publicly visible methods, including the trivial stuff. Because the trivial stuff grows into non-trivial stuff, and before you know it, the whole world knows that your `Person` object stores its phone number as an `Int` instead of a `String` and is accessing it directly, making reversing that questionable decision very messy. Better to have a `phoneNumberAsInt()` method for any object that needs, well, the phone number as an `Int`.

Design patterns

We will facilitate communication between layers of our code in such a way that those layers need to know absolutely nothing of other layers, except how to request and send data to and from each other.

In principle, truly isolated layers of an app don't even need to reside in the same building, let alone within the same app instance, on one machine. We will try to imagine that each layer has to communicate with other layers that are being written by somebody else, who has no knowledge of what we are writing ourselves.

Where possible, we will prefer to hide groups of entities behind a facade, to facilitate simpler communication with such entity groups. This allows us to split, for example, a `financialReports` object into several distinct and more manageable objects, such as `archivedReports`, `pendingReports`, and `lastIssuedReports`, without complicating the picture for the rest of the app.

Summary

We have no need to be dogmatic about the concepts introduced in this chapter; we will use them *à la carte* as befits our needs. Think of this chapter as having sown the seeds of several concepts that you'll be using fluently later on; we will certainly revisit them again in this book.

Checking out this stuff elsewhere, in depth, is an extremely good idea. But do remember, whatever you might read, that there is no single best solution, style, or paradigm. Software development is a vast field, there's a lot of stuff out there, and it is entirely up to us to use it appropriately and skillfully.

In this chapter, you have learned the meaning of programming paradigms, the ways in which OOP differs from FP, some of the ways in which concepts from FP are applicable within an OOP context, and the importance of applying encapsulation consistently. Finally, you have also learned the rationale behind some of the coding strategies adhered to in this book.

The next chapter will introduce you to more advanced Swift programming topics, including many features of the language that have been mentioned in this chapter.

5
Advanced Swift

Swift encapsulates many different programming philosophies, it supports a number of different programming paradigms, and includes many of the most proven and successful developments in programming languages from the last decade or so.

Some of the borders have moved over time too: enumerations (or *enums*) and protocols have become so much more powerful that they can often replace the class-based hierarchies that have ruled the object-orientated roost for so long; control flow statements have become incredibly flexible; custom operators are easy to create; and perhaps most importantly of all, functions have become first class entities (we'll see what that means in a while).

In this chapter, you will learn about the following:

- Control flow
- Functions
- Enumerations
- Protocols
- Custom operators
- Array and dictionary operations

We can't cover all of Swift here, but we can ensure that there will be no obstacles to understanding what the subsequent chapters cover in terms of the Swift language.

Control flow

Some of Swift's control flow and control transfer statements are either considerably more flexible than their counterparts in other languages, or behave a little differently to what one may be accustomed to.

Using switch

We saw in Chapter2, *Basic Swift* that a Swift switch statement will test for the equality of any type, not just Int, and that we can test for values within a range.

That's just the start. The switch statement is an extremely flexible mechanism, and is capable of reducing large amount of if else code to much more concise, readable, and elegant blocks of code.

Compound cases

Cases can be combined on one line, if they are required to share the same block of code:

```
let a = 1

switch a
{
case 1,3,5,7,9:
  print("a is a single digit positive odd number")
case 0, 2,4,6,8:
  print("a is a single digit positive even number")
default:
  print("a is not a single digit positive number")
}
```

Tuple matching

If we are dealing with tuples in a switch statement, we can test against them too:

```
let b = 0
let c = 1
let t = (b, c)

switch t {
case (0,0):
  print("cannot divide by a or b")
case (0,_):
    print("cannot divide by a")
case (_,0):
      print("cannot divide by b")
default:
  print("can divide by both a and b")
}
```

Note how the underscore denotes a value in which we are not interested, as is the case with `for in` loops.

Value binding

If we need to access the values that are being tested against, we can bind them to variables within the scope of the `switch` statement.

Staying with our a, b, and t definitions, we could write the following:

```
switch t {
  case (let x, 0 ):
    print("cannot divide \(x) by b")
  case (0, let x ):
    print("cannot divide \(x) by a")
  default:
    print("can divide by both a and b")
}
```

Although we tested against one value, we are still able to extract the other for use inside the `switch`.

Using the where keyword

We use the `where` keyword to add additional tests within the `case` statement:

```
switch a
{
    case 0..<10 where a%2 == 0:
      print("a is a single digit positive even number")
    case 0..<10:
      print("a is a single digit positive odd number")
    default:
      print("a is not a single digit positive number")
}
```

Control transfer statements

We have already seen that there is no implicit fall-through in `switch` statements, which in turn makes a `break` statement within each case unnecessary. However, both these statements are available to us should we require them.

The break statement

We can add a `break` statement where we want to exit a block of code before it finishes:

```
switch a
{
case (let a) where a >= 1:
  print("a is a positive integer")
  if a >= 10
  {
    break
  }
  print("a is less than 10")
default:
  print("a is zero or less")
}
```

A second, perhaps more frequent use of `break` is to ignore some cases. Since `switch` statements must be exhaustive, we cannot simply leave them out, but we can insert `break` into whatever cases we wish to ignore:

```
switch a
{
case 0:
  print("can't divide by this")
case 1:
  print("dividing by one is pointless")
default:
  break
}
```

The fallthrough statement

Similarly, we may occasionally need the fall-through behavior that C `switch` statements exhibit. We can do this by adding the `fallthrough` keyword to a case:

```
switch a
{
case (let x) where x > 0:
  print("a is positive")
```

```
    fallthrough
case 0..<10:
  print("a is single digit")
default:
  break
}
```

With judicious use of these additional matching and control transfer features, we can often write extremely neat code. As usual, with power comes responsibility (if only I had a dollar for every blog post that says that), and it's worth reiterating the point that clarity trumps brevity; less is not *always* more.

The guard statement

The guard keyword is a little like a specialized edition of if else. It tests a Bool value, and if that value is true, then the guard statement has finished its work, and code execution continues with the next statement. If, however, the Bool value is false, then its else clause is executed. This clause *must* end in a return statement, which will leave the function in which the guard statement is used.

Here is an example:

```
func processEvenNumber(i: Int)
{
  guard i%2 == 0 else {
    return
  }

  print("\(i) is an even number)")
}
```

Now, on seeing that for the first time, you may think, as many do, "yeah big deal, I could have done that with an if statement." And that would be absolutely true, but the story's not over yet.

A `guard` statement offers three advantages to using an `if` statement:

- The code that comes after the (successful) test does not need to be wrapped in curly braces
- The `guard` statement enforces a return block (which may also contain any warnings and clean-up code that you may wish to include); failing to add one will result in a compiler error
- It encourages an early exit if the test fails

We'll look at some of the most common use cases for `guard` when we get to the optionals, later in this chapter.

Functions

Functions in Swift are more flexible than those of many other languages that you may have used. They'll certainly do most, if not all, the things you would expect when coming from C, Objective C or Java, but they also do more, in that they are also objects, just like any other types.

Function declarations offer considerable flexibility, much more so than Objective C, if you are coming from that background.

Arguments

Swift has some method parameter features not available in some languages, such as default and *variadic* arguments, and it is these that we will investigate first.

 Arguments or parameters? Both terms get used, as do `argument list` and `parameter list`, in both Apple's documentation and other documentation. For the purposes of this book, they are interchangeable.

Default arguments

Function parameters maybe given default values, in the following form:

```
func paintFace(color: String = "white")
{
  print("I have painted my face \(color)")
}
```

It's probably clear already that the function can be called with `color`, or with none, in which case the default value is used:

```
paintFace()
paintFace(color: "red")
```

If we run the code above, we'll see the following output:

```
I have painted my face white
I have painted my face red
```

This can also be used with optional type parameters. This allows us to test for the presence of an argument to the function:

```
func paintWagon(color: String? = nil)
{
  if let color = color {
    print("I have painted the wagon \(color)")
  }
}
```

Anonymous arguments

For some functions, the requirement to use an argument name at the call site can either produce somewhat ungainly--looking code, or can be made superfluous by the name of the function itself. In such cases, we can precede the argument name in the method declaration with an underscore, indicating to the compiler that the argument's name will not be included when calling the function:

```
func triple(_ a: Int) -> Int
{
  return a * 3
}
```

This code can now be called as follows:

```
let oldStockPrice  = 134
let x = triple(oldStockPrice )
```

Variadic arguments

We can include an arbitrary number of arguments (of a single type) using the following variadic parameter syntax:

```
func introduceNumbers(string: String, numbers: Int...)
{
  for number in numbers
  {
    print(string, number)
  }
}
```

We can now call this function with as many `Int` arguments as we need to:

```
introduceNumbers(string: "This is a", numbers: 1)
introduceNumbers(string: "This is a", numbers: 1,2,3)
```

 Variadic arguments once needed to be the last argument in the parameter list, but this is no longer the case. However, this is another one to watch out for when browsing older documentation of posts on the web.

Function overloading

If a function could reasonably be expected, from its name, to apply to different data types, which is certainly the case with our `triple` function, then we can overload it, meaning that we use the same symbol, but provide different argument types.

We could expand our `triple` function to apply to `Double` values, by providing this new function signature:

```
func triple(_ a: Double) -> Double
{
  return a * 3.0
}
```

If we should decide that `triple("la")` makes perfect sense in the context of our program, we can again provide an additional implementation with the appropriate signature:

```
func triple(_ a: String) -> String
{
    return "\(a)\(a)\(a)"
}
```

Now we have useful implementations for all three of the p named types. Running the following code will make that clear in the console:

```
print(triple(3))
print(triple(3.0))
print(triple("3"))
```

Function naming in Swift 3.0

We often need to have more than a verb in a function symbol in order for it to be unambiguous. A function named `ring`, for example, could apply to a number of situations, and it is not clear from the name which is the case here. So, in the case that our `ring` function should, in fact, apply to a telephone number, we'll need to add something to the function name to reflect that.

The Swift 3 API guidelines have something to say on this matter, and we should adhere to those guidelines for the sake of consistency, and therefore clarity:

Don't do this:

```
func ringNumber(_: Int) {...}
```

Do this instead:

```
func ring(number: Int) {...}
```

You may or may not agree that this is more readable, and more appropriate for function overloading, but either way, conforming to the conventions of a language are an important part of learning to use it.

First class functions

You have probably heard this before, but here it is again anyway: Swift functions are *first class* entities. This is not some commentary about the quality of the functions we write (unfortunately); rather it means that functions are objects themselves and like any other object can be passed as arguments to other functions.

It also means that functions can return other functions.

Functions that either take other functions as an argument, or have a function return value type are called *higher order* functions.

This is a big thing in Swift. Whereas in Objective C, passing code blocks was bolted on as an afterthought (and not very elegantly at that), first class functions are central to the Swift language, forming an essential part of its standard library, as well as being one of its more powerful, future-orientated features.

Many functions in Swift take a function as an argument, usually in the form of a closure, as we shall see shortly.

Functions are typed

Being objects, Swift functions are typed, which is an essential aspect of being able to be passed to and from higher order functions. A function that takes an Int as its single argument, and has no return value, has the type (Int) ->Void, for example, and this is exactly as it appears in a higher order function's parameter list.

Here is a function that takes that (Int) ->Void function type as one of its arguments:

```
func appraise(int: Int,
              f: (Int) ->Void)
{
   f(int)
}
```

This function, then, simply applies the function passed to it, f, to the Int passed to it, int.

Let's whip up a function of the required type:

```
func isBinary(i: Int)
{
  switch i
  {
  case 0: print("zero")
  case 1: print("one")
  default: print("not binary")
  }
}
```

We'll now call the `appraise` function, using the `isBinary` function as the second argument:

```
appraise(int: 3, f: isBinary)
```

This is a simple example which illustrates the syntax and principle of passing functions as arguments to other functions. We'll soon come to see the type of situation in which this idea is essential, but first, let's make things a little more readable, using type aliases.

We can use `typealias` declarations to improve readability, since functions are typed:

```
typealias Subroutine = () ->Void
```

Now we can refer to the type of function that takes no arguments and returns nothing as `Subroutine` **instead of** `()  -> void`.

Just as an aside, this name `Subroutine` is borrowed from the **Fortran** language, which distinguishes between functions that take a value and return some other value, and subroutines that take no value and return none. Thus, functions guarantee no side effects (see `Chapter 4`, *MVC and Other Design Patterns*), and subroutines do nothing *but* side effects.

This is an approach that produces clear and robust code in situations in which a purely functional approach is not possible, and I highly recommend adopting it.

Of course, we can `typealias` a function type that also returns a value:

```
typealias SingleIntegerOperation = (Int) ->Int
```

Now that we have such an alias, we can simplify the argument list of a higher order function like so:

```
func performMathOperation(int: Int,
                          f: SingleIntegerOperation)
{
   f(int)
}
```

We can have any number of arguments, just as in any function's argument list.

Here is an example that is useful in any program that deals with HTTP requests:

```
typealias HTTPRequestCompletionHandler
           = (Data, URLResponse, Error) ->Void
```

To see this function type, and its alias, in action, see Chapter 14, *The Benefits of Core Data*. This type of alias really tidies up the code.

Closures

We don't necessarily have to have previously defined a function in order to pass code to a higher order function. We can pass a closure, a (usually) nameless block of code. A closure may look something like these two examples:

```
{ print("I am a closure") }
{ return "I am a closure" }
```

The first of these is of type () -> Void, which we defined in the preceding Subroutine alias. The second is of type () -> String.

Now let's define a couple of artificially simple higher order functions, that can take these closures as arguments:

```
func executeSubroutine(f: Subroutine)
{
   f()
}

func executeStringGenerator(f: () ->String )
{
   let message = f()
   print(message)
}
```

So, all that these two functions do is call the functions that they have been passed in their argument list.

We call these higher order functions as we would any other function, passing the closure as the single parameter:

```
executeSubroutine(f: { print("I am a closure") } )
executeStringGenerator(f: { return"I am a closure" })
```

Both these calls will print the message to the screen, of course.

Before we move on to closures that themselves take arguments (which is where their usefulness starts to become apparent), there is an alternative syntax that should be mentioned. The two lines of code above can be written with so-called **trailing closures**, meaning that when the last argument of a function is a closure, we can write it outside of any brackets, as follows:

```
executeSubroutine { print("I am a closure") }
executeStringGenerator { return"I am a closure" }
```

Now, this syntax doesn't look anything like the standard syntax which we know from the C language family. It has its advantages, a discussion of which is beyond the scope of this book. If you are comfortable with it, including when it is nested inside other functions that use this syntax (where things start to get a little unclear sometimes), then go ahead and use it.

We will not use it in this book, for reasons of familiarity, and therefore clarity. But that should not be taken as an implicit rejection of the syntax.

We can also assign a closure to a variable, like this:

```
let myGreeting = {print("G'day, mate!")}
```

Now we can use myGreeting as the parameter in a call to executeSubroutine:

```
executeSubroutine(f: myGreeting)
```

Why wouldn't we just call the `print` statement directly? Well, we might want to make use of the fact that `executeSubroutine` doesn't know or care anything about the details of the function that it executes. We could pass it a different function, like this one:

```
let myOtherGreeting = {
 if loggedIn==true
    {
       print("G'day, matc!")
    }
 }
```

The `executeSubroutine` is completely unaware of any `loggedIn` status that may exist, and may or may not need to be checked. The part of the program responsible for checking whether being logged in is important or not can make that decision, and pass the appropriate function to `executeSubroutine`.

The syntax and use of closures really underscores the objective nature of functions.

Closures that take arguments

A higher order function may require a closure that takes an argument itself, and/or returns a value:

```
func processInt(f: (Int) ->Int )
{
  let x = f(42)
  // do something with x
  print(x)
}
```

This function takes a closure of type `(Int) -> Int`. Having defined a type alias, we could have used that instead:

```
func processInt(f:SingleIntegerOperation)
{
  let x = f(42)
  // do something with x
  print(x)
}
```

The `processInt` function doesn't know whether the `SingleIntegerOperation` that it is passed will print an `Int`, or use it to make an HTTP request, or whatever. It will simply supply that closure with an argument (in this case `42`).

So, we could pass the following closure:

```
{x in return x / 2}
```

This is the same as if we had defined a function:

```
func nameless(x: Int) -> Int {
   return x / 2
}
```

We can pass this closure to the `processInt` function:

```
processInt(f: {x in return x / 2})
```

What `processInt` does with the result of that closure is its own business; the closure itself, and indeed the code that passes that closure to `processInt`, knows nothing of the context in which it is called.

Closures with multiple arguments

Just like any function, a closure may take as many arguments as necessary:

```
let myIntOp: (Int, Int) -> Int = {x, y in return x * y}
```

Alternative closure syntax

There is a way to automatically name the arguments in a closure, leading to a slightly more concise syntax. The preceding closure could have been written as follows:

```
let myIntOp: (Int, Int) -> Int = { return $0 * $1 }
```

So $0, $1... are symbols for the arguments passed to a closure.

In the case of such one-liners, we can even omit the *return* keyword:

```
let myIntOp: (Int, Int) -> Int = { $0 * $1 }
```

This may look odd at first, but you get used to it pretty quickly.

Closures are functions; functions are closures

Anywhere that you can pass a closure, whether inline or as a named variable, you can also pass a function defined with the more familiar `func` statement.

The `follow` function in the following code makes use of a declared function, `audioWisdom`, a declared closure, `visualWisdom`, and an inline closure:

```
func audioWisdom() { print("Hear no evil") }
let visualWisdom = { print("See no evil") }

struct Acolyte
{
  func follow(theWay: Subroutine)
  {
    theWay()
  }
}

struct WiseOne
{
  func impartKnowledge(acolyte: Acolyte)
  {
    acolyte.follow(theWay: audioWisdom)
    acolyte.follow(theWay: visualWisdom)
    acolyte.follow(theWay: { print("Speak no evil") })
  }
}
```

The higher order `follow` function has been passed both a function and closures as its `theWay` parameter.

There are a few differences between a function defined with `func` and a closure defined with `let`. The closure cannot be recursive, for example. However, in the majority of cases, the choice between function and closure declaration is a matter of taste and style, guided by convention and the situation at hand. Defining a dozen simple `string` operations with `let` will look a lot more concise, and therefore easier to read, than a dozen function declarations.

Using map, reduce, and filter

Next, we'll look at a specialized set of standard library functions that take closure parameters:

- map returns an Array containing the results of applying a function to each item in a collection.
- filter returns a collection containing only those items of a collection that satisfy a specified match
- reduce returns a single value calculated by iterating through a collection, and applying a supplied function to each element and the accumulated results of the previous elements

Each of the functions and matches in this list are typically supplied as inline closures.

Map with arrays

The map function is simply the equivalent of looping through a collection (an Array, Set, or Dictionary object), applying a function to each element, adding the result of that function application to a new array, and returning that array once the iterations are complete.

So here are two ways to derive one Array object from another. First, an algorithm that will be familiar to most readers:

```
let units = [0,1,2,3,4,5,6,7,8,9]

func timesTen() -> [Int]
{
  var result: [Int] = []
  for i in units
  {
    result.append(i * 10)
  }
  return result
}
```

We'll pass the units array to the timesTen function:

```
let tens = tensFunc()
```

However, we can condense both the function implementation and the line of code that calls it to a single line, using map:

```
let tens = units.map({$0 * 10})
```

This essentially means take each element, apply the closure code to it, and add it to the array that is returned. The `units` array remains unchanged.

The resulting `tens` is the same in each case, but the `map` syntax automatically performs the iteration through the array and returns the new array.

The `map` function does not necessarily return an array of the same type as the array on which it is called:

```
let strings = units.map {"\($0)"}
```

Here we map the `units` array of `Int` objects to an array of `String` objects.

> Note that `map` is defined as a method of `Array` type objects. The same is true for `Set` and `Dictionary` types.

This makes the code significantly more concise where the implementation of the closure is only a small number of lines long.

There is a special case of `map`, called `flatmap`, with which we can unpack an `Array` of `Array` objects, combining them into a single `Array`:

```
let unitsAndTens = [units, tens]
let flatUnitsAndTens = unitsAndTens.flatMap({$0})
```

Running this code will produce an array of `Int` objects from an array of `[Int]` arrays.

Map with dictionaries

We can also map over the `(key, value)` pairs of a dictionary:

```
let numbers = ["1": "one",
               "2": "two",
               "3": "three"]
let other = numbers.map({(key, val) in
             (Int(key), val.uppercased())
             })
```

This syntax takes a little getting used to; just remember, you need to create a tuple when reading the key and value of each dictionary element into the closure, and similarly return the new values as a tuple.

reduce

The `reduce` function is applied to a collection of a given type, taking two parameters--an initial value of any type, and a closure. This closure takes two parameters--the first is of the initial type and the second is the same type as the collection. Then `reduce` applies the closure to the initial value and the first element of the collection. The result of that application is used as the first argument to another call of that closure, the second element being the next element of the collection, and so on. When all elements in the array have been processed, the accumulated result is returned:

```
let totalUnits = units.reduce(0, {$0 + $1})
```

This code returns the sum of the elements in the `totalUnits` array.

As was the case with `map`, the returned value does not need to be the same type as the type of the collection elements:

```
let unitsString = units.reduce("", {"\($0)\($1)"})
```

This code produces a `String` object, `"0123456789"`.

The initial value passed to `reduce` is not necessarily 0, or an *empty* value:

```
let totalUnits = units.reduce(1, {$0 * $1})
```

filter

The way `filter` works is quite simple. It iterates through a collection, applying a test to each element. Each element that passes the test is added to a new collection, which is returned:

```
let primes = [2,3,5,7,11,13,17,19,23]
let singleDigitPrimes = primes.filter({$0 <10})
```

The preceding code returns an array of single digit primes, leaving the `primes` array unchanged.

```
let intStrings = [1:"1",2:"4", 3:"3"]
let results = intStrings.filter { key, str in"\(key)"== str }
```

The preceding code returns a dictionary that does not contain the entry `2: "4"`, since it failed the test in the closure.

Nesting and chaining map, reduce, and filter

We can use multiple applications of map, reduce, and filter in a single statement. Take the following Array of [Int] objects:

```
let collections = [[5,12,17],[4,18],[9,11,3]]
```

Nesting

We can nest a filter application within a flatmap application:

```
let results1 = collections.flatMap
{
    intArray in intArray.filter { $0 <10 }
}
```

See if you can work out what type and value results1 will have, before running the code.

Chaining

We can also chain applications:

```
let results2 = collections.flatMap({$0}).filter({ $0 <10 })
```

Again, see if you can work out what type and value results2 will have, before running the code.

Knowing when to stop:

Like so many things in code writing, the extent to which you can reasonably chain and nest such statements should depend on code readability. It's not very smart to write code that looks very clever, if nobody can understand it.

Enumerations as data structures

Although we have already seen in Chapter 2, *Basic Swift*, that enum in Swift goes a lot further than merely representing integers with more memorable symbols; we have only just scratched the surface. The enum in Swift is so powerful that its use encroaches far into terrain that once belonged exclusively to heavyweight data structures such as classes.

For that reason, enum plays a huge part in Swift; give yourself some time to play around with them, and start to uncover the many ways in which they can offer a lightweight and clear option for structuring your data.

In this section, we'll look at three areas that are particularly powerful, one of which we might not expect to associate with an enum:

- enum methods
- Associated types
- Recursive enum definitions

Adding methods to enums

The first feature of a Swift enum that makes them so much more than just names of integer values (or any other type) is the ability to add methods to them.

Let us create an enum of traffic light colors, which also defines a method that can be called on any instances of that enum type:

```
enum TrafficLightColor
{
    case red, amber, green

    func inFrench() ->String
    {
        switch self
        {
          case .red:
            return "Rouge"
          case .amber:
            return "Jaune"
          case .green:
            return "Vert"
        }
    }
}
```

Note that no default case is necessary here, since our switch statement is exhaustive in terms of the possible TrafficLightColor cases.

Now, we have an enum that encapsulates not only the definition of the new type and its cases, but also a method with which we can have the instance return a String object that is computed from within the enum itself:

```
let stop: TrafficLightColor = .red
print(stop.inFrench())
```

Already it is becoming clear that there are many situations in which we would traditionally have created a class, but for which we can instead create a much more lightweight enum.

 Note that enum instances are passed by value, not by reference.

Associated values

Enum cases can include different types in Swift. When cases are declared to be of different types like this, we speak of an enum having associated values.

In this section, we will look at two valuable use cases for associated values:

- Using an enum to group together different data types
- Using an enum to create multiple distinct types from a single type

Grouping together different data types

Imagine a situation in which we need a function that will handle one of a limited number of types, though we don't know in advance which of those data types will be passed. Let's say we receive a response to an HTTP request, but we may get either a String or an Array of strings. To write a method that will take either of these types could mean that we have to use the Any type as an argument to that method. Yet we know that an attempt to pass, say, an Int is a mistake, and should not compile. Our method that takes an Any argument won't catch that.

We could override the method, providing a version for each data type, but we don't know at compile time which method will be called. So the conditional code starts to spread its ugly traces across our program.

However, there is a better way; we can define an `enum` that has two cases, each of which is a different type:

```
enum Response
{
    case string(String)
    case array([String])
}
```

When we create an instance of either case of this `enum`, we are required by the compiler to provide a value, which is type-checked against the case's type:

```
let response = Response.string("hi there")
let response = Response.array(["fox", "socks", "box"])
```

The method that we write simply has to test the `case` for its type:

```
func handleResponse(response: Response)
{
    switch response
    {
      case .string(let s):
          // do one thing
          print(s)
      case .array(let a):
          // do something else
          print(a)
    }
}
```

Nothing outside the method needs to start throwing `if` clauses around and covering the different scenarios. The `handleResponse` method knows what to do in each case, and accepts complete responsibility for dealing with the different types that may be passed.

Creating multiple distinct types from a single type

The flipside of that principle is a situation in which we pass values of the same type, but which may have different meanings. A method may need to accept both inches and centimeters as `Double`, but will need to know which it is dealing with. We could add a second argument, a `Bool` that states whether or not the argument is in inches; but what about if there is also the need to accept millimeters? Or even lightyears?

This problem can also occur in compound data types; coordinates, for example, can be `Cartesian` or `polar`, but both would be expressed as a combination of two `Double` values.

Well, once again, there is a way. We can define an `enum` that consists of different cases wrapping the same type of data:

```
enum Coordinate
{
    case cartesian(x: Double, y: Double)
    case polar(r: Double, theta: Double)
}
```

So. we have created a type, `Coordinate`, which groups together two distinct cases that just happen to have the same associated value type.

Nevertheless, `Coordinate.cartesian` and `Coordinate.polar` are different types as far as the compiler's type-checking is concerned.

Let's see this in action:

```
let myCartesianPosition = Coordinate.cartesian(x: 100.0, y: 100.0)
let myPolarPosition = Coordinate.polar(r: 50.0, theta: 0.5)

var myCoordinates: [Coordinate] = []
myCoordinates.append(myCartesianPosition)
myCoordinates.append(myPolarPosition)

for coordinate in myCoordinates
{
  switch coordinate
    {
    case .cartesian(let c):
      // do something with Cartesian coordinate
      print("Cartesian coordinate: x = \(c.x), y = \(c.y)")
    case .polar(let p):
      // do something with polar coordinate
      print("Polar coordinate: r = \(p.r), theta = \(p.theta)")
    }
}
```

This is a useful technique, and is worth experimenting with.

Mixed type arrays, anybody?

Did you notice something there? Look at these lines again:

```
myCoordinates.append(myCartesianPosition)
myCoordinates.append(myPolarPosition)
```

Using an `enum` as an array type, `[someEnum]`, we can store different types, using the associated types mechanism, within one `Array`.

And all of that in complete type-safety.

Recursive definitions

Some data structures need to be able to refer to instances of themselves within their own definition. You can't do this with a `struct`, but the lowly `enum` offers a solution.

Let's look at boxes that can contain either a number of books, or another box. We'll start by defining a `Book` type:

```
typealias Book = String
```

Yes, I know, the suggestion that a book is nothing more than a mere string of text is a little off the mark, but you know what I mean.

Next, we'll define a `Box` type, which can either contain `Book` objects (so an array of type `[Book]`), or another `Box` object:

```
enum Box
{
  case books([Book])
  case box(Box)
}
```

And straight away we get a compiler error.

However, this easily fixed, by declaring the `.box` case to be `indirect`:

```
enum Box
{
 case books([Book])
 indirectcase box(Box)
}
```

 We can also declare the whole `enum` to be `indirect`, by placing the `indirect` keyword before the `enum` keyword: `indirect enum Box`.

Now we can have books in a box, or a box in a box, or a box of books in a box.

Making constants with an enum

Here's a really good use for `enum`: We can use `enum` to create a restricted subset of some type, much as we did with the preceding `Coordinate` enum.

For example, when we are defining HTTP request code, we don't want any typing mistakes to find their way into our `String` objects, rendering the keys (silently) unusable.

A common solution is to create a list of constant strings like so:

```
let kUserName = "userName"
let kPassword = "password"
let kvideoPath = "/video"
```

And so on.

The prefix k indicates that this constant is used as a `key` for something, perhaps a `Dictionary` destined for passing to an HTTP request body. This is not dictated by the syntax, it is just a widely-used convention.

But these keys can still get mixed up, since they are simply `String` objects, and so the compiler cannot check that we are passing the right strings. Any `String` will keep the compiler happy.

By using an `enum`, we can gather together any number of `String` objects under one type:

```
enum APIKey: String
{
    case userName, password, email
}
```

Remember that Swift automatically assigns raw String values to `enum` cases that are declared to be of type `String`, as discussed previously.

Now when we need to specify method parameter types, and any other type-related definitions, we can use the `APIKey` type instead of the `String` type, thereby ensuring that the string `"/video"` can never be passed as an API key--the compiler will complain (and refuse to compile, of course).

In our data layer, far away on the other side of the program, we may declare something like the following:

```
typealias APIParams = [APIKey: String]
```

And now we can't mess up assigning one of the valid strings to anything declared to be of type APIKey:

```
let userCredentials: APIParams = [.userName: "Ali Baba",
                                  .password: "Open Sesame",
                                  .email: "notinvented@themoment"]
```

Back in the HTTP service layer, we can then safely extract the String values from the APIKey typed values:

```
var httpParameters: [String: String] = [:]
for apiKey in userCredentials.keys
{
  httpParameters[apiKey.rawValue] = userCredentials[apiKey]
}
```

This leads to significantly safer code when passing strings around, strings that would otherwise happily compile and lead to complete confusion when the HTTP request comes back with the following error message:

"What??"

Replacing classes

We have seen that enum types can be powerful and useful constructs, and in many cases they will replace classes as the go-to data structure. Where value-passing semantics are needed instead of reference passing, and where no inheritance is needed, it's always worth considering whether an enum is, in fact, all that is needed.

Protocols

A protocol is a guarantee made by any type that conforms to (or *adopts*) that protocol, that it will comply with certain requests when required to do so.

If we have a `Tractor` type, a `Helicopter` type, and a `Submarine` type, we may wish that they all implement a `takeMeToTheBeach` method. We don't care how they do it, each type will take care of the details itself, in possibly very different ways (depending on who's flying the submarine), but we do know that they will implement a method of that name.

Declaring protocols involves specifying either or both the following:

- Methods that conformant types must implement
- Properties that conformant types must implement

Once we have types that conform to protocols, we can often dispense with the need for subclassing abstract classes.

Declaring method requirements

Let us start by declaring a simple protocol and having a look at what it all means:

```
protocol Talkative
{
   func sayHi()
}
```

The `Talkative` protocol says that any type declaring itself to conform to the protocol will implement its own version of the `sayHi` function.

That's all it does, and yet simple though it is, this idea turns out to be immensely powerful. Keep reading.

Conforming to a protocol

Declaring a type to conform to a protocol is very straightforward:

```
struct ChattyStruct: Talkative
{
}
```

At this point, the compiler will point out the fact that your type does *not* yet conform to the protocol, since it doesn't yet implement the `sayHi` function, so let's fix that:

```
struct ChattyStruct: Talkative
{
  func sayHi()
    {
      print("hi")
    }
}
```

Now we can call the `sayHi` method on any `ChattySruct` type object:

```
let anon = ChattyStruct()
anon.sayHi()
```

Note that we didn't include any default implementation of the required method in the protocol declaration. To do that, we would need to create an extension of the protocol:

```
extensionTalkative
{
   func sayBye(){
     print("bye!")
   }
}
```

Now we can call that method, and since `ChattyStruct` has not provided its own implementation, the default is used, so both these lines of code will print the appropriate text to the console:

```
anon.sayHi()
anon.sayBye()
```

Protocol advantages over classes

There are some tricks that we can do with protocols that we cannot do in a class/subclass hierarchy.

Extending existing types with a protocol

We can declare a type that we haven't declared ourselves, including Swift's own types, to conform to our custom protocol by using an `extension`:

```
extension Int: Talkative
```

```
  {
    func sayHi()
    {
      print("Hey, I'm \(self)")

      if self%2 != 0
      {
        print("Isn't that odd?")
      }
    }
  }
```

We can now call the `sayHi` method on any `int`:

```
1.sayHi()
```

 Note that by using `self`, we can access the instance's value.

This is something you couldn't do with subclassing--we now have the ability to customize any and all Swift types in any way that we need to, including *primitives* such as `Int` and `Double`.

Creating collections of mixed types

Using the code we have written so far, we can create an `Array` that contains both an `Int` and a `ChattyStruct`:

```
var talkativesArray: [Talkative] = []
talkativesArray.append(anon)
talkativesArray.append(42)
```

In the code above, it can be seen that an `Array` (or any other collection) can be of type `<SomeProtocol>`, rather than be restricted to a specific type.

This means that we can perform any operation with the elements of `talkativesArray` that are specified by the protocol:

```
for entity in talkativesArray
{
    entity.sayHi()
}
```

Note that we cannot use any methods that are not in the protocol specification, since all we know about the contents of the array is that each element conforms to the given protocol; at least, not without some extra work. To use methods specific to the specific types, we must first try to cast the element to that type:

```
if let entity = entity as? Int
{
    print("... and twice \(entity) makes \(entity * 2)")
}
```

Protocols can conform to protocols

Protocols that declare themselves to conform to another protocol or protocols can be said to *inherit* from those protocols:

```
protocol TalkativePerson: Talkative
{
    ... additional requirements
}
```

We might now begin to see what was meant by making subclassing unnecessary. There is no limit to the number of protocols to which a type, or another protocol, may conform. Similarly, there is no limit to the *depth* of inheritance; we could have `ProtocolA`, which inherits from `ProtocolB`, which in turn inherits from `ProtocolC`, and `ProtocolD` and so on.

This is a much more lightweight principle than subclassing, and also introduces the ability to mix and match protocols in a manner that many languages don't support in their class mechanism.

In the next section, we'll add some properties to our `TalkativePerson` protocol.

Declaring required properties

Not surprisingly, we can also add properties to a protocol. Protocol properties must be declared with `var`, and can be declared to be settable (that is, read--only) or settable and gettable (meaning read and write).

Let's add a couple of properties to the `TalkativePerson` protocol:

```
protocol TalkativePerson: Talkative
{
    var name: String { get }
    var address: String { getset}
}
```

`TalkativePerson` contains everything from `talkative`, and adds two further properties. We assume (for the sake of the demonstration) that people don't change their names, but do change their addresses.

 Using `{ get set }` will prevent types that conform to the `TalkativePerson` protocol from declaring their `address` property with `let`.

Implementing required properties

The implementation of protocol properties looks just the same as any other property declaration:

```
struct MarketingGuy: TalkativePerson
{
    let name: String
    var address: String

    func sayHi() {
        print("Yes, I'm \(name), here's my card. Say, may I blah
        blah blah...")
    }
}
```

The compiler will help you with two things here:

- It will not let you declare a `{ get set }` property with `let`
- It will insist that the properties (just like the methods) are implemented

Class-only protocols

If a protocol is to apply to types that are assumed to use reference semantics (rather than being passed by value), then we can create a class protocol that restricts its use to classes:

```
protocol ClassyProtocol: class
{
   func addClassToClassesList() // or whatever
}
```

Any attempt to declare a value type, whether `struct`, `Int` or any other, will be met with a compiler error.

Class considerations

When declaring a class to conform to a protocol, any superclass declarations must come first:

```
class MyClass: NSObject, ClassyProtocol
{
   func addClassToClassesList()
   {
      //
   }
}
```

Protocol composition

We can declare types to conform to more than one protocol, creating a type that satisfies the requirements of both protocols. This is called **protocol composition**.

Let's first declare another protocol:

```
protocol Pensive
{
   func reactToStimulus()
}
```

Now we can declare a type that conforms to both the `Talkative` and `Pensive` protocols:

```
struct Philosopher: Talkative, Pensive
{
  func sayHi()
  {
    print("hi")
  }

  func reactToStimulus()
  {
    print("I thing therefore I am")
  }
}
```

The syntax of declaring protocol compliance looks much like the syntax for declaring subclasses, but value types cannot inherit from other types (that is, declare themselves as subclasses). However, adopting a protocol is to all intents and purposes a form of inheritance.

Customizing operators

In addition to the operators provided by the Swift language, we can both override existing operators and, where necessary, create new ones.

Adding operator implementations to types

This sounds so complicated, but it is, in fact, really easy. All we need to do is define an implementation of any given operator for any given type.

 For the time being, we'll use a custom type, although what we are doing can be used equally effectively for Swift and Cocoa types.

We'll start by defining a custom type:

```
struct GridMovement
{
  let rows: Int
  let cols: Int
}
```

Now that we have it, we notice that it would make perfect sense to be able to apply some basic arithmetical operators to our type. We could add these to the main type declaration, but convention (young though it is) suggests we put it in an extension:

```
extension GridMovement
{
  static func + (lhs: GridMovement,
                  rhs: GridMovement) -> GridMovement
  {
    let rows = lhs.rows + rhs.rows
    let cols = lhs.cols + rhs.cols
    return GridMovement (rows: rows, cols: cols)
  }
}
```

As you can see, we're treating the + operator as we would any method name, though we do need to declare it to be static, making it a type method rather than an instance method.

So, we can now add two GridMovement together. How about multiplying a GridMovement by an Int?

```
static func * (multiplier: Int,
                movement: GridMovement) -> GridMovement
{
  let rows = multiplier * movement.rows
  let cols = multiplier * movement.cols
  return GridMovement (rows: rows, cols: cols)
}

static func * (movement: GridMovement,
                multiplier: Int) -> GridMovement
{
  let rows = movement.rows * multiplier
  let cols = movement.cols * multiplier
  return GridMovement (rows: rows, cols: cols)
}
```

Note that we have to provide (Int, GridMovement) and (GridMovement, Int) signatures, because we don't know in which order they will be called.

Now let's round it off with the += operator:

```
static func += (lhs: inout GridMovement,
                rhs: GridMovement)
{
  lhs = lhs + rhs
}
```

Pretty simple, having already implemented the + operator.

Run the following code to check it all worked out:

```
var movementA = GridMovement (rows: 3, cols: 5)
movementA = movementA * 2
print(movementA)
var movementB = GridMovement (rows: 11, cols: 13)
let movementC = movementA + movementB
print(movementC)
```

Equivalence

We can also implement the == operator, since again it makes sense to be able to compare two GridMovement objects:

```
extension GridMovement
{
    static prefix func -><- (movement: inout GridMovement)
                                        -> GridMovement
    {
        return GridMovement (rows: movement.col, cols: movement.row)
    }
}
```

These GridMovement objects are usable now as, say, chessboard moves that can be added together, multiplied by an integral number of moves, and compared with each other. Now go write a chess program.

Just kidding.

Custom operators

We are not limited to coding implementations of the operators we know already. If we need to implement an operator for functionality for which +, % and so on make no sense (or are already in use), we can define our own, using any of a set of characters allowed by Swift.

The following is a list of characters that may make up custom operators:

```
/ = - + ! ? * % <>& | ^ ~
```

Operators may also start with a . character.

There are also some other Unicode characters that are allowed, but are not valid as first characters. See Apple's documentation if you need to go beyond the set listed previously.

To write a custom operator, we need to complete two steps:

- Define the operator itself
- Implement the behavior of the operator

Remember that we can do this by extending existing types, including those provided by Swift, such as `Int` and `String`.

In the next section, we will write an operator that swaps the rows and columns dimensions of our `GridMovement` struct.

Defining a custom operator

Firstly, we need to tell Swift about how our operator looks:

```
prefixoperator-><-
```

This declaration must take place at file scope, meaning outside of any `class`, `func`, or other declarations.

So what does `prefix` mean in this context? There are three categories of operator, defined according to their position with regards to their operands:

Prefix operators

These are operators that are placed before their operand, for example the – operator:

```
Let a = -3
```

Postfix operators

These are operators that are placed after their operand, for example the ? operator:

```
if unwrapped = myVar? {...}
```

Infix operators

These are operators that are placed between two operands, for example the % operator:

```
let a = 23 % 5
```

So the syntax for using our new operator will be -><-someGridMovement.

Implementing a custom operator

Having defined what it looks like, and how we use it, we now need to define what the new operator actually *means*. We could include an implementation in the main definition of the GridMovement class, but a convention is emerging to put such code in an extension. This makes sense when we consider that what we are actually doing is defining something that belongs not so much to the type itself, as to the code that uses it:

```
extension GridMovement
{
static prefix func -><- (movement: inoutGridMovement)
               ->GridMovement
  {
    return GridMovement(rows: movement.col, cols: movement.row)
  }
}
```

Since this method mutates a variable (as opposed to returning a new one) we need to declare it as an inout parameter.

 The inout keyword forces us to be explicit about the fact that we want to change a variable in place. Without that, a function assumes its arguments to be immutable. This is a good example of Swift's safety as default philosophy.

Try it out with something like the following code:

```
print(movementB)
-><-movementB
print(movementB)
```

In the console, we will see we have mutated the `movementB` variable.

We have chosen a deliberately provocative set of characters for the operator here. Given that any such operator could also be implemented as a function, any operators we create should be immediately readable.

There should be a strong rationale for creating an operator instead of a function.

Collection types

Although we don't have space here to discuss all the methods that are made available by `Array` and `Dictionary` types, we should cover, albeit briefly, the most common operations on those objects.

This section provides examples of these most common operations, and it is assumed that they are mostly self-explanatory; elaborations are added where that is possibly not the case.

Arrays

We'll start, as one usually does, with arrays.

Comparing arrays

Arrays, being value types, are compared according to their contents:

```
let arrA = [1, 2, 3]
let arrB = [1, 2, 3]
let arrC = [3, 4, 5]

arrA == arrB
arrA != arrC
```

Both these comparisons return `true`, as one would expect.

Mutating an array

Adding and inserting individual elements or several elements is performed as follows:

```
var arr = [2, 3, 5, 7]
arr.append(11)

let tens = [10, 20, 30]
arr.append(contentsOf: tens)

arr.insert(13, at: 5)
arr.insert(40, at: arr.endIndex)
arr[6...8] = [17, 19, 23]
```

Using arrays to create new arrays

These methods do not mutate the array, but return new ones:

```
let tail = arr.dropFirst()
let truncated = arr.dropLast()
let fragment = arr.dropFirst(3)
let rearFragment = arr.dropLast(3)
```

Testing array elements

We can access single elements, or a subgroup of elements, according to the results of a supplied test:

```
let firstBiggerThan10 = arr.first(where: { $0 >= 10 })
let allBiggerThanTen = arr.filter({ $0 >= 10}
```

We can also easily extract maximum and minimum values from an array of a type that conforms to the Comparable protocol:

```
let max = arr.max()
let min = arr.min()
```

Removing elements from an array

When using the various methods that remove elements, we must be careful to distinguish those that mutate the array and return the removed element(s), and those that simply mutate the array.

Methods that mutate and return a value

The following methods all return the elements that they remove from the array, as well as mutating the array:

```
let thirdElement = arr.remove(at: 2)
let firstElement = arr.removeFirst()
let lastElement = arr.removeLast()
```

The methods above will cause a runtime error if called on an empty array. However, the following method returns an optional value, which will be `nil` if the array is empty:

```
let lastInt = arr.popLast()
```

The `lastInt` value will need to be unwrapped before being used as an `Int`.

Mutating non-returning methods

The following methods do not return the removed elements:

```
arr.removeLast(2)
arr.removeFirst(3)
arr.removeAll()
```

It's particularly confusing that the methods `removeFirst` and `removeLast` behave differently depending on whether an `Int` argument is supplied, so watch out for that one.

Sorting arrays

The sort methods available on arrays come in two flavors:

The `sorted` method returns a new, sorted array:

```
var randomInts = [233, 6, 85, 1, 6, 24]
let sortedInt = randomInts.sorted()
print(randomInts) //unchanged
```

The `sort` method mutates the array in place:

```
randomInts.sort()
print(randomInts) //mutated
```

Dictionaries

Just like `Array` objects, `Dictionary` objects have a set of methods that we can't cover completely here, but we can look at the most common operations.

Accessing all keys or values

If necessary, we can access all of a dictionary's keys or values, as follows:

```
var dict: Dictionary<String, String> = ["one": "drum",
                                        "two": "shoe",
                                        "three": "knee"]

for key in dict.keys { print(key) }
for value in dict.values { print(value) }
```

Mutating dictionaries

We saw in `Chapter 2`, *Basic Swift* that we can change a dictionary element's value like so:

```
dict["someKey"] = someValue
```

Using the `updateValue` method instead returns the old value:

```
let oldThree = dict.updateValue("tree", forKey: "three")
print("oldThree was", oldThree)
let oldFour = dict.updateValue("door", forKey: "four")
print("oldFour was", oldFour)
```

If we run the preceding code, we get the following debug console output:

```
oldThree was Optional("knee")
oldFour was nil
```

Since there was no element with the key `"four"`, `oldFour` holds the value `nil`.

Removing dictionary elements

We can remove an element from a dictionary by setting its value to `nil`:

```
dict["three"] = nil
```

If we need to retrieve the old value as well, we can use the `removeValue` method:

```
let val = dict .removeValue(forKey: "three")
```

If we need to remove dictionary elements one at a time in no particular order, and have their values returned, we can use the `popFirst` method:

```
let poppedElement = dict.popFirst()
```

In this case, the `dict` dictionary had been mutated, and `poppedElement` now contains either the value of the key/value pair, or `nil` if the dictionary was empty.

We can remove all elements from a dictionary using either of these two methods:

```
dict.removeAll()
dict = [:]
```

Optionals

In `Chapter 2`, *Basic Swift*, we looked at the raw basics of Swift's optionals. In this section, we'll flesh that out to cover their most essential use cases.

Conditional downcasting

We have already seen how to safely unwrap an optional value:

```
if let id = Int("12364677")
{
  print("Valid id: \(id)")
}
```

In this case, we know that the `Int` `init` method that takes a `String` argument returns an optional `Int`. We only need to test whether it contains a value or `nil`, and if it contains a value, we know that we can unwrap the value to get an `Int`.

If, however, we don't know what type may be returned by a function, we can attempt a downcast with the `as?` keyword:

```
let jsonResponse: [String: Any] = ["user": "Elliot",
                                   "id": "Elliot2016"]

if let userString = jsonResponse["user"] as? String
{
  print("User string contains \(userString.characters.count)
  characters")
}
```

This code will print the required information, since the downcast succeeds.

Now try this code:

```
if let id = jsonResponse["id"] as? Int
{
  print("Valid id: \(id)")
}
else
{
  print("Invalid id")
}
```

This will print the `else` statement, since the `id` downcast has returned `nil`.

Unwrapping optionals with guard

The `guard` statement will only allow further execution within a scope if a test passes, and so is suitable for testing whether binding an optional to a value has succeeded:

```
guard let id = Int("42") else { return }
let myID: Int = id
print(myID)
```

The preceding code will print `myID` to the console, since the downcast succeeded.

Perhaps the most common usage for the `guard` statement is at the beginning of a function that takes an optional argument:

```
func printId(int: Int?)
{
  guard let myInt = int else {
    print(#function, "failed")
    return
```

```
    }

    // .. do lot of code with int
    print(int)
}
```

In the preceding code, we test for the presence of a value, and if there is `nil`, we print an error and then return immediately from the function. However, if there is a value in the `int` argument, it is unwrapped, and the rest of the function needs no extra braces, and no further unwrapping and/or testing of the `myInt` variable.

```
printId(int: Int("34a"))
```

What will this code print?

Implicitly unwrapped optionals

The following code will produce an error:

```
let a:Int
a = 3
let b: Int = a
let c: Int = a * 2
```

Even though variable `a` does contain a value, its type is still an optional `Int`, and cannot be assigned to the values of `b` and `c`, which are declared to be non-optionals of type `Int`.

Rather than force unwrap `a` each time we use it, we can declare it to be an implicitly unwrapped optional, using the ! operator, which kind of bakes the unwrapping into the variable itself:

```
var a:Int!
a = 3
let b: Int = a
let c: Int = a * 2
```

We would only do this when we can guarantee that `a` can never be `nil`, but there are occasions when we can do just that. The `IBOutlet` from an Interface Builder storyboard is a common example.

If an implicitly unwrapped optional is unexpectedly `nil` *at runtime, your program will, of course, drop dead on the spot.*

Summary

This chapter has been a pretty rapid run through most of the Swift concepts and practices we will need throughout the rest of this book. It by no means covers all that Swift has to offer; that must be the subject of a book of its own. But understanding the material here will serve to make understanding the rest of the book much easier.

You have learned the following in this chapter:

- How `switch` and `guard` can improve clarity, economy, and readability in our code
- Making the most use of Swift functions, and how to use first class functions as objects
- Making use of enumerations as data structures that can replace some classes
- The use of protocols, and particularly their strengths as an alternative to class inheritance
- How to override operators and create new ones
- Handling the most common operators on collection types

The next chapter will take us into the Cocoa landscape, where we will begin to take a thorough look at how it works as a framework, and the programming concepts we will need to make the most effective use of its vast functionality.

6
Cocoa Frameworks - The Backbone of Your Apps

We suggested a metaphor in Chapter 1, *Hello macOS*, making a comparison between an artist's brushes and paints and the frameworks available to the macOS developer through Cocoa. In this chapter, we'll take a look at some of the concepts we will need to make effective and creative use of all the tools that Cocoa puts at our disposal. Like using any tool, using Cocoa's frameworks means being aware of how they work and how they were intended to be used. This is not to say that macOS development is nothing more than learning to connect up a few pre-prepared framework objects, far from it. The very power of Cocoa is that it gives you an enormous amount of control over its seemingly innumerable features, allowing you to dive deeply into the nuts and bolts wherever you need that level of access.

But it does mean adhering to some ground rules as a kind of default strategy, and veering away from that when you have good reason to. You won't become the best developer you can be without a firm grip on Cocoa's way of doing things.

If that sounds a little restrictive, remember that Johann Sebastian Bach, Brian Eno, and Jimi Hendrix used the same twelve notes, but sound, well, slightly different.

In this chapter, you will learn the following:

- The significance and features of Foundation Kit
- How to make your classes a subclass of NSObject, and why you'd want to
- Importing Foundation, AppKit, or Cocoa
- How to make your classes compliant with key-value coding
- How to use Cocoa bindings to remove a large amount of UI synchronization code

Understanding Foundation Kit

The `Foundation` **Kit** framework that comes with Cocoa (officially it's got the Kit appended to it, but not many people bother) provides us with a number of basic utility classes, which were originally written to extend the Objective C programming language. These include strings, arrays, sets, dictionaries, and dates, for example.

Some of the more basic classes are, strictly speaking, no longer needed for Swift development, since Swift already provides support for strings, text, and collections such as dictionaries and arrays. However, we will see later that they can often be of use to us. `Foundation` is baked into the core of Cocoa, so we will need to make use of most of what it has to offer.

Then there are a larger number of classes that go way beyond basic data types and structures, such as those providing us with classes for network connectivity, notifications, threading, user defaults, and many others.

In addition to its classes, `Foundation` also defines a number of protocols that we use frequently, including the `NSObject` and `NSKeyValueObserving` protocols, both of which we'll be looking at more closely in this chapter.

Another aim of `Foundation` is to encapsulate a range of technologies that can be used across all of Apple's platforms, thus enhancing portability. Although Cocoa provides us with many user interface elements, which are generally not portable across platforms, it should not be forgotten that there are extensive amounts of Cocoa code that reside under the hood, and which use frameworks that would be equally at home on iOS, tvOS, or of course, macOS.

Understanding NSObject

Using Cocoa (and therefore `Foundation`) requires a certain level of familiarity with `NSObject`, but what exactly is this entity that seems to lie at the root of everything?

Well, in Objective C at least, `NSObject` was pretty much exactly that; it was the **root object** of most of the classes used in Objective C, and it defines many behaviors that are inherited by all of its subclasses, including those that we use in Swift.

Now, Swift itself has no explicit base object. You can declare a class, for example, like this:

```
class MySwiftClass
{
   var someProperty = 0
}
```

In the preceding code, `MySwiftClass` is not declared to be the subclass of any other class, and indeed, trying to make any call to `super` will trigger an error, since it has no superclass:

`'super' members cannot be referenced in a root class`

 Any class declared without a superclass is considered a root class in Swift.

So what about all the functionality encapsulated in `NSObject`, how do we get our hands on that?

First of all, do we even need to? I think the only fair answer to that is *sooner or later, almost certainly sooner, yes*. There are many things you can do in Swift without using `NSObject`, but there are too many things that you can't. We really do need it in a number of critical situations, which we will cover as we work through the code in this book. There is no need to do this habitually; many of your classes, perhaps most of them, will never need the `NSObject` protocol, but some will.

Adding that NS-goodness to our classes is very easy; we simply declare our class to be a subclass of `NSObject`:

```
class MySwiftClass:NSObject
{
   var someProperty = 0
}
```

With this one small addition to your class declaration, your class will now slip gracefully into the Cocoa/NSObject world.

Import statements

Your `.swift` files must import frameworks in order to use them, but we don't necessarily need to import the whole of Cocoa.

If you have, for example, a model class that has no need of interacting with any UI elements (and a model class should certainly not be interacting with UI elements), you don't need to import Cocoa, `Foundation` will suffice:

```
import Foundation
class MyFoundationClass: NSObject
{
 var someDate = Date()
}
```

So here, `MyFoundationClass` is using the `NSObject` class and the `Date` class, both of which require `Foundation`. If you comment out the `import` statement, you'll get two errors, with the compiler complaining it doesn't know what those two classes are:

```
15
 16    class MyFoundationClass: NSObject        ❶ Use of undeclared type 'NSObject'
17    {
 18        var someDate = Date()                 ❶ Use of unresolved identifier 'Date'
19    }
20
```

This is in contrast to the `MySwiftClass` we created previously. That class declared only an `Int` property, which is part of Swift, not `Foundation`, and also declared no `Foundation` superclass. So there was no need to `import Foundation`.

If our class needs to use user interface classes, which are not included in `Foundation`, such as the `NSColor` class, we need to import the `AppKit` framework:

```
importAppKit
class MyAppKitClass: NSObject
{
  var someColor = NSColor.red
}
```

Here again, if you see something like the following screenshot, you've probably used the wrong `import` statement (most likely `Foundation`):

```
20
21    class MyAppKitClass
22    {
23        var someColor = NSColor.red        ⊘ Use of unresolved identifier 'NSColor'
24    }
25
```

Since `AppKit` imports `Foundation` itself, there is no need for us to explicitly import it.

If we also need a framework such as Core Data (more of which is in Chapter 9, *Getting More from Interface Builder*), which is not the case here, we would need to import Cocoa in its entirety.

 `Foundation` is imported by `AppKit`, which is imported by Cocoa.

So now that we have a grasp of why we need `Foundation` and how to make sure we can subclass `NSObject` when we need to, we can turn to another idiom of Cocoa programming, one that is very widely used and can save you a lot of coding, **key-value observing**.

Leveraging key-value observing

Key-value observing, generally abbreviated in literature to KVO, is a mechanism by which an object can observe properties of another object, so that when, for example, the data in your data model changes, that change is automatically reflected in the user interface. There are different ways for objects to notify one another in Cocoa; KVO, which is used for a number of purposes within Cocoa itself, including Cocoa bindings, Core Data, and AppleScript support, is a well-established pattern.

It doesn't take a huge amount of effort to set up, and does save you a fair amount of repetitive boilerplate code writing.

Coding for KVO

There are three steps involved in setting up KVO, and one cleanup step when we have finished observing:

1. We need to prepare our classes for KVO.
2. We need to let the system know when we wish to observe an object, and which change(s) we wish to observe.
3. We need to override NSObject's method that handles the change notification.

   And when we are done, the last step:

4. Let the system know that we have finished observing the object (either because we no longer need to observe changes to properties of the object, or because the observing object is to be deallocated).

Once we have done that, we will have created a fully KVO--compliant class and implemented the observation code in another class.

KVO - compliant classes

Let's first create a class that will satisfy the very simple demands of KVO.

 Both the observable class and the observing class that wish to make use of KVO must be subclasses of NSObject. That means we don't use KVO with structs and enums, and we cannot use it with generics.

Create a new Xcode project, and name it PeopleWatcher:

1. Using *command + N* to create a new file, select **Swift File** and name it Person.swift.
2. Change the import statement in the file to this:

   ```
   import AppKit
   ```

   This will allow us to use the classes of AppKit.

3. Below the `import` statement, add the following code:

```
class Person: NSObject
{
 dynamic var name: String
 dynamic var busy: Bool
 dynamic var shirtColor: NSColor

 init(name: String,
        busy:Bool,
        shirtColor: NSColor)
    {
        self.name = name
        self.busy = busy
        self.shirtColor = shirtColor

        super.init()
    }
}
```

We can see that the `Person` class has three properties: `name`, which is a `String` object; `busy`, which is a `Bool`; and `shirtColor`, which is an `NSColor`, which is a class from `AppKit`. So here we have properties both from Swift and AppKit.

As one would expect, `Person` objects will be ranked according to the color of their shoes.

So what's with the `dynamic` keyword? Well, this asks the Swift compiler to use something called **dynamic dispatch**, which in turn allows something called **interception**, which is part of the *Objective C messaging* system, and is basically something that falls outside of the scope of this book except to say:

Class properties that are to be used in key-value observation need to be marked as dynamic.

And the rest we'll leave for another day.

The `Person` class has an `init(name: busy: shirtColor:)` method, and notice there's no `override` here, since `NSObject`, the superclass, has an `init()` method, but no `init(name: busy: shirtColor:)` method. `Person` is a `class`, not a `struct`, so we don't get a member--wise initializer for free.

So that's done. With the addition of `dynamic` to the properties, the class becomes KVO--compliant. How easy was that?

Adding the observer

So let's add an observer. We will create a `PeopleWatcher` class that holds a reference to a `Person` object, and will observe changes in the busy property of `Person`:

1. Create a new Swift file and name it `PeopleWatcher.swift`.
2. Replace the `import` statement with the following code:

```swift
import AppKit

class PeopleWatcher: NSObject
{
  privatevar myContext = 0
  var myPerson: Person


  init(person:Person)
    {
      self.myPerson = person
      super.init()

      myPerson.addObserver(self,
                           forKeyPath: "busy",
                           options: [.new],
                           context: &myContext)
    }
}
```

So what's going on here?

First we create a private context variable, `myContext`, which we will use to identify the change notifications when they come in. The value of this variable is completely arbitrary; we will only be using its location in memory for identification. More of this shortly.

Next create an `init` method that takes a `Person` object as its argument, and retain this reference in the class's `myPerson` property.

In the `init` method, we add this `PeopleWatcher` instance to the `Person` list of observers:

- The `self` argument refers to the particular `PeopleWatcher` instance
- The `keyPath` argument, `"busy"`, is a `String` representation of the name of property that we wish to observe
- There are a number of `NSKeyValueObservingOptions` that we can pass in the `options` array, but in our case we are only interested in the new value, so we specify only the `.new` case of the `NSKeyValueObservingOptions enum`

Then, we use `&myContext` to pass a pointer to the `myContext` object. The handler method for the notification (which we'll code next) will check this pointer to make sure this notification is our one.

Reacting to value changes

We now need to add a handler method to the class, which will be called whenever an observed property changes. Add the following method to the `PeopleWatcher` class:

```swift
override func observeValue(forKeyPath keyPath: String?,
                          of object: Any?,
                          change: [NSKeyValueChangeKey : Any]?,
                          context: UnsafeMutableRawPointer?)
    {
        if context == &myContext {
            if let keyPath = keyPath
            {
                print("\(keyPath) has changed to",
                "\(change![NSKeyValueChangeKey.newKey]!)")
            }
        }
    }
```

We override NSObject's `observeValue(keyPath: object: change: context:)` method. This is a terribly named function, since we are *observing* already; the method is about *handling* property changes.

If the context pointer passed is the one created by this instance of the class (remember, they're all 0, but are different *instances* of 0, and it is the memory address of that instance that we are checking), we react to the notification.

For the moment, we'll just log the change.

Removing the observer

And finally, we need to remove ourselves as observer once we have finished observing. If we only need to react to the first occurrence of the property change, we might do that in the `observeValue(keyPath: object: change: context:)` method itself, but assuming we want to catch all of the property's changes, we put this in the class's `deinit` method.

Add the following code to the `PeopleWatcher` class:

```
deinit
{
    removeObserver(self,
                    forKeyPath: "busy",
                    context: &myContext)
}
```

The code here is clear enough, methinks.

Trying it out

So let's test the code. To keep things simple, we'll have the `ViewController` class maintain a `PeopleWatcher` property.

Modifying ViewController

Next, we must modify our `ViewController` class. Add the following line of code to the `ViewController` class:

```
var thePeopleWatcher: PeopleWatcher?
```

Our `ViewController` class maintains an optional `PeopleWatcher` property, which we will initiate in the `viewDidLoad` method.

Replace the `viewDidLoad` method with the following code:

```
overridefunc viewDidLoad()
    {
      super.viewDidLoad()

      let thePerson = Person(name: "McCoy",
                        busy: true,
                        shirtColor: NSColor.blue)

      thePeopleWatcher = PeopleWatcher(person: thePerson)
```

```
DispatchQueue.main.asyncAfter(
    deadline: .now() + 3.0,execute: {
        thePerson.busy = false
    })

}
```

Most of this code is not hard to follow:

- We initialize a `Person` instance
- We use that as the single argument to initialize the `ViewController` `PeopleWatcher` property
- We queue up a change to the `busy` property of the `Person` object using Foundation's `Dispatch` framework (more on that in Chapter 14, *The Benefits of Core Data*)

Now run the app. A few seconds after the app has launched and the window has appeared, you'll see the `print` statement appear in the console:

busy has changed to 0

 Welcome to the world of C, where `false` equals 0. In dealing with `Foundation` codem, you'll sometimes need to understand a little C.

So to wrap up KVO, we have now seen that it is a very simple task to add KVO to subclasses of `NSObject`. Yes, the code looks a little prehistoric (it's about thirty years old, in fact), but it is not really hard to understand.

Cocoa bindings

A technology central to macOS development, Cocoa bindings is a feature that allows you to establish connections between the AppKit classes that we use to provide an app with standardized UI elements, and your model object's (or objects') data. There are other ways to do this, but at the moment we will concentrate on bindings, since they can save us large amounts of what is generally referred to as *glue* code, the stuff that tells your data model what the user has done, and tells your user interface what change the model has made to its data.

Using Cocoa bindings, we can keep the data and the UI synchronized at all times. And the amazing thing is, we do it without a single line of code.

If you already have a fair amount of experience in programming for OS X/macOS, you will probably have some idea of how to use Cocoa bindings, but we will nevertheless run quickly through how to connect your UI in Interface Builder with your data model.

Since we have the `PeopleWatcher` app lying around, we will use that as our test bed. In order to do that, we will need to do the following:

1. Create a data structure (an extremely simple one), which is an array of `Person` objects, and make it the content of an `NSArrayController` object.
2. Add an `NSTableView` object to our UI and bind it to the array controller.
3. Bind the selection of the table view to the array controller.

None of this is complicated from our perspective, although under the hood, Xcode, Interface Builder, and Swift will be working feverishly to hook up your UI and data.

Adding the data model

For simplicity's sake, we will add a property to the `PeopleWatcher` app's `ViewController` class, which will be an array of `Person` objects.

 Normally we would not create the date model in a View Controller! But at the moment our focus is on KVO and bindings, so we'll allow ourselves this tiny fragment of data model in the wrong place.

Add the following code to the `ViewController` class:

```
var people: [Person] =
[
    Person(name: "Scottie", busy: true, shirtColor: .red),
    Person(name: "Kirk", busy: false, shirtColor: .yellow)
]
```

Adding an NSArrayController

Now that we have a data structure that we can bind to, select the `Main.storyboard` file in the navigator and go through the following steps:

1. From the Object Library (`Command_Option_control_3`), drag an `NSArrayController` object onto the **View Controller Scene**, as illustrated in the following screenshot:

2. With the array controller selected, expand the **Controller Content** section's **Content Array** subsection of the Bindings Inspector in the utilities view (*command + option + 7*).
3. Bind it to **View Controller** in the **Bind to** menu.
4. Set the **Model Key Path** to `people`:

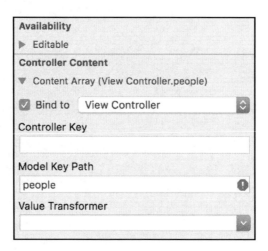

Binding the table view

Now, we'll add a table view to display the data, and then bind it to the Array controller. Binding the table view is done as follows:

1. From the Object Library, drag an `NSTableView` object onto the **View Controller Scene** view.

2. With the table view selected, expand the **Table Content** section in the Bindings Inspector, and bind the table view to **Array Controller**:

3. Leave the **Controller Key** set to `arrangedObjects`.

   If you hit the **Run** button now, you'll see that the number of table rows reflects the number of objects in the `people` of the `ViewController`, but that there is no data showing. This is because we still need to bind the table columns to the desired `Person` properties.

4. In the **View Controller Scene**, select the first **Table Column | Table Cell View | Table View Cell** of the table view:

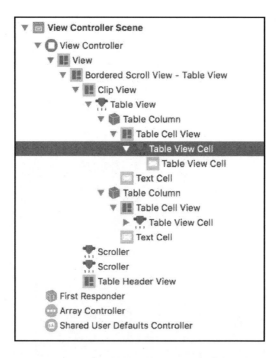

5. Expand the **Value** section in the Bindings Inspector, and bind the Table View Cell to **Table Cell View**.

6. Leave the **Controller Key** blank, and set the **Model Key Path** to objectValue.name:

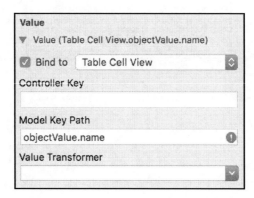

7. Repeat steps 7 to 9 for the second **Table Column**, setting the Table View Cell's **Model Key Path** to **objectValue.busy**.

> Now when you build and run, you'll see the `people` contents reflected in the table:

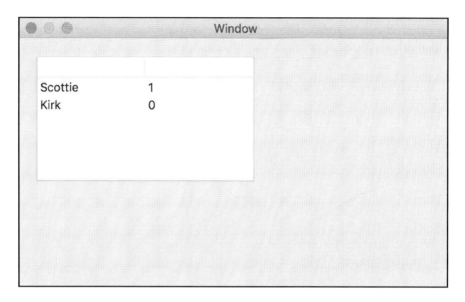

> Now, what about that `shirtColor` property?

8. Select the first **Table Column | Table Cell View | Table View Cell** again.
9. In the Bindings Inspector, expand the **Text Color** section and bind it to **Table Cell View**.
10. Leave the **Controller Key** blank, and set the **Model Key Path** to `objectValue.shirtColor`.

Now when you run the app, you'll see those colors used to set the text color of the first column's text.

So now that we have the table view displaying the properties of each entry of `people`, either textually or graphically, let's get things working in the opposite direction, and have the app reflect the user's selection.

Binding the table selection

This is also very simple:

- We must bind the NSArrayController to the table selection
- We add a text field to reflect the user selection
- We then bind the properties of the selection object in the NSArrayController to the new text field

Once we have done that, we will see changes in the user's selection reflected in the text of the text field.

Adding the binding

Follow these steps to bind the Table View's selection:

1. Select **TableView** in the **View Controller Scene**.
2. In the Bindings Inspector, expand the **Table Content** section.
3. Expand the **Selection Indexes** section.
4. Set the **Controller Key** to selectionIndexes.

The parameters should now look like this:

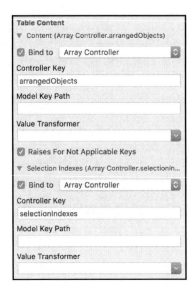

Adding and binding a text field

Now we'll add the text field and bind it to the **People Array Controller**:

1. From the Object Library, add a **Text Field** object to the view.
2. With the text field still selected, expand the **Value** section of the Bindings Inspector, and bind it to **Array Controller** in the **Bind to** menu.
3. Leave the **Controller Key** set to selection.
4. Set the **Model Key** path to name.

If you build and run now, you'll see the name property of the selected Person object in the text field:

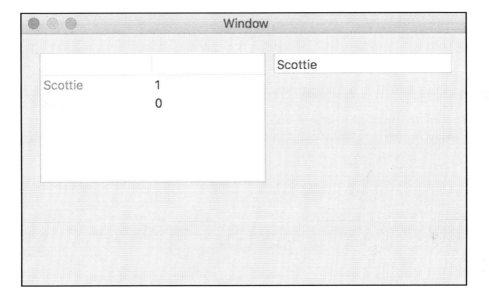

Changing array values

What happens when the people array changes?

We'll return to the ViewController class and add some code to change the array, simulating, perhaps, an update over the network. We'll also need an outlet to the array controller we added in Interface Builder.

Add the following outlet to the `ViewController` class:

```
@IBOutlet var arrayController: NSArrayController!
```

In Interface Builder, connect the **Array Controller** in the **View Controller Scene** with the new outlet.

Add the following function to the `ViewController` class:

```
func queueUpChanges()
    {
        DispatchQueue.main.asyncAfter(
            deadline: .now() + 2.0, execute: {
                self.arrayController.addObject(Person(
                        name: "Spock",
                        busy: true,
                        shirtColor: .blue))

                print(self.people)
                })
    }
```

We fire off a call to dispatch to add another `Person` object to `peopleArrayController`, which is now in charge of `people`. If we change `people` directly, we won't see any update in the UI. We have added a `print` statement with which we can see in the console that the array controller has also updated the array.

This function will be called from the `ViewController` class's `viewDidLoad` method. Add that call, so that the functions code looks like this (we'll leave aside the code to initialize the `thePeopleWatcher` variable for now, but you can leave it in if you want):

```
overridefunc viewDidLoad()
    {
        super.viewDidLoad()

        queueUpChanges()
    }
```

Go ahead and hit **Run**, and you'll see a third row being added after two seconds. If your system's selection color is still the default blue of macOS, you might wish that Spock's shirt was a different color.

Pretty Boolean

Let's just clear up that annoying `busy` value showing up as `0` or `1`.

We will return to our `Person` class, and add a new computed property called `busyString`:

```
dynamic var name: String
var busy: Bool
dynamic var shirtColor: NSColor
dynamic var busyString: String {
    return busy ? "Busy" : "Not busy"
    }
```

We use the ternary operator to return a `String` representation of the `Person` object's `busy` state.

 We have removed the `dynamic` keyword from the **Busy** property. This indicates that this property is not being used in Cocoa bindings. Should we need to access the **Busy** property for some other binding, we can put the `dynamic` keyword back, but it's a good practice to keep things tidied up as we progress.

We're not quite done yet; we need to change the value of the second column's **Table View Cell**'s **Model Key Path** to `objectValue.busyString`:

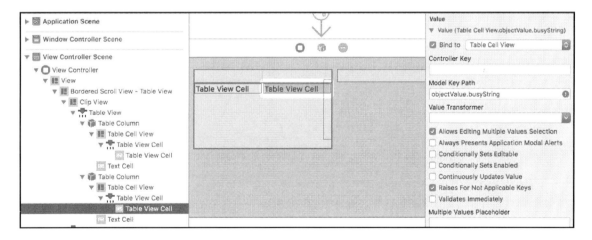

Now the table will show **Busy** or **Not busy** instead of **1** or **0**. And I think we can assume users will prefer that.

Just to round it off, select each **Table Column**, and set the **Title** properties to **Name** and **Status** in the Attributes Inspector. The table should now look as follows:

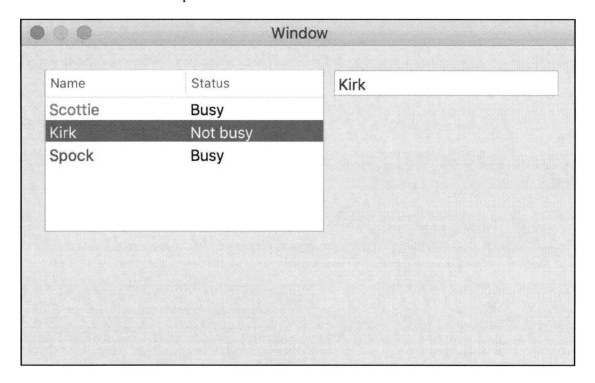

Summary

In this chapter, you have learned the following:

- The ways in which Foundation Kit, AppKit, and Cocoa relate to each other
- When and how to use NSObject as a superclass of your custom classes
- How to code your classes for key-value observation
- How Cocoa bindings can help keep your code clean, minimal, and consistent with Cocoa's own design patterns

In the next chapter, we will build on this knowledge as we explore more advanced techniques, enabling us to populate View Controllers by coding, as an alternative to Interface Builder.

7
Creating Views
Programmatically

In the last chapter, we used Interface Builder to create a window containing a table view and text field, which we then hooked up to the app's data model using Cocoa Bindings. This is an excellent way to go about constructing user interfaces, since it takes much of the complicated background machinery out of the picture, allowing the developer to focus on the visual aspects of the interface.

In many cases, this method of building is perfectly adequate, and can save a lot of boilerplate code writing, but there are also many occasions in which it is necessary, or at least preferable, to create an interface in code, and this is the topic of this chapter.

In this chapter, you will learn about the following:

- The advantages that coding an interface offers
- Creating and configuring an `NSTableView` and other controls from scratch
- Adding a property list to a project and editing its XML data
- Reading data from an app's main bundle
- Wrapping Swift data structures to enable key-value observing
- Extensions for adopting data source and delegate protocols
- Implementing key-value observing without using Cocoa Bindings

Let's start with looking at why we should go to the effort of coding an interface when Interface Builder seems to offer a much easier way.

Why code instead of IB?

There are several reasons why we may need, or choose, to create a user interface in code, rather than using Interface Builder:

- It may be necessary to configure the interface according to runtime criteria. The user may perhaps be given a choice of how the interface is presented, for example, or the number of some UI elements may depend on data that cannot be foreseen at compile time.
- Code is easier to read than a storyboard. To find out all the property values of an interface built with Interface Builder requires endless clicking on the various panes and inspectors. Reading through the same properties set in code, on the other hand, will generally entail no more than scanning over a few classes.
- Code shows structure. The interaction and relationships between the various elements of the interface are written explicitly into the code, with no behind-the-curtains magic being supplied by the IB development team.
- To code it is to understand it. However adept we may become at dragging and dropping NSView and its many subclasses into the IB window, a true understanding of the complex structure of modern desktop program interfaces is better gained by building it *by hand*.

To a certain extent, developers will have different preferences as to when to use Interface Builder and when to code (and the Web is full of lively exchanges of opinion on the topic), but most would agree that building an interface entirely in code is an essential skill to have, and is a process with which we should feel comfortable.

Setting our goals

In this chapter, we will recreate the window we created in the previous chapter, including its table view and text view. We'll also add a couple of tweaks here and there, to produce the familiar looking window illustrated here:

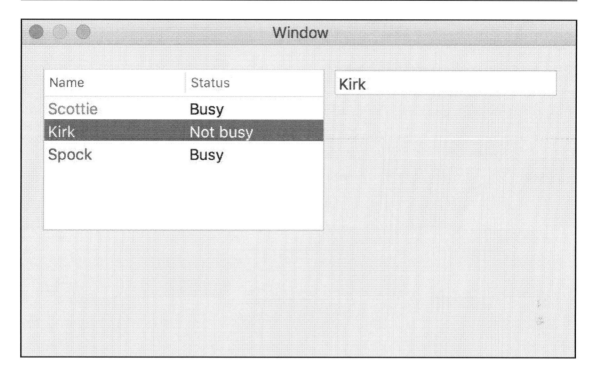

The steps involved

Broadly speaking, the process will look like this:

- We will add `NSTableView` and `NSTextView` properties to the View Controller
- We will then build and configure the views and their subviews, including their various visual aspects
- We will adopt data source and delegate protocols in the `ViewController` class and implement their required methods

Beyond the visuals

In order to reproduce the functionality, as well as the appearance of the previous chapter's window, we will perform these additional steps:

1. We will create a property list XML file in the app's main bundle.
2. We will look at how to load data from the main bundle and decode it for use in the app.

3. We will create a wrapper object for Swift data structures to make them compatible with key-value observing.
4. We will use key-value observing to create a relationship between the app's data and its presentation in the interface.

So, with that overview in place, let's start with getting an NSTableView up and running.

Coding a table view

Firstly, we need to start a new project. All we need here is the standard macOS template with which we started the project in Chapter 6, *Cocoa Frameworks: The Backbone of Your App*, so create that first.

Preparing the View Controller

Before we can get going on the code for the table view itself, we need to add a couple of properties to the View Controller that will manage the window in which that table view is built.

Add the following lines of code to the ViewController class:

```
class ViewController: NSViewController
{
    var tableView: NSTableView!
    var infoLabel:NSTextField!
}
```

The table and label

We will create both of these UI elements without the aid of Interface Builder. This means we have three tasks to perform:

1. Create an NSTableView.
2. Configure that table view.
3. Add an NSTextField info label.

We'll create a method for each of those steps, but since they will only ever be used once, we will declare them within the scope of an umbrella function, `buildUI`. While it would be an exaggeration to talk of encapsulation here, we could argue that the mental fence we erect around the `buildUI` method is a step towards cleaner code. Just collapse the method in the code editor window, and all of the UI-building methods collapse with it.

So, the structure of this umbrella method and its child methods (if they may be called that) is as follows:

```
func buildUI()
{
  func addTable()
  {
  //...
  }

  func configureTable()
  {
  //...
  }

  func addInfoLabel()
  {
  //...
  }

  addTable()
  configureTable()
  addInfoLabel()
}
```

Add that code to the `ViewController` class. This will be called later from the View Controller's overridden `viewDidLoad` method.

Adding the table

An `NSTableView`, as used in Interface Builder, is in fact a whole nest of objects working together, as you can see if you inspect the document organizer pane in IB. In this chapter, we will populate the view ourselves:

1. Complete the stubbed `addTable` method with the following code:

```
func addTable()
{
    let tableRect = CGRect(
```

```
                         x: 20,
                         y: 115,
                         width: 240,
                         height: 135)

        let tableScrollView = NSScrollView(frame: tableRect)
        self.tableView = NSTableView(frame: tableRect)

        tableView.dataSource = self
        tableView.delegate = self

        tableScrollView.documentView = tableView
        view.addSubview(tableScrollView)
    }
```

2. This method firstly creates an `NSScrollView`, and sets an `NSTableView` as its `documentView` property (meaning the view that gets scrolled).

3. We set our `ViewController` class to be the table view's data source and delegate.

> We haven't yet made the ViewController class conform to the NSTableViewDataSource and NSTableViewDelegate protocols, so for the moment we have a compiler error. If you're like me, you'll comment out those lines for a while, to get rid of those disconcerting red warning signs in the code editor.

4. Finally, we add the `tableScrollView` to the View Controller's `view`'s `subview` array.

Now we have a table view, but it's a table view without content.

Configuring the table's columns

Next, we need to add our two columns to the `tableView`.

Complete the stubbed `configureTable` method with the following code:

```
func configureTable()
{
    let nameColumn = NSTableColumn(identifier: "nameColumn")
    nameColumn.title = "Name"
    nameColumn.minWidth = 100
    tableView.addTableColumn(nameColumn)
```

```
    let statusColumn = NSTableColumn(identifier: "statusColumn")
    statusColumn.title = "Status"
    statusColumn.minWidth = 130
    tableView.addTableColumn(statusColumn)

    tableView.intercellSpacing = CGSize(width: 5.0, height: 5.0)
    tableView.usesAlternatingRowBackgroundColors = true
}
```

I'd imagine this code is easy enough to understand at first glance:

1. An NSTableColumn view is initiated with an identifier string that is used by the table's data source.
2. We specify the text to appear in each column's header view by setting the column's title property.
3. We can set maximum and minimum widths for each column within the table view.
4. The last two lines of code are gratuitous visual formatting; mostly just because we can, but also to demonstrate where we would undertake much of the customization of an NSTableView appearance. Have a play around with those values; I would.

 A command-click on those last two properties reveals a veritable treasure trove of properties that can be customized in a table view; no developer should be deprived of such a wealth of valuable information and programming entertainment.

Adding the info label

Finally, we must add the text field that will show the name property of a user's selection.

Complete the stubbed addInfoLabel method with the following code:

```
func addInfoLabel()
{
    let infoLabelFrame = NSRect(
            x: 268,
            y: 228,
            width: 192,
            height: 22)
```

```
    self.infoLabel = NSTextField(frame: infoLabelFrame)
    view.addSubview(infoLabel)
}
```

There is nothing here that we have not seen before.

Now we can override the `ViewController` class's `viewDidLoad` method, to set the UI-building code in motion:

```
override func viewDidLoad()
{
  super.viewDidLoad()
  buildUI()
}
```

If you're wondering how far we've come, comment out the data source and delegate declarations from the `addTableView` method (if you haven't already) and run the app.

You should be greeted by an app window that looks like this:

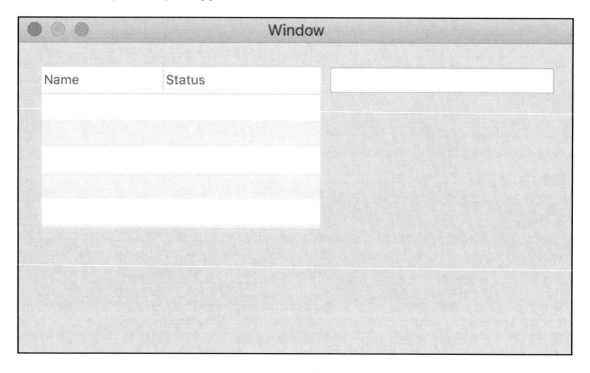

As you can see, we're well on the way to having a coded table view. Perhaps before moving on, it would be a good idea to experiment with the values we have used so far.

Providing the app with data

Until now, we've hard coded whatever data we have needed for demonstration purposes, but this is not a very realistic scenario. In the real world, data will generally come from user input, local storage, or from the network.

Even carved-in-stone immutable data is better kept separately from the code of an app, and a common approach is to put such data into a property list, which is a file written in XML format.

 If you haven't dealt with XML before, you'll be pleased to learn that property list XML doesn't get very complicated. As far as we are concerned here, XML is no more than a cross-platform compatible way of expressing arrays and dictionaries using standard text. You'll see when we get to it, it's dead easy, and if you've had any experience with HTML, you'll recognize the close relationship immediately.

Within the app itself, we will represent the data with objects familiar to you already, including our old friend, the `Person` object.

Importing the Person class

Since we are programmatically recreating the table view we used in the last chapter, we'll need to have a `Person` class.

Rather than rewriting the code, or copying and pasting it, we'll simply import it from the previous chapter's project:

1. Type `Command-Option-A`.
2. Navigate to the `Person.swift` file in the previous chapter's project directory.

3. Click the **Options** button and make sure that **Copy items if needed** is ticked.

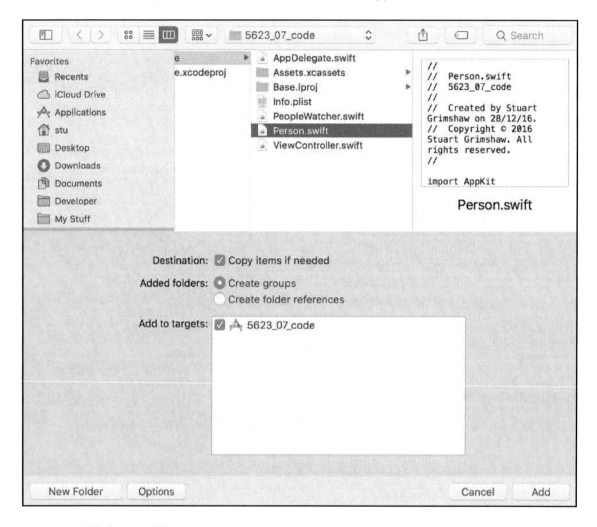

4. Click on **Add**.

We can now create a custom class that will hold an array of type [Person].

The data model

In the last chapter, we maintained an array of `Person` objects. We will follow a similar approach here, with the difference being that we will not be using Cocoa Bindings or an `NSArrayController`.

We could use a simple array of type `[Person]`, but if we want to add key-value observing later on (and we do), we need to wrap the array of `Person` objects in an `NSObject`, which then enables us to make use of the KVO mechanism.

Create a new Swift file, name it `PeopleArrayWrapper.swift`, and add the following code below the `import` statement:

```
class PeopleArrayWrapper: NSObject
{
    dynamic var content: [Person]

    init(content: [Person])
    {
        self.content = content
    }

    var personCount: Int { return content.count }

    func add(person: Person)
    {
        content.append(person)
    }
}
```

Most of this code will be familiar from the previous chapter.

It's worth mentioning the fact that we offer the outside world a `personCount` variable and an `add(:Person)` method, so that we can change the internal logic of the class, should we wish to, without disturbing any code elsewhere in the app. Who knows, perhaps some law of nature stipulates that all `Person` arrays start with a hundred people, or that adding a `Person` to the array means triggering some code to alter the amount of train seats available. We want to be able to take care of all of that without having to change the code that uses this class.

> Providing a consistent interface means that the internal representation is isolated from the client code. This is a *good thing*.

Now add an instance of the `PeopleArrayWrapper` class to the `ViewController` class:

```
var peopleArrayWrapper = PeopleArrayWrapper(content: [])
```

So, now that we have our array of `Person` objects, all we need to do is find some people.

Creating a property list with XML

In the last chapter, we created an `Array` literal to provide the table with some data. This time, we're going to push the list of `people` data out to a property list, or `plist` (pronounced *p - list*):

1. Type `Command-N` to bring up the new file templates.
2. Scroll down to the **Resource** section and select **Property List**.
3. Name it `People.plist`.
4. Click on **Create**.

The code editor window will present itself, as illustrated in the following screenshot:

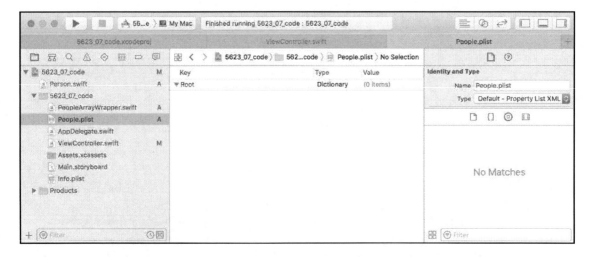

In the navigator pane, right-click on the `People.plist` file, and select **Open As | Source Code**.

This will display the list as raw XML code, which is a more transparent representation of the data contained in it:

All we need to do now is add an XML list of the people we wish to load into the app once it has launched.

Between the `<dict>` and `</dict>` tags, insert the following XML:

```
<key>PeopleData</key>
<array>
  <dict>
    <key>name</key>
    <string>Kirk</string>
    <key>busy</key>
    <true/>
    <key>shirtColor</key>
    <string>yellow</string>
  </dict>
  <dict>
    <key>name</key>
    <string>Scottie</string>
    <key>busy</key>
    <false/>
    <key>shirtColor</key>
    <string>red</string>
  </dict>
</array>
```

The structure of the XML data is self-explanatory, and this is one of the great strengths of XML; anyone who knows the basics of dictionaries and arrays, regardless of which language they learnt it in, will immediately be able to visually parse and understand the file's contents.

Getting data from the property list

Our next task is to get the data from the XML and turn it into an array of `Person` objects that we can assign to the `content` property of `personArrayWrapper`. We can break this down into a few discrete steps:

1. Get the location of the `People.plist` file within the app's main bundle.
2. Decode the XML data in that file.
3. Parse that data to create an array of `Person` objects.
4. Assign that array to the `personArrayWrapper` property of `ViewController`.

In order to make use of some of the data we get from the property list, we will need a dictionary of type `[String: NSColor]`, which we will use to convert the XML's `String` representation of a color to an `NSColor` object. Rather than bloat the `ViewController` with this code, we will place the data management code in files of their own.

> A View Controller need not, and indeed should not, know anything about the original source and format of the data. We should be able to alter any and all aspects of data retrieval without having to change code in the View Controller.

So, let's get that dictionary done:

1. Create a new Swift file, and name it `ColorUtilities.swift`.
2. Replace the `import` statement with the following code:

```
import Cocoa
let colors = ["red": NSColor.red,
              "blue":        .blue,
              "yellow":        .yellow]
```

`NCColor` is defined in Cocoa, not foundation, so we must change the `import` statement. We have only used three colors here, but the reader is invited to expand the list *ad libitum*.

We can now write a class that will locate and decode the property list data:

1. Create a new Swift file, and name it `DataManager.swift`.
2. Add the following code after the `import` statement:

```
class DataManager
{
  static let sharedInstance = DataManager()

  private init() {}
}
```

The `DataManager` class is given a static `sharedInstance` variable, with which we guarantee that there can only be one instance of the class. In order to ensure this, we make the `init` method private, to prevent circumventing the `sharedInstance` variable.

This class will do all the work involved in obtaining data for the app. In our case, we will get it from a property list, but none of the classes elsewhere in the app will need to know this. If we get our XML data from another source, it won't affect the `ViewController` class.

We now add the following methods to the `DataManager` class:

```
private func getData() -> Data?
{
  if let path = Bundle.main.path(forResource: "People",
                                 ofType: "plist")
  {
    return FileManager.default.contents(atPath: path)
  }
  return nil
}
```

This method does nothing more than fetch the raw data from the app's main bundle:

1. We declare the method to be `private`. It is for class-internal use only; we do not want it accessed from outside the `DataManager` class.
2. We get the file path to the property list, and pass it to the `FileManager` class's `default` instance.
3. The `FileManager` instance then converts the XML to a Swift `Data` object.

At this point, we have obtained the necessary `Data` object. The next method will be responsible for serializing that raw data, and converting it to an array of dictionaries. Each of those dictionaries will contain the data for a single person.

Add the following method to the `DataManager` class:

```
private func serialize(data: Data) -> [[String: Any]]
{
  var format:PropertyListSerialization.PropertyListFormat = .xml

  do
  {
    let plistData = try PropertyListSerialization.propertyList(
      from: data,
      options: .mutableContainersAndLeaves,
      format: &format)

    let plistDictionary = plistData as! [String: Any]

    let peopleDataArray
      = plistDictionary["PeopleData"] as! [[String: Any]]

    return peopleDataArray
  }
  catch
  {
    print(error)
    return []
  }
}
```

This method contains a few steps:

1. The `PropertyListSerialization` class that we will use to convert the XML into data can accept a few formats; we specify `.xml` as the source format, and assign that to a variable, which we will access in a moment.
2. We then pass the `data` object, along with a mutability option and the format variable.

    > The ampersand (`&`) means that we pass the actual `format` variable, not a copy of it. In Swift, this is called an `input` variable; the method is permitted to mutate the variable that is passed to it as an argument.

3. We add the `plistData` object to a dictionary of type `[String: Any]`. We force-unwrap the result of that downcast, because if there are any errors in the XML formatting, we want the app to crash.

If we were obtaining the XML data from an external server, we would probably want to handle invalid XML data differently.

4. We parse the dictionary for the `"PeopleData"` key, and cast it to an array of `[String: Any]` dictionaries. Again, we have chosen to crash the app during development rather than permit the shipping of faulty data in the app's main bundle.
5. We return that array.
6. If the serialization fails and throws an error, we print that error to the console and return an empty array.
7. The next step is to parse the array and build an array of `Person` objects.
8. Add the following method to the `DataManager` class:

```
private func peopleFrom(dictionary: [[String: Any]]) -> [Person]
{
  var peopleArray = [Person]()

  for person in dictionary
  {
    if
      let name = person["name"] as? String,
      let busy = person["busy"] as? Bool,
      let shirtColor = person["shirtColor"] as? String,
      let color = colors[shirtColor]
    {
      let nuPerson = Person(name: name,
                       busy: busy,
                       shirtColor: color)

      peopleArray.append(nuPerson)
    }
  }
  return peopleArray
}
```

This is very simple code, using the `colors` dictionary that we defined earlier to determine which `NSColor` to assign for a given color `String`.

9. Finally, we need a method that will call the methods we have added to the `DataManager` class previously:

```
func getPeople() -> [Person]
{
  guard let data = getData() else { return [] }
  let xmlData = serialize(data: data)
  let peopleData = peopleFrom(dictionary: xmlData)
  return peopleData
}
```

10. This class is not declared private, since we need to access it from another class, the `ViewController`.

11. The method is declared to return an array of type `[Person]`, meaning that it has no knowledge of what happens to the data it returns; this is preferable to mutating the `ViewController` properties directly.

We have coded an encapsulated data management class, albeit a simple one, that keeps the data fetching and formatting code separate from the View Controller.

Adopting datasource and delegate protocols

If we want the table view to talk to the rest of the app, we'll need to provide it with a data source and a delegate, which we did, much to the annoyance of the compiler, in the `addTable` method of the `ViewController` class.

So, let's uncomment those lines, and adopt both of the necessary protocols.

Datasource extension

It's worth mentioning again that Swift conventions are recent ones, but they're all we've got at the moment, so we'll follow the newly-established pattern of adding protocol compliance in an extension to the `ViewController` class.

Before we do that, we must add an instance of the `PeopleArrayWrapper` class as a property of the `ViewController` class:

1. Add the following property to the `ViewController` class:

    ```
    var tableView: NSTableView!
    var infoLabel:NSTextField!
    var peopleArrayWrapper = PeopleArrayWrapper(content: [])
    ```

2. Add the following method to the `ViewController.swift` file, after the end of the `ViewController` class's closing bracket:

    ```
    extension ViewController: NSTableViewDataSource
    {
        func numberOfRows(in tableView: NSTableView) -> Int
        {
            return self.peopleArrayWrapper.personCount
        }
    }
    ```

This extension declares the `ViewController` class to conform to the `NSTableViewDataSource` protocol.

It then defines the `numberOfRows` method that is required of any class adopting the `NSTableViewDataSource` protocol.

The compiler will now stop complaining about us having set the ViewController class to be the data source of a table view.

The `numberOfRows` method is called by the table view each time it needs to know how many rows it will be required to display.

Delegate extension

In addition to a data source, we must supply the table view with a delegate that will provide it with the `View` objects that make up the cells that it will display. We will provide the protocol conformance declaration, as well as the necessary methods, by adding another extension.

Add the following extension declaration to the `ViewController.swift` file, outside of either the `ViewController` class declaration or the data source extension:

```
extension ViewController: NSTableViewDelegate
{
}
```

Now we need to fulfill the promise implicit in our protocol adoption. We will add two methods to this extension:

- `tableView(NSTableView, viewFor: NSTableColumn?, row: Int)`
- `tableViewSelectionDidChange(Notification)`

We'll implement these methods next.

Returning table view columns

First, let's supply the table with some details of how it should display its content, by providing it with table column views.

Add the following method to the `NSTableViewDelegate` extension:

```
func tableView(_ tableView: NSTableView,
               viewFor tableColumn: NSTableColumn?,
               row: Int) -> NSView?
{
  //....
}
```

We won't add the whole implementation of this method in one go; we'll start with the code for just the first table column.

Add the following code to the `tableView(NSTableView, viewFor: row:)` method:

```
if tableColumn == tableView.tableColumns[0]
{
  let cellIdentifier = "NameCellID"
  var cell = tableView.make(withIdentifier: cellIdentifier,
                            owner: self) as? NSTextField

  if cell == nil
  {
    cell = NSTextField(frame: NSRect(
      x: 0,
      y: 0,
      width: tableView.frame.size.width,
```

```
          height: 0))
    }

    if let cell = cell
    {
      cell.identifier = cellIdentifier

      cell.stringValue = peopleArrayWrapper.content[row].name
      cell.textColor = peopleArrayWrapper.content[row].shoeColor
      cell.backgroundColor = .clear

      cell.isBezeled = false
      cell.isEditable = false
    }
    return cell
}
```

The code breaks down as follows:

1. The `cellIdentifier` is an arbitrary string with which we can distinguish different cell types within the table.
2. We then call the table view's `make` method, which will return an existing (off-screen) cell if one is available, or `nil`, if there is none. This saves us from creating cells unnecessarily when scrolling through long lists.
3. If that method returns `nil`, then we create an instance of `NSTextField` (though we could use custom classes if we needed to).

> The `height` property of the text field is unimportant, since it will be overridden by the table row's height property.

4. If we now have a cell instance that is not `nil`, we populate it with the relevant data from the `peopleArrayWrapper.content` array.
5. This is the time to perform any visual customization we may require, which will depend on the context of the cell.
6. We set the cell's `isEditable` value to `false`, since the table does not need any editing functionality in this particular case.

This code creates a `view-based` table view, as opposed to a `cell-based` table view. This is the recommendation of Apple, and offers a superior level of customization.

The code for the second column is almost the same.

Add the following code to the `tableView(NSTableView, viewFor: row:)` method:

```
else if tableColumn == tableView.tableColumns[1]
{
  let cellIdentifier = "StatusCellID"
  var cell = tableView.make(withIdentifier: cellIdentifier,
                        owner: self) as? NSTextField

  if cell == nil
  {
    cell = NSTextField(frame: NSRect(
      x: 0,
      y: 0,
      width: tableView.frame.size.width,
      height: 0))
  }

  if let cell = cell
  {
    cell.identifier = cellIdentifier

    cell.stringValue
      = peopleArrayWrapper.content[row].busy ? "Busy" : "Not busy"
      cell.backgroundColor = .clear

    cell.isBezeled = false
    cell.isEditable = false
  }
  return cell
}
```

Finally, we must return `nil` if the table column is not one of the first two table columns.

Add the following code as the last line of the `tableView(NSTableView, viewFor: row:)` method:

```
return nil
```

Let's test what we've got so far.

To do that, we just need to add the following two lines of code to the `viewDidLoad` method of the `ViewController` class:

```
peopleArrayWrapper.content
= DataManager.sharedInstance.getPeople()
tableView.reloadData()
```

Now, when you run the app, you should see this window:

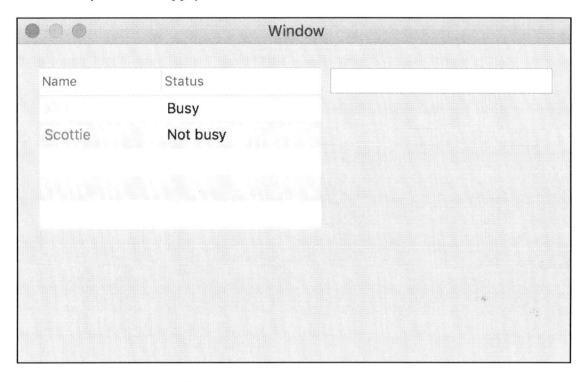

Troubleshooting tip

You *did* uncomment these lines, didn't you?

```
tableView.dataSource = self
tableView.delegate = self
```

Congratulations. Without any smoke and mirrors from Interface Builder, you have constructed a functioning table view using nothing but code. This may be a good moment to address a couple of frequently asked questions:

Er... that took ages.

Yes, it does at first. But it will get faster, and with some practice and some advanced code-snippet-ninja stuff, it will be way faster.

But would I even bother?

I'm glad you asked. Here are a few points to consider:

- Everything is explicit; there is nothing there that you didn't put there, giving you a far more thorough understanding of how the table view and its data fit together.
- Everything is explicit; everything you put there can be read by someone else much more quickly than endlessly clicking through a hundred Interface Builder editor panes.
- Debugging code is a lot easier than debugging storyboards.
- You can customize your table right down to the smallest detail, and add custom subclasses wherever you need functionality that goes beyond what Cocoa supplies out of the box. I've never met a developer yet that didn't think total control was a *really good thing*.

Just to prove that last point, let's add the following method to the `NSTableViewDelegate` extension:

```
func tableView(_ tableView: NSTableView,
        heightOfRow row: Int) -> CGFloat
{
  return 22.0
}
```

The results look pretty standard, so try changing that float value. And when you're done, *command-click* on the method name in the editor window to find out what else you can get up to.

Okay, I get it. But selecting a row doesn't do anything.

True. Let's fix that.

Reacting to selection events

The table view's delegate must also implement the `tableViewSelectionDidChange` method, which will receive a notification whenever the selection of the table changes, whether programmatically or through user interaction.

Our method is very simple, it will just display the `name` property of whichever `Person` is selected by the user, just as we did in the previous chapter, but without using Cocoa Bindings.

Add the following code to the `ViewController`'s `NSTableViewDelegate` extension:

```
func tableViewSelectionDidChange(_ notification: Notification)
{
  let theTableView = notification.object as! NSTableView

  let indexes = theTableView.selectedRowIndexes
  if let index = indexes.first
  {
    self.infoLabel.stringValue
        = peopleArrayWrapper.content[index].name
  }
}
```

This is straightforward enough:

1. A reference to the table view that has sent the notification is contained in that notification's `object` property.
2. Since some tables allow multiple selections, the selections' indexes are contained in the `selectedRowIndexes` array. But we only need to access the first element of that array, since we have not enabled multiple selections.
3. We use that index to access the `peopleArrayWrapper.content` array for the `name` property of the selected object, to which we set the `stringValue` property of the `infoLabel`.

If you run the app again, you'll see that the selection is reflected in the text field's text.

Observing without bindings

We haven't yet quite caught up with the table we built in the previous chapter using Interface Builder.

At the moment, we are manually triggering the table view's `reloadData` method. If we were to continue with that approach, we would need to ensure that we triggered the reload every time something in the data changed that needed to be reflected in the table view.

Our previous version used bindings in Interface Builder to do this automatically, and we are able to reproduce this functionality through the use of the key-value observing mechanism, which we also saw in the last chapter.

Adding KVO to the View Controller

The first step is to add two properties to the `ViewController` class:

```
    class ViewController: NSViewController
{
    var tableView: NSTableView!
    var infoLabel:NSTextField!
    var peopleArrayWrapper = PeopleArrayWrapper(content: [])

    let kContentKeyPath = "content"
    private var myContext = 0

    ...
```

We need these to add the `ViewController` class as an observer to the `peopleArrayWrapper`, which we need to do in the `viewDidLoad` method.

Adding an observer

Add the following code immediately after the `super.viewDidLoad()` call, and delete the `tableView.reloadData()` call:

```
    override func viewDidLoad()
    {
      super.viewDidLoad()

      peopleArrayWrapper.addObserver(self,
                                forKeyPath: kContentKeyPath,
                                options:[.new, .old],
                                context: &myContext)
      buildUI()

      peopleArrayWrapper.content = DataManager.sharedInstance.getPeople()
    }
```

We need to add the observer *before* we get the people data from the `DataManager` instance because, now that we are using KVO, we can dispense with the manual table view reload. So, in order for the initial table view data load to take place, we must already have the observer in place.

Handling changes in the data

This is where the table view gets instructed to refresh its data (making any other calls to `tableView.reloadData()` unnecessary).

Add the following code to the `ViewController` class:

```
override func observeValue(forKeyPath keyPath: String?,
                           of object: Any?,
                           change: [NSKeyValueChangeKey : Any]?,
                           context: UnsafeMutableRawPointer?)
{
  if context == &myContext
  {
    tableView.reloadData()
  }
  else
  {
    super.observeValue(forKeyPath: keyPath,
        of: object,
        change: change,
        context: context)
  }
}
```

This is exactly as we saw in the previous chapter.

Removing an observer

We must take care to remove the View Controller from the observers of the `peopleArrayWrapper` property when the View Controller is deallocated.

Add the following method to the `ViewController` class:

```
deinit
{
  removeObserver(self, forKeyPath: kContentKeyPath)
}
```

It's true, that in this artificial context, the View Controller will never get as far as a `deinit` call, but we should maintain best practices (or *form sensible habits,* as they like it to be called).

Triggering changes to the data

With all that KVO code in place, we have nothing more to do than to repeat the person-adding code from the last chapter:

```
func queueUpChanges()
{
  DispatchQueue.main.asyncAfter(
    deadline: .now() + 2.0,execute: {
      self.peopleArrayWrapper.content[0].name = "Jim"
      self.peopleArrayWrapper.add(person: Person(
        name: "Lt. Uhura",
        busy: true,
        shoeColor: .red))
  })
}
```

We have also changed the name of the first person in the array. Because we can.

Advantages of KVO in code

Assuming the same frequently asked questions, which we mentioned previously, all the previous answers still apply. Here are a couple of additional points:

- This way is how I've always seen it done. In all the enterprise code I have ever worked on that I didn't write myself, KVO was coded, not bound in Interface Builder.
- The iOS and tvOS platforms do not have Cocoa Bindings, but are able to reuse code that includes KVO. Given the high degree of code reused across these platforms, it obviously pays to keep one's options open by keeping classes and their methods compatible with as many of the Apple platforms as possible.

I think it's fair to say that, despite the convenience of Cocoa Bindings, the use of coded KVO is not a skill that we can do without, beyond a very basic level of app functionality.

The final line of code

Add the following code to the `viewDidLoad` method of the `ViewController` class:

```
queueUpChanges()
```

Running the app now will make it clear that the table view is automatically updated any time its underlying data is changed.

Having wired up the table view to the data model with KVO, many of the tasks that would otherwise involve coding changes to the table view's presentation of the data, and synchronizing it with the app's data, become obsolete. KVO just takes care of it.

In this way, actions such as sorting the data and removing elements from the array (and, thus, the table view) become much simpler - and safer - to implement. We have already seen that this works with triggering the addition of an array element using `dispatch`.

Adding further control elements in code

Let's now add a button, programmatically of course, with which the user can alphabetically sort the table view's rows and the underlying data.

Adding the sort button

Firstly, we need to build the button itself.

Add the following method inside the `buildUI` method of the `ViewController` class:

```swift
func addSortButton()
{
  let frame = CGRect(x: 268,
                     y: 178,
                     width: 192,
                     height: 32)

  let sortButton = NSButton(frame: frame)

  sortButton.bezelStyle = .rounded
  sortButton.title = "Sort"

  view.addSubview(sortButton)
}
```

And add a call to that method within the `buildUI` method:

```
addTable()
configureTable()
addInfoLabel()
addSortButton()
```

The interface should now look as follows:

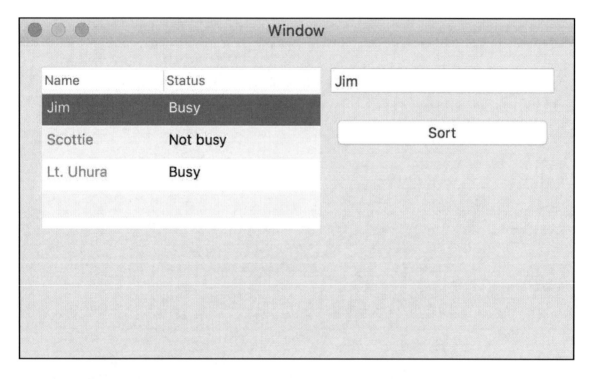

It's a fine looking button, but it doesn't do anything yet. For this, we need to add a `target` and an `action` to the button.

Add the following lines of code to the `addSortButton` method:

```
sortButton.target = self
sortButton.action
    = #selector(ViewController.sortButtonClicked)
```

The first line says that `self`, that is the `ViewController` class, will receive a notification when the user clicks the `sortButton`.

Note how the second line uses `#selector` to pass the name of the `sortButtonClicked` method to the `action` property of the `sortButton` method.

Now we need to add that `sortButtonClicked` method.

Implementing a button's action

To implement the `sortButtonClicked` method, add the following code to the `ViewController` class:

```
func sortButtonClicked()
{
  let sortedArray
    = peopleArrayWrapper.content.sorted(by: { $0.name < $1.name })

  peopleArrayWrapper.content = sortedArray
}
```

Look how elegant this code is. The array's `sortedBy` method takes a closure, to which it passes each pair of elements to be sorted. These two elements are given the symbols `$0` and `$1`, and Swift's type inference works out that these are instances of the `Person` type, enabling us to access their `name` properties.

The `name` property's `String` type already gives us an implementation of the comparison operator, `<`.

Because of the context, we can omit the `return` keyword, although the compiler would be just as happy to accept the closure in this form:

```
{ return $0.name < $1.name }
```

Or even this more explicit one:

```
{
  a, b in
  return a.name < b.name
}
```

However, once we have grown accustomed to the abbreviated form, it seems sensible to use it.

In this way, `sortedBy` returns a new array, containing the sorted contents of the array it is called to perform on.

> It won't have escaped your notice that this is way cleaner than the equivalent in many other languages, not least objective C.

It's worth pointing out that we could have sorted the array in place, but we have chosen to create a new array returned by the `sortedBy` method. This is a much safer approach than reaching into the `peopleArrayWrapper` object (and data structures in general) and messing around with the data.

Running the app

Now run the app again and test the button.

We haven't touched the table view's code, but everything *just works*, to borrow Mr. Job's famous claim from the 2011 WWDC.

It is left as an exercise for the reader to implement reverse sorting and sorting by the `Person` object's `status` property.

Summary

Hopefully, this chapter has given you some insight into the techniques of coding an interface, some of the main reasons for doing so, and the increased level of control that it gives us as developers.

You have learned the following in this chapter:

- How coding an interface can give you greater control than Interface Builder
- How to manually create, configure, and customize views in code
- How to use XML property lists to store data
- How to read that data from disk and format it for use in the app
- How to write data source and delegate protocol extensions
- How to keep the user interface in sync with the app's data by using KVO

The next chapter will take an in - depth look at strings and text.

8
Strings and Text

Ever since Charles Babbage's amazing difference engine, computers have communicated with homo sapiens using text. It's true the Starship Enterprise's bridge was full of lights flashing across the screens, but the only one who ever needed to understand anything was Spock, and he stared into that little glowing monitor; and I'm guessing it displayed text.

A few years after that, Steve Jobs got the idea in his head that computers should not just produce text, they should produce beautiful text, and desktop publishing was born.

Within a few years of that, we were all spending huge amounts of time reading computer-generated text, on our desks, on our laps, and then on our phones; and we wanted it as cool and glossy as the most sophisticated magazines in print.

As a result, the presentation of text has become an essential part of writing software, at least for anyone writing desktop programs. As a macOS developer, you're in the company of people who produce the most elegant--looking operating system, including its text, and users of our software (like it or not) have the highest expectations.

In this chapter, you will learn the following:

- How Swift represents characters and strings
- The roles of Unicode compliance and grapheme clusters
- Escape characters and string interpolation
- Strings represented as `NSString` and other string types
- Adding styles, effects, and URL functionality to text
- Creating text views with custom functionality

Strings and characters

At an intuitive level, we understand text to consist of words that themselves consist of letters, all chained together in some meaningful fashion (Dr. Seuss books and the poetry of E.E. Cummings excepted). However, the further we look into the technicalities of providing the user with numerous alphabets, symbols, and emojis, the more we realize that this simple intuitive perception of text hides a large number of issues that we, as developers, must grapple with.

Drawing text using default fonts and styles is very easy. But the more we understand about strings and text, the better we are equipped to make use of the rich set of tools at our disposal. And toolsets don't come much richer than macOS.

What is a String in Swift?

A Swift `String` is a `struct` that adopts the `Equatable` and `Comparable` protocols (as well as several others). As all structs, it is passed by value. It has a `CharacterView` property (with which we will seldom interact explicitly), which is a collection (*not* an array) of `Character` objects.

The `String` type provides a range of methods for accessing and changing parts of the `String`, as well as getting information about the `String`.

What is a Character?

In the context of the Swift language, a `Character` is the intuitive notion of a character, which is to say a drawing (**glyph**, in technical terms), something that represents a letter, or numeral, or an emoji, and something that can be combined into words. Characters such as é or ö can be a single **Unicode scalar**, or a combination of scalars that combine to make a single character. Such groups of scalars are called **extended grapheme clusters**. But as far as we're concerned (or most of us, at least), it doesn't matter what the underlying structure of any given `Character` is, because Swift provides us with an abstraction that presents characters (with a small c) as `Character` (with a capital C) type objects.

Unicode compliance

Swift provides complete Unicode support. Unicode is the international standard text encoding that goes beyond ASCII's 16-bit limit, to provide support for most alphabets, as well as math and other symbols, and of course those damned emojis.

Both `String` and `Character` types are fully Unicode compliant.

 Here is an excellent blog post on the subject of Unicode, and Swift's model of dealing with it, discussed at a level of detail for which we don't have room here: `https://www.mikeash.com/pyblog/friday-qa-2015-11-06-why-is-swift s-string-api-so-hard.html`.

Combining strings and characters

We can create a `String` from an array of type `[Character]`:

```
let chars: [Character] = ["b","l","u","e"]
var string = String(chars)
```

The `String` type's `append` method can take a `String` or `Character` as its sole argument:

```
let char: Character = "s"
string.append(char)
string.append("ey")
```

It's not that often that we'll need to access the characters of a string in this way, since the operations performed directly on the `String` type are much more efficient. It should be noted that accessing the `Character` property is not a trivial operation, since it involves parsing the entire string.

 If you really do need to work with the `Character` property of a long, document-length string, you might want to consider extracting a substring, and performing any necessary work on that.

String indices and subranges

The `String` object contents cannot be treated as an array of characters, due to the fact that `Character` objects consist of varying numbers of Unicode scalars, but Swift exposes the characters to us in the `String` type's `CharacterView` object, and this is subscriptable using a `String.Index`, a struct that sound like an integer, but isn't.

This makes dealing with Unicode both easier and more consistent between one character and the next. The price we pay for that is the fact that accessing specific character indices (and by extension, subranges) is less than completely intuitive.

So rather than make a method call such as `myString[3]` or something similar, we must first obtain the correct index as a `String.Index` value; only then can we access the character at that index.

Obtaining a String.Index

The indexing system is based upon a `String` having a `startIndex` property. If we were to access the `Character` at that `startIndex`, we would get the first `Character`. Any index beyond that can be obtained by applying an offset to this `startIndex`, or, if it makes more sense, we can use a negative offset from an `endIndex` property of `String`.

A few examples will help us here more than any further explanation:

```
let question = "What will you do?"
question.startIndex
question.index(after: question.startIndex)
question.index(before: question.endIndex)
question.endIndex
question.index(question.startIndex, offsetBy: 3)
question.index(question.endIndex, offsetBy: -3)
```

It is tempting to pause at this point to write an extension on the `String` type, with which to abstract away this rather messy--looking syntax. But we have a way to go yet, and for clarity and compatibility's sake, we'll resist that temptation for now. However, it is certainly very easy to create an `idx` method (or call it what you will) that takes an `Int`, and executes the preceding code behind the scenes.

Once we have an index, we use it as a subscript to access `Character`:

```
let i = question.index(after: question.startIndex)
question[i] //"h"

let j = question.index(question.endIndex, offsetBy: -3)
question[j] //"d"
```

The reverse of this is to access the index of a given character:

```
let charIndex = question.characters.index(of: "l")
```

Where there are multiple occurrences of the character, the index of the first occurrence is returned.

Obtaining a subrange

Subranges of a `String` are simple and intuitive, once we have obtained the indices:

```
let rangeStart = question.startIndex
let rangeEnd = question.index(question.startIndex,
                              offsetBy: 4)
let subrange = rangeStart ..< rangeEnd
```

We can also get the range of a given substring:

```
let youString = question.range(of: "you")
```

Modifying strings

So now that we know how to specify the indices and ranges that interest us, we can perform all of the standard operations on a `String` variable.

You may notice a strong resemblance to the operations we can perform with `Array` and `Dictionary` object types. This is because they all conform to the `Collection` protocol, and so share a number of methods; only the argument types differ.

Removing characters

Removing individual characters of subranges from a `String` is done as follows:

```
var badBoys = "The Rolling Stones"

let s = badBoys.remove(at: badBoys.index(before: badBoys.endIndex))

let range1Start = badBoys.startIndex
let range1End = badBoys.index(badBoys.startIndex,
                                offsetBy: 4)
let range = range1Start ..< range1End

badBoys.removeSubrange(range)
```

Note that `remove` returns a `Character`, while `removeSubrange` returns nothing.

Inserting characters

We can insert individual characters as follows:

```
badBoys.insert(" ", at: badBoys.startIndex)

var wannaBeBad = "Justin"

let range2Start = wannaBeBad.index(wannaBeBad.endIndex,
                                     offsetBy: -2)
let range2End = wannaBeBad.endIndex

let range2 = range2Start ..< range2End

wannaBeBad.replaceSubrange(range2, with: " Like A")

let bobSong = wannaBeBad + badBoys
```

You may be tempted to distil several lines of code into a single statement, as follows:

```
var stillTrying = "Justin"
stillTrying.replaceSubrange(stillTrying.index(
stillTrying.endIndex, offsetBy: -2) ..<
stillTrying.endIndex, with: " Like A \(badBoys)")
```

My advice is don't. Abstract it into an extension if you like, but the native Swift String operations quickly become difficult to read when nested inside each other. Clarity trumps brevity every time.

String interpolation

We have already seen that we can include object descriptions in strings, as follows:

```
let houseNumber = "221B"
let string = "I live at number \( houseNumber), Baker Street"
```

We can also put a complete expression within the \():

```
let x = 0b001
let y = 0b010
let z = 0b100
let t = "The total is \(x + y + z)"
```

This includes function calls:

```
let gift = "Jaguar"
let wishfulThinking
    = "My wife bought me a \(gift.uppercased()) for my birthday!"
```

It's probably not a good idea to include huge chunks of code though, again for reasons of clarity.

Writing long strings

Unlike some languages, such as C, we can't spread a single String over separate lines, but there is an easy workaround for those occasions when we have to use really long string literals:

```
let multilineString = "Supercalla"
    + "fragilistic"
    + "expialidocious"
```

We'll be needing this in the next section.

Escape characters

There are a number of characters that cannot be contained in a String without being **escaped**. The escape character in Swift is the backslash.

In the spirit of a demonstration being worth a thousand words, run the following code for the rest of this section's text:

```
print(
    "Use the \\ character to print \"quotes\"\n"
    + "And \\n to print a new line\n"
    + "\twith tabs\n"
    + "\tby using \\t")

print(
    "You can also use:\n"
    + "\t\\0 for the null character\n"
    + "\t\\r for the carriage return\n"
    + "\t\\' for single quotes"
    + "and \n\t\\\\ for the backslash itself")
```

And let's not forget our emoji friends, if for no other reason than Apple's evident enchantment with the idea of adding them to messages in different sizes:

```
print(
    "Use \\u{unicode} to produce unicode "
    + "characters like \u{1f480}")
```

The Unicode code is a number, up to eight digits long, giving you access to an almost inexhaustible supply of ice creams, thumb gestures, and puppy dogs.

If your native alphabet is not the Latin one, you'll doubtless be aware of other, more business-like uses for Unicode characters.

Other representations

Depending on what we need to do with `String` objects in our code, we may need to access other representations of the string it contains. One frequent case is interfacing with ASCII strings, in either UTF 8 or UTF 16 encodings.

We will look at these four representations:

- UTF-8, as frequently used in database columns
- UTF-16, which is the basis of `NSString` objects
- UTF-32, the format of so-called Unicode **code points**
- Unicode scalars

There are two `String` methods, `utf8` and `utf16`, which return strings in the required formats:

```
let answer = "Enjoy the trip ☺"
answer.utf16.count    // 18
answer.utf8.count     // 20
```

We see here that the smiley character gives different character counts in the two UTF formats.

Let's compare the contents of these types. For readability's sake, we'll shorten the string to this:

```
let shortAnswer = "trip ☺"
shortAnswer.characters.map({ print($0, terminator: " ") })
print()

shortAnswer.unicodeScalars.map({ print($0, terminator: " ") })
print()

shortAnswer.unicodeScalars.map({ print($0.value, terminator: " ") })
print()
```

```
shortAnswer.utf16.map({ print($0, terminator: " ") })
print()
shortAnswer.utf8.map({ print($0, terminator: " ") })
print()
```

 We are using the print statements for separating the individual lines, since we have specified the non-empty print statements to use a space rather than a new line to terminate their outputs.

Running that code produces this output at the debug console:

```
t  r  i  p ☺
t  r  i  p ☺
116 114 105 112 32 128512
116 114 105 112 32 55357 56832
116 114 105 112 32 240 159 152 128
```

As you can see, the representations are the same for the standard Latin alphabet characters, but diverge significantly for the extended characters.

The unicodeScalars method returns a collection of raw Unicode scalar values, and is the same as the characters property we saw in Chapter 2, *Basic Swift*.

C strings

The cString method will return an Array of type [CChar] :

```
let swiftString = "string"
let cStringUTF8
    = swiftString.cString(using: String.Encoding.utf8)
```

NSString

There is another very important string representation that we need to look at, and that is Cocoa's own NSString type.

Swift's String type is bridged to Cocoa's NSString class, meaning basically that we can always successfully cast between them when necessary. Foundation also *extends* Swift's String type to expose NSString methods directly, without the need for casting.

When is it necessary to use NSString? Well, there are still many Foundation methods that require parameters of type NSString (or its subclasses), some of which we will be using in this chapter, including subclasses of NSString such as NSAttributedString and NSMutableAttributedString.

Some NSString gotchas

While the compatibility between String and NSString types has developed to the point where we may seldom be aware of the difference between the two (and the occasions when it is necessary to use NSString are becoming less and less frequent), there are still a few things that we need to bear in mind when working with the latter.

Indexing

NSString is indexed by integer values and String is, as we have seen, indexed by String.Index values. This means that, depending on which characters are used, String.count and NSString.length may differ for a given string.

And that could be a seriously difficult bug to find.

Mutability

An NSString is an immutable string; and mutable strings are wrapped in one of its subclasses, NSMutableString. This mutable version of Cocoa objects is the model for many complex object types in Objective C, including arrays and dictionaries.

Since Swift uses a different model, whereby any type can be declared to be mutable or immutable using let and var respectively, we are faced with some behavior that seems, at first glance, a little inconsistent.

Imagine we declare an NSMutableString with let, like so:

```
let aString: NSMutableString = "Changeable"
```

We have an apparent conflict of philosophies here--is aString mutable or not?

The following will compile without problems:

```
aString.replaceOccurrences(of: "able",
                with: "d",
                options: [],
                range: NSRange(location: 0, length: a.length))
```

But an attempt to change the entire string will fail:

```
aString = "Mutated" // complier error
```

What is happening here is that NSString and its subclasses, including NSMutableString, are reference values. So while we can change the content of the object that the aString variable points to, we can't change the variable to which it points.

Value and reference

The fact that NSString objects are reference types rather than value types also leads to String and NSString behaving differently when it comes to copying:

```
let a: NSMutableString = "Copyright"
let b = a
```

In the preceding code, we have not copied the contents of a, only its location in memory.

Run the following code:

```
a.replaceOccurrences(of: "right",
                with: "left",
                options: [],
                range: NSRange(location: 0, length: a.length))
print(a, b)
```

We see that a and b still return the same value as each other (albeit a new one).

Compare this with Swift's String behavior:

```
var c = "Copyright"
let d = a
c.replacingOccurrences(of: "right", with: "left")
print(c, d)
```

In this case, c and d return different values. String is actually a struct type, and is thus copied by value, not memory location.

String comparison

We dealt with the equivalence operator, `==` ,in `Chapter 2`, *Basic Swift*. We can also search a string for substrings, as follows:

```
let str = "Henry the V"

str.hasPrefix("H")
str.hasSuffix("V")
str.contains("the")
```

Note that `hasPrefix` and `hasSuffix` take `String` parameters, not `Character`. These parameters are not limited in length.

Formatting strings

Writing strings into the user interface can be very simple, using whatever defaults are used by whichever flavor of text view we are using. However, we also have fine-grained control over the appearance of on screen text, down to the smallest of details. Given the generalized nature of this book, there is a limit to the extent that we can cover customized text, but given just a few tools, we can address probably ninety percent of what most developers need ninety percent of the time.

Broadly, there are two distinct areas in which we can tailor on screen text to our requirements:

- We can set the text's font and size
- We can use a Foundation `NSAttributedString`, setting all manner of properties to whichever color, size, and style we need

Let's look at these in more detail.

Formatting using fonts

Setting a font is very straightforward:

```
textView.string = "Salut!"
textView.font = NSFont(name: "Impact", size: 12.0)
```

This doesn't involve the `string` property itself, simply the font.

Formatting using NSMutableAttributedString

We have, however, much more control with an `NSAttributedString`. This is a subclass of `NSString`, that has its own properties that pertain to the string's appearance. These properties include the font, but as we shall see in the next few paragraphs, there's a lot more on offer than that.

Adding an attribute

One of the most valuable aspects of `NSAttributedString` is that the various attributes are each associated with a range of characters within the string. Thus, we are not limited to a single style, font, or any other property, within one string.

 Since we wish to mutate the properties of the string we will need to use an instance of `NSMutableAttributedString`.

```
let str1
  = NSMutableAttributedString(string: "Hello attributions!\n")

let range = NSRange(location: 6,
                    length: 12)

str1.addAttribute(NSForegroundColorAttributeName,
                 value: NSColor.brown,
                 range: range)

textView.textStorage?.setAttributedString(str1)
```

The preceding code produces a single string with two different colors.

 Don't worry about the `textStorage` property for now, we'll cover that when we come to `NSTextField` in its own right.

Multiple attributes

We can mix and match attributes of different types, for example color attributes and font attributes. We can add them individually, as we did previously, or we can combine them first into a `Dictionary` object, in which each attribute is identified by a `String` constant, with a value of the requisite type:

```
let myAttributes: [String: Any] = [
  NSForegroundColorAttributeName: NSColor.darkGray,
  NSBackgroundColorAttributeName: NSColor.init(red: 0.8,
                                          green: 0.8,
                                          blue: 0.8,
                                          alpha: 1.0),
  NSFontAttributeName: NSFont(name: "Courier", size: 18.0)!]

let str2 = NSMutableAttributedString(string: "Great to be here",
                                     attributes: myAttributes)
str1.append(str2)

textView.textStorage?.setAttributedString(str1)
```

And now we have text in different fonts and colors, on different lines, but there is nothing stopping us from mixing attributes within one line, or even one word, as we shall see soon.

One mistake to be extra careful of avoiding is missing the unwrapping (!) operator when creating a value for the `NSFontAttributeName` key. The dictionary values are declared to be of type `Any`, so the compiler will quite happily add an `optional<NSFont>` type value to a dictionary that requires a non-optional `NSFont` value.

If you do forget to unwrap the font, you'll see an error message in the debug console, accompanied by a blank view in your app:

```
2016-10-18 14:10:46.640057 cb8sketch[28801:2191226] -
[_SwiftValue _isDefaultFace]: unrecognized selector sent
to instance 0x6000000498d0 2016-10-18 14:10:46.640401
cb8sketch[28801:2191226] Failed to set
(contentViewController) user defined inspected property
on (NSWindow): -[_SwiftValue _isDefaultFace]:
unrecognized selector sent to instance 0x6000000498d0
```

Links in text

We can go beyond the mere appearance of the text to even specify aspects of functionality, using an NSLinkAttributeName, which is the key to a String value representation of a URL:

```
let linkAttributes
    = [NSLinkAttributeName: "http://www.grimshaw.de"]

let link = NSMutableAttributedString(string: "\nClick me already",
                                     attributes: linkAttributes)

str1.append(link)

textView.textStorage?.setAttributedString(str1)
```

One thing to note here is that the link text will adopt the color specified as the system's http link color (usually blue).

Styles and effects

We frequently use a dictionary to group together a number of attributes to be applied to a particular text style, like headers, sub-headers, and so on.

In the following code we'll combine several attributes of different types to produce a rather over-the-top emphasis text style:

```
let emphasisTextAttributes: [String: Any] = [
  NSUnderlineStyleAttributeName: NSUnderlineStyle.styleSingle.rawValue,
  NSTextEffectAttributeName :
      NSTextEffectLetterpressStyle,
  NSForegroundColorAttributeName:
      NSColor.black,
  NSStrokeWidthAttributeName : 2.0]

str1.addAttributes(emphasisTextAttributes,
                   range: NSRange(location: 29,
                                  length: 2))
```

Running all the `NSMutableAttributedString` preceding code will produce the rather messy input text pictured here:

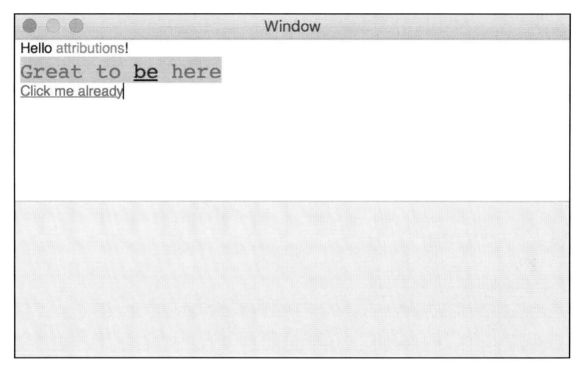

Finally, we can't leave attributed strings without adding some shadow:

```
let myShadow = NSShadow()
myShadow.shadowBlurRadius = 1
myShadow.shadowOffset = CGSize(width: 8, height: -8)
myShadow.shadowColor = NSColor.init(red: 0.9,
                                    green: 0.9,
                                    blue: 0.9,
                                    alpha: 1.0)
```

Here we can see that we have full control over the blur, color, and offset values of text shadows.

So let's apply that to a portion of the string:

```
str1 .addAttribute(NSShadowAttributeName,
                   value: myShadow,
                   range: NSRange(location: 46,
                                  length: 7))

textView.textStorage?.setAttributedString(str1)
```

Note how attributes of *different types* can overlap each other, without affecting each other.

It's an amusing fact of life that while developer conferences continue to discuss how passé shadows and skeuomorphism is, designers continue to use them.

NSTextView

We have our strings, we have our attributes, and we'll now take a look at the place where we put them to use: NSTextView.

An NSTextView, a subclass of NSText, is actually a complex, multi-facetted object, consisting of a small, specialized stack of object types, all hidden behind what appears to the user to be nothing but a blank part of the screen. If only they knew.

NSTextView provides the view in which the text is displayed, exposing the properties textContainer and textStorage, with which we can supply it with text, and display that text on the screen. The two objects that these properties expose communicate with each other via a LayoutManager object.

The MVC pattern of text views

Cocoa's text view is in fact a microcosmic version of the *Model-View-Controller* design pattern followed by so much of Apple's frameworks:

- NSTextStorage is the model, containing all the string and attributes data
- NSTextContainer is the view, providing the *de facto* page onto which we draw text
- NSLayoutManager is the controller, taking the data from the text storage and conveying it to the text container

We won't go into too much detail here as it could fill entire book on its own, but we will take a brief look at each of these classes and how they fit together, in order for us to understand how to design text views with custom behavior.

NSTextStorage

The NSTextStorage class is a subclass of NSMutableAttributedString (itself a subclass of NSString), which, through its string property, exposes a collection of text characters, as well attributes specifying color, font, and style of the text.

It also holds an array of NSLayoutManager objects, each of which gets notified of any changes to the string or attributes of the text storage.

NSTextContainer

An NSTextContainer models the geometric layout of the page on which the text is drawn. The area defined by the text container may be an infinitely long rectangle (well, in theory, anyway), in which case the text will continue to accept text forever, scrolling into infinity. The area may also be a finite rectangle, representing, for example, the page of a magazine, in which case it will limit the amount of text it can accept.

The region in which text may be drawn doesn't have to be a rectangle; areas can be defined around which the text should *flow*, perhaps around an image, or to produce text that will fit into an irregularly shaped graphic like a speech bubble.

NSLayoutManager

The NSLayoutManager sits between NSTextStorage and NSTextContainer objects: The text storage passes text to the layout manager, which then turns characters into glyphs (that is the drawings that you and I recognize as letters and so on), consults the text container for the required drawing area, and then constructs appropriately sized lines of glyphs, taking into account things like line-break specifications, before drawing the finished item into the drawing area of the text container.

Custom text view

So NSTextView saves us from having to write thousands of lines of boilerplate text-drawing code. It may be the case, however, that we wish to extend the abilities of the vanilla NSTextView, and it is such a situation to which we direct our attention in this section.

We will design a text view that will display its text differently according to the content of the string it is displaying. Typing the word red will result in that portion of the text being displayed in red, the word blue will be displayed in blue, etc.

Doing this requires us to subclass NSTextStorage, providing it with the means to parse its own content.

But having coded the subclass, we cannot just replace the textStorage property of an NSTextView initiated from a storyboard; it's a read-only property. So we'll be building the full stack of text view objects, component by component. That may sound like an arduous task, but in fact it's only a page or two of code, and once you have built a text view from scratch, you'll understand much better some of the inner workings of the standard NSTextView, and your text view will do *more*, which has got to be good, right?

To do this, we will need to go through the following steps:

1. Create a custom NSTextStorage subclass.
2. Create instances of NSLayoutManager and NSTextContainer.
3. Associate the text container with the layout manager.
4. Create an NSTextView, initiated with the text container.
5. Create an instance of our custom text storage class, and associate it with the layout manager.

In doing that, we will have implemented an entire customized (and further customizable) stack of objects with all the features of the native NSTextView, but with the addition of the new custom text storage class's functionality, enabling it to inspect its own string value.

Creating the custom storage class

So let's get going on the custom text storage class, declaring it to be a subclass of NSTextStorage, and adding two properties:

```
class CustomTextStorage: NSTextStorage
{
  let textContent = NSMutableAttributedString()

  override var string: String {
  return textContent.string
  }
}
```

The textContent property is an NSMutableString, and as such we declare it with let. We won't change the instance to which the variable points, but we will change the instance's contents.

We then override the superclass's string property, to return the textContent's own string value.

Next we need to override a number of methods of the superclass, much of which is self-explanatory, with the possible exception of the somewhat clunky NSRange code, which is a result of the fact that we dealing with NSMutableAttributedString, and must therefore use the methods declared in its superclass, NSMutableString.

Add the following method overrides to the CustomTextStorage class:

```
override func attributes(
        at location: Int,
        effectiveRange range: NSRangePointer?)
        -> [String: Any]
{
  return textContent.attributes(
        at: location,
        effectiveRange: range)
}
```

The one thing we need to note here is that the attributes are of various types, and so the dictionary returned by this method needs to be of type [String: Any].

Next, we must override the replaceCharacters method:

```
override func replaceCharacters(
        in range: NSRange,
        with str: String)
{
  beginEditing()

  textContent.replaceCharacters(
        in: range,
        with:str)

  edited([.editedCharacters, .editedAttributes],
    range: range,
    changeInLength: (str as NSString).length - range.length)

  endEditing()
}
```

Note that we place the actual character replacement code between calls to `beginEditing` and `endEditing`. The call to `beginEditing` causes the changes in characters or attributes to be buffered and optimized until a matching `endEditing` call is made, after which it can consolidate changes and notify any observers that it has changed.

Overriding the `setAttributes` method is very similar:

```
override func setAttributes(_ attrs: [String : Any]?,
                            range: NSRange)
{
  beginEditing()

  textContent.setAttributes(
          attrs,
          range: range)
  edited(
    .editedAttributes,
    range:range,
    changeInLength: 0)

  endEditing()
}
```

The last thing that we need to override is the `processEditing` method:

```
override func processEditing()
{
  var range = NSUnionRange(
    self.editedRange,
    NSString(string: textContent.string).lineRange(
      for: NSMakeRange(self.editedRange.location, 0)))

  range = NSUnionRange(
    self.editedRange,
    NSString(string: textContent.string).lineRange(
      for: NSMakeRange(NSMaxRange(self.editedRange), 0)))

  applyStyles(range: range)
  super.processEditing()
}
```

This method is automatically called in response to the `endEditing` call (after the edits within the `beginEditing` blocks of the `replaceCharacters` and `setAttributes` methods).

At the moment the compiler will be complaining that it doesn't know anything about an `applyStyles` method; this will be the final method to be added to our `CustomTextStorage` class. But first we must add the following two constants to the class:

```
class CustomTextStorage: NSTextStorage
{
  let textContent = NSMutableAttributedString()
  override var string: String { return textContent.string }

  let normalAttributes = [NSForegroundColorAttributeName:
                          NSColor.darkGray]
  let highlights = ["red": NSColor.red,
                   "blue": .blue,
                   "green": .green]
  ...
```

We have only used three colors here for brevity.

Note that once the `highlights` object type is known, by adding `"red":` `NSColor.red` to the dictionary, the following entries can be abbreviated to `.blue` and `.green`, without explicitly including the `NSColor` enumeration.

We will use these constants in the `applyStyles` method, which it will add to the `CustomTextStorage` class now:

```
func applyStyles(range: NSRange)
{
  for (string, color) in highlights
  {
    let regexStr = "\\b\(string)\\b"

    do {
      let regex = try NSRegularExpression(pattern: regexStr,
                                          options: [])

      regex.enumerateMatches(
        in: textContent.string,
        options: [],
        range: range,
        using: {
          match, flags, stop in

          guard let match = match else {return}

          let matchRange = match.rangeAt(0)
```

```
            self.addAttributes(
                    [NSForegroundColorAttributeName: color],
                    range: matchRange)

            let maxRange = matchRange.location + matchRange.length
            if maxRange + 1 < self.length
            {
                self.addAttributes(normalAttributes,
                                    range: NSMakeRange(maxRange, 1))
            }
        })
    }
    catch { print(error) }
    }
}
```

As you may have spotted, we search the text for a match using regular expressions.

If **regular expressions (regex)**, is a new thing for you, it would be worth doing a little extra homework some time, since the topic itself is beyond the scope of this book. But a deep understanding is not needed here, it suffices to know that we ask an NSRegularExpression object to search for the string that we define with "\\b\(string)\\b", representing a color from the highlights dictionary.

So what's going on here? We iterate through the highlights dictionary:

1. For each color string, we create a regular expression, using standard regex syntax, and use that to initialize an NSRegularExpression
2. We pass the text content and the range to that NSRegularExpression's enumerateMatches method, which also takes as its last parameter a closure which is to be executed for each match
3. That closure simply applies the changes, using the addAttributes method we have overridden

The rangeAt(0) needs to be called on the match variable, which is an array of matches; we don't deal with match groups in this code, but we need to extract that single match nevertheless.

And that completes the CustomStorageClass.

Creating the custom text view

We're very close to being done, as we did the bulk of the work in creating our custom text storage. These are the steps we have still to complete:

1. Create an NSTextView programmatically, using native implementations of the NSTextContainer and NSLayoutManager classes.
2. Declare the ViewController instance to be its delegate.
3. Add the text view as a subview of the View Controller.
4. Create an instance of CustomTextStorage and add the text view's layout manager as an observer, to be notified when changes occur.

We'll put all of those steps into a createTextView method, which we will call from the viewDidLoad method of the ViewController.

Add the following method to the ViewController class (*not* the CustomTextStorage class):

```
func createTextView()
{
    let newTextViewRect = CGRect(x: 0,
                                 y: 0,
                                 width: view.bounds.width,
                                 height: 130)

    let container = NSTextContainer()
    container.size = CGSize(
        width: newTextViewRect.width,
        height: CGFloat.greatestFiniteMagnitude)

    container.widthTracksTextView = true

    let layoutManager = NSLayoutManager()
    layoutManager.addTextContainer(container)

    customTextStorage = CustomTextStorage()

    let attrs = [NSForegroundColorAttributeName: NSColor.darkGray]
    let attrString
        = NSAttributedString(string: "Type some colors here...",
          attributes: attrs)

    customTextStorage.append(attrString)
    customTextStorage.addLayoutManager(layoutManager)
```

```
textView = NSTextView(
        frame: newTextViewRect,
        textContainer: container)

textView.delegate = self

view.addSubview(textView)
}
```

Don't forget, this method is called from the `viewDidLoad` method of the `ViewController`.

Running the code should produce a window much like the following screenshot:

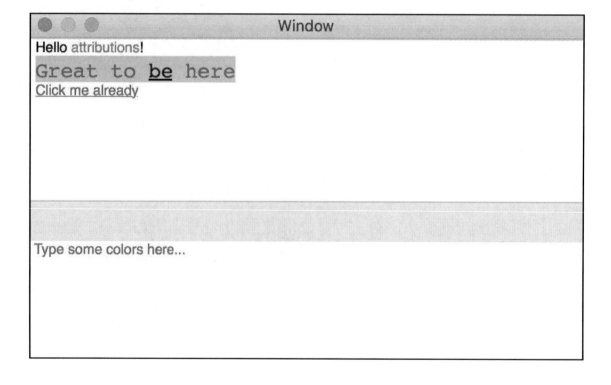

Typing into the lower, dynamically created text view will respond according to the (lowercase) colors you type in:

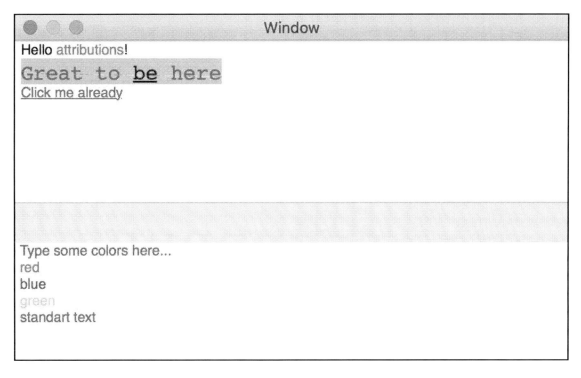

This looks a little underwhelming in gray-scale, but it should look great on your screen.

 So now you've got the syntax-coloring done, you can write an IDE for your own programming language.

Summary

Text plays a central role in desktop computing, and it is likely you will frequently need all the skills you gained in this chapter. It's likely you'll also need several more, and hopefully, your understanding of the material here will stand you in good stead when it comes to discovering and absorbing more of the huge flexibility afforded to us by Swift strings and the Cocoa string and text classes.

You have learned the following in this chapter:

- The structure and representations of strings and characters
- Using indices and subranges when accessing and mutating strings
- Fonts and string formatting
- Understanding the internal structure of `NSTextView`, and the roles of `NSTextStorage`, `NSTextContainer`, and `NSLayoutManager`
- Creating custom text storage for a text view

The next chapter, we'll go beyond drawing text, as we look at one of the most powerful frameworks available on macOS: Core Graphics.

9
Getting More from Interface Builder

This chapter is about making your life with **Interface Builder** (**IB**) a little more comfortable. Although it is possible to write a complete app without doing any work in IB, it's fair to say that most projects are completed with at least some help from the editor that Apple likes to claim meets all your user-interface design needs. Sometimes, it even does.

The main challenge with Interface Builder is the sheer amount of information it holds. A storyboard may contain scores of View Controllers, navigation, and tab controllers; views may be nested deep inside a hierarchy of other views, some of which are never even visible, and increasingly, interfaces are built with a large number of separate storyboards.

Maintaining a clear overview of a project can become quite tricky, but there are a number of things we can do to make all of the challenges listed above more manageable, without compromising our design and development flow.

In this chapter, you will learn about the following:

- The project navigator HUD
- Using the live Debug View Hierarchy
- Using Stack Views to simplify UI layout
- Refactoring large storyboards into multiple, smaller units
- Understanding the XML basis of storyboards

Advanced IB navigation

It is tempting to open every view we are working on in a separate tab, and this is often perfectly plausible. But, especially during the design phase, when we are coordinating any number of views and the subclasses they represent, the luxury of unlimited tabs starts to become as much of a burden as the problem it is meant to solve.

A large part of getting around this problem is getting used to navigating quickly between the various panes and tabs that we have open, and using some of the navigation features to make such a plethora of open tabs unnecessary in the first place. I find that, with fewer other tabs open, I am more inclined to open storyboards in several tabs at once, each showing a different part of a storyboard (or different storyboards, which we'll see later), saving me a lot of scrolling and zooming.

The little-known HUD

One feature that gets little publicity is the heads-up display (**HUD**), or so Apple calls it, which is available in the project navigator.

Simply *option* + *shift* + click on a file that you wish to open, and you'll be greeted with the contextual screen shown in the following screenshot:

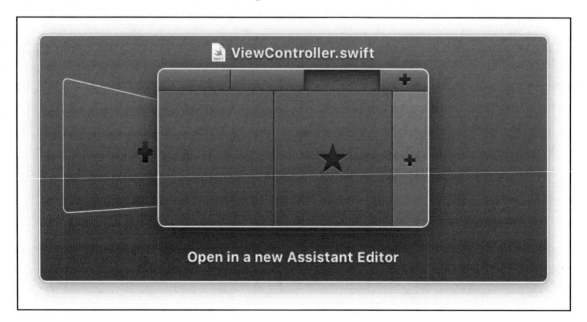

It's surprising how many people haven't discovered this yet. From this pane, we have a number of options beyond opening the file in a new assistant editor, as shown in the preceding screenshot.

We can *replace* the contents of a tab, for example, by clicking first on the mini tab bar shown in the pane:

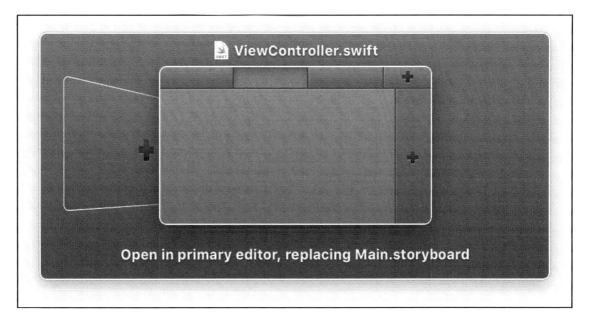

That mini tab bar will show as many tabs as you have open in the main Xcode window, and you can insert the desired file into any one of them, by first selecting it, and then by hitting *return*.

 Personally, I find this more convenient than having a large number of tabs open, especially when working on the laptop. The one downside is that there appears to be no way to do this without the mouse/trackpad.

Showing all views under the cursor

Another challenge in IB, once a project's UI starts to grow in size and detail, is selecting deeply nested or hidden views.

The first solution to this is mostly using the Document Organizer, by which I mean this one:

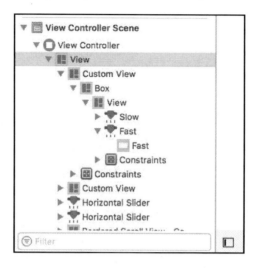

But, there are times when the Document Organizer pane is unwelcome; it does take up a lot of space on screen, and designing the interface is the point at which we need the space most.

But there is another way to select a view. Look at the following storyboard screen:

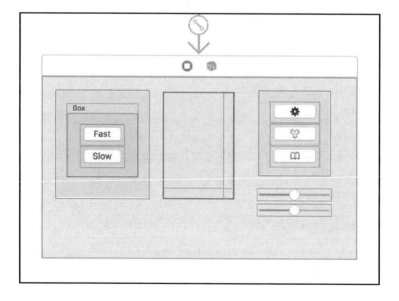

If we wish to select the **Button Cell** of a **Push Button** object, we can't do so by simply clicking on it, which would select the **Button** object itself.

So, we might open the Document Organizer and select it there:

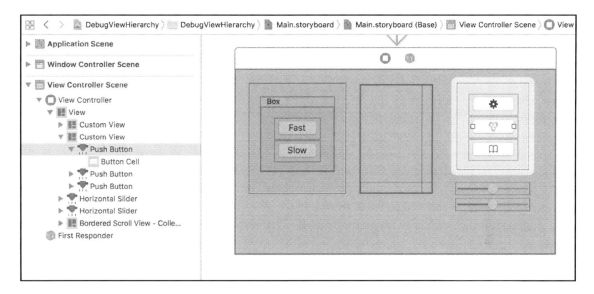

If we do not wish to lose a sizeable portion of the screen to the Document Organizer, we can *shift + control + click* on an element in the main Interface Builder window. This will bring up a contextual menu of all the views that are currently under the mouse.

In the following screenshot, I have clicked on the middle of the group of three buttons:

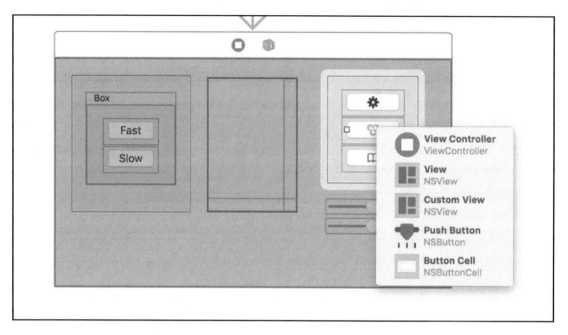

This shows us the complete view hierarchy of **Button Cell**, **Push Button**, **Custom View**, **View**, and **View Controller**.

This doesn't just save us screen real estate; it's also faster, and is often a great source of instruction in itself.

Debug View Hierarchy

The next feature we'll look at is anything but little known, probably because it makes for such spectacular viewing during presentations. Once again, this is a feature to help us cope with the depth and complexity of the view hierarchy that we are frequently faced with.

We are talking here about the **Debug View Hierarchy** feature, which is available to us once the app is running.

The button we need for this is shown in the following screenshot:

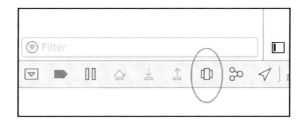

When we first click on this button, the storyboard disappears and is replaced by the following:

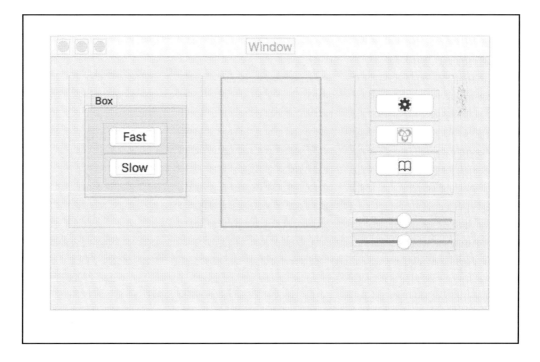

This doesn't look that exciting, it's true. But drag anywhere with the mouse, and you'll see that the UI representation starts to rotate:

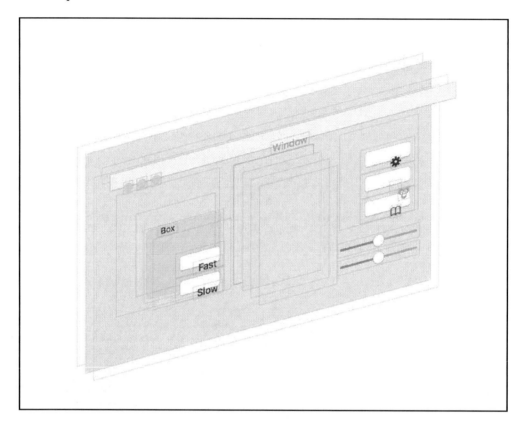

This affords us a much clearer view of what is going on in our interface. Given that so many UI elements are composed of several layers, this can be an invaluable help.

With this view open, we can still select elements. Opening up the Object Inspector (*command + option + 3*) and selecting an element gives us the following:

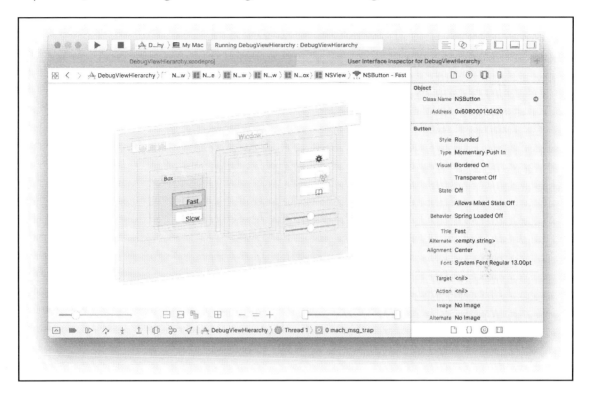

This provides us with a wealth of information about each view's properties. The larger the project, the more valuable this feature becomes.

Controlling the amount of information

Various controls in the window allow us to set exactly how much information we view at one time.

The depth adjustment allows us to set how much separation there is between the layers:

We can also adjust the range of visible views, using these sliders:

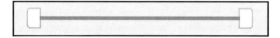

We remove the background views by moving the left slider inwards, that is, to the right. We can remove the foreground views by moving the right slider inwards.

Adjusting the depth and range values gives us control over how much information is shown in the Debug View Hierarchy:

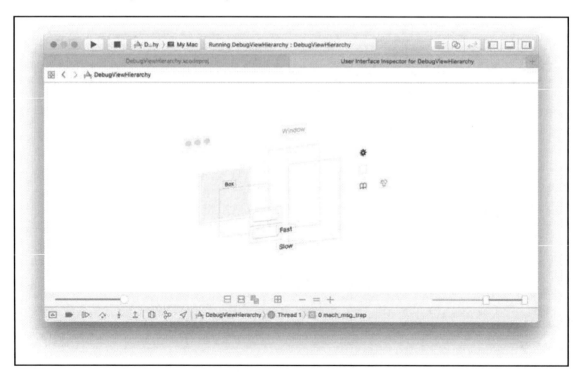

Other view settings

A few other settings are available during a debug session. The following sections cover them in more detail.

Wireframe view

We can also set the controls to show a wireframe view of the UI, or remove the borders completely showing us only the views' contents. The default view is to show both wireframes and contents.

Zooming

The + and - buttons control the zoom level.

Showing constraints

We can also see the constraints of any selected view(s) using the following button:

This can quickly clear up any constraints-related confusion:

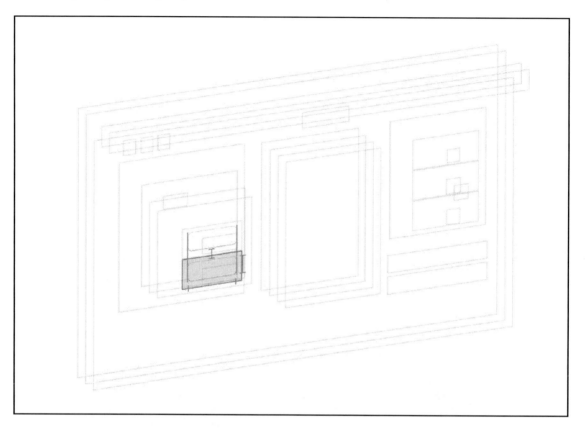

And who doesn't suffer from constraints-related confusion?

Encapsulating views with NSStackView

One of the most useful views in a storyboard UI is, ironically, one that the user never sees. That view is NSStackView.

The idea is simple: Put views that are spatially related to each other into a containing view that offers support for automatically aligning, distributing, and spacing the items that are placed within it.

This offers a number of advantages:

- It's a really quick way to lay out a set of UI elements, particularly when you need to align text baselines and such, which can get a bit fiddly at times.
- It's really robust, in terms of design, since the elements within an NSStackView will retain their relative layout regardless of what happens outside of the view.
- The default values give an immediately Apple-typical look.

This is a good example of *if you can use Apple's little helpers, you probably should.*

Let's take a rather messy, not yet laid out interface:

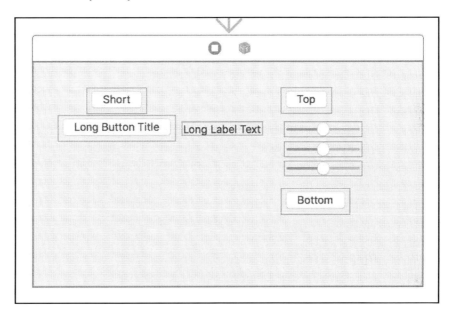

We can group-select the two buttons and the label on the left, and hit the Embed in Stack button at the bottom of the IB window:

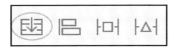

Then we do the same for the group on the right.

Now we drag the two stack views to whichever positions we require:

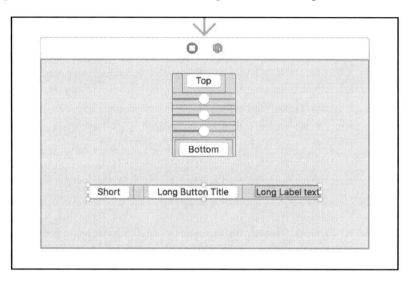

The settings we have chosen for the two stack views are as follows:

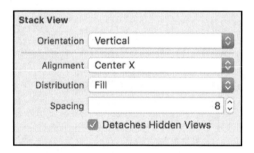

The second stack view is as shown in the following screenshot:

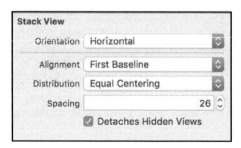

When we run the app, all we see is beautifully aligned, perfectly spaced UI elements:

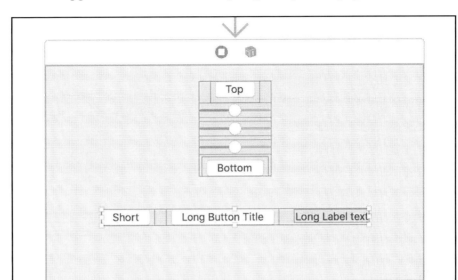

 If you need to do any further laying out using constraints, set up the stack views first, then add the constraints.

And of course, you can select two or more stack views, and embed them in a stack view.

If you are working on really tight design specifications, NSStackView might not be the thing for you this time, but if you're doing your own layout, do give stack views some consideration. They'll save you a lot of time, both in the immediate term and during later tweaks.

Taming the storyboard

Storyboards can become huge, unwieldy things. I've assumed ownership of projects in the past that had many dozens of views and controllers, which forced even the most-up-to-date machine to its knees when scrolling or doing any other redrawing of the Interface Builder window.

So, let's look at a couple of ways we can tame the mighty storyboard.

Refactoring large storyboards

There was a time when refactoring storyboards was an arduous and complicated process, but it has now become so easy that there is little reason not to make our lives much easier by splitting a large, monolithic storyboard into several smaller ones.

In the following screenshot, we can see that our screen space is starting to be an issue:

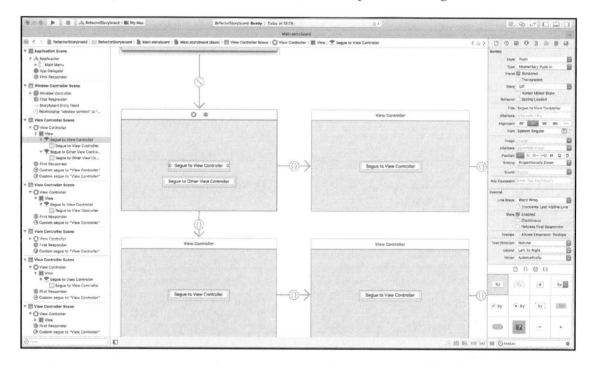

We see that there are segued View Controllers off to the right (in fact, there are another four), and it is clear from the View Controller architecture that we could quite logically separate the second row of controllers into a storyboard of its own (we are assuming here some kind of functional similarity to the storyboard's layout).

So, we'll do just that:

1. Select all the View Controllers in that second row, checking in the Document Outline that we have all the correct ones selected:

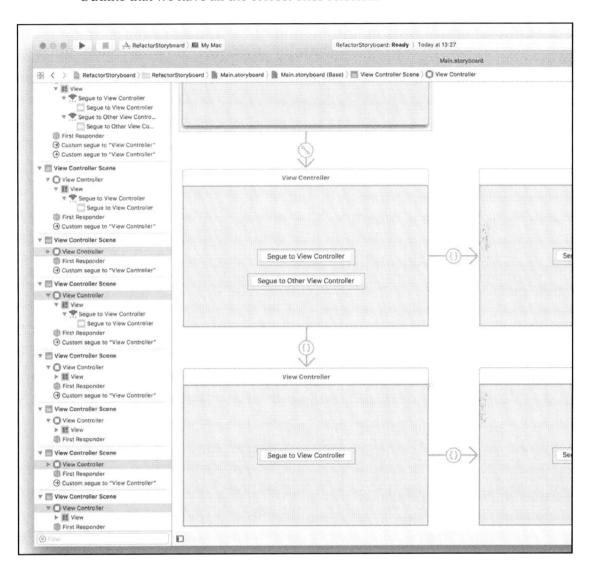

2. We now select **Editor | Refactor to Storyboard...**:

The file-save dialog should automatically select the `Base.lproj` directory, but make sure anyway.

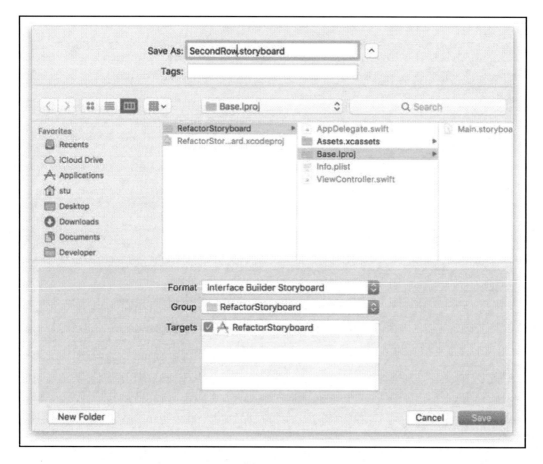

3. Give the storyboard a suitable filename.

4. Hit the **Save** button, and you'll see that we now have a new `.storyboard` file:

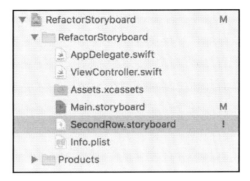

This will not only make working with storyboards much easier, but it also makes the process of collaborating on storyboards, a much-dreaded thing in many dev teams, much safer and easier to coordinate.

Under the hood of a storyboard

Despite the fancy graphics, and the ever-expanding list of tools to help us make the most of storyboards (and Interface Builder in general), the fact remains that the UI of an app is just a heap of XML:

1. To prove it, create a new project, ticking **Use Storyboards**, obviously.
2. Navigate to the `Main.storyboard` file.
3. *Control* + click on that file and select **Open As | Source Code** from the contextual menu.

The file I'm looking at is just short of seven hundred lines of XML. Now, nobody is going to suggest we want to create storyboards by typing that much code. But it really is worth reading through it, to see just how much work we *can* do at this level.

We can rapidly scroll through, for example, menu items, changing their `title` attributes (that is, the text shown on screen) or key equivalent attributes.

We can refer to every single element in the storyboard by its unique object identifier, which looks like this:

```
id="AYu-sK-qS6"
```

If you ever work collaboratively on a storyboard, you're very likely to find this useful, since it's the clearest way of referring to a single element of the UI.

Let's add a few control elements to our UI, and see how that looks.

 One irritating aspect of Interface Builder is that it won't let us open the storyboard as source code and as storyboard, not even in a separate window. So, we'll have to lose our XML view for a moment. You could open it in Text Edit or some such, but you'll need to refresh it after every change in Xcode, so we'll leave that for another time, to save confusion.

Follow these steps:

1. *Control* + click on the file in the project navigator again, and this time choose **Open As | Interface Builder Storyboard**.
2. Add three buttons to the **View Controller Scene**.
3. Select all three buttons, and select **Editor | Embed In | Custom View**.
4. Change the **Title** property of the first button to `Carrots`.

 The reason we are choosing `Carrots` over something like `one`, or `first`, is that we can be quite sure that nothing else in the XML file will contain the word `Carrots`.

Our interface should look roughly as follows, but it's not important how things are laid out:

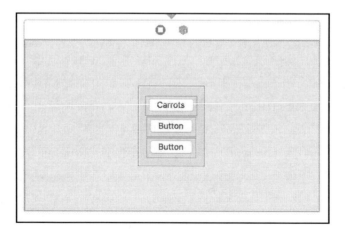

5. Return to the XML view by selecting **Open As | Source Code** from the contextual menu.

6. Search the file for Carrots (*command + F*, as usual). There should only be one hit.

You should find it within the subviews section of the viewController object:

```
<subviews>
  <customView fixedFrame="YES"
    translatesAutoresizingMaskIntoConstraints="NO"
    id="Ma7-lz-Jar">
  <rect key="frame" x="186" y="71" width="109" height="127"/>
  <autoresizingMask key="autoresizingMask"
    flexibleMaxX="YES"
    flexibleMaxY="YES"/>
  <subviews>
    <button verticalHuggingPriority="750"
    fixedFrame="YES"
    translatesAutoresizingMaskIntoConstraints="NO"
    id="3vG-MA-73B">
    <rect key="frame" x="12" y="79" width="85" height="32"/>
      <autoresizingMask ...
      <buttonCell
          key="cell"
          type="push"

          bezelStyle="rounded"
          alignment="center"
          borderStyle="border"
          imageScaling="proportionallyDown"
          inset="2" id="9no-Ft-3Ki">
        <behavior ...>
        <font ...>
      </buttonCell>
    </button>
    <button ...>
    ... more of the same
    </button>
    <button ...>
    ... more of the same
    </button>
  </subviews>
```

As you can see, everything you ever wanted to know about a button in a storyboard is set out before you. And with a little experimentation (and, inevitably, a few mistakes along the way), you'll start to appreciate the extent to which we can drop down into XML to do much of our housekeeping code:

1. Locate the `title` attributes of the next two buttons, which are named `Button`.
2. Change their titles to something like `Orange` and `Ginger`.
3. Swap back to the **Interface Builder Storyboard** view.

You want those buttons a little taller, to match another element somewhere? Look at the following line, within the `<button>` and `</button>` tags of each button:

```
<rect key="frame" x="14" y="79" width="81" height="32"/>
```

Change the `height` property of each button to `42`, and either run the code, or flip back to the IB Storyboard view.

We don't have room here for an exhaustive list of things that are much quicker in the XML view, but for anything to do with renaming or reordering several elements, or changing several properties, such as alignment, for example, all this is a lot quicker when we can type it directly into the XML code.

Summary

Interface Builder can save you a *lot* of work, even if you're the code-as-much-as-possible type. The more time you can invest in getting into its deeper features, the easier and faster it will be to use.

You have learned the following in this chapter:

- Using the project navigator's HUD
- Using `NSStackViews` to simplify UI layout
- Using the Debug View Hierarchy to gain clarity around the UI
- How to navigate the Debug View Hierarchy, and restrict the information shown using the filters provided
- The hows and whys of refactoring storyboards
- Editing a storyboard's underlying XML code

In the next chapter, we will look at how to get the most out of Cocoa's drawing framework, Core Graphics.

10
Drawing on the Strength of Core Graphics

Stop me if you've heard this before, but a picture is worth a thousand lines of text.

And sometimes, a few lines of text can be the source of a great picture. It could be a sleek and minimalist icon; it might be the subtly textured border of a UI control; it might even be a dynamically rendered background texture that changes slightly from one window to the next. There really is no end to the opportunities we have to model the appearance of our software's user interface in almost any fashion we choose.

Everyone loves drawing. Except those who, like me, are absolutely rubbish with a pencil. Which makes it all the more encouraging to experience how engaging a UI can look with the application of a few coding skills rather than a paintbrush and canvas (or Photoshop and a graphics tablet).

With Core Graphics, we can reach into the macOS draw routines, gaining a deep level of control over the user interface. We can draw our own buttons, create our own backgrounds, we can code icons and other symbols. And because it's all in code, it all resizes perfectly, without a trace of pixilation.

In this chapter, you will learn about the following topics:

- How AppKit and Core Graphics work together
- How to create completely custom controls and other views
- Using gradients to add shading
- Using paths to define draw areas and masks
- What a graphics context is and why you need one

But before we learn how, we'll take a look at some of the reasons why we would choose to code rather than images and native controls.

Why not use an image?

There are, of course, many images that we cannot create in code, but for those we can, such as icons, control views, and such, it is worth considering what advantages drawing with Core Graphics has over simply importing an image.

Here are just a few:

- Coding an image is way faster than waiting for a graphic artist to find time to create and send you a bunch of images. And changing, say, the color of a background is way faster still.
- Code is smaller than an image. Your app bundle is smaller, so it downloads more quickly.
- No more pixelated images. With Core Graphics, we store the instructions of how to draw an element, not an image of the ready-drawn element itself.
- There is no need for @2x or @3x resolution images. This is more of a consideration on mobile devices, but resources for a desktop app are frequently reused for iOS and friends.

Why not use native views?

The same arguments apply to the choice between standard button and other controls, and building your own. Often, you will want to use the familiar controls provided as is by Cocoa.

And often, you won't.

The modern requirements of branding, corporate identity, or just an app studio's own style, means that having buttons, faders, and other elements that conform to a particular image or style, are easy to incorporate into an app's UI, especially once a small library of code templates has been built up (and it's amazing just how quickly that happens).

Hopefully, by the end of this chapter, you'll be fully convinced that drawing in code is as productive as it is fun.

Core Graphics and AppKit drawing

Essentially, we have two ways to access the functionality made available by Core Graphics:

- We can use AppKit code, which wraps Core Image code in a simple and abstracted, though limited, interface
- We can call the CG methods directly, leveraging all its power, but with the additional workload that that entails

Using AppKit

The graphics code that starts with the NS prefix is generally from AppKit. This includes NSBezierPath, NSColor, and a whole host of other objects and methods that you will almost certainly have used in the past. Core Graphics used to be harder to use than it is now, and during that time, a lot of effort was put into making it more manageable for those whose background does not include a semester or two of memory management.

The benefits of AppKit's graphics methods are still a most welcome addition to the raw Core Graphics code that is the subject of this chapter.

Using Core Graphics

Core Graphics code is recognizable by the CG prefix. This includes CGFloat, CGRect, and all those other CG's you've been using for so long.

Core Graphics is lower--level code, giving you far more control over the appearance of on screen user interface elements. And with greater power comes greater responsibility, meaning you'll have to give CG a lot more information than you pass to AppKit.

Which to use

I think the best piece of advice at this point is this:

Don't worry about it.

That sounds like a low-intensity bout of Douglas Adams, but it doesn't really matter which you use at first, since you need to get to know both frameworks. By the time you have done that, you will know which to use and when. By all means, read all those blog posts that argue passionately for the highest level of abstraction possible, or whatever else is the topic of the month, but in my view, it's a distraction from the serious and enjoyable business of getting to know all the cool visual stuff that is just a few keystrokes away.

Creating custom views

In this chapter, we are going to use both AppKit and direct Core Graphics code to create custom views. Two of those views will be clock faces, which will give us ample opportunities to explore the most common drawing methods. The other view will be a fairly straightforward custom button.

We are not actually designing an app, so much as designing subclasses of NSView that can be added to any app we wish. We are designing views outside of an actual app project.

This is a good way to ensure that your code is well encapsulated, as well as helping us to focus on the task at hand, rather than being distracted by the rest of an app's implementation.

So, each of these views will hold all the methods and properties needed to draw itself, without needing to refer to the environment in which it is created. When we initiate one of these views, we will only need to supply the frame in which it is to be drawn, much as we would do with any other view.

Custom buttons

We will start with a simple custom button, which will serve as an uncomplicated first look into AppKit and Core Graphics.

We will design the view in a standard template macOS app, so create a new project and call it CoreGraphicsTest or something. The name doesn't matter, since it's the classes that we design that we will use in other apps (whose names presumably do matter).

Drag a **Custom View** object onto the **View Controller Scene**, as illustrated in the following screenshot:

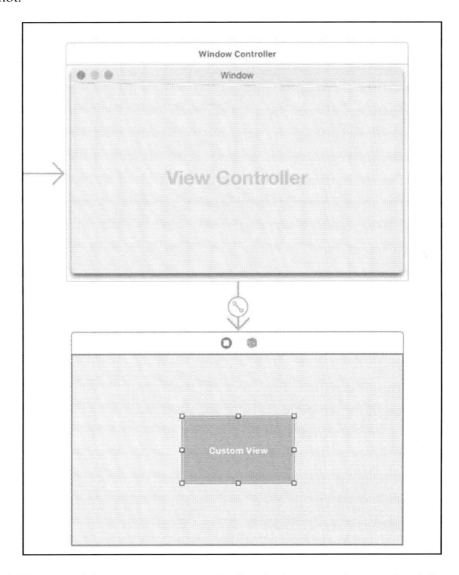

Set its **Width** and **Height** properties as 200 in the size inspector (*command* + *option* + *5*).

Before we start coding, let's take a look at what the finished result will look like:

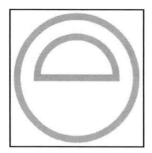

Defining the custom button's properties

To begin with, we'll create a class and make the Interface Builder custom view an instance of that.

Follow these steps:

1. Create a new Cocoa class file, name it ButtonView, and make it a subclass of NSButton.
2. This will give you a stub implementation of the ButtonView class in a file named ButtonView.swift.
3. In Interface Builder, set the custom view's custom class property to ButtonView in the Identity Inspector (*command + option + 3*).
4. Open the assistant editor window (*command + option + return*) and use the jump bar to navigate to the ButtonView.swift file.
5. Now add the following properties to the ButtonView class:

```
@IBDesignable
class ButtonView: NSButton
{
  @IBInspectable var borderColor: NSColor = .white
  @IBInspectable var normalButtonColor: NSColor = .blue
  @IBInspectable var highlightedButtonColor: NSColor = .gray
  @IBInspectable var roundIcon: Bool = true
  var fillColor: NSColor {
    return isHighlighted ? highlightedButtonColor
            :normalButtonColor
  }

    override func draw(_ dirtyRect: NSRect) {
```

```
        super.draw(dirtyRect)

        // Drawing code here.
    }

}
```

The @Inspectable properties will allow us to experiment in Interface Builder with different color schemes.

The fillColor variable is a computed variable, which depends on the runtime value of the button's isHighlighted property, so it needs to be calculated at runtime. By the time the variable is used, all of the necessary data (that is, the view's bounds) are in place, and can be safely used.

We can set such variables in an init method, but I find this way to be more convenient.

 Don't omit the @IBDesignable declaration before the class keyword.

Overriding the button's draw method

This is the method where it all starts to happen:

```
override func draw(_ dirtyRect: NSRect)
```

Any time the view needs drawing, whether because it has just appeared on the screen, or has been half covered by another window, or for whatever other reason, this method gets called.

You don't have to worry about which part of the view needs redrawing, the system takes care of that for you, you simply need to tell it what should be drawn inside the view.

So that we can see the view more clearly, we'll give it a temporary black background:

Replace the commented-out code // Drawing code here with these lines of code:

```
NSColor.black.setFill()
NSRectFill(dirtyRect)
```

Here, we are using AppKit's NSRectFill method, which is just a convenient wrapper for the underlying Core Graphics code.

The results of the drawing code on the view should now be visible in Interface Builder:

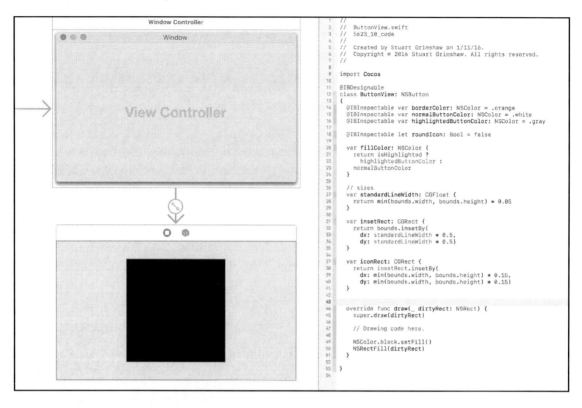

Because we do not know at compile time how large the button will be (the class creating the instance can choose any frame it wants), we need to express all measurements as a percentage of the total button frame size.

Add these computed variables to the `ButtonView` class:

```
var standardLineWidth: CGFloat {
  return min(bounds.width, bounds.height) * 0.05
}

var insetRect: CGRect {
  return bounds.insetBy(
    dx: standardLineWidth * 0.5,
    dy: standardLineWidth * 0.5)
}

var iconRect: CGRect {
  return insetRect.insetBy(
```

```
            dx: min(bounds.width, bounds.height) * 0.15,
            dy: min(bounds.width, bounds.height) * 0.15)
    }
```

These three computed values are all that we will need in positioning the drawings in the view.

We will see later why the `insetRect`, the one that will define the button's visible size, is inset from the actual edges of the view.

The `iconRect` is smaller still; this will be the `CGRect` into which we draw the button's icon.

Filling a path

Next up, we're going to draw and fill a circle, which will be the actual visible background of the button.

To do this, we use an `NSBezierPath`, which is AppKit's model of a shape, or line.

Add the following code to the `draw` method of the `ButtonView` class:

```
let circlePath = NSBezierPath(ovalIn: insetRect)
fillColor.setFill()
circlePath.fill()
```

That was easy enough; we declare the `circlePath` with `NSBezierPath`'s `init(ovalIn:)` method. A circle is just an oval drawn into a square rectangle.

The path doesn't actually draw anything; it's more of an instruction as to where to draw when the time comes.

We call `setFill` on the predefined `fillColor` variable, which is the equivalent of dipping our brush into a particular color, and then tell the `circlePath` to fill its bounded area with the current `fill` color. This performs the actual drawing.

Interface Builder should now be showing this:

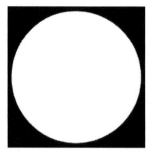

Now we need to add a border to the circle.

Stroking a path

Whereas the `fill` method fills up a shape, the `stroke` method draws around its edges, thus creating a border.

Add the following code to the `draw` method:

```
circlePath.lineWidth = standardLineWidth
borderColor.setStroke()
circlePath.stroke()
```

We set the `lineWidth` property to specify how thick a *brush* we use to paint the border.

The `setStroke` method is akin to the preceding `setFill` method, meaning we select which color to use for the `stroke` method.

The `stroke` method does the actual drawing. The view should now look like this:

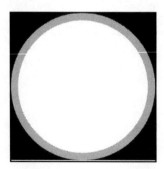

Now we see why the `insetRect` was necessary - the stroke method draws on the path, not inside it, and so it increases the overall size of the drawing. Since the view will cut off anything outside its borders, we need to have made adjustments for that. Which is just what we did when defining the `insetRect` variable.

Drawing the icon with code

Let's add another temporary background color, to make it easier to understand what's going on, this time in the `iconRect`.

Add the following code to the `draw` method:

```
NSColor.gray.setFill()
NSRectFill(iconRect)
```

Now we can see the area into which we will be drawing the icon:

It's time to draw the icon into the button's `iconRect`. We will have one of two icons, depending on the value of the `roundIcon` variable. First, we'll draw the icon when `roundIcon` is `true`.

Add the following code to the `draw` method:

```
let iconPath = NSBezierPath()
if roundIcon == true
{
  iconPath.appendOval(in: iconRect)
}

//  add else {...} here in a moment
```

```
iconPath.lineWidth = standardLineWidth
borderColor.setStroke()
iconPath.stroke()
```

Nothing new here, this is the same as the button's border; the view in Interface Builder will now look like this:

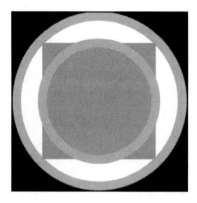

Adding an alternative icon

Now to the other icon, when `roundIcon` is `false`.

Add the following `else` clause to the `if` clause we added previously:

```
let iconPath = NSBezierPath()
if roundIcon == true
{
   iconPath.appendOval(in: iconRect)
}
else
{   iconPath.appendArc(withCenter: CGPoint(
                x: iconRect.midX,
                y: iconRect.midY),
                radius: min(
                    iconRect.width,
                    iconRect.height) / 2.0,
                            startAngle: 180.0,
                            endAngle: 0)
    iconPath.close()
}

iconPath.lineWidth = standardLineWidth
borderColor.setStroke()
iconPath.stroke()
```

Change the `roundIcon` value to `false` and you'll see the newer icon in Interface Builder.

While we're at it, let's remove the temporary rectangle fill-colors.

Delete these lines of code from the `draw` method:

```
NSColor.black.setFill()
NSRectFill(dirtyRect)
...
NSColor.gray.setFill()
NSRectFill(iconRect)
```

The button should now look just as we wanted it:

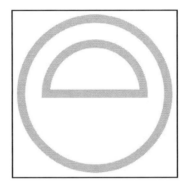

So where's all the button stuff, like actions? Well, they will be specified by whichever class creates an instance of our custom button. Don't forget, we have inherited all the `NSButton` functionality by subclassing it. So, all of the familiar methods of creating a button and assigning it an action are available to use here too.

Testing the button

To check out that the button does actually work, we'll need to run the app. However, there's something we haven't mentioned yet, and that is the fact that we dragged an `NSView`, not an `NSButton`, into the Interface Builder canvas.

The reason for this is that an `NSButton` doesn't render in live view in Interface Builder. Whether this is a bug or not is unclear at the time of writing, but either way, we needed a workaround, and using an `NSView` is the easiest.

Now that the button is finished and ready to test, we can swap out the `NSView` that shows live rendering (but isn't a button), for an `NSButton` that doesn't render in Interface Builder, (but will function as a button):

1. Delete the `NSView`, and drag an `NSButton` from the Object Library. In the Attributes Inspector, set the button's **Style** property to **Square**, so that it becomes fully resizable, and deselect **Bordered**, as shown in the following screenshot:

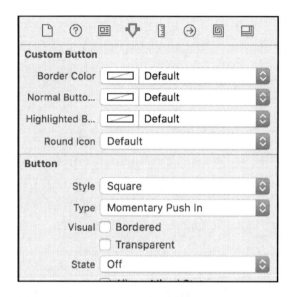

2. Set the class in the Identity Inspector to **ButtonView**.
3. Resize the button appropriately, perhaps to something more button-like, such as 40x40 points, and hit **Run**.

You'll now be able to click on the button to check that it shows its highlighted state.

Copy and paste to create a second button and, in the Attributes Inspector, set the **Round Icon** property to **Off**. When you run the app, it should now look something like this:

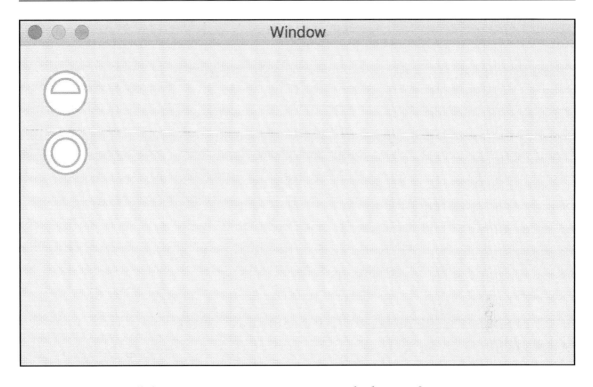

Now, what about all that inviting empty space next to the buttons?

Dial clock

Time for the first clock. No pun intended.

We'll start with a figure that shows how our finished clock view will look:

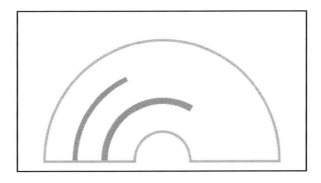

The outer, thinner arc will display minutes and the inner arc will display hours, so the preceding figure is showing the time to be 08:22.

I guess this is a clock for those who don't need to be too fussy about the exact time.

In this view, we will not use Core Graphics code directly; rather, we will use AppKit's wrapper functions, which simplify much of the drawing code to a set of standard calls with standard default values.

Don't worry; in the next section we'll be getting our hands dirty with direct Core Graphics manipulation.

Creating a custom view with AppKit

The first thing we need to do is create a class and make the custom view an instance of that:

1. Create a new Cocoa class file, name it `DialClockView`, and make it a subclass of `NSView`.
2. This will give you a stub implementation of the `DialClockView` class in a file named `DialClockView.swift`.
3. In Interface Builder, change the custom view's custom class property to `DialClockView` in the Identity Inspector (*command* + *option* + *3*), so that we'll be seeing that class as it progresses, rather than the finished `ButtonView`.
4. Open the assistant editor window (*command* + *option* + *return*) and use the jump bar to navigate to the `DialClockView.swift` file.
5. Now add the following properties to the `DialClockView` class:

```
@IBDesignable
class DialClockView: NSView
{
    @IBInspectable var outlineColor: NSColor    = .orange
    @IBInspectable var innerColor: NSColor      = .white
    @IBInspectable var lineColor: NSColor       = .gray
    var timeHours: CGFloat = 8.0
    var timeMinutes: CGFloat = 42.0
    ...
}
```

These are just a set of values that we can use during the design of the view; it's not important what they are.

> Don't forget the `@IBDesignable` declaration before the class keyword.

Next, add the following computed variables to the class:

```
var radius: CGFloat {
  return min(bounds.width,
            bounds.height) * 0.4
}
var radiusHours: CGFloat {
  return bounds.width * 0.2
}
var radiusMinutes: CGFloat {
  return bounds.width * 0.3
}
var center: CGPoint {
  return CGPoint(x:bounds.width / 2.0,
                y: bounds.height / 2.0)
}
```

The `bounds` and `frame` are both `CGRect` type `structs`.

> A view's `frame` pertains to its location (its top--left coordinates) within its containing view, as well as its `width` and `height`.
>
> A views `bounds` is in its own frame of reference; it contains the view's `width` and `height`, but its `x` and `y` coordinates will always be zero.

So, now that we have the view set up to show anything we draw into it in Interface Builder, let's get to work on some actual drawing.

Overriding the custom view's draw method

Once again, let's get things going by coloring the view's background, this time in white.
Add the following lines of code to the `draw` method:

```
NSColor.white.setFill()
NSRectFill(dirtyRect)
```

You should now see this in Interface Builder:

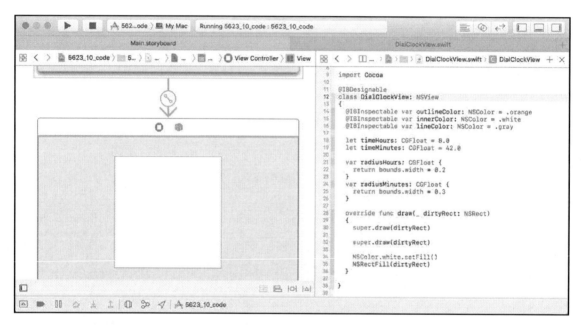

Now that we can see the view, it's time to draw something interesting in it.

Drawing arcs

To draw the clock's *dial*, we'll need to first draw one arc, and then join it to another arc, to
make a complete path. The `appendArc` method of `NSBezierPath` that we used to draw the
custom button's icon will serve us well here; the end of the first arc will be joined to the
beginning of the second automatically, and we then just need to join the end of the second
arc to the beginning of the first, by calling the `close` method on the path.

Add the following code to the `draw` method of the `DialClock` class:

```
let path = NSBezierPath()

path.appendArc(withCenter: center,
               radius: radius,
               startAngle: 0.0,
               endAngle: 180.0)

path.appendArc(withCenter: center,
               radius: radius * 0.25,
               startAngle: 180.0,
               endAngle: 0.0,
               clockwise: true)

path.close()
```

The first call to `appendArc` is just as we have seen before, but the second includes a Boolean `clockwise` argument, with which we can specify in which direction the arc is drawn. The default is anticlockwise, and so we need this to draw the second arc in the opposite direction to the first.

Drawing the outline

Now, with the path in place, we can stroke the outline:

```
outlineColor.setStroke()
path.lineWidth = 4
path.stroke()
```

In addition to the width of the path's line, we can also set how its ends and corners look.

To see this, add the following line of code:

```
path.lineJoinStyle = .roundLineJoinStyle
```

If you look carefully, you'll see that the corners are now rounded, as in the following figure:

Whether or not that line of code stays there is entirely left up to the reader, but the rest of this chapter assumes the default corners.

Adding the fill color

Adding a fill color introduces nothing new:

```
innerColor.setFill()
path.fill()
```

With the background set to white, we don't see much difference. But we don't know what the case will be when a real instance is created in an app, and of course, we can't assume white.

Adding the minutes curve

To add the minute *hand*, we'll draw another arc, one which won't be filled. To know how far round to draw the arc, we need to do some pretty light math, but otherwise the following code contains nothing new:

```
let pathMinutes = NSBezierPath()

pathMinutes.lineWidth = 4

let arcSweepMinutes = CGFloat(timeMinutes) / 60.0 * 180.0
pathMinutes.appendArc(withCenter: center,
                radius: radiusMinutes,
                startAngle: 180.0,
                endAngle: 180.0 - arcSweepMinutes,
                clockwise: true)

lineColor.setStroke()
pathMinutes.stroke()
```

Interface Builder should now show the view to look as follows:

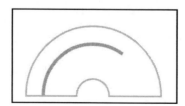

If we were so inclined, we could have a dashed line and add the round cap style as follows:

```
pathMinutes.lineCapStyle = .roundLineCapStyle
let dashes: [CGFloat] = [10, 5]
pathMinutes.setLineDash(dashes, count: 2, phase: 0)
```

The two values of the `dashes` array we pass to the `setLineDash` method specify the length of the dashes and spaces respectively. The `phase` value specifies how far through a dash the line should begin - in this case we have set it to 0, so the line will start with a full-length dash:

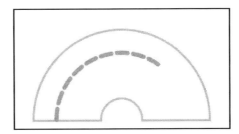

Leave the rounded cap style in place for the moment; we'll be revisiting that in a moment.

Next, we need to add the *hour hand*.

Adding the hours curve

Adding the hours curve uses the same process, with some slightly different math:

```
let pathHours = NSBezierPath()
pathHours.lineWidth = 5

let arcSweepHours = CGFloat(timeHours) / 12.0 * 180.0
pathHours.appendArc(withCenter: center,
                radius: radiusHours,
                startAngle: 180.0,
                endAngle: 180.0 - arcSweepHours,
                clockwise: true)

lineColor.setStroke()
pathHours.stroke()
```

The view will now look as follows:

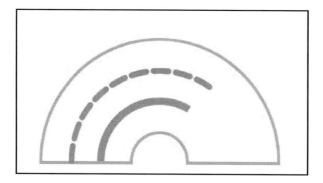

Hmm. If you look closely, you'll notice that the minutes curve, with its protruding rounded corners, is overlapping the border, which doesn't look good.

Correcting the order of drawing

We need to have drawn the minutes and hours curves before we draw the border.

So, move these lines to immediately after the hours curve has been drawn:

```
outlineColor.setStroke()
path.lineWidth = 4
path.stroke()
```

Now the minutes arc ends neatly against the border, as we intended it to look.

It might be worth experimenting with the values of the dashes array and turning the rounded caps on and off; aesthetically, it makes quite a difference:

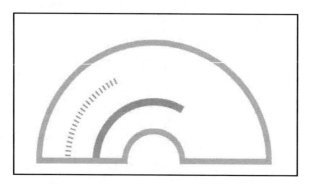

You may even be tempted to add some math to make the minute hand dashes correspond to the sixty minutes of an hour.

And if you're wondering how you would add the hours as curved text, then read on!

Pie clock

The next clock is a little more complicated, so let's take a look at the finished result before we start to look at how we will go about putting it together:

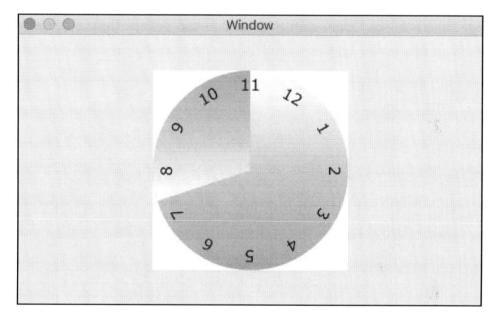

The clock is showing the time at 11.42. The hour text rotates to show the hours, and the segmented face shows the minutes.

This clock was inspired by a real clock that I picked up in Covent Garden once; the hour hand stays in the same position while the whole clock rotates. It's completely impractical, and very cool.

As you might guess, this design involves some amount of drawing on top of previous drawings, as well as a small dose of text rotation.

Creating a custom view with Core Graphics

In this section, we'll move a little closer to the metal, making direct use of some Core Graphics functions.

> *You are leaving the green zone. From now on, it's just you and the graphics; no AppKit safety harness. If you like hot chili and strong coffee, you'll love CG.*

As is generally the case with the core libraries, Core Graphics requires a bit more work from the developer, and in return offers a greater degree of control and detail than is possible with AppKit's methods.

Before we start using Core Graphics code, we need to take a look at the concept of the **graphics context**, which is central to our understanding of lower--level graphics.

Understanding CGContext

As we have seen, drawing to a view has a lot in common with the familiar idea of drawing or painting on a canvas. The `NSView` is that canvas, so what is this context thing?

Imagine that, on top of the canvas you are drawing on, you have a wooden frame. You can only draw inside this frame, and the frame is free to move independently of the canvas. Outside of this frame, the canvas cannot be painted. The frame may be the same size as the canvas - and this is what you have so far experienced - but it may also be resized, moved around, and even rotated.

This wooden frame (which has nothing to do with a view's `frame` property, by the way) is the graphics context, and we have a concrete type for that called `CGContext`.

Why do we need a graphics context?

Imagine sitting at a table, with a piece of paper taped to it, on which you wish to draw.

Now imagine you wanted to take a roller brush to paint just a small corner of the canvas. Being able to resize and reposition the context means you can redefine the area of the view that is paintable, and now you can *fill* just that part of the canvas.

Perhaps you wish to draw some text (or anything else, it doesn't matter), but you wish to draw it upside down. How would you do it? You could try to turn the whole table around through 180 degrees, but it would be easier to move around to the other side of the table to write your text. Rotating the context does the same thing. The graphics content doesn't need to know how to write upside down, it just needs to be moved around the table.

So, broadly speaking, the view we draw into is fixed, while the context is free to move around, and in so doing, defines the part of the view we can draw to. We can specify which areas we want to be able to draw to, and mask off areas we don't want to draw to, by using the graphics context. We can stretch, compress, rotate, and flip the context; we can even save it and restore it.

That may all seem a little abstract right now, but by the end of this chapter, you will have grasped the basic concept of graphics context. It's really not that complicated once you have played with it a little bit.

So far, using the AppKit methods, those that start with NS, has meant that a context was managed for you. When using Core Graphics directly, you'll have the opportunity to manipulate the context to achieve a huge range of drawing functionality that is not possible with the higher level AppKit. And you'll need to specify a CGContext.

Understanding the CG coordinates system

In Core Graphics, the point 0, 0 is at the bottom left-hand corner of the view. So, increasing values of the y coordinate are higher in the view. Increasing values of the x coordinate move to the right.

So, let's see what Core Graphics can do for us.

Creating the custom class

We will begin by creating the new class and making it visible in Interface Builder:

1. Create a new Cocoa class file, making it a subview of NSView, and name it PieClock.swift.

2. Precede the class declaration with @IBDesignable:

```
@IBDesignable
class PieClockView: NSView
{
    override func draw(_ dirtyRect: NSRect) {
        super.draw(dirtyRect)

        // Drawing code here.
    }
}
```

Just as we did with the dial clock, we need to set up some properties, including a couple of computed variables.

3. Add the following code to the `PieClock` class, before the `draw` method:

```
@IBInspectable var darkColor: NSColor = .orange
@IBInspectable var lightColo: NSColor = .white

var center: CGPoint {
  return CGPoint(x: bounds.midX,
                 y: bounds.midY)
}

var timeHours: CGFloat = 11.0
var timeMinutes: CGFloat = 42.0

let numberRectSize: CGFloat = 25.0

var context: CGContext {
  return NSGraphicsContext.current()!.cgContext
}
```

There is only one new thing here, and that's the `context` variable. AppKit's `NSGraphicsContext` holds a reference to the current context in its `cgContext` property.

4. In Interface Builder, use the Identity Inspector to change the class of the custom view from `DialClockView` to `PieClockView`.

Overriding the class's draw method

Since the drawing here gets slightly complicated, we'll break down the clock face into a few separate elements, each with its own drawing method, which we will call from the class's `draw` method. We'll put these methods into an extension of the `PieClockView` class.

Write an extension to `PieClockView`, including the following methods:

```
extension PieClockView
{
  func drawFace(clockRect: CGRect)
  {
  }
```

```
    func drawMinutes(minutes: CGFloat,
                     clockRect: CGRect)
    {
    }

    func drawHours(context: CGContext,
                   hours: CGFloat,
                   clockRect: CGRect)
    {
    }
}
```

Now we need to call those methods, so that we can see what's happening as we add code to them.

The draw method

Let's fill the view with a temporary white background first.

Add the following code to the `draw` method of the `PieClockView` class:

```
NSColor.white.setFill()
NSRectFill(bounds)
```

Below that, we call the individual drawing methods that we created in the extension:

```
drawFace(clockRect: bounds)
drawMinutes(minutes: timeMinutes, clockRect: bounds)
drawHours(context: context, hours: timeHours, clockRect: bounds)
```

We need to draw the *background* first, and work our way to the front, just as we would if we were painting in the physical world.

We use the entire view's `bounds`, since we are not adding a border around the clock face, so we have no need for an `insetRect` as we did in the `DialClockView`.

Note that we need to send the `context` to the second and third of these methods. This is an indication of the fact that those methods will be using Core Graphics methods directly, instead of through AppKit.

Interface Builder should now be showing a white square, since those drawing methods are still empty.

The drawFace method

The face itself is very simple, the only new thing being that we use a gradient to fill it, instead of a solid color.

> We are using quite a bold combination of colors here to make what we are doing easier to follow, particularly in print, but you will probably find that much more subtle differences in color generally produce more pleasing gradient textures.

Adding a gradient with AppKit

Add the following code to the `drawFace` method of the `PieClockView` extension:

```
let circle = NSBezierPath(ovalIn: clockRect)

if let gradient = NSGradient(
  starting: color1,
  ending: color2)
{
  gradient.draw(in: circle, angle: 90.0)
}
```

Using an `NSGradient` is very easy, as we can see here. Later, we'll see that using Core Graphics directly gives us significantly more flexibility.

The results should look like this:

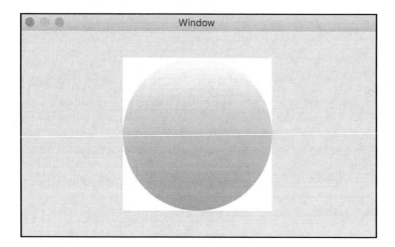

You can see that the `angle` parameter specifies the direction that the `ending` color *points* to. Like all angular things in Core Graphics, gradient angles start at 3 o'clock (or along the *x*-axis, if you prefer) and rotate anti clockwise. Try moving the angle around; you might like something a little less conservative than the 90 degrees parameter we have used here.

The drawMinutes method

You might have already guessed that the minutes are shown by drawing an arc on top of the clock face.

We'll set the radius of the minutes arc to be the same as the radius of the clock face oval and, once again, we'll need some lightweight math to calculate the sweep of the minute hand.

Add the following code to the `drawMinutes` method of the `PieClockView` class:

```
let sweep: CGFloat = (60.0 - minutes) / 60.0 * 360
let radius = (clockRect.size.width, clockRect.size.height) / 2.0
```

Now add the arc, with the following code:

```
let path = NSBezierPath()
path.move(to: center)
path.appendArc(withCenter: center,
            radius: radius,
            startAngle: 90.0,
            endAngle: 90.0 + sweep)
path.close()

darkColor.setFill()
path.fill()
```

There's nothing here that we haven't seen before and Interface Builder should be showing this:

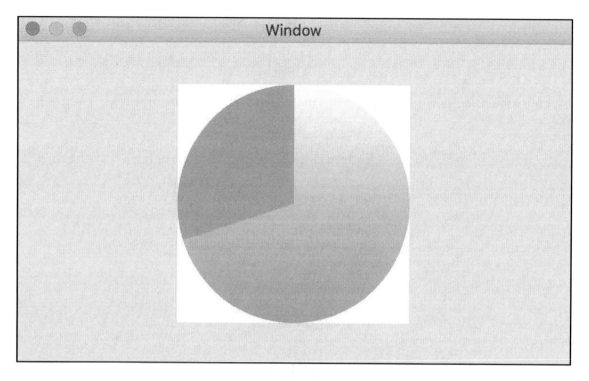

 You might like to experiment with the value of the radius of the arc, either now or when we have added the numbers.

Adding a gradient with Core Graphics

Now we'll replace the solid orange color with a gradient, but this time, a gradient that faces the other way:

1. Delete the following lines of code from the `drawMinutes` method:

```
darkColor.setFill()
path.fill()
```

This time, instead of initiating an NSGradient as we did for the clock face, we will draw into the graphics context, using CGGradient. The Core Graphics methods that we use to do that work a little differently to AppKit's methods, as we'll see shortly.

To begin with, we need to specify three values with which to configure the CGGradient object. We'll go through these one at a time.

Firstly, we need to define a CGColorSpace, which will inform Core Graphics that we are using **RGB** colors.

2. Add the following to the code:

```
let colorSpace = CGColorSpaceCreateDeviceRGB()
```

We could have also used **CMYK** or **grayscale** for the color space.

3. Next, we need to define the colors of the gradient:

```
let colors = [
darkColor.cgColor,
lightColor.cgColor]
```

As you can see, this is an array of colors, but they need to be CGColor objects. We can use the cgColor property of the NSColor objects we have been using up till now to get the CGColors we need.

4. Next, we specify at which positions, relative to the gradient, the colors reach their full values:

```
let colorLocations:[CGFloat] = [0.0, 1.0]
```

The locations are expressed as values between 0.0 (the start point of the gradient) and 1.0 (the end of the gradient).

At the moment, we have specified two colors and two locations, which will produce the same effect as the `NSGradient` method we used before. A bit later, we'll look at adding more colors and locations.

We can now create the gradient and define its start and end points.

5. Add the following lines of code:

```
let gradient = CGGradient(colorsSpace: colorSpace,
                          colors: colors as CFArray,
                          locations: colorLocations)!

let startPoint = CGPoint(x: 0.0,
                         y: 0.0)

let endPoint = CGPoint(x:bounds.width,
                       y:0.0)
```

This code shows how Core Graphics affords us greater control over where the gradient starts and stops within the area drawn to. The `NSGradient` only allowed us to specify an angle.

It's worth playing around with these values later, to get a feel for how the gradient's appearance responds to them.

One thing we need to take care of is the area that is drawn to. We are filling a `CGContext`, not the arc path we created, and that context covers the whole view at the moment. So, we need to clip the context to the arc path--imagine we have a template with an arc-shaped hole cut into it, and we will be spraying our gradient onto that.

However, we only want to clip the context temporarily, since it's only this one arc we're drawing, and after that we will want to draw into the whole view again. So, we need to follow these steps:

- Save the state of the context before we clip it
- Clip the context to the shape of the path we have defined
- Draw the gradient itself
- Restore the original context, as it was prior to clipping

With that overview, we can complete the drawing code for the minute hand.

Add the following code to the `drawMinutes` method of the `PieClockView` extension:

```
context.saveGState()

path.addClip()

context.drawLinearGradient(
    gradient,
    start: startPoint,
    end: endPoint,
    options: [])

context.restoreGState()
```

The `options` parameter allows us to set the values `drawsBeforeStartLocation` or `drawsAfterStartLocation` to extend the fill beyond the start and end points, but we don't need that here.

Adding more color locations

We said earlier that the `colors` and `colorLocations` arrays could contain more than two values, and we'll give that a spin before we move on.

Try these values instead:

```
let colors = [darkColor.cgColor,
              lightColor.cgColor,
              darkColor.cgColor,
              lightColor.cgColor,
              darkColor.cgColor
    ]

let colorLocations:[CGFloat] = [0.0, 0.3, 0.5, 0.7, 1.0]
```

It won't win any awards for good taste, but it amply illustrates the point that Core Graphics is capable of flexible and fine-tuned drawing.

The drawHours method

Now we get to the most exciting bit, where we draw the hour numbers around the outside of the clock, rotating them as we go.

To do this, we'll need to both move and rotate the context.

Context translation

Moving the context up and down, or left to right, or a combination of those, is called **translation**. A nice piece of jargon for a very straightforward concept.

Context rotation

Rotating the context around a point is deemed unworthy of its own jargon and is called **rotation**.

But there is one point to note about CGContext rotation--the point of rotation is the *lower left-hand corner* of the context, which is to say, at the coordinate 0, 0.

This means that if we want to rotate around another point, we need to move the context such that its bottom--left corner is at the point around which we wish to rotate.

We'll do this step by step, so you can follow what's going on.

To start with, add the following code to the drawHours method of the PieClockView class:

```
let numbersRadius = (min(
    clockRect.size.width,
    clockRect.size.height) - numberRectSize) / 2.0

let numberRect = CGRect(
    x: 0 - numberRectSize * 0.5,
    y: numbersRadius - numberRectSize / 2.0,
    width: numberRectSize,
    height: numberRectSize)

let path = NSBezierPath(rect: numberRect)
NSColor.white.setFill()
path.fill()
```

You should now see a white rectangle (into which we will draw the number later) on the far--left side of the view:

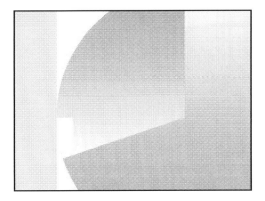

Its top edge is aligned exactly half the way up the side of the view, and its mid--point is aligned with the edge of the view (so half of it is not visible, since it is outside of the view's bounds).

A look at the preceding code should make it clear how we achieved that.

Now, imagine what would happen if we were to stick a pin in the context's bottom--left corner (its 0, 0 coordinate) and rotate it anticlockwise. The rectangle would quickly disappear from the view.

What we need to do is move the bottom left--hand corner of the context to the center of the clock face. Only then can we rotate the numbers around the clock.

Translating the context

To move the context's origin to the center of the clock face, add the following code to the drawHours method, before the call to path.fill():

```
let path = NSBezierPath(rect: numberRect)
NSColor.white.setFill()

context.translateBy(x: bounds.width * 0.5,
                    y: bounds.height * 0.5)

path.fill()
```

And now we have our number rectangle at the 12 o'clock position:

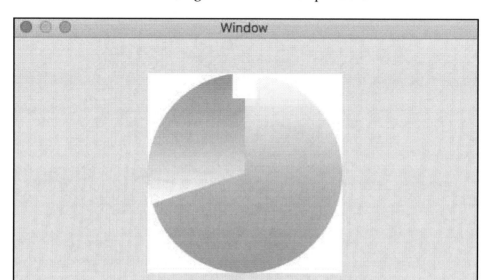

We are now nearly ready to rotate the context. Before we do, we're going to need PI (all code with circles needs PI sooner or later), so we'll define that at the top of the file, outside of any class scope.

Add the following line of code to the `PieChartView.swift` file:

```
let π: CGFloat = CGFloat(M_PI)
```

This isn't really the right place for such constants, and in a real app we would put it along with other constants in a separate file.

We are now going to loop through a block of code 12 times, doing the following in each iteration of the loop:

- Save the graphics context so that we can restore it to its unrotated position
- Rotate the context by 1/12 of a full rotation
- Draw the rectangle
- Restore the context

Now add the following code immediately to the `drawHours` method:

```
for i in 0..<12
{
context.saveGState()

let rotation = 2.0 * π / 12.0 * CGFloat(i)
context.rotate(by: rotation)

path.fill()

context.restoreGState()
}
```

(You can also delete the `path.fill()` call that comes immediately after the translation it's now superfluous).

Now you have all 12 rectangles drawn on the clock face:

At the moment, it's looking more Aztec than hi-tech, but those squares won't be with us for much longer.

Rotating the text

All we need to do to add the text is to draw the appropriate `String` into the `numberRect` on each iteration of the loop.

First, we'll write a function that constructs the text attributes dictionary that we will pass to the text drawing method.

Add the following method to the `PieClockView` extension:

```
func hourTextAttributes(clockRect: CGRect) -> [String: Any]
{
  let paragraphStyle = NSMutableParagraphStyle()
  paragraphStyle.alignment = .center

  let textSize = min(clockRect.size.width,
                     clockRect.size.height) * 0.08

  let textAttributes: [String: Any] = [
    NSParagraphStyleAttributeName: paragraphStyle,
    NSFontAttributeName: NSFont(name: "Verdana",
                                size: textSize)!]
  return textAttributes
}
```

This is all code that we have seen before, only this time, instead of being passed to an NSMutableAttributedString, it will be passed to the String type's draw(in: withAttributes) method.

This isn't the place for a refresher course in trigonometry, suffice to say that 2.0 * π radians equals 360º.

Add the call to `hourTextAttributes` *before* the start of the loop, and the number-drawing code *inside* the loop:

```
let textAttributes = hourTextAttributes(clockRect: clockRect)

for i in 0..<12
{
  context.saveGState()

  let rotation = 2.0 * π / 12.0 * (CGFloat(i))
  context.rotate(by: rotation)

  path.fill()

  let numberString = "\(12 - i)"
  numberString.draw(in: numberRect,
                    withAttributes: textAttributes)

  context.restoreGState()
}
```

Note that we *don't* make the mistake of putting code that only needs to be calculated once into the body of the loop.

Now we can get rid of those white squares.

Delete these lines from the `drawHours` method:

```
let path = NSBezierPath(rect: numberRect)
NSColor.white.setFill()
```

Delete this one from the `drawHours` method too:

```
path.fill()
```

You should now be looking at a recognizable clock face in Interface Builder:

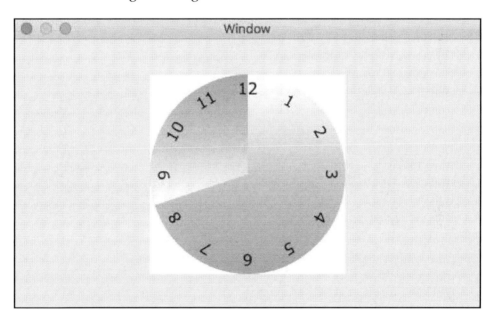

Adding the hour displacement

Our clock is close, but not quite there--it's not yet showing the hour by rotating the number *dial*. This is easily fixed.

Change this line of code:

```
let rotation = 2.0 * π / 12.0 * (CGFloat(i))
```

To the following line of code:

```
let rotation = 2.0 * π / 12.0 * (CGFloat(i) + hours)
```

And, hey presto:

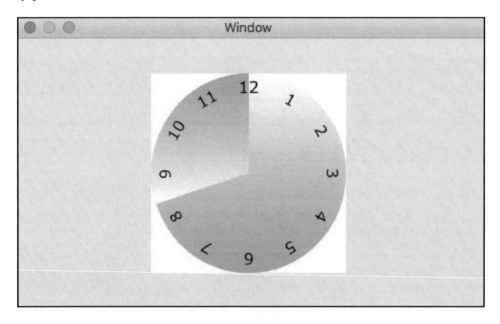

If you've been following attentively, you might have noticed that we have done a lot of stuff to the context, and it is, in fact, still in its translated state.

So, add this call to the very beginning of the drawHours method:

```
context.saveGState()
```

And this one at the very end:

```
context.restoreGState()
```

And, with that, our clock is complete.

 24-hour clock, anyone? Try replacing 11.0 with 23.0 for the timeHours value. Why does that work?

If you try resizing the view in Interface Builder, you can get an idea of how the clock reacts to being drawn in non-square views. Think about how you might ensure that the clock's dimensions follow the smaller of the two dimensions of the view it is being drawn in. Or, even better, use it as is to construct a sun dial in code!

Adding shadows

Adding shadows to Core Graphics is easy, effective, and totally out of fashion. Three good reasons for learning how to do it.

Add this to the start of the drawHours method, immediately after the call to context.saveGState():

```
context.setShadow(
    offset: CGSize(width: 3.0, height: -5.0),
    blur: 5,
    color: NSColor.gray.cgColor)
```

If it's not to your taste, try changing the color values of the shadow, especially the alpha values.

Context scaling

Last but not least, we want to look at **scaling** the context, meaning that we can change a context's width and height independently, and everything in it will adjust accordingly.

Add this line of code in the drawRect of the PieChartView class:

```
context.scaleBy(x: 1.0, y: 0.5)
```

Removing the view's white background helps to make the effect a little more convincing:

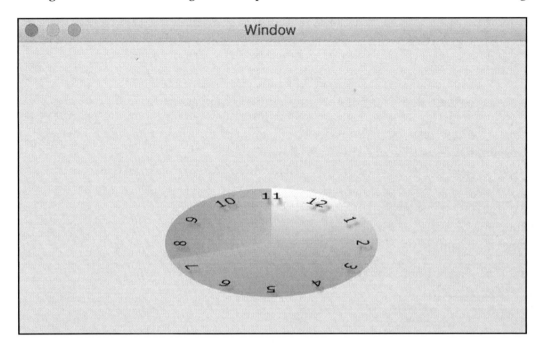

Summary

This was a long chapter. Desktop software graphics is a big topic. And, of course, this is only the beginning. We have covered here the day-to-day requirements of drawing with Core Graphics, but the reader is urged to continue to explore the field, to make the most of the visually rich desktop platforms out there.

In this chapter, you have learned the following:

- Drawing custom controls and views
- Stroking and filling graphics paths
- The methods available through `CGContext`
- Translation, rotation, and scaling of graphics contexts
- Saving and restoring contexts

All splendid stuff. Wouldn't it be great to animate it?

In the next chapter, we will add the code to animate the correct time on these clocks.

11
Core Animation

It's a funny thing how mobile computing, meaning chiefly smart phones, has led the way in animated user interfaces. The restricted space in which the mobile developer must build an interface between an app and the user has meant that animation has developed an essential role in providing the user with cues as to how to engage with apps that might show three or four buttons, where a desktop program would have a dozen or more.

Arguably, desktop computing has not really kept up with the mobile, and even the HTML 5-based browser experience. In many, if not most, apps, there is little in terms of animation beyond the drawing of a focus ring, highlighted-on-click buttons, and a few other system-provided flourishes.

Although things are changing slowly, there is still a massive amount of untapped potential when it comes to animating the UI in subtle but engaging ways. It is this that we will address in this chapter.

 We should mention right at the beginning that we are talking here about animating user-interface elements to add clarity and interest to your app. Writing the next Pixar film in code is way beyond the scope of this chapter.

The topic of animation, whether in 2D or 3D, is a huge one. The approach that this chapter will take in presenting the vast palette of functionality offered by the Core Animation framework is practice over theory, firstly because there is simply too much theory for one modest chapter. Secondly, an intuitive grasp of writing animation code is much better achieved through hands-on experience, through a set of examples designed to present the material with a set of typical property values, followed by as much experimentation as possible. At least, that's the place to start. Later on, with many hours of experience, the theory will make more sense and be considerably easier to digest.

This chapter is much more concerned with what you can *do* with the CAAnimation and CALayer frameworks than it is with the details of how that is achieved at a technical level. It's the declarative way.

It is, of course, perfectly true that the more we understand about the background of the tools we are using, the better placed we are to make optimal use of them. But the great painters and composers of history didn't master their crafts by beginning with lessons in the chemical composition of oil paints, or a physics lesson on the harmonic series that underlies our notion of what music is.

In this chapter, you will learn the following:

- How Core Animation relates to other graphics layers of the Cocoa frameworks
- How to use CALayer and its subclasses
- How to code Core Animation transformations, including rotating, resizing, and translating layers
- The difference between implicit and explicit animations, and how to use them
- How to add 3D drawing and perspective to your interface
- How to use NSView animation methods

What is Core Animation?

Core Animation is, rather strangely, not just a framework for animation, but also a higher-level abstraction of what we have learned with Core Graphics. A large part of this chapter will deal with the CALayer class and its subclasses. Drawing into Core Animation layers is often easier and quicker than dropping down to Core Graphics. Subclassing, or customizing, Cocoa's own views and controls is mostly done through their CALayer properties. But the really magical thing about these layers is the extent to which their properties are already primed for animation. If you can set it on a CALayer, chances are you can animate it, and, generally, animate it very easily.

Core Animation relieves us of the burden of thousands of lines of animation code, presenting us with abstractions that give us as much or as little control over animated user-interface elements as we are likely to need.

Where does Core Animation fit in?

Core Animation is built on top of Core Graphics and Open GL, giving us powerful but manageable abstractions of those frameworks' features. AppKit is then built upon **Core Animation**, enabling us to access the large number of pre-configured controls that we so often add to our interfaces with drag-and-drop, or with just a few lines of initialization code:

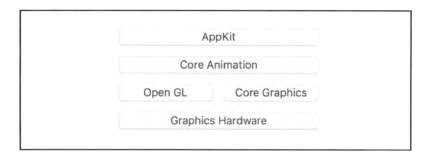

Core Animation takes care of the calculations, interpolation points, and timing that make up an animation, and shields us from having to deal directly with threading issues (and too many more others to list here).

It uses a declarative style API, with which we tell it what we want to see drawn on the screen without having to worry about the technical details. But, it also offers us a great deal of control and flexibility, and it is not often that we'll run into insurmountable barriers when dreaming up the perfect animated user interface.

Layer backed and layer hosting

There are two ways in which an NSView can interact with a CALayer object. The one we will look at in this chapter (and the one that is used 99% of the time) is the **layer backed** view. We will not cover **layer hosted** views here.

Drawing, then animating

This chapter is more or less divided into three parts:

- We will first look at CALayer types, their properties, and their appearance on screen

- We will then take those same layers and turn them from static drawings into animations, using the various types of CAAnimation at our disposal
- Finally, as a short coda, we will look at how we can animate NSView objects directly

Introducing CALayer

We could think of Core Animation layers as a lightweight version of NSView. Layers don't come with many of the properties that we generally associate with views, particularly those associated with user interaction, but much of a view's appearance is in fact the product of its underlying layer.

Almost any CALayer property is animatable--check the CALayer docs for anything that is labeled CAAnimatable.

Subclasses of CALayer can implement the drawInContext method to use Core Graphics drawing methods, or they can set a delegate that implements a drawLayer:inContext method. But Core Graphics is a 2D framework, whereas CALayer offers support for perspective and 3D drawing.

Creating a project

To look at what Core Animation can do, we'll need a window to view it in, so let's get that set up first:

1. Create a new project and navigate to the Main.storyboard in the project navigator.
2. In the document organizer, expand the **Window Controller Scene**, then expand the **Window Controller**, and then select the **Window**.
    1. In the Size Inspector (*Command* + *Option* + 5), set the window's **Width** property to 700 and its **Height** property to 500.
3. Now, in the document organizer, expand the **View Controller Scene**, then expand the **View Controller**, and select the **View**.
4. Set the view's **Width** to 700 and its **Height** to 500, to match the dimensions of the **Window** object.

Adding a custom view

Although we can add objects to the view controller's view directly, we will be putting all our custom layers into a custom view, which we can modify to out heart's content, as and when the need arises:

1. From the Objects Library (*Command + Option + Control + 3*), drag a **Custom View Controller** object onto the **View Controller | View**.
2. In the **Size Inspector**, set the custom view's **X** and **Y** values to **0**, and set the **Width** and **Height** properties to `700` and `500`, respectively.
3. Set the view's **Autoresizing** behavior to resize with the window. The settings should now look as follows:

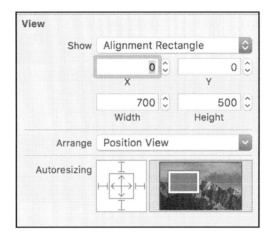

4. Now add an outlet to the custom view, in the `ViewController` class:

```
@IBOutlet weak var customView: NSView!
```

5. Connect the outlet to the custom view in **Interface Builder**.

Extending CGColor

`CALayer` objects have a couple of color properties, as we shall see shortly; they are not `NSColor` instances, but instances of `CGColor`.

Create a new Swift file and name it `CGColorExtension.swift`.

Add the following code to the file:

```
extension CGColor
{
  static var white: CGColor {
    return CGColor(red: 1, green: 1, blue: 1, alpha: 1)}
  static var black: CGColor {
    return CGColor(red: 0, green: 0, blue: 0, alpha: 1)}
  static var silver: CGColor {
    return CGColor(gray: 0.5, alpha: 0.7)}
}
```

This will enable us to easily refer to a set of pre-configured colors in the code, much as we do with some NSColor convenience computed variables.

So much for black, white, and gray. Now let's get a little style.

Add the following variables to the CGColor extension:

```
static var transparentGold: CGColor {
  return CGColor(genericCMYKCyan: 0.1,
              magenta: 0.2,
              yellow: 0.8,
              black: 0.0,
              alpha: 0.7)}

static var gold: CGColor {
  return CGColor(genericCMYKCyan: 0.1,
              magenta: 0.2,
              yellow: 0.8,
              black: 0.0,
              alpha: 1.0)}

static var niceRed: CGColor {
  return CGColor(genericCMYKCyan: 0.4,
              magenta: 0.9,
              yellow: 0.7,
              black: 0.0,
              alpha: 0.7)}
```

If you are accustomed to creating RGB colors using red, green, and blue components, it will certainly be worth your while playing around with the CMYK colors. If you're after those pastel-like 1960s colors rather than bold up-front colors, then CMYK is the way to go.

There's much to be said about CGColor, and RGB/CMYK color design in general, but space is limited, and we are here to look at Core Animation, so the reader is encouraged to read up on, and experiment with, custom color design. There's no easier and more satisfying way to give an app its own unique identity than creating a custom color set.

With our color palette set up, we're ready to turn to the ViewController class.

Preparing the ViewController class

Before we get to coding any custom layers and methods, we'll add a bunch of properties to our View Controller, which we will code up as the chapter progresses.

Add the following variables to the ViewController class:

```
var goButton: NSButton!

var cosmicDoor:   CALayer!
var subLayer:     CATextLayer!
var shapeLayer:   CAShapeLayer!
var textLayer:    CATextLayer!

var circleLayers: [CALayer] = []
var squareLayers: [CALayer] = []
var cubeLayers:   [CALayer] = []

var transformLayer: CATransformLayer!

var colors: [CGColor] = [.transparentGold,
                         .silver,
                         .transparentGold,
                         .silver,
                         .transparentGold]

let easeInOut = CAMediaTimingFunction(
        name: kCAMediaTimingFunctionEaseInEaseOut)

let strings = ["Reading","Loading","Ready..."]
let lockedString = "Locked"
let unlockedString = "Unlocked"
```

We don't need to go into detail here; look at it as a foretaste of the classes we will be dealing with.

In production code, we would probably put the string constants in a separate file along with other string values.

We also need to add a couple of lines to the `viewDidLoad` method:

```
override func viewDidLoad()
{
  super.viewDidLoad()
  customView.wantsLayer = true
  setUpButton()
}
```

By setting the `customView` object's `wantsLayer` property to `true`, we are creating a `CALayer`-backed view, which basically means that we are telling AppKit that we want it to do all the magic caching stuff that it can do with a layer-backed view in the background. If that's not technical enough, *option* + click on the property in the code editor for a fuller explanation, but don't get lost in the detail yet.

The compiler will complain that there is no `setUpButton` method, but we'll cover that soon.

We will also override the `viewDidAppear` method with the following code:

```
override func viewDidAppear()
{
  customView. layer?.backgroundColor = .black
}
```

Don't forget the ? character, since the compiler cannot know that we have indeed required AppKit to provide and manage a layer for the `customView` object.

Adding a button in code

So why are we adding a button in code? Well, it's a great way to see how a `CALayer` fits into the overall button-creation code.

Add the following method to the `ViewController` class:

```
func setUpButton()
{
  goButton = NSButton(
    title: "Go",
    target: self,
```

```
      action: #selector(ViewController.buttonClicked))
    goButton.wantsLayer = true
    goButton.frame = NSRect(x: 620, y: 10, width: 60, height: 20)

    goButton.bezelStyle = NSBezelStyle.recessed
    goButton.layer?.backgroundColor = .gold
    goButton.layer?.cornerRadius = 5.0

    customView.addSubview(goButton)
}
```

Having set the wantsLayer property to true, we can already start to make use of the CALayer properties that afford us such a great degree of control over the appearance of layer-backed views.

Next, we need to silence the compiler by implementing the buttonClicked method that we have set as the action property of the goButton.

Add the following method to the ViewController class:

```
func buttonClicked()
{
}
```

As we add the various animation methods, we will add the relevant calls to this method.

Hit **Run** to make sure that everything is running OK, although there's not much to see yet, just a golden **Go** button.

But now the project is ready for some Core Animation.

Building CALayer objects

We'll kick it off with a simple CALayer instance.

Add the following method to the ViewController class:

```
func buildCosmicDoor()
{
  cosmicDoor = CALayer()

  cosmicDoor.bounds = CGRect(
        x: 0,
        y: 0,
        width: 200.0,
        height: customView.bounds.height * 0.8)
```

```
    cosmicDoor.position = CGPoint(x: 120.0,
                           y: customView.bounds.height * 0.5)

    cosmicDoor.backgroundColor = .black
    cosmicDoor.borderWidth = 1.0
    cosmicDoor.borderColor = .black

    customView.layer?.addSublayer(cosmicDoor)
}
```

Let's have a look at what we're doing here.

Creating the layer's bounds is straightforward enough; we have chosen to make its width absolute, while making its height proportional to the height of (what will be) its super layer.

Note that we use the layer's position property to place it in its super view, rather than setting its frame property. We'll see later on that animating the layer's position property is a breeze to implement, as it is animated by default.

Since the backgroundColor and borderColor properties are both the same color as the customView background, you won't see much if you run the app now. Unless, of course, you take a few minutes to change those values, along with the borderWidth property, which can also produce radically different effects (try setting it to 80.0, for example, and it looks less like a border than a shape in its own right).

Adding CA sublayers

Just like NSView, CALayer has a sublayer property, to which we may add any layer that we require as a sublayer.

Since we add the cosmicDoor layer as a sublayer to the customView layer, the position property will refer to the coordinates within the customView. All of this is pretty intuitive once we have worked with NSView objects and subviews for a while.

Exploring glows and shadows

Now, there is a good reason for setting the background color of the layer to the same as its superlayer's instead of making it transparent. We will be using the layer's shadow properties to achieve a particular effect, and with no background color, you get no shadow (logically enough, I suppose).

We have said elsewhere that shadows are currently out of fashion. Or so everyone claims, although in fact they are found everywhere, in perhaps more subtle forms than the wild days of Snow Leopard. But layers have a shadowColor property, which just begs to be abused, swapping out a shadowy black for something a little more radical. Let's see this in practice.

Add the following code to the buildCosmicDoor method:

```
cosmicDoor.shadowColor = .gold
cosmicDoor.shadowOffset = CGSize(width: 5.0, height: -5.0)
cosmicDoor.shadowRadius = 15.0
cosmicDoor.shadowOpacity = 1.0
```

Now we just need to add the following call to the ViewController class's viewDidAppear method:

```
buildCosmicDoor()
```

Now when you hit **Run**, you should see the following:

Who knew? A colored shadow is a glow! Try messing around with the layer's shadow property values, to get a feel for the various effects that you can achieve with them and to see what their limits are. Don't be shy about using absurd values (it's not like you're going to break anything, is it?), say, a shadow whose radius is as wide as the object itself.

As you might expect, we can also add sublayers to sublayers.

Add the following method to the `ViewController` class:

```
func buildCircleLayers()
{
    let layer = CALayer()
    layer.bounds = CGRect(x: 0.0,
                          y: 0.0,
                          width: 40.0,
                          height: 40.0)
    layer.position =  CGPoint(x: 130,
                              y: 40)
    layer.borderWidth = 2.0
    layer.borderColor = .gold
    layer.cornerRadius = layer.bounds.width * 0.5

    circleLayers.append(layer)
    cosmicDoor.addSublayer(layer)
}
```

We'll be returning to this method later on, when it will become apparent why we are adding layers to the `circleLayers` array. For the moment, we'll just note in passing that an easy way to make a square layer into a circle is to use its `cornerRadius` property set to half its width (or height).

Add the following call to the `viewDidAppear` method:

```
buildCircleLayers()
```

Run the code, and you'll see a golden ring floating in the `cosmicDoor` layer.

Adding a CAShapeLayer

Now that we have created a circle shape using a standard Core Animation layer, it's a good time to introduce `CAShapeLayer`, a subclass of `CALayer`.

The advantage of using CAShapeLayer is that it draws itself using a CGPath, which, as you might guess, is analogous to NSBezierPath. This gives us all the flexibility afforded by Bezier paths, meaning that there is practically no limit to the kind of shapes we can create.

Add the following method to the ViewController class:

```
func buildShapeLayer()
  {
    shapeLayer = CAShapeLayer()
    shapeLayer.bounds = CGRect(x: 0.0, y: 0.0,
                               width: 60.0,
                               height: 60.0)
    shapeLayer.position =  CGPoint(x: 334.0,
                                   y: 45)
    shapeLayer.shadowColor = .white
    shapeLayer.shadowOffset = CGSize(width: 0,
              height: 0)
    shapeLayer.shadowRadius = 15.0
    shapeLayer.shadowOpacity = 1.0

    // CAShapeLayer properties
    shapeLayer.fillColor = .transparentGold
    shapeLayer.strokeColor = .niceRed

    let path = CGPath(ellipseIn: shapeLayer.bounds,
                      transform: nil)
    shapeLayer.path = path

    customView.layer?.addSublayer(shapeLayer)
  }
```

We start by creating the layer just as we would a standard CALayer. Adding the shadow also presents nothing new.

CAShapeLayer properties

CAShapeLayer introduces a number of properties that are not available in its superclass. We will be adding more later, but it's worth noting here that we are setting the fillColor and strokeColor properties of its path property, rather than the background and border colors of the layer. This is because we want to color the shape's path, and not the *rectangle* that the CAShapeLayer occupies.

CGPaths

Because this is not a book exclusively dedicated to macOS drawing and graphics, we can't really delve into all the full flexibility and creative potential of using CGPath to create layers; the interested reader is encouraged to look into the topic in much more depth.

 Resources on this topic are not hard to find, particularly when one includes iOS's use of the same Core Animation framework.

However, we're not done with CGPath yet. Let's look at what we have so far.

First, add the following call to the viewDidAppear method:

```
buildShapeLayer()
```

Now run the app, and you'll see we have added a glowing sphere. Or is it a disc?

Read on...

Adding CA transformations

A **transformation** simply means changing a layer's size, rotation, or position, or a combination of those things.

Core Animation supports three-dimensional transformations (which the good people at Apple endearingly refer to as *two-and-a-half D*), meaning that we also have a z axis to consider.

 The z axis is the one perpendicular to both the x and y axis, which comes out of the screen at you.

Ironically, this is the axis we use more than any other when rotating a layer; turning a rectangle clockwise by 90 degrees on the screen actually means rotating it around the z axis.

Each CALayer object has a transform property, and it is this property we need to address here.

Add this line of code to the buildShapeLayer method:

```
var transform = CATransform3DMakeScale(1.0, 1.0, 1.0)
shapeLayer.transform = transform
```

The `CATransform3DMakeScale` function takes three `CGFloat` values, for the *x*, *y*, and *z* axis respectively. Before we move on, you might want to play around with those values (although changing the `z` value won't do much at the moment).

Rotating a layer in 3D

Okay, we have one little thing to sort out before we get rotating.

Many APIs in Core Animation (and Core Foundation in general) use **radians**, not degrees, to measure angles. Many books and tutorials add a method to convert degrees to radians, in order to use these APIs.

 This book assumes that anyone writing computer software is quite able to remember that 360 degrees equals 2 pi radians, that pi radians are equal to 180 degrees, and that a right angle is pi/2 radians.

 Darwin (and therefore Foundation) gives us access to Unix's `M_PI` value, which is a `Double` in Swift.

So, let's add some of that.

Add the following two lines of code to the `buildShapeLayer` method:

```
var transform = CATransform3DMakeScale(1, 1, 1)
let rotation = M_PI * 0.55
transform = CATransform3DRotate(transform,
                    CGFloat(rotation),
                        1.0, 1.0,0.0)
shapeLayer.transform = transform
```

We set the rotation to be a little over 90 degrees with `pi * 0.55`, and then pass that to the `CATransform3DRotate` function, along with three `CGFloat` values, which specify the factor by which we multiply the given rotation, individually for each axis. Thus, we have specified that we want a rotation of `pi * 0.55` for the *x* and *y* axis, but no rotation around the *z* axis.

The function returns a new CATansform3D object, which is assigned to the layer's transform property.

Now run the code--you'll see a basic approximation of a galaxy.

Mess around with those transform values; it's time well spent. Maybe create a few more galaxies, spread them around the window, and compare the effects of different transformations, perhaps with a few additions to our palette of celestial colors, using the CMYK extensions to CGColor.

Using CATextLayer

We have one more subclass of CALayer to introduce before we start animating our interface, CATextLayer.

Add the following method to the ViewController class:

```
func buildTextLayer()
  {
    textLayer = CATextLayer()
    textLayer.backgroundColor = .gold
    textLayer.opacity = 0.3
    textLayer.shadowColor = .gold
    textLayer.shadowOffset = CGSize(width: 5.0,
                                    height: -5.0)
    textLayer.shadowRadius = 15.0
    textLayer.shadowOpacity = 1.0

    textLayer.bounds = CGRect(x: 0,
                              y: 0,
                              width: 200,
                              height: 34.0)
    textLayer.position = CGPoint(x: 394,
                                 y: 430)
    customView.layer?.addSublayer(textLayer)
  }
```

There is nothing new here, except that we have set the layer's `opacity` property to `0.3`. We will be brightening it up later, but for the moment we'll leave it somewhat faded.

Add the following call to the `viewDidAppear` method:

```
buildTextLayer()
```

If you run the code now, you'll see the layer and its shadow, but we haven't yet added any text, so let's do that next.

Add the following code to the `buildTextLayer` method:

```
let fontName = "Luminari" as CFString
textLayer.font = CTFontCreateWithName(fontName,
                                      0.0,
                                      nil)
textLayer.fontSize = 24.0
textLayer.string = lockedString
textLayer.foregroundColor = .black
textLayer.isWrapped = true
textLayer.alignmentMode = kCAAlignmentCenter
textLayer.contentsScale = (
    NSScreen.main()?.backingScaleFactor)!
```

Given the similarity to `NSTextView` methods, most of this code should be easy to understand. However, the first two lines warrant some closer attention.

We set the `font` property of a `CATextLayer` with a call to Core Text's `CTFontCreateWithName` method, which takes three arguments:

- A Core Foundation string representation of the font name (hence the cast to `CFString`)
- A `CGFloat` for the size, which the text layer will ignore anyway since it will use its own `fontSize` property to set the size of the text drawn
- A pointer to a `CAAffineTransform` object, which we will not use yet

Run the code again, and you should see the following:

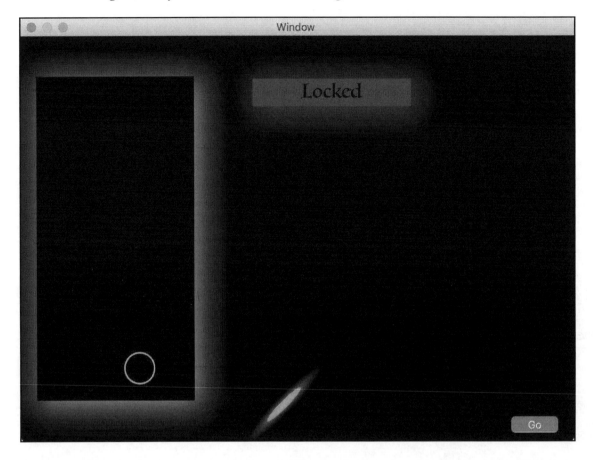

Notice that the shadow's opacity is reduced, because the layer's own opacity is less than 1.0.

And now it's time to get things moving, in every sense.

Animating CALayer objects

As we noted at the beginning of this chapter, the great thing about using `CALayer` and its subclasses is that most of the properties are pre-configured for animation. How simple or how complex those animations are is entirely up to us, but it makes the implementation very easy.

In this section, we will start with some one-liner animation code and work our way up to some pretty intense 3D animations that will consist of a page of code each. But by using CALayer objects to compose our slightly sci-fi inspired UI, we have completed much of the work that is needed to get Core Animation to do what it says on the box, namely animation.

CA implicit animations

Core Animation provides us with default animation of many of its property changes, which requires no extra code at all. Let's see this in action.

Add the following method to the ViewController class:

```
func moveShapeLayer()
{
  shapeLayer.position = CGPoint(
          x: customView.bounds.width * 0.5,
          y: customView.bounds.height * 0.5)
}
```

Add the following line of code to the buttonClicked method:

```
moveShapeLayer()
```

Now run the app. When you click the button, the shapeLayer changes its position as specified in the moveShapeLayer method, with the change occurring in a one-second animation.

Animation doesn't get any easier than this. Although the default is one second, we can customize that with one line of code.

Add the following line of code to the moveShapeLayer method (before the changes in position):

```
CATransaction.setAnimationDuration(3.0)
```

And hey presto, we've customized our first animation. Having done that, it seems a shame to remove the call to moveShapeLayer from buttonClicked, but we're going to need the button for more spectacular things than that, and the moveShapeLayer will collide with the more controlled animations anyway, so go it must.

CA explicit animations

Core Animation provides us with a number of animation methods that afford us a much greater degree of control than the default values.

CABasicAnimation

The most basic explicit animation type provided by Core Animation is the appropriately named CABasicAnimation, which we will put to use first:

Add the following method to the ViewController class:

```
func cosmicDoorExplicitAnimation()
{
  let animation = CABasicAnimation(
                    keyPath: "bounds.size.height")
  animation.duration = 3.0
  animation.fromValue = 0.0
  animation.toValue = view.bounds.height * 0.8
  cosmicDoor.add(animation,
                    forKey: nil)
}
```

Add the following method call to the buttonClicked method:

```
cosmicDoorExplicitAnimation()
```

Run the code, and you should see the cosmicDoor layer expand, from a height of zero to its original height. So, what's happening here?

- As you can see, CABasicAnimation takes a String parameter that specifies the key path of the property that is to be animated.
- We have chosen to set the duration to 3.0 seconds, but there is also a default value which we could have used, by not specifying the duration (comment out that line and see how the animation changes).
- The animation's fromValue is also optional. If we do not specify it, the animation begins at the current value of the animated property.
- However, we do need to set the toValue, which is, of course, the final value that the animation is to reach.

- We add the animation to the `cosmicDoor` layer's animations array, which sets the animation in motion.
- At the moment, we do not need to specify a unique key for the animation, so pass `nil` to the `forKey` parameter. This key is used when we call the `removeAnimationForKey` method of a layer, to cancel its animation.

Why does the `shapeLayer` move? Because its `position` property is in relation to its `superlayer`, which is the `cosmicDoor` layer that is animating. This means that the `shapeLayer` is blissfully unaware that it is moving at all, much like a sleeping railroad passenger.

CABasicAnimation and the view model

Now try swapping the `fromValue` and `toValue` property values. What happens? Why does the layer return to its original height as soon as the animation is over?

`CABasicAnimation` does not affect the *model layer values* of the view, that is, the view model. As far as the layer is concerned, its height property remained unchanged at all times, even during the animation. `CABasicAnimation` changes the *appearance* of the layer, but not its properties.

There are many alternatives to this if we need different behavior, which we will get to very soon.

Delaying an animation

Animations provided by Core Animation conform to the `CAMediaTiming` protocol, meaning that they implement (among many other things) a `beginTime` variable, with which we can delay the start of an animation.

This allows us to coordinate the timing of separate animations. To demonstrate this, we will do the following:

- We will create a visual row of identical `CALayer` objects.
- We will then pass identical animations to each of the layers, which differ only in their `beginTime` property values. We'll do this in a loop in the code.

So first, we need to create the layers.

Add the following method to the `ViewController` class:

```
func buildSquareLayers()
{
  for i in 0..<colors.count
  {
    let  layer = CALayer()
    layer.bounds = CGRect(x: 0.0,
                          y: 0.0,
                          width: 30.0,
                          height: 30.0)
    layer.position =  CGPoint(x: 52 + 34 * i,
                              y: 30)
    layer.borderColor = colors[i]
    layer.borderWidth = 2.0
    squareLayers.append(layer)
    customView.layer?.addSublayer(layer)
  }
}
```

Apart from the fact that we are using the `for in` loop to populate the `squareLayers` array, there is nothing new here. For each object in the `colors` array, we create a `layer` object, offsetting its `position` property by a multiple of the iteration value `i`, that is valid for the current loop iteration.

 A list of color objects is an unlikely source of data for the number of layers, but it will suffice for our purposes, and it allows a lot of playing around with different colors later on, if we are so inclined. Our example produces a neat little line of five alternating gold and silver squares.

Note that `CGPoint` has an initializer that takes integer arguments instead of `CGFloat`, which leads to somewhat tidier code.

Because we will need to refer to the layers in order to animate them, we add them to the `squareLayers` array.

Add the following call to the `viewDidAppear` method:

```
buildSquareLayers()
```

Run the code to ensure that the layers are being drawn correctly. You should see something close to the following:

Now we need to add the animation code.

Add the following method to the ViewController class:

```
func squareLayersTimingAnimation()
  {
    for i in 0..<squareLayers.count
    {
      let layer = squareLayers[i]

      let newPosition = CGPoint(x: layer.position.x,
                                y: layer.position.y + 50.0)

      let animation = CABasicAnimation(keyPath: "position.y")
```

```
            animation.toValue = newPosition.y
            animation.duration = 1.0
            animation.beginTime = CACurrentMediaTime() + Double(i) * 0.2;

            layer.add(animation, forKey: nil)
        }
    }
```

Now add the following call to the `buttonClicked` method:

```
    squareLayersTimingAnimation()
```

Run the app to see what we've got.

Hmm. On the one hand, we've definitely managed to produce the staggered effect we were after, using the `beginTime` property. But it's still not the sweetest of animations.

Let's fix that.

Add the following line to the `squareLayersTimingAnimation` method:

```
    animation.autoreverses = true
```

Run the code again, and you'll see that the animation has indeed turned itself into an animated palindrome, by appending the reversed animation to the end of the original one.

 Note that this doubles the length of the animation.

But, the animation is still very jerky.

To fix this, we can make use of a `CAMediaTimingFunction` object, which we can assign to the animation's `timingFunction` property. If you look back at the constants we set up near the beginning of this chapter, you'll see we have already defined the `easeInOut` constant.

So, add this line to the method:

```
    animation.timingFunction = easeInOut
```

Run the code again. The results are now much better, as the speed of the animation is gradually increased at the beginning and decreased at the end.

 You might like to try creating constants for the other values of the timing function. These are as follows:

```
kCAMediaTimingFunctionLinear
kCAMediaTimingFunctionEaseIn
kCAMediaTimingFunctionEaseOut
kCAMediaTimingFunctionDefault
```

There is one more property we will set here, and that is the number of times the animation is to repeat.

Add the following line to the method:

```
animation.repeatCount = 3
```

Running the code again will produce the expected result.

 Note that this line of code also extends the duration of the animation.

There is also a `repeatDuration` property, which enables us to specify how long an animation should be repeated, instead of how many times. Apple states in the docs that setting both the `repeatCount` and `repeatDuration` on the same animation properties produces undefined behavior. Worth exploring, I'm sure (but don't put it in production code).

Using CAKeyframeAnimation

Now that we have looked at how to coordinate the timing of separate animations, we will look at a method provided by Core Animation that enables us to control the timing and values within a single animation.

The API of `CAKeyframeAnimation` exposes two properties, each of which is expressed as an array of arbitrary length, specifying the values through which an animation passes.

Add the following method to the ViewController class:

```
func keyframeShapeAnimation()
  {
    let kfaY = CAKeyframeAnimation(keyPath: "position.y")
    kfaY.values = [shapeLayer.position.y,
                   80.0, 30.0, 60.0, 30.0, 120.0,
                   layer.position.y]
    kfaY.duration = 10.0
    shapeLayer.add(kfaY, forKey: nil)
  }
```

The basic syntax of the preceding code shows some similarity to that of CABasicAnimation, but there is also an important difference. We have provided an array of CGFloat values, instead of a fromValue and a toValue, which will be applied to the specified key (in this case the *y* coordinate of the position property of the layer).

For the moment, we are supplying a duration parameter, just as we would with the basic animation. We will get to an array of times in a moment.

To see this in action, add the following method call to the buttonClicked method:

```
keyframeShapeAnimation()
```

If you run the code, you'll be able to follow the animations between the values supplied to the .values property. The values are distributed evenly across the time-space defined by the duration of the animation.

The animation is somewhat jerky, as we have seen before. CAKeyframeAnimation has no timingFunction property, but has instead a calculationMode property, which is one of the following string constants:

- kCAAnimationCubic
- kCAAnimationDiscreet
- kCAAnimationLinear
- kCAAnimationPaced
- kCAAnimationCubicPaced

The effect of the cubic mode is similar to the easInOut timing function's behavior, and we'll try that first.

Add the following line of code to the `keyframeShapeAnimation` method:

```
kfaY.duration = 10.0
kfaY.calculationMode = kCAAnimationCubic
shapeLayer.add(kfaY, forKey: nil)
```

If you run the code again, you'll see a much smoother animation. Since the distances covered by the animation are different, the speed of movement varies accordingly, to reach each value of the `.values` array at equally spaced time intervals. If we should prefer the speed of movement to be made even, with the timing of each step adjusted accordingly, we can use either the paced or paced cubic calculation modes.

You might expect to be able to specify the values of the `.values` array as computed values, instead of absolute ones, and you'd be right.

Add the following code to the `CAKeyframeAnimation` method (either before or after the existing code--it makes no difference):

```
let kfaX = CAKeyframeAnimation(keyPath: "position.x")
kfaX.values = [shapeLayer.position.x,
               shapeLayer.position.x - 10.0,
               shapeLayer.position.x + 20.0,
               shapeLayer.position.x - 10.0,
               shapeLayer.position.x]
kfaX.duration = 10.0
kfaX.calculationMode = kCAAnimationCubic
shapeLayer.add(kfaX, forKey: nil)
```

Here we have added a second animation, this time affecting the *x* coordinate of the layer's `position` property, with the values of the array calculated at runtime.

 We can combine any number of separate animations in this way, although we'll look at an alternative method in the next section.

Not all animations will produce a smooth transmission between values, depending on the nature of the animated property. Text is one such property value.

Add the following method to the `ViewController` class:

```
func textLayerKeyFrameAnimation()
{
  let kfa = CAKeyframeAnimation(keyPath: "string")
  kfa.values = strings
  kfa.duration = 5.0
```

```
    textLayer.add(kfa, forKey: nil)

    textLayer.string = strings.last
}
```

Here we are supplying the array of `String` objects we defined earlier to the `.values` property. We have also set the `string` property of the layer to the last entry of that array, so that when the animation is finished, it does not return to the original value that would otherwise still be stored in the layer's model.

We also need to add the following method call to the `buttonClicked` method:

```
    textLayerKeyFrameAnimation()
```

Running this code will show the animation simply swapping out one string for the next. If you want something a little more flash than this, you'll need to compose several animations.

Controlling animations with CAAnimationGroup

We mentioned just now that there was an alternative way to combine multiple animations (of whatever type), and this we achieve through the use of a `CAAnimationGroup` object. Instead of adding animations directly to a layer, we add them to an animation group, and then add that group to the layer, once it contains all the animations we require.

This allows us to configure several animations at the same time, perhaps with an overall duration (which will cap the duration of the animations within the group) or a common timing function. Animating layers that contain animated sublayers can benefit from belonging to the same group, and we can call the `removeAnimation` method on a layer, supplying the group's `key` property as a parameter, to cancel all the animations within that group.

To try this out, add the following method to the `ViewController` class:

```
func groupAnimation()
{
  let groupAnimation = CAAnimationGroup()
  groupAnimation.duration = 5.0
  groupAnimation.timingFunction = easeInOut

  let kfa1 = CAKeyframeAnimation(keyPath: "opacity")
  kfa1.values = [1.0,
                 0.2, 1.0, 0.2, 1.0, 0.6,
                 1.0]
  kfa1.duration = 2.0
  kfa1.calculationMode = kCAAnimationLinear
```

```
    let kfa2 = CAKeyframeAnimation(keyPath: "position.y")
    kfa2.values = [shapeLayer.position.y,
                   100.0, 20.0, 100.0,
                   200.0]
    kfa2.calculationMode = kCAAnimationCubicPaced

    groupAnimation.animations = [kfa1, kfa2]
    shapeLayer.add(groupAnimation, forKey: nil)
}
```

You'll need to add the following method call to `buttonClicked`:

```
    groupAnimation()
```

You also need to comment out the call to `keyframeShapeAnimation` (otherwise, you'll see a combination of the two methods).

Try running the code. You may have already spotted that the animation ends in a position from which it will jump back to the *real* position of the layer, stored in the view model. There are very many circumstances in which we want to show an animation without changing the underlying model.

But if we want both to change the `CALayer` values in the model and animate those changes, we need to turn to a different Core Animation mechanism, namely, `CATransaction`.

Wrapping changes in CATransaction objects

Before we put `CATransaction` to use, we will modify our `shapeLayer` object to include a border, which we will then animate.

Add the following lines of code to the `buildShapeLayer` method:

```
    ...

    shapeLayer.fillColor = .transparentGold
    shapeLayer.strokeColor = .niceRed

    shapeLayer.lineWidth = 3.0
    shapeLayer.lineDashPattern = [5.0, 3.0]
    shapeLayer.lineDashPhase = 0.0
    shapeLayer.strokeStart = 0.0
    shapeLayer.strokeEnd = 0.0
```

```
let path = CGPath(ellipseIn: shapeLayer.bounds,
                  transform: nil)
shapeLayer.path = path
```

...

As you can see, not only can we specify a border on a `CALayer` (and its subclasses), we also have further control over its appearance:

- The `.lineDashPattern` property is an array of `CGFloat` values that specify the length of the dashes and gaps between them. The code we have written here specifies dashes of length `5.0` and gaps between them of length `3.0`, but we could have used any number of values here.
- The `.lineDashPhase` property specifies how far into the dash pattern the border starts (the default being `0.0`).
- The `strokeStart` and `strokeEnd` properties specify how far around the layer's edge the border is drawn. A border that starts at `0.0` and ends at `1.0` will be complete; one that starts at `0.5` and ends at `1.0` will only be half-drawn, starting 180 degrees from the zero rotation (which is horizontally to the right, just as when drawing arcs).

So, let's use some of these properties to illustrate the use of `CATransaction`:

1. Add the following method to the `ViewController` class:

```
func shapeLayerTransaction()
{
    CATransaction.begin()

    CATransaction.setAnimationDuration(5.0)

    shapeLayer.shadowOffset.height = 5.0
    shapeLayer.shadowOpacity = 1.0

    shapeLayer.lineDashPattern = [10.0, 3.0]
    shapeLayer.lineDashPhase = 90.0
    shapeLayer.strokeEnd = 1.0

    CATransaction.commit()
}
```

The basic structure of the CATransaction API is not hard to grasp at first sight. Simply pack all the desired property changes between calls to the .begin and .commit methods. Here we have mixed border dash animations with a slight change in the shadow's appearance.

2. Now add the following method call to buttonClicked:

```
shapeLayerTransaction()
```

3. Comment out the call to groupAnimation.

4. Finally, just for the moment, comment out this line from the buildShapeLayer method:

```
shapeLayer.transform = transform
```

This will remove the layer's rotation so that we can more easily follow what is going on with the border.

Run the code. This is a subtle, but quite complicated, mix of animations, so you may also wish to try commenting them all out, and then adding them singly.

The important point here is not so much the animated border properties than the fact that the appearance of the layer does not revert to its original properties once the animation is over. In contrast to CABasicAnimation (and its key frame and group siblings), a CATransaction actually changes the underlying view-model data.

 This also includes all points in between, so you don't want to be using this method anywhere that KVO is watching the state of any of those properties or you'll get a flood of notifications.

When you're done, don't forget to uncomment this line, because next we'll be animating that transform property:

```
shapeLayer.transform = transform
```

Affine transformation

An affine transformation is a 3×3 matrix that is used in drawing 2D graphics, and the CGAffineTransform type provides functions for creating, concatenating, and applying affine transformations.

The subject of affine transformations is a complex one, and we will follow a strategy here of providing examples as a starting point for experimentation, rather than trying to condense a few chapters' worth of material into half a dozen paragraphs.

Fortunately, we don't always need to actually *create* an affineTransformation ourselves. If all we need to do is rotate, move, or scale a layer, we are provided with a set of functions that create affine transformations that do just that, and for the moment, we will limit our transformations to those (don't worry, it'll get more complex soon enough).

Add the following method to the ViewController class:

```
func affineTransformAnimation()
{
    CATransaction.begin()
    CATransaction.setAnimationDuration(10.0)

    shapeLayer.setAffineTransform(CGAffineTransform(
                                  translationX: 0.0,
                                  y: 10))

    CATransaction.commit()
}
```

Now, before we call this method, decide what you expect the layer to do (obviously, there's a reason for doing this, which we'll get to in a moment).

Now, add the following method call to buttonClicked:

```
affineTransformAnimation()
```

Run the code. Is this what you expected? Naturally, the layer is moving along the *y* axis, and you are sure to have expected that. By why the rotation? Well, we haven't changed the affine transformation that we had previously; we've completely replaced it, and so the 3D rotation has been replaced by a (2D) translation, and the layer animates to the new affineTransform values.

Since we used a CATransaction to perform the animation, the model's values are now changed accordingly, and the layer stays put once the animation completes.

So, when we look at the other two setAffineTransform methods, we need to bear in mind that we don't mix them, since the last set will overwrite any previous set command.

Replace the preceding translation call with this one:

```
shapeLayer.setAffineTransform(
                 CGAffineTransform(rotationAngle: 20.0))
```

It will come as no surprise that the rotation is replaced by a different one.

Just to complete the threesome, replace the `affineTransform` rotation with this one:

```
shapeLayer.setAffineTransform(CGAffineTransform(
                            scaleX: 0.2,
                            y: 0.2))
```

The overloaded `CGAffineTransform` initializer offers us a quick and succinct way to achieve simple but frequently needed affine transformations.

Adding CATransaction completion blocks

`CATransaction` has another handy trick; it has an optional `completionBlock` property, which we can use to fire off any code that needs performing once all the animations in the `CATransaction` block have completed (or been canceled):

```
func squareLayersCompletionAnimation()
  {
    for (i, layer) in squareLayers.enumerated()
    {
        let nextPosition = CGPoint(x: layer.position.x + 20,
                                   y: layer.position.y)
        CATransaction.begin()

        CATransaction.setAnimationTimingFunction(easeInOut)
        CATransaction.setAnimationDuration(5.0)

        CATransaction.setCompletionBlock({
           layer.opacity = 0.5
      })

     layer.position = nextPosition
     CATransaction.commit()
   }
 }
```

Note that no layer property changes in the completion block are committed to the `CATransaction` block itself; it is simply code that will be triggered by the animations' completion.

Add the following method to the `ViewController` class:

```
squareLayersCompletionAnimation()
```

Disable the following line in the `buttonClicked` method, if you haven't done so already:

```
squareLayersTimingAnimation()
```

Run the code, and you'll see how the opacity of the square layers changes once the `CATransaction` block's animations are complete. The opacity change is not governed by the `CATransaction` block's `duration` property, since it lies outside of the animation block, in the completion block, so it adopts the default one-second animation duration.

Nesting CATransaction blocks

Now things start to get interesting. We can nest a `CATransaction` block inside another. Replace the body of the `squareLayersCompletionAnimation` with the following code:

```
for (i, layer) in squareLayers.enumerated()
{
  let nextPosition = CGPoint(x: layer.position.x + 20,
                             y: layer.position.y)
  CATransaction.begin()

  CATransaction.setAnimationTimingFunction(easeInOut)
  CATransaction.setAnimationDuration(5.0)

  CATransaction.setCompletionBlock({
    print("CATransaction block \(i) done :)")
    layer.opacity = 0.5
  })

  // begin nested block
  CATransaction.begin()
  CATransaction.setAnimationDuration(3.0)
  CATransaction.setAnimationTimingFunction(easeInOut)
  CATransaction.setCompletionBlock({
    print("inner block \(i) done")
  })
  if i == 2
  {
    layer.position = nextPosition
  }
  CATransaction.commit()
  // end of nested block

  if i != 2
```

```
    {
        layer.position = nextPosition
    }
    CATransaction.commit()
}
```

We have made a few crucial changes here:

- We have added a `print` statement to the completion block that we had already
- We have added a `CATransaction` block inside the block that we had already, with its *own* completion block and `print` statement
- The nested block's duration is *longer* than the outer block's (what do you imagine will happen?)
- We have changed the code so that one of the layers in the `squareLayers` array is moved, not by the original `CATransaction`, but by the new, nested one

If you run the code again, you'll see the following debug console output:

```
inner block 0 done
inner block 1 done
inner block 3 done
inner block 4 done
outer block 0 done
outer block 1 done
outer block 3 done
outer block 4 done
inner block 2 done
outer block 2 done
```

Because the nested transaction is part of the outer transaction's block, layer 2's completion block is not run until the nested block has completed itself--including the nested completion block.

This idea can be used to set up some very complex relationships between different animations, in a way not possible (or at least, not at all easy) with `CAMediaTimingProtocol`.

Two-and-a-half dimensional animations

I love that term. This is Apple's way of admitting that we can't *really* do 3D graphics on a single screen, but we *can* add perspective to create the illusion of depth. We have already had some very limited contact with the z axis when using CATransform3D objects, and now we'll push that idea somewhat further. It is, of course, along the z axis that we'll be pushing it.

Adding perspective

Before we can animate our z axis, we need to add perspective to our user interface.

Replace the buildCircleLayers method with the following code:

```
func buildCircleLayers()
{
  for i in 0..<colors.count
  {
    let  layer = CALayer()
    layer.bounds = CGRect(x: 0.0,
                          y: 0.0,
                          width: 40.0,
                          height: 40.0)
    layer.position =  CGPoint(x: 130,
                              y: 40)

    layer.zPosition = CGFloat(-3 * i)
    layer.borderColor = colors[i]
    layer.borderWidth = 2.0
    layer.cornerRadius = layer.bounds.width * 0.5
    circleLayers.append(layer)
    cosmicDoor.addSublayer(layer)
  }

  var perspective = CATransform3DIdentity
  perspective.m34 = -0.2
  cosmicDoor.sublayerTransform = perspective
}
```

We iterate through the colors array, as we have done before, and as you can see, we have set the layer's zPosition property to a multiple of each iteration's value of i. If that's all we did, then we'd only see the last of the five circle layers, which would cover the others, so we need to move the "camera," or user's point of view, slightly to one side.

This we do by creating a mutable CATransform3DIdentity. As the name might suggest (at least if you have a mathematical background), the *identity* transform is the equivalent of multiplying everything by 1, that is, no transformation at all. But then the weird stuff begins. The meaning of m34 is the position 3, 4 in the 4×4 matrix with which we represent a 3D transformation.

> Warning: Matrices are the invention of mathematicians, and mathematicians don't seem to like zero-based arrays, so the top-left position in a matrix is position 1, 1.

> Try to approach this from two angles (no pun intended). First, experiment with the matrix values (and not just m34), and try to develop an intuitive understanding of what's going on, before making a second approach, with the help of a search engine, the term *graphics matrix*, and a lot of time. Even if your linear algebraic skills are second to none, you're likely to need some time before the transform matrix becomes something with which you are completely comfortable.

You should now be looking at something like this:

So, let's get animated.

Add the following method to the `ViewController` class:

```
func circleLayersAnimation()
  {
    let newPosition = CGPoint(
        x: circleLayers[0].position.x - 40.0,
        y: circleLayers[0].position.y + 300.0)

    for (i,layer) in circleLayers.enumerated()
    {
      let groupAnimation = CAAnimationGroup()
      groupAnimation.duration = 15.0
      groupAnimation.timingFunction = easeInOut

      let animationY = CABasicAnimation(keyPath: "position.y")
      animationY.fromValue = layer.position.y
      animationY.toValue = newPosition.y
      animationY.duration = 2.0
      animationY.repeatCount = 3
      animationY.autoreverses = true
      animationY.timingFunction = easeInOut

      let animationX = CAKeyframeAnimation(keyPath: "position.x")
      animationX.values = [layer.position.x,
                           layer.position.x - 80.0,
                           layer.position.x + 40.0,
                           layer.position.x]
      animationX.duration = 4.0
      animationX.autoreverses = true
      animationX.timingFunction = easeInOut
      animationX.beginTime
        = animationY.duration * 2.0 + (Double(i) * 0.2)

      groupAnimation.animations = [animationX,
                                   animationY,]

      layer.add(groupAnimation, forKey: nil)
    }
  }
```

This code doesn't actually contain anything new; it's just a mash up of what we have seen before. The animations in the group are of different types, one `basicAnimation` and one `keyframeAnimation`, and the combination of the `duration`, `autoreverses`, and `beginTime` properties makes for a relatively complex-looking composite animation.

Next, add the following method call to `buttonClicked`:

```
circleLayersAnimation()
```

Remove or comment out the following one, if you haven't done so already:

```
cosmicDoorExplicitAnimation()
```

Run the code, enjoy the show, and then change some of the property values and run it again. Repeat endlessly. Add more colors to the `colors` array, add more colors to the `CGColor` extension, change the timing functions, and then animate a few more properties. Repeat.

The next section gets quite hardcore, so take your time.

Getting even closer to 3D

So far, we have added some perspective to individual layers, and that was easy enough to manage as far as it went; but often, we need to group together several transformed layers into a composite whole, which we can then transform in its entirety.

Introducing CATransformLayer

`CATransformLayer` is a special case of `CALayer`; it only exists to host other layers, and as such lacks many of the properties generally found in `CALayer` subclasses, for example, `backgroundColor` or `strokeColor`. All such properties are already found on the sublayers that make up the `CATransformLayer`, and so it has no need to maintain such properties itself.

The animation code that we will write later will be very simple, but in using `CATransformLayer`, we'll have to do a fair amount of preparatory work before we can start morphing things around the screen (although it will be worth it, I promise you).

Our goal here is to compose a cube. A cube is the *Hello World* of 3D, and our cube will look like this:

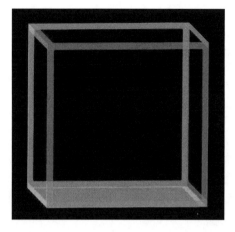

At least, it will look like this until we unleash a barrage of animations at it.

Each side of the cube is a separate layer, with its own color, opacity, and other properties. To build it, we will do the following:

- Create the CATransformLayer
- Populate it with sides made of a single individual layer each
- Rotate and translate the sides until they're all in the right place and looking cubic
- Rotate the whole thing so we can see it's a cube and not a square.

Composing CALayers onto CATransformLayer

To begin with, add the following method to the ViewController class:

```
func buildTransformLayer()
{
   let sideLength = CGFloat(160.0)
   let rightAngle = CGFloat(M_PI) * 0.5
   transformLayer = CATransformLayer()

   func sideLayerWithColor(_ color: CGColor) -> CALayer
   {
      // code to follow
   }

   func addLayersToTransformLayer()
```

```
{
  // code to follow
}

addLayersToTransformLayer()

transformLayer.anchorPointZ = sideLength / -2.0
applyRotation(xOffset: 6.0,
              yOffset: 8.0)

customView.layer?.addSublayer(transformLayer)
}
```

We'll get to the locally defined methods in a moment, but first let's see what we've got here:

1. We declare a couple of constants and initiate the `transformLayer` property of the `ViewController` class.
2. We add sublayers to the `transformLayer` (which we'll get to soon).
3. We set the anchor point in relation to the *z* axis, and then apply a rotation to the whole `transformLayer`. We'll leave the compiler complaining about that for the moment.

Looked at from this high level, it all seems harmless enough, but the devil is in the detail, so we'll drop down a level and look at how we create each individual layer.

First, we need to fill out the `sideLayerWithColor` stub:

```
func sideLayerWithColor(_ color: CGColor) -> CALayer
{
  let layer = CALayer()
  layer.frame = CGRect(
                  origin: CGPoint(x:0, y:0),
                  size: CGSize(width: sideLength,
                               height: sideLength))
  layer.position = CGPoint(x: 500,
                           y: 100)
  layer.borderColor = color
  layer.borderWidth = 6.0
  cubeLayers.append(layer)

  return layer
}
```

The preceding code seems suspiciously simple for a cube, doesn't it? All we are doing is creating a standard CALayer, setting a couple of property values, and adding it as a sublayer to the cubeLayers array. So, you might guess that the bulk of the work is not in creating the layers, but in organizing them, and you'd be quite right.

Add the following method call to the viewDidAppear method so that we can run the drawing code as we go:

```
buildTransformLayer()
```

We'll be using various translations and rotations to assemble the layers, within the transformLayer, to build up the cube.

This we'll do by filling in the addLayersToTransformLayer stub, but we won't do it all at once. We'll start with just two of the sides.

Add the following code to the addLayersToTransformLayer method:

```
let frontLayer = sideLayerWithColor(.silver)
transformLayer.addSublayer(frontLayer)

let rightLayer = sideLayerWithColor(.silver)
var transform = CATransform3DMakeTranslation(
                             sideLength / 2.0,
                             0.0,
                             sideLength / -2.0)
transform = CATransform3DRotate(transform,
                             rightAngle,
                             0.0, 1.0, 0.0)
transformLayer.addSublayer(backLayer)
```

The amount of work we need to do varies with the orientation and position of each side of the cube. In the preceding code, we start off with the simplest layer, the front layer, which is just a call to the sideLayerWithColor method. We then add the layer to the transformLayer, and the job's done.

The next layer is a bit more complicated:

1. First, we create a layer, as we did before.
2. We then create a CATransform3D object.
3. We move the layer back by half a side length, and to the right, by a side length.

4. We then take that transform and pass it to another `CATransform3D` method--one that adds a rotation. This takes a rotation parameter, the `rightAngle` that we defined earlier, and values for the (x, y, z) vector of the transform matrix. Or to put it in English, we set the rotation to be about the *y* axis, by setting the *y* value to `1.0` and the other two axes' values to `0.0`.

This is the manner in which we compose 3D transformations. Translations, rotations, and scales can be added one at a time to an instance of the `CATransform3D` class.

5. We then add the transform to the layer.

If we were to simply rotate the layer, without translating it, it would look like this:

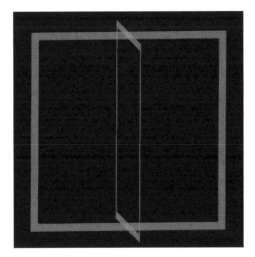

This probably gives us a better intuition of what is going on than a more theoretical explanation. By adding the translations, we get the following:

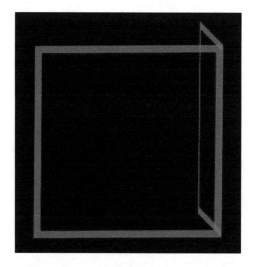

This is certainly closer to the cube we are aiming for.

Before we go any further, take a few minutes (at least) to play around with the transform values, particularly those pertaining to the rotation. This is a much better way to get an initial grasp of what is going on than wading through countless pages of matrix graphics and linear math theory. If you get seriously into 3D, you'll have time enough to consult those more technical resources later.

Now we'll add the other sides:

```
rightLayer.transform = transform
transformLayer.addSublayer(rightLayer)

let backLayer = sideLayerWithColor(.transparentGold)
backLayer.transform = CATransform3DMakeTranslation(
                              0.0,
                              0.0,
                              -sideLength)
transformLayer.addSublayer(backLayer)

let leftLayer = sideLayerWithColor(.transparentGold)
transform = CATransform3DMakeTranslation(
                              sideLength / -2.0,
                              0.0,
                              sideLength / -2.0)
```

```
transform = CATransform3DRotate(transform,
                                rightAngle,
                                0.0, 1.0, 0.0)
leftLayer.transform = transform
transformLayer.addSublayer(leftLayer)

let bottomLayer = sideLayerWithColor(.transparentGold)
bottomLayer.backgroundColor = .transparentGold
transform = CATransform3DMakeTranslation(
                           0.0,
                           sideLength / -2.0,
                           sideLength / -2.0)
transform = CATransform3DRotate(transform,
                                rightAngle,
                                1.0, 0.0, 0.0)
bottomLayer.transform = transform
transformLayer.addSublayer(bottomLayer)

let topLayer = sideLayerWithColor(.silver)
transform = CATransform3DMakeTranslation(
                           0.0,
                           sideLength / 2.0,
                           sideLength / -2.0)
transform = CATransform3DRotate(transform,
                                rightAngle,
                                1.0, 0.0, 0.0)
topLayer.transform = transform
transformLayer.addSublayer(topLayer)
```

This is simply more of the same, with the values adjusted appropriately. Again, take time to play around with these values and get a strong intuitive grasp of what's going on.

If you run the code now, you should be seeing something very similar to the illustration at the beginning of this section.

Rotating the CATransformLayer

Now that we have rotated and translated so many layers, we are in an excellent position to tackle the rotation and translation of the whole transformLayer. We add the transform directly to the subLayerTransform property of the CATransformLayer, which then applies those transform values to its sublayers, thereby doing almost all the heavy lifting for us.

Add the following method to the `ViewController` class:

```
func applyRotation(xOffset: Double, yOffset: Double)
{
   let offset = sqrt(xOffset * xOffset + yOffset * yOffset)
   let rotation = CGFloat(offset *  2 * M_PI / 360.0)

   let rotationX = CGFloat(offset) / rotation
   let rotationY = CGFloat(offset) / rotation

   let translation = CATransform3DTranslate(
                        transformLayer.sublayerTransform,
                        0.0, 0.0, 0.0)

   let completeRotation = CATransform3DRotate(
       transformLayer.sublayerTransform,
       rotation,
       rotationX * translation.m11
         - rotationY * translation.m12,
       rotationX * translation.m22
         - rotationY * translation.m21,
       rotationX * translation.m32
         - rotationY * translation.m31)

   transformLayer.sublayerTransform = completeRotation
}
```

This is a complicated set of property values, and to understand them fully we'd need whole chapters full of 3D graphics theory. One way to get an idea of what the values mean is to replace them with mundane values, typically `0.0` or `1.0`, and build upon that.

For example, we could run the code with the following values:

```
let completeRotation = CATransform3DRotate(
   transformLayer.sublayerTransform,
   1,
   1 * translation.m11
     - rotationY * translation.m12,
   1 * translation.m22
     - rotationY * translation.m21,
   1 * translation.m32
     - rotationY * translation.m31)
```

That would produce the following rotation:

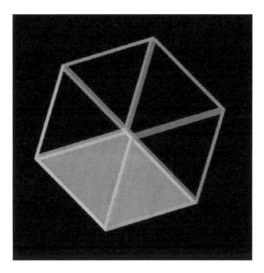

For the purposes of this chapter, we will take the values as presented in the original method implementation, which nicely showcase some of the possibilities available through using CATransformLayer.

Much of this needs to be animated to make sense, and as promised, the animation code is very simple.

Adding 3D animation

Add the following method to the ViewController class:

```
func animateTransformLayer()
{
  CATransaction.begin()
  CATransaction.setAnimationDuration(5.0)

  CATransaction.setCompletionBlock({
    [unowned self] in
    self.textLayer.opacity = 1.0
    self.textLayer.string = self.unlockedString
  })

  applyRotation(xOffset: -290.0, yOffset: -60.0)

  for layer in cubeLayers
```

```
   {
     layer.cornerRadius = 80
     layer.backgroundColor = nil
   }

   CATransaction.commit()
 }
```

There is nothing here that is new to us (although the values of the `xOffset` and `yOffset` will seem a bit obscure).

- The animation changes the rotation of the `transformLayer`, and iterates through the `cubeLayers` array, changing the square borders into circular ones
- Each layer's `backgroundColor` property is set to `nil`, but this will only affect the `bottomLayer`, since this is the only side that was assigned a `backgroundColor` anyway
- The animation's completion block speaks for itself.

Add the following method call to `buttonClicked`:

```
addLayersToTransformLayer()
```

Time to run the code. I think it is fair to say that the animation looks as complicated in action as it does in code. I'm not sure I'd include this in an app of my own, but it does demonstrate some of the behaviors we can govern by the use of a unifying `CATransformLayer` to host several instances of `CALayer`.

Animating NSViews

We will finish off this chapter by returning to `NSView`, which also has animatable properties.

We will let the examples speak mostly for themselves. Often, it will be sufficient for us to apply animations to a view at this higher level, and the experience we have gained in animating `CALayer` objects, together with the material covered in the previous chapter on Core Graphics, will make understanding this code reasonably easy.

Firstly, `NSView` and its subclasses can also make use of implicit animations:

```
func NSViewImplicit()
{
  NSAnimationContext.current().allowsImplicitAnimation = true
  NSAnimationContext.current().duration = 5.0
  customView.animator().alphaValue = 0.0
}
```

Just a few points here:

- The first line of code is not actually necessary--implicit animations are enabled by default--but it shows how you would also disable implicit animations if the need should arise
- We do, however, need to set the `duration` property of the `NSAnimationContext` to be more than `0.0`; otherwise, we'll see no animation
- The `animator` method returns a proxy object with which we can specify the details of the desired animation

You could add the following method call to `buttonClicked`, or to one of the completion blocks of some other animation:

```
NSViewImplicit()
```

If we need more control, we can use the `CABasicAnimation`, just as we did with `CALayer`, as in the following method:

```
func NSViewBasic()
{
  let basic = CABasicAnimation()
  basic.beginTime = 0.0
  basic.duration = 3.0

  NSAnimationContext.runAnimationGroup({
      context in
      customView.animations = ["alphaValue": basic]
      customView.animator().alphaValue = 0.0},
                                    completionHandler: {
                                    self.customView = nil

  })
}
```

Here too, we can specify a completion block, `beginTime`, and other properties.

Finally, we have access to a `runAnimationGroup` method, which takes two closure parameters, one for the animation, and an optional one for the completion block:

```
func NSViewContextAnimationGroup()
{
  NSAnimationContext.runAnimationGroup(
    {
      context in

      context.duration = 1.5
      context.timingFunction = CAMediaTimingFunction(
        name: kCAMediaTimingFunctionEaseOut)

      customView.animator().alphaValue = 0.0
  },
    completionHandler:
    {
      [unowned self] in

      NSAnimationContext.current().duration = 3.5
      NSAnimationContext.current().timingFunction
        = self.easeInOut
      self.customView.animator().alphaValue = 1.0
  })
}
```

Once you have worked through these examples, refer to Apple's documentation for a full list of animatable properties, which should provide you with plenty of material for experimentation. Here, as in so many areas of development, experimentation is at least as valuable as pouring over those docs.

Summary

What a long chapter that turned out to be. As mentioned already, the available space only allows us to introduce a subset of the features accessible through Core Animation.

You have learned the following in this chapter:

- How to use `CALayer` for graphics rendering
- Using CALayer's subclasses: `CAShapeLayer`, `CATextLayer`, and `CATransformLayer`
- Rotating, resizing, and translating layers
- Using implicit animation with `CALayer`
- The purposes and methods of several flavors of animation, including basic, key-frame, and group animations
- Using `CAMediaTiming` objects to coordinate several staggered animations
- Wrapping property changes in `CATransaction` blocks, and how to nest transactions
- 3D drawing and a brief look at its matrix-based model
- Animating NSViews directly using `NSAnimationContext`

In the next chapter, we'll take a look at Swift's error-handling features.

12
Handling Errors Gracefully

Errors are your friend.

This is a pretty bizarre claim, so let's back it up.

The problem with errors, as opposed to mere *errors*, is that the name is a public relations disaster. Math assignment errors at school got you bad grades; driving errors cause bumps and scrapes and endless letters from insurance companies; tax office errors mess with your tax bill.

In this chapter, we will cover the following topics:

- Swift error handling mechanisms
- Error type enums
- Throwing and catching errors
- Error propagation

Errors aren't mistakes

But our errors are different in two fundamental ways. The first is that they contain information - as much information as you want. The second is that when they occur, you have a lot of flexibility as to what to do about them. They're like the Marine Corps of code-branching statements; when something unanticipated crops up, just stand back and let the specialists take over. Errors aren't mistakes, they are solutions.

None of which you can say for your math assignments.

But who wants to be delving into error handling when we could be animating the transition of a table view cell into a web-browsing-enabled emoji? Are errors not inherently unattractive? Does error handling mean that we're lousy developers really? Can we just leave this for later and get on with using the Core3DAugmentedSocialVideo framework?

As a result of their understandably less-than-stellar image, errors are not only poorly understood, they are also chronically underused, and it is the intention of this chapter to put aside any ideas that error handling is no fun at all, as well as demonstrate the hows and whys of getting the most from error-type objects. By the time we're done here, error handling will be your new best friend.

As we progress through the chapter, try to remember this:

- Error-handling code is as creative and rewarding as any other area of code
- Error handling is not one of the dark arts of other peoples' programming
- Kicking the can down the road really isn't an option
- Swift makes it all really easy to understand
- Swift makes it all really easy to implement

Those last two points are particularly worthy of expansion. Objective C's NSError - and the handling thereof - was bulky, ugly, and not much fun to use, and some other languages would rather your app crash than get a chance to recover gracefully. Swift's error-handling support is a breeze to understand and a joy to use. In fact, Swift does this stuff so well that even using NSErrors is much simpler, and we'll cover that toward the end of this chapter.

Expecting the unexpected

Programming was challenging enough in the days when scientists in lab coats were writing code for their own use on a single mainframe computer located in a cellar just a few meters away.

But the apps that we write - that *you* write - today, now run on thousands or millions of machines, operated by thousands or millions of users, who are connected to millions or billions of other machines. There is simply no way that all those users and connections are going to behave themselves, and as for the other developers (who are filling servers all over the globe with code that has to deal with millions of apps like yours) that expect to have things their own way, well, you can imagine, it's a bit of a jungle out there.

So, we need to deal with unanticipated situations occurring constantly. We need strategies to deal with one piece of code being told to do something it can't that will keep our apps running smoothly and predictably when something says:

Sorry, it didn't work out.

Optionals

We have already looked at one very useful tool, optionals, in `Chapter 2: Basic Swift`. They are good for a lot more than error handling, but they're certainly a great way to deal with two types of error situations:

- A situation in which a `nil` value is so unlikely to occur that we're checking purely on principle
- A situation in which a `nil` value is quite compatible with the unproblematic execution of the app's code

But returning optionals has limits. A function returning `nil` is something we can handle in code, but `nil` doesn't tell us very much, except that no value could be returned.

Explicit error handling

Many is the occasion when we need to do more than shrug our shoulders and break out of an `if` statement (or similar). Sometimes, we need to understand what has gone wrong, or where it went wrong; we may need several branches of code to deal with an unexpected outcome. We need *information*.

By using Swift's support for error handling, we can write code that not only lets us change course according to the source and nature of the error, but also *requires* us to explicitly deal with those errors. Once you have marked a function with the `throws` keyword, your calling code *has* to have a way to deal with any errors that get thrown.

This is better for developers: we have a way to make clear to consumers of a function that it may throw an error type, and we have a way to model that error type in any way necessary.

And, of course, it's better for users, since code that expects the unexpected is inherently more robust than code that assumes the world is full of benevolent and well-formed HTTP responses.

Swift error handling

Swift offers first class support for catching, propagating, and manipulating recoverable errors at runtime. By recoverable, we mean errors that can be foreseen and handled suitably.

What Swift's `Error` handling approach offers us is a dedicated branching mechanism and a syntax to support it. It's a kind of specialized `if-else` mechanism, but one that, crucially, *forces* a calling function to deal with an error that may occur, by declaring itself as a throwing function, using the `throws` keyword.

Error handling thus becomes a graceful and uncomplicated way of dealing with functions that can fail.

The four ways of handling errors

Sounds a bit esoteric, I admit, but no worries, there is no magic involved. We'll get to the details shortly, but there are basically four ways to handle Swift errors:

- Assert that the error will not occur
- Handle the error as an optional value
- Handle the error using a `do-catch` statement
- Propagate the error to the calling function

Exactly how all that works will be revealed as we progress through this chapter. In order to understand error handling in Swift, we must complete three steps:

1. Create an error-type object
2. Create a function that will throw an `Error` type
3. Write code that will handle an `Error`

Before we can start throwing and catching errors, we'll need an `Error` type that we can throw.

Error types

So, what is an error type, then? Nothing but good news here. There is no concrete error type that you must use; you don't even subclass an abstract class.

The fact is, an `Error` type in Swift is literally anything you want it to be; you simply create a `struct`, or a `class`, or an `enum`, and declare it to conform to the `Error` protocol. Beyond that, do with it as you see fit.

The simplest and most common way to create an error type is to use an `enum`. This provides us with a single umbrella structure, under which we can create different error types according to the differing needs of our code.

Creating the simplest Error enum

The basic syntax around `Error` enums is as follows:

```
enum MyAppError: Error
{
  case myError
}
```

Now we can use the `MyAppError.myError` type anytime we need to throw an error (which we'll get to in a moment).

The name of the `enum` itself is in `CapitalizedCamelCase`, and the individual cases are in `uncapitalizedCamelCase`.

This is a part of the new Swift 3 API specifications, but it wasn't always that way, so don't be surprised to see capitalized `enum` cases in older resources. Be sure to stick to the new convention.

It's true that `MyAppError.myError` doesn't contain any information about what caused the error, where it occurred, or what type of error it was, but it already serves to give us an opportunity to react in a controlled way to something occurring that our happy path code can't deal with.

Creating a better Error enum

Usually, we will want our `Error` type to do much more than just, well, be an error. The following `enum` is a little more useful:

```
enum MathError: Error
{
  case divideByZeroError
  case negativeNumberError
  case lousyNumberError(objection: String)
}
```

Firstly, we now have three distinct `Error` types, which we can deal with separately in code as appropriate.

Secondly, we have declared one `enum` case with an **associated value**, which we can populate according to our needs. This `enum` merely uses a `String` object to convey information about whatever is causing the error, but it could be any type you want, and we'll make use of that later in this chapter.

These errors have been conjured up from nowhere and then declared to be of type `Error`. They are not in any way provided by the system, and their names are purely descriptive. They would work just as well if we called them `redError` and `yellowError`.

Try saying `redError yellowError` quickly three times.

Okay, we have some errors. Let's throw one and see if it sticks.

Throwing an error

Throwing an error is simple enough once you have defined your `Error` type.

When we talk about throwing an `Error`, we are talking specifically about using an object that conforms to the `Error` protocol, so this has nothing to do with out-of-bounds array errors and the like.

We simply add the `throws` keyword to the function declaration:

```
func divide(_ a: Double,
            by b: Double) throws ->Double
{
 if b == 0.0
  {
     throw MathError.divideByZeroError
  }
 return a / b
}
```

We might choose to use the guard statement to trim this down slightly:

```
func divide(_ a: Double,
            by b: Double) throws ->Double
{
  guard b != 0 else { throw MathError.divideByZeroError }
```

```
    return a / b
}
```

Whichever way you prefer, what we have now is a function that checks if it can actually perform the calculation it is required to perform. If it cannot (in this case because dividing by zero does not produce a number), it throws an `Error`. It can throw anything that is declared to conform to the `Error` protocol. Great; we have an easy way to force an error. So, now that we have an `Error` type `enum` and we are able to throw it, what then?

Handling an error

Before we take a detailed look at the four ways of dealing with Swift `Error` throwing, we need to look at the `try` keyword and the life cycle of an error.

The error life cycle

There are basically three stages involved in handling errors:

- `try`: We prepend a function that can throw an error with the `try` keyword, using the following syntax:

  ```
  let x = try myErrorThrowingFunction()
  ```

- `throw`: That function throws an `Error` type object with the `throw` keyword, as we have seen already:

  ```
  if b == 0.0
      {
        throw MathError.divideByZeroError
      }
  ```

- `catch`: The scope in which that function was called needs to `catch` the `Error`, or `rethrow` it further up the chain.

Our calling code, that is, the scope in which `try myErrorThrowingFunction()` occurs, then needs to deal with the error that is thrown. Using `try` requires us to think explicitly about what we will do with that error.

Asserting that the error will not occur

We could insist that this error will not occur. If we can guarantee, for example, that we are not going to pass an invalid argument, we can overcome the fact that a function is declared to throw an error by using `try!`:

```
let jsonDict = ["accountString": "ABC123",
"authString": "123xyz"]

func disabledPropagation() ->Data
{
   let data = try! JSONSerialization.data(withJSONObject: jsonDict,
                                  options: .prettyPrinted)
   return data
}
```

That's it. No more safety net, so you'd better be sure. In this case, we are sure because we provide a constant value in the throwing method's parameters.

But what happens if the function does fail? Our app will crash. And there are indeed situations in which we would rather our app crash than continue in an undesirable (and possibly unknown) state.

There is a saying:

> *Crash early, crash hard.*

Although, googling it only returned articles about racing cars and hard drives, so we can't credit it here.

It's often good advice during development. If passing an invalid argument to a function means that we have made a mistake in the code because that invalid argument should simply never arise, then we want to crash the app, rather than risk releasing it with that potential error:

```
func crashOnError() ->Double
{
   return try! divide(1.0, by: x)
}
crashOnError()
```

If x is equal to zero, you'll get an error in the debug console along the following lines:

```
fatal Error: 'try!' expression unexpectedly raised an Error:
ch11sketch.MathError.divideByZeroError: file /Library/...
```

So, not the most elegant error handling, but if an error can only occur due to a programming mistake, try! is sometimes what you need.

Handling the error as an optional value

In some sense, try! has a sibling, try?.

When using try?, the value returned by the function will be wrapped in an optional. We can then test the return value for nil and proceed accordingly. This is a lightweight method to deal with a function that throws an error and is appropriate in situations in which we don't care about the cause of that error.

 The return value is an optional, regardless of whether or not the function fails.

Try out the following code:

```
func returnOptional() -> Double?
{
    return try? divide(1.0, by: 0.0)
}
print(returnOptional())
```

You'll see in the debug console that the value is nil.

Handling an error with do-catch

Now let's do some proper error handling.

If we want to handle the error differently according to which error type has been thrown or an property of that error, we use the try keyword on its own. We can now do one of two things:

- Catch the error immediately
- Propagate the error upwards

In this section, we will catch and deal with the error at the first opportunity.

To do this, we use a `do-catch` statement, as follows:

```
func useDoCatch() ->Double?
{
  do {
      return try divide(1.0, by: 0.0)
   }
  catch {
      print(#function, error)
   }
  return nil
}
print(useDoCatch())
```

When the `divide` function throws an error, it becomes available in the `catch` block, as the `Error` variable. We don't do much with it here; we just print it to the console (also adding the `#function` for good measure), and your code will likely do substantially more, perhaps even depending on which error has been thrown. Cue pattern matching.

Pattern matching

This is a very cool and elegant part of Swift's error handling. We can have a number of `catch` blocks, each of which deals with a specific error type:

```
func patternMatchedDoCatch() ->Double?
{
  do {
     let result = try divide(1.0, by: someDouble)
     return result
  }
  catch MathError.divideByZeroError {
     print (#function, "oh oh, divide by zero")
   }
  catch {
     print(#function, error)
  }
  return nil
}
```

This saves us a ton of `if-else` or `switch` statements, making the code much more readable. The final `catch` block is the equivalent of a switch's `default` case; it deals with anything not specifically listed in the other blocks.

Matching associated values

The pattern matching doesn't stop there. If the error type we define has an associated value, as is the case with our `.lousyNumberError`, we can test its value in a `catch` block. In the following code, we do just that (we also use a shortcut in the `do` block to throw an error, although this would be pointless in real code):

```
func doCatchWhere()
{
 do {

     throwMathError.lousyNumberError(
     objection: "I don't do primes")

 }
 catch MathError.lousyNumberError
 where Error =="I don't do primes" {

     print("You were told not to attempt a prime")

 }
 catch MathError.lousyNumberError (let Error) {

     print("Some other objection")

 }
 catch {

     print(error)

 }
}
print(doCatchWhere())
```

Here, we test not only the type of error, but also its value. Since the enum case `.lousyNumberError` has an associated value that is a `String`, we can handle that error as if it were a `String` itself, making a direct `==` comparison with the string against which we are testing.

Propagating an error

We don't have to catch an error at the site at which it was thrown.

Let's say we have a function; `innerFunc`, which is declared to be a throwing function:

```
func innerFunc() throws
{
   throw MathError.lousyNumberError(objection: "Bad day")
}
```

This `innerFunc` is called by a function; `outerFunc`, which is also declared to be a throwing function:

```
func outerFunc() throws
{
   try innerFunc()
}
```

No `do-catch` here, or `try!`, or `try?`. What happens here is that any error thrown by `innerFunc`, instead of being caught and handled, is being thrown by `outerFunc` itself. Any function that calls `outerFunc` will therefore need to provide explicit error handling (just as if `outerFunc` has its own `throw` statement):

 Getting techy: A throwing function propagates errors that are thrown inside of it to the scope from which it is called.

```
func innerFunc() throws
{
   throw MathError.negativeNumberError
}

   func outerFunc() throws
{
   try innerFunc()
}

func consumerFunc()
{
   do {
      try outerFunc()
   }
   catch {
      print(error)
   }
}
```

With this general pattern in mind, let's take a look at a couple of examples.

Propagation - case study: handling in scope

To test this, we'll write an `innermost` math function that returns one of two errors; if the divisor is zero or negative, an error is thrown:

```
func innermost(_ a: Double,
                 by b: Double)
throws ->Double?
{
   if a < 0.0
     {
        throw MathError.negativeNumberError
     }
   if b == 0.0
     {
        throw MathError.divideByZeroError
     }
   return a / b
}
```

That function will be called by a `middle` function, which will not handle the errors thrown by `innermost`. But because `middle` is itself declared with `throws`, it will propagate (that is, throw) that error to the scope that calls it, namely, the `outermost` function:

```
func middle(_ a:Double,
              by b: Double)
throws ->Double?
{
    let result = try innermost(a, by: b)
    return result
}

func outermost()
{
   for (dividend, divisor) in [(1.0, 0.0),
     (-1.0, 0.0),
     (1.0, 1.0)]
   {
     do {
          let d = try middle(dividend, by: divisor)
          print(d)
     }
     catch {
          print(error)
     }
   }
}
```

```
}
outermost()
```

Running that code will print the following three logs to the debug console:

```
divideByZeroError
negativeNumberError
Optional(1.0)
```

As we can see, the `MathError` thrown in the `innermost` function have bubbled all the way up to the `outermost` function, where they are dealt with. It is often the case that we need errors to propagate up to a scope in which we can handle them, rather than dealing with them at the throw site. The next section will present such a case.

Propagation - case study: propagation

In the previous case study, all of the functions were declared in the same scope. But this does not need to be the case; errors will quite happily propagate upward through as many different classes and structs as necessary. In this second case study, we will see how arguments are passed through several structs before being evaluated, and how the error produced by doing so then propagates its way back up through that same chain, but in the opposite direction. This means that we can decide exactly where and how the errors are handled.

Let's start coding:

1. Just to keep the code a little tidier, and therefore easier to follow, we will start by declaring a couple of type aliases:

```
typealias MathQuestion = (Double, Double) throws ->Double
typealias MathQuestionArgs = (Double, Double)
```

2. With that done, we will define a `Student` `struct`, whose job it will be to act as a guinea pig for a new examination set by the examination board of a hypothetical top-league university:

```
struct Student
{
  let name: String
  func checkExam(question: MathQuestion,
                 args: MathQuestionArgs) rethrows
  {
    let x = try question(args.0, args.1)
    print("Homework answer = \(x)")
  }
```

```
        }
```

Note that the `question` argument to the `StudentcheckExam` method is a function that takes two `Doubles` and returns a single `Double`, as defined by the `MathQuestion` type alias. Those two `Doubles` are provided in the `args` parameter of type `MathQuestionArgs`.

So, what's with the `rethrows`? This means that the function propagates any errors thrown by its parameters (arguments). If a throwing function is passed to a `Student`, he/she must either handle the error, or rethrow it. In this way, the compiler will refuse to let you pass a throwing function to the `checkExam` method until you state what you intend to do with it.

1. Let's now create a couple of students:

   ```
   let students = [Student(name: "Dennis"),
   Student(name: "Gnasher")]
   ```

2. Next up, we create a `Struct` that will also receive a `MathQuestion` and `MathquestionArgs` object, the `Lecturerstruct`:

   ```
   struct Lecturer
   {
      func assignExam(question: MathQuestion,
                  args: MathQuestionArgs) rethrows
        {

          for student in students
            {
               print("Attempt by \(student.name)")
   //        do {
               try student.checkExam(question: question,
                 args: args)
   //        } catch {
   //            print("Exam Error found by \(student.name)")
   //        }
          }
        }

   func handleNewExam(question: MathQuestion,
                   args: MathQuestionArgs) rethrows
      {
   try assignExam(question: question,
                   args: args)
      }
   }
   ```

The lecturer will not deal with any errors that are received by the
`assignExam` method, having been rethrown by the student's `checkExam`
method; `assignExam` will rethrow the error itself to its calling function,
which was called from within the `Lecturer` struct by the `handleNewExam`
method.

Don't remove the commented-out lines of code; we'll need them later.

3. We'll create one `Lecturer` instance:

```
let grumpy = Lecturer()
```

4. Finally, we'll create the `struct` (that will actually handle any errors that occur),
`ExaminationBoard`:

```
struct ExaminationBoard
{
  func testNewExam(question: MathQuestion,
    args: MathQuestionArgs)
  {
    do {

      try grumpy.handleNewExam(question: question,


        args: args)
      print("Great new curriculum")

    } catch {

      print("Bad curriculum: \(error)")


    }
  }
}
```

At last we see a `do-catch` statement in which the error is handled. The `testNewExam` method takes the same parameters as the methods further down the chain, but the buck stops here. We're close to being able to try out this code.

5. We'll create an `ExaminationBoard` instance:

```
let oldAndGrumpies = ExaminationBoard()
```

Pass an exam question (no pun intended) to the old and grumpies of the examination board, for the purposes of testing the new syllabus:

```
oldAndGrumpies.testNewExam(question: divide,
    args: (1.0, 0.0))
```

Hmm, there's going to be trouble; we're passing a zero divisor. The debug console tells us the following:

```
Attempt by Dennis
Bad curriculum: divideByZeroError
```

The examination board is not happy.

Only one attempt? Does `Gnasher` not get a go?

Not once an error is thrown; then it's game over for that function call (the one that is iterating through the `students` array.

If we were to uncomment those commented out lines of code in the `Lecturer` struct, what would happen? Give it a go (naturally). Yep, the `Lecturer` reports that a `Student` has found an `Error`. And the `ExaminationBoard` doesn't need to deal with it.

Such is life.

As a last experiment, try changing the `args` parameter values in the call to `testNewExam`. What happens when there is no error?

Verbose errors

We have used very terse error messages up till now. But it may be the case that more information could be useful to the function that handles the error. Here is an example of a more complicated, and garrulous, `Error`:

```
enum DevelopmentError: Error
{
  enum DevelopmentErrorDomain
  {
    case specsErrorDomain
    case managementErrorDomain
    case highlyImplausibleDeveloperErrorDomain
  }

  case undefined
  case networkError(ErrorCode: Int)
  case verboseError(userInfo: [String: Any])
  case seriouslyVerboseError(
    date: Date,
    domain: DevelopmentErrorDomain,
    userInfo: [String: Any],
    payload: Any)

  var ErrorTypeString: String {
    return "DevelopmentError"
  }
}
```

The first thing you'll notice is probably that this `enum` contains a nested `enum` of its own. One of the `DevelopmentError` cases associated types is `DevelopmentErrorDomain`, an `enum` in itself. Since `DevelopmentErrorDomain` is only needed within the `DevelopmentError` enum, it is also declared there.

Then come the various cases, all with different associated types. The `seriouslyVerboseError` associated type is a compound object in itself. And to really make the point, one of the elements of the `seriouslyVerboseError` associated type is itself a `Dictionary` of type `[String: Any]`.

This emphatically demonstrates that `Error` types are first-class constructs in Swift. There really is no limit - apart from good taste and judgment - to what you can do with them.

To top it all off, the `enum` declares an `ErrorTypeString` variable too, which has the same value for each `case` of `DevelopmentError`.

Test `DevelopmentError` with the following code:

```
func testErrors(verbose: Bool)
{
  do {
    let problematicData = [2, 3, 5, 6, 7]
    // find some issue with problematicData

    let info: [String: Any] = ["reason": "found non-prime"]
    if verbose
    {
      throw DevelopmentError.seriouslyVerboseError(
        date: Date(),
        domain: .specsErrorDomain,
        userInfo: info,
        payload: problematicData)
    }
    else
    {
      throw DevelopmentError.undefined
    }
  } catch let error as DevelopmentError {

  // do something special
  print(error.ErrorTypeString, error)

  } catch {

    // all other Errors
    print(error)
  }
}

testErrors(verbose: false)
testErrors(verbose: true) // almost as bad as NSLog!
```

It's worth spending some time playing around with the preceding code, and seeing what works and what doesn't. If nothing else, it may at least soak up some over-enthusiasm for massively bloated `Error` types.

Anything can be an error

Remember we said that anything that declares itself to conform to the error-type protocol can be used as an `Error`?

The following code demonstrates one case in which it may be unnecessary to create a dedicated error type at all:

```
struct Person: Error
{
  let name:String
  let address: String?
  let age: Int
}

func grantCredit(to candidate: Person) throws ->Int
{
  if candidate.address == nil
    {
      throw candidate
    }
    return candidate.age > 21 ? 10_000 : 100
}
```

Look at that. We just `throw` the `Candidate` if its `address` property is `nil`. All we need now is some code to put that to use:

```
func processRequest(customer: Person) ->Int?
{
  do {
      let availableCredit = try grantCredit(to: customer)
      return availableCredit
    } catch let failedCandidate as Person {

      print("Request Error:",
        failedCandidate.name,
        "needs a valid address")

    } catch {

    print(error)

  }
    return nil
}

let customer = Person(name: "Zaphod", address: nil, age: 42)
```

```
let availableCredit = processRequest(customer: customer)
print("Available credit:", availableCredit)
```

The trick here is to put `let failedCandidate as Person` after the `catch` keyword. Having done that, all of the `Peron` object's properties are accessible.

NSError handling

Now and again we will still need to deal with `NSError`. Although the Cocoa APIs are being updated for Swift very rapidly, it's likely that `NSError` will be with us for some time to come. The good news is that Swift makes it very easy to do.

Anatomy of an NSError

An `NSError` object has four properties of interest to us here:

- The `domain` is a `String` and is used to differentiate groups of error `codes`
- The error `code` is an `Int`, specific to the `domain` to which it belongs
- The `userInfo` property is a `Dictionary`, the values of which are strings that convey any information the throwing function wants to include
- The `localizedDescription` is a `String` and is intended for presentation to the user; examples include `"You don't have permission..."` and such

Catching NSErrors

One common framework that still returns NSErrors is the `FileManager` framework, which is part of Foundation Kit. Here is an example of how to catch and deal with the errors it throws:

```
let url1 = URL(fileURLWithPath: "/non-existent")
let url2 = URL(fileURLWithPath: "/someLocation")
do {
    try FileManager.default.moveItem(at: url1, to: url2)
} catch let error as NSError {
    print(error)
}
```

This is way simpler than Objective C, don't you agree? Running this code will print the following error to the debug console:

```
Error Domain=NSCocoaErrorDomain Code=4 ""non-existent" couldn't be
moved to "Macintosh HD" because either the former doesn't exist, or the
folder containing the latter doesn't exist."
UserInfo={NSSourceFilePathErrorKey=/non-existent, NSUserStringVariant=(
    Move
), NSDestinationFilePath=/someLocation, NSFilePath=/non-existent,
NSUnderlyingError=0x100d32c00 {Error Domain=NSPOSIXErrorDomain Code=2 "No
such file or directory"}}
```

Here we can see, from the `UserInfo`, `Domain`, and `Code` entries, that this is an `NSError` and not a Swift error.

Pattern-matched Cocoa catches

We can employ the same pattern-matching support we saw when using Swift error catching. The following code allows us to separate the `.fileNoSuchFile` error case from any other error types that may occur:

```
do {

    try FileManager.default.moveItem(at: url1, to: url2)

} catch CocoaError.fileNoSuchFile {

    print("oh oh, no such file")

} catch let error as NSError {

    print("some other failure")
}
```

Creating NSError instances in Swift

Occasionally, you may find yourself in a position where you need to return an `NSError` from your own functions.

The following code demonstrates how to rewrite our `divide` function to return an `NSError` if the divisor parameter is `0`:

```
func divide(a: Double, b: Double) throws ->Double
{
  if b == 0.0
  {
    throw NSError(domain: "CustomErrorDomainString",
              code: 5001,
              userInfo: ["ErrorType": "DivideByZeroError"])
  }
  return a / b
}
```

Let's give it a spin with the following code:

```
do{
  let x = try divide(a: 1, b: 0)
} catch let error {
  print(error)
}
```

You'll see that the output from our own `NSError` is considerably less verbose than NSFileManager's:

```
Error Domain=CustomErrorDomainString Code=5001 "(null)" UserInfo=
{ErrorType=DivideByZeroError}
```

Summary

I hope we have delivered on the promises made at the beginning of this chapter, and that you have begun to appreciate the value, importance, and sheer elegance of Swift's error-handling support.

In this chapter, you have learned the following:

- When to use optionals and when to use explicit error handling
- How to create custom error types of varying complexity
- How to throw an `Error` type in your code

- The four ways of handling a Swift `Error`
- How to `catch` or `rethrow` an error
- Using pattern matching to distinguish between error types
- Using an error's associated types to convey information
- How to handle and write `NSError` code

You'll be glad about this in the next chapter, in which we address the topics of file storage - both local and in the cloud - areas in which clear error-handling code are of the utmost importance. Read on!

13
Persistent Storage

In this chapter, we will look at some of the most useful and commonly used options available for persisting data to disk.

You will learn about the following:

- The Foundation-supplied user-defaults object
- Storing simple and complex object types
- The NSCoding protocol
- NSKeyedArchiver and NSKeyedUnarchiver
- Creating NSCoding--compliant classes
- Presenting the user with open and save dialog boxes

This chapter will use a simple interface that will allow the user to save and load various types of data using different frameworks and file locations.

Creating a project

Before we get coding, we'll assemble a window with a few buttons and a text field, which will facilitate trying out the code as we progress:

1. Create a new project using Xcode's **Cocoa Application** template.

2. Add six buttons and a text field to the **View Controller Scene**, arranged something like this:

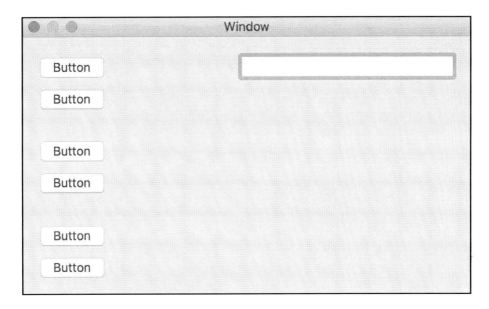

As we move on, we'll make the buttons' titles a little more descriptive.

Creating the project's file manager

We won't put any file reading or writing capabilities in the **ViewController** class, since that's not its job, so we must create a class to manage file IO:

1. Create a new Swift file, and name it `CustomFileManager.swift`.
2. Add the following class definition to the new file:

```
class CustomFileManager
{
  static let sharedManager = CustomFileManager()
  let userDefaults = UserDefaults.standard
}
```

All we're doing here is setting up the class as a singleton (we will only ever need one instance, from wherever we access it in the app), and then declaring a property that will maintain a reference to the `standard` defaults provided by `UserDefaults`.

3. Add a property to the `ViewController` class to hold a reference to this singleton:

```
class ViewController: NSViewController
{
    let customFileManager = CustomFileManager.sharedManager
}
```

We will add all our file read and write methods to this class. To keep the class well organized, we will create an extension for each type of file IO that we wish to implement:

- Using Foundation's `UserDefaults`
- Using the write methods provided by `String` objects
- Using `NSCoding` in tandem with `NSKeyedArchiver` and `NSKeyedUnarchiver`

We'll also be adding a few helper functions, and methods that use a dialog box to provide file paths.

We'll start with the one that most of us have at least some experience with, `UserDefaults`.

Using UserDefaults

The name `UserDefaults` rather undersells the wide range of uses for which this feature of the Foundation framework is suitable. Any data that is reasonably simply structured can be stored with very little code in `UserDefaults`, and there is no limit to the amount of data that can be stored (apart from the obvious limit to the device's storage).

However, if you're storing large amounts of data, we'll be looking at more suitable alternatives later in this chapter, and in the next.

`UserDefaults` can save the following data types:

- `Bool`
- `Number types`
- `Array`
- `Dictionary`

Other types can be stored if they can be coded into `Data` type objects:

- `Data`

Foundation also provides convenience methods for the following commonly stored types that need serializing first:

- `Date`
- `String`
- `URL`

For the `UserDefaults`, we will create an extension.

Add an extension code to the `CustomFileManager` class:

```
extension CustomFileManager
{
}
```

Storage of simple objects

We will start with storing and retrieving simple Foundation objects.

Storing simple objects

First, let's create some string constants for our default keys, with which we will specify our objects once we have stored them:

1. Add the following code to the top level of the `CustomFileManager` class:

```
let kBoolValue = "BoolValue"
let kIntValue = "IntValue"
```

```
let kDoubleValue = "DoubleValue"
let kFloatValue  = "FloatValue"
let kAnyValue = "AnyValue"
```

These strings are never visible to the user, and so their actual values are completely arbitrary. We have chosen the preceding values to make the debug console output as clear as possible.

Next, we'll create an example instance of each type that `UserDefaults` will store.

2. Add the following, also to the top level of the `CustomFileManager` class:

```
let myInt = 42
let myDouble: Double = 3.142
let myFloat: Float = 1.414
let myObject = "My object"
```

We use a `String` as object here for simplicity's sake.

Now we can use all variations of the overloaded `set` method of the `userDefaults` instance.

3. Add the following code to the the `CustomFileManager` class:

```
func saveSimpleDefaults()
{
  userDefaults.set(true,
                   forKey: kBoolValue)
  userDefaults.set(myInt,
                   forKey: kIntValue)
  userDefaults.set(myDouble,
                   forKey: kDoubleValue)
  userDefaults.set(myFloat,
                   forKey: kFloatValue)
  userDefaults.set(myObject,
                   forKey: kAnyValue)
}
```

This method accepts, as its first parameter, all the types used previously.

Any object that conforms to NSCoding (which we'll deal with shortly) can be used as an object as the first parameter, as we do in the final line of code.

Using the synchronize method

We could force the defaults to be stored immediately to disk with the following line of code:

```
userDefaults.synchronize()
```

But, because this method is automatically invoked at periodic intervals, we use it only if we cannot wait for the automatic synchronization to kick in (for example, if the application is about to exit).

Writing the defaults to disk writes *all* the data at once, that is, **atomically**, and calling the synchronization method manually, and unnecessarily, just uses up a ton of file IO traffic, and doesn't usually benefit the program.

So, generally, you will not need this method.

Loading simple objects

Having stored the data, we'll want to retrieve it sooner or later. There are two ways to do this.

If we want to retrieve only a *stored* value, and nil if no value has been stored, we can use the object(forKey:) method. This method returns a value that we can then downcast to the type we expect it to be.

Add the following method to the CustomFileManager extension:

```
func loadSimpleDefaults()
{
  print(#function)

  if let value = userDefaults.object(
    forKey: kBoolValue) as? Bool
  {
    print("object forKey: \(kBoolValue), value: \(value)")
  }

  if let value = userDefaults.object(
    forKey: kIntValue) as? Int
  {
```

```
        print("object forKey: \(kIntValue), value: \(value)")
    }

    if let value = userDefaults.object(
        forKey: kDoubleValue) as? Double
    {
        print("object forKey: \(kDoubleValue), value: \(value)")
    }

    if let value = userDefaults.object(
        forKey: kFloatValue) as? Float
    {
        print("object forKey: \(kFloatValue), value: \(value)")
    }

    if let value = userDefaults.object(
        forKey: kAnyValue)
    {
        print("object forKey: \(kAnyValue), value: \(value)")
    }

    if let value = userDefaults.object(
        forKey: "WrongKey")
    {
        print("object forKey: WrongKey, value: \(value)")
    }
    else
    {
        print("Wrong key loads nil")
    }
}
```

This is very safe code: either we get a stored value of the type we are expecting for any given key, or we get nil.

Look at that last call, which uses a non-existent key. This will fail, and return nil, so we will never see the code inside its braces executed. Instead, we should expect the else clause to execute every time.

 See the following sections for methods that will return a default value if none is stored.

Testing the code

Before we can see if everything is being stored and retrieved as it should be, we need to modify the UI in Interface Builder:

1. First, we'll add the actions for the first two buttons:

```
@IBAction func saveUserDefaults(_ sender: Any)
{
   customFileManager.saveSimpleDefaults()
}

@IBAction func loadUserDefaults(_ sender: Any)
{
   customFileManager.loadSimpleDefaults()
}
```

2. And we may as well update the button titles as well, as illustrated here:

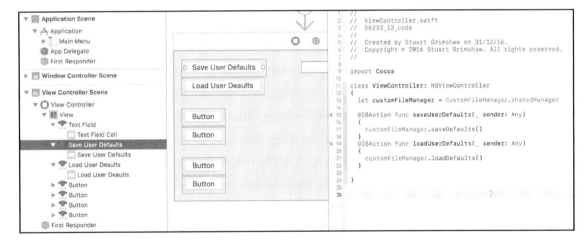

3. Now hit **Run** and, once the window is visible, click the **Save User Defaults** button.

4. Click on **Load User Defaults** and the console will display the following:

```
object forKey: BoolValue, value: true
object forKey: IntValue, value: 42
object forKey: DoubleValue, value: 3.142
object forKey: FloatValue, value: 1.414
object forKey: AnyValue, value: My object
Wrong key loads nil
```

As we can see, all our stored defaults have loaded properly, and the use of a wrong key returns `nil`.

Storing structured data

By no means are we limited to *primitive* types. `UserDefaults` will also store more complex objects, such as collection types, as we will see next.

Saving structured data

We'll start with a few string constants, as we did with the simple data types:

1. Add the following code to the top level of the `CustomFileManager` class (not the extension, which the compiler will not allow you to do):

```
let kStringsArrayValue = "StringsArrayValue"
let kIntsArrayValue = "IntsArrayValue"
let kDictValue = "DictValue"
```

And just as we did before, we'll create a few example instances.

2. Add the following, also to the top level of the `CustomFileManager` class:

```
let stringsArray = ["a", "b", "c"]
let intsArray = [1, 2, 3]
let myDict = ["one": 1,
              "two": 2]
```

As mentioned previously, we'll create a new extension to `CustomFileManager` that will contain the methods to save these values.

3. Next, we'll create a new method in the new extension to `CustomFileManager`:

```
func saveComplexDefaults()
{
  userDefaults.set(stringsArray,
                   forKey: kStringsArrayValue)
  userDefaults.set(intsArray,
                   forKey: kIntsArrayValue)
  userDefaults.set(myDict,
```

```
                              forKey: kDictValue)
        }
```

These calls are examples of the `set(object:` `forKey:)` method.

Loading structured data

Retrieving these values is just as simple as with any other data type.

Add the following method to the `CustomFileManager` extension:

```
func loadComplexDefaults()
{
  print(#function)

  if let value = userDefaults.object(
    forKey: kStringsArrayValue) as? [String]
  {
    print("object forKey: \(kStringsArrayValue), value: \(value)")
  }
  if let value = userDefaults.object(
    forKey: kIntsArrayValue) as? [Int]
  {
    print("object forKey: \(kIntsArrayValue), value: \(value)")
  }
  if let value = userDefaults.object(
    forKey: kDictValue) as? [String: Int]
  {
    print("object forKey: \(kDictValue), value: \(value)")
  }
}
```

Testing the code

Let's add these defaults to the two methods we have defined already:

1. Add this call to the `saveUserDefaults` action method of the `ViewController` class:

   ```
   customFileManager.saveComplexDefaults()
   ```

2. Add this call to the `loadUserDefaults` action method of the `ViewController` class:

   ```
   customFileManager.loadComplexDefaults()
   ```

3. Run the app again. In addition to the previous logs, the console will now show the following output:

```
object forKey: StringsArrayValue, value: ["a", "b", "c"]
object forKey: IntsArrayValue, value: [1, 2, 3]
object forKey: DictValue, value: ["one": 1, "two": 2]
```

Loading by type

We can make our code more succinct by calling the defaults' type-specific loading methods, such as this one:

```
userDefaults.bool(forKey: kBoolValue)
```

Rather than returning an optional value for us to test, this method returns either a value stored with the specified key, or a default value if none is found. In the case of `bool(forKey:)`, that default value is the Boolean `false`.

Add the following code to the `CustomFileManager` extension:

```
func loadDefaultsByType()
{
  print(#function)

  let ud = userDefaults

  print(
    "bool forKey: \(ud.bool(forKey: kBoolValue))",
    "bool WrongKey: \(ud.bool(forKey: "WrongKey"))",

    "integer forKey: \(ud.integer(forKey: kIntValue))",
    "integer WrongKey: \(ud.integer(forKey: "WrongKey"))",

    "double forKey: \(ud.double(forKey: kDoubleValue))",
    "double WrongKey: \(ud.double(forKey: "WrongKey"))",

    "float forKey: \(ud.float(forKey: kFloatValue))",
    "float WrongKey: \(ud.float(forKey: "WrongKey"))",

    "url forKey: \(ud.url(forKey: kUrlValue))",
    "url WrongKey: \(ud.url(forKey: "WrongKey"))",

    separator: "\n")
}
```

We have included a call to each method using a non--existent key, which will log the default values returned when the specified key does not exist.

 The only reason I have added a shortened symbol, `ud`, to refer to the `userDefaults` property, is to get the method calls onto one line of text, since a `String` literal cannot be written across several lines. There is no need for you to do this in Xcode; use `userDefaults` instead.

Testing the code

We now need to add the following method call to the `loadUserDefaults` action method of the `ViewController` class:

```
customFileManager.loadDefaultsByType()
```

Running the app again, add the following output to the debug console:

```
bool forKey: true
bool WrongKey: false
integer forKey: 42
integer WrongKey: 0
double forKey: 3.142
double WrongKey: 0.0
float forKey: 1.414
float WrongKey: 0.0
```

UserDefaults convenience methods

Some types of object are stored so often that Foundation provides convenience methods that both serialize and store the object. These types are as follows:

- URL objects
- String objects
- Date objects

Again, we'll set the keys' string constants first:

1. Add the following code to the top level of the `CustomFileManager` (not the extension):

```
let kUrlValue = "UrlValue"
let kStringVlaue = "StringVlaue"
let kDateValue = "DateValue"
```

Then we'll create some example instances.

2. Add the following code to the top level of the `CustomFileManager`:

```
let myUrl = URL(string: "/Some/Url")!
let myString = "My string"
let myDate = Date()
```

Saving with convenience methods

Now we need a method to store these values. Add the following methods to the `CustomFileManager` extension:

```
func saveDefaultsWithConvenience()
{
  print(#function)

  userDefaults.set(myUrl,
                   forKey: kUrlValue)
  userDefaults.set(myString,
                   forKey: kStringVlaue)
  userDefaults.set(myDate, forKey: kDateValue)
}
```

Loading the data

We also need a method to load the data back into the app. Add the following methods to the `CustomFileManager` extension:

```
func loadConvenienceDefaults()
{
  print(#function)

  if let url = userDefaults.url(forKey: kUrlValue)
```

```
  {
    print(url)
  }
  if let string = userDefaults.string(forKey: kStringVlaue)
  {
    print(string)
  }
  if let date = userDefaults.object(forKey: kDateValue)
  {
    print(date)
  }
}
```

These methods retrieve the object stored in the defaults and downcast them to the type specified. Note that these convenience methods return an optional value, just like the `object(forKey)` method. For a non-existent key, they return `nil`.

Testing the code

To test the code, perform the following steps:

1. Add this call to the `saveUserDefaults` action method of the `ViewController` class:

   ```
   customFileManager.saveDefaultsWithConvenience()
   ```

2. Add this call to the `loadUserDefaults` action method of the `ViewController` class:

   ```
   customFileManager.loadConvenienceDefaults()
   ```

3. Run the app again. The following output is added to the debug console logs:

   ```
   /Some/Url
   My string
   2017-01-01 23:49:46 +0000
   ```

These methods are provided by the system, since those object types are frequently stored in `UserDefaults`, but we will soon see how we can apply the same functionality to our own objects.

Security considerations

One thing to be aware of when storing data to `UserDefaults` is that it is not secure.

`UserDefaults` are stored as property lists, with no encryption, and are stored in your app's directory. Any user who is inclined to do so can access this data with a few minutes' hacking.

 Don't store password and other sensitive information in `UserDefaults`. Ever.

Saving text to the Documents folder

We started with `UserDefaults` because you are likely to have used them before. Most tutorials that deal with data storage start with text. This is true for most platforms; macOS is no exception, and this section will bring us up to speed with the ease with which we can store text files.

Foundation `String` objects provide methods for storing and loading text data. The text can be stored in a number of common formats, meaning that we can store text files that can be read by other programs, and of course, reading in different formats allows us to load text files that have been created outside our app. Once we have the path of the file to be saved, storing or loading is just a couple of lines of code.

We'll start with a text file IO extension to `CustomFileManager`.

Create an extension and helper function

Keeping the code tidy, we'll create a new extension to the `CustomFileManager`, to which we'll directly add a helper function that will return a URL at which we will store a text file:

```
extension CustomFileManager
{
  var textFileUrl: URL?
  {
    let file = "file.txt"

    if let dir = FileManager.default.urls(
    for: .documentDirectory,
```

```
      in: .userDomainMask).first
      {
        let path = dir.appendingPathComponent(file)
        return path
      }
      return nil
  }
}
```

The `textFileUrl` method gets a reference to the `Documents` folder with the `documentDirectory` (note the missing s character) that is passed to Foundation's `FileManager` default instance `urls` method.

Don't ever create your own class with this name as it will mask the Foundation class, preventing you from being able to access it.

Other commonly used directory parameters that we could have used here include:

- `libraryDirectory`
- `desktopDirectory`
- `applicationSupportDirectory`
- `picturesDirectory`
- `musicDirectory`
- `moviesDirectory`

These, and others, are all declared in an `enum` in the `NSPathUtilities` object (*command* + click on the `documentDirectory` parameter to get there):

```
public enum SearchPathDirectory : UInt
```

However, the `Documents` folder will serve as well here.

In addition to the fact that a user cannot write files to directories for which he does not have the appropriate security privileges, apps are also expected to follow certain conventions regarding the location of different files for different purposes. The user's files should be kept separate from the files that the app needs, such as preferences data, which should be stored where they will not get in the user's way.

The `userDomainMask` parameter specifies the user's own home directory - the one that includes `Documents`, `Desktop`, and so on.

The `urls` method returns an array, of which we need the first element.

The `textFileUrl` method then adds the name of the file itself to that URL, giving us the complete URL at which the data is to be stored.

Storing textual data

Now, saving the data is very simple.

Add the following method to the new `CustomFileManager` extension:

```
func save(text: String)
{
  if let path = textFileUrl
  {
    do {
      try text.write(to: path,
                     atomically: true,
                     encoding: String.Encoding.utf8)
    }
    catch { print(error) }
  }
}
```

The first line of this code makes use of the helper function to get a valid location at which to store the file.

We then call the `write` method on the `String` itself, providing the following parameters:

- `to` is the path mentioned in the preceding code.
- `atomically` means that we write the whole file to a buffer before it is saved to disk, rather than directly to a file. This means that, if the write process is suddenly interrupted, let's say by a power failure, the original file will not be corrupted; the file is written completely or not at all.
- `encoding` specifies the text format; in our case, we have chosen the most basic text format, `utf8`, which can be read by just about anything that can read text files.

Before we write a method to load the file back into memory, let's check that we can see the file in the **Finder** once it has been created.

Testing the save function

We'll need to add an action for the save button in the ViewController:

```
@IBAction func saveText(_ sender: Any)
{
    customFileManager.save(text: "Here is some text to save")
}
```

Let's change the title of the buttons as well:

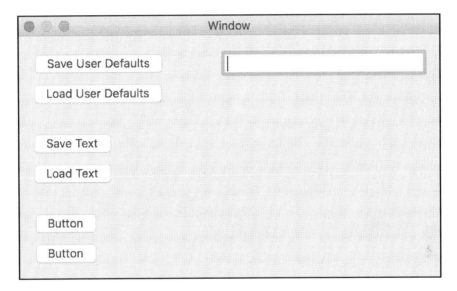

Now, when you run the app and hit the **Save Text** button, you'll see the file.txt file appear in your Documents folder. You should be able to open this file with Text Edit, or any other app that opens text files, including Xcode itself.

Loading text files

So, having successfully saved a text file, it's only logical to open it again and read the data into our app's memory. This is also very simple.

Add to the following method the text IO extension of `CustomFileManager`:

```
func loadText() -> String?
{
  if let path = textFileUrl
  {
    do {
        let loadedText = try String(contentsOf: path,
                                encoding: String.Encoding.utf8)
        return loadedText
    }
    catch {
      print(error)
    }
  }
  return nil
}
```

At the moment, we're using a hard--coded URL, which we would be unlikely to do in the case of general-purpose text files. Presenting the user with a dialog box to locate a file is covered later in this chapter.

The `String` object's `contentsOf` initializer can throw an error, so the whole thing is done inside a `do catch` block.

We provide the same `encoding` parameter here that we used to store the file, but a `utf16` format would work just as well (`utf8` is just a subset of `utf16`).

Testing the load function

Add an action for the **Load Text** button in the `ViewController`:

```
@IBAction func loadText(_ sender: Any)
{
  let text = customFileManager.loadText()
  print(text ?? "No file found")
}
```

Note the use of the `??` operator. This means, if there's a non-nil value, return it; otherwise, return the following default value, in this case, a `"No file found"` string. The result of the `??` operation is returned to the `print` statement.

Once again, run the code, and read the contents of `file.txt` into memory. Assuming you have not deleted the file (or made any coding errors), the `text` variable now holds the `String` data.

NSCoding/NSKeyedArchiver

Okay, so we've stored a number of data types in `UserDefaults`, and we've saved textual data to the user's `Documents` folder. How do we save our own custom objects to the file system?

We need to make our custom objects conform to the `NSCoding` protocol. This means, firstly, that the object in question knows how to serialize itself (or, at least, tell the system to serialize itself), and secondly, that it provides an interface to the code outside the object, through which we can instruct the object to **encode** and **decode** data.

`NSCoding` is a very simple protocol; it requires two methods:

- `initWithCoder`
- `encodeWithCoder`

Objects that conform to `NSCoding` can then be serialized and de-serialized into data that can be saved to disk (or, indeed, sent across a network). So, we have three tasks to complete:

- Create an `NSCoding`--compliant class
- Write a save-to-disk method
- Write a load-from-disk method

Once we have completed the first step of making our object `NSCoding`--compliant, the rest is as simple as saving a `String` object, as dealt with in the previous section.

Creating an NSCoding--compliant class

For the purposes of demonstration, we'll create a very simple class with a single property. The first thing to note is that we must subclass `NSObject`, which is a class, so we cannot use a `struct` here:

1. Create a new swift file, and name it `Person.swift`.

2. Add the following class declaration to the new file, after the `import` statement:

```
class Person: NSObject, NSCoding
{
  var name: String

  init(name: String) {
    self.name = name
  super.init()
  }
}
```

We will get a protocol error, since the class does not yet conform to `NSCoding`, but we'll solve that very soon.

The `init` method is the so-called **designated initializer**; it provides a way for the code to initialize an instance of the class, and will also be called by the decoding method we will write in a moment.

A `designated` initializer is the initializer method that must be called either directly by client code, or by any internal, specialized auxiliary initializer methods. All classes must have one, and this is ours. Every initialization sequence ends up here.

3. The single property of the class, `Name`, will need to be stored under a key, so we need a string constant for that:

```
let kName = "Name"
```

Strictly speaking, this constant is not that important, since no code outside of the class will access it, and the class is very small; but I personally adhere to the "No magic strings are good magic strings" school of thought. Who knows, maybe that class will turn into a huge object with dozens of properties sometime in the future.

4. Add the following method to the `Person` class:

```
required convenience init?(coder aDecoder: NSCoder)
{
  guard let name
    = aDecoder.decodeObject(forKey: kName) as? String
  else {return nil}

  self.init(name: name)
}
```

But what's all that stuff before `init`?

The `convenience` keyword means that we are providing a secondary initializer that will perform some specialized function, in addition to calling the designated initializer.

This particular convenience initializer calls on Foundation's `NSCoder` class to decode serialized data.

If the coder fails to decode the `name` object as a `String`, the class returns `nil`; if it succeeds, it calls the class's designated initializer, providing it with the decoded `name` object.

Getting the class to serialize itself is even easier.

5. Add the following method to the `Person` class:

```
func encode(with aCoder: NSCoder)
{
  aCoder.encode(name, forKey: kName)
}
```

All we do here is provide the coder with the value and key of the property that needs to be stored, along with the class instance.

Handling NSCoding--compliant objects

Now that we have an object that we can serialize, we can move on to writing the code that will do just that.

Add another extension to the `CustomFileManager` class, adding a helper function that will once again provide us with a valid path:

```
extension CustomFileManager
{
  func personFileUrl(person: Person) -> URL?
  {
    if let dir = FileManager.default.urls(
                for: .documentDirectory,
                in: .userDomainMask).first
    {
      return dir.appendingPathComponent("\(person.name).person")
    }
    return nil
  }
}
```

The `personFileUrl` method is basically the same as the `textFileUrl` method we wrote in the previous section.

Saving NSCoding--compliant objects

Now we add a method that will perform two duties:

- Serialize (that is, encode) a `Person` object
- Save that serialized data to disk

Add the following method to the `CustomFileManager` extension:

```
func archiveToDisk(person: Person)
{
  if let url = personFileUrl(person: person)
  {
    let data = NSKeyedArchiver.archivedData(
              withRootObject: person)

    do {
        try data.write(to: url)
        print(
              "Successfully archived \(person.name) to \(url.path)")
```

```
    }
    catch { print(error) }
  }
}
```

To encode the object, we pass it to the `NSKeyedArchiverarchivedData` method, which takes an object as its single parameter and returns a `Data` object.

Just like the `String` object in the previous section, the `Data` object provides a (throwing) method for storing the data to a given location, which is the only parameter it requires.

Serialize, archive, or encode?

These terms, in this context at least, mean essentially the same thing. They all mean that a structured object (however simple or complicated) is turned into a stream of 1s and 0s that can be stored on-disk.

The program *archives* an object, by instructing it to *encode* itself, producing *serialized* data. Don't worry about it too much.

We'll print any `Error` that gets thrown, but we shouldn't ever get to see that. Hopefully.

Loading NSCoding--compliant objects

Loading the stored data back into the app is done as follows.

Add the following method to the `CustomFileManager` extension:

```
func unarchiveFromDisk(person: Person) -> Person?
{
  if let url = personFileUrl (person: person)
  {
    let result
        = NSKeyedUnarchiver.unarchiveObject(withFile:url.path)

    return result as? Person
  }
  return nil
}
```

Again, there is a parallel with what we have seen already. If the unarchiving fails (which means the `Person` class has failed to decode the data), `nil` is returned; otherwise, we get an initialized `Person` object.

Testing the code

We'll create a `Person` object using the `stringValue` of the text field for its `name` property:

1. Add an outlet to that text field in the `ViewController` in Interface Builder:

```
@IBOutlet weak var textField: NSTextField!
```

2. Add the following actions to the `ViewController` class and connect them up to the final two buttons in the interface:

```
@IBAction func saveCustomObject(_ sender: Any)
{
  let name = textField.stringValue
  let person = Person(name: name)
  customFileManager.archiveToDisk(person: person)
}

@IBAction func loadCustomObject(_ sender: Any)
{
  let name = textField.stringValue
  let person = Person(name: name)
  if let unarchivedPerson
     = customFileManager.unarchiveFromDisk(person: person)
  {
    print(
    "Successfully retrieved person: \(unarchivedPerson.name)")
  }
  else
  {
    print(
    "Couldn't find person: \(name)")
  }
}
```

3. Rename the buttons appropriately:

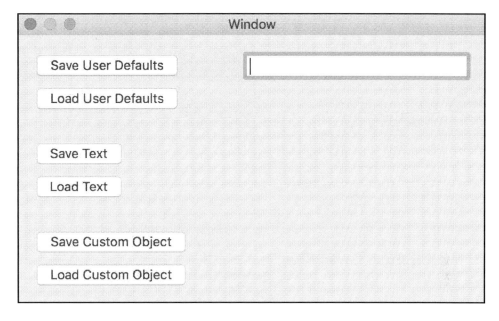

4. Run the code and add some text in the text field:

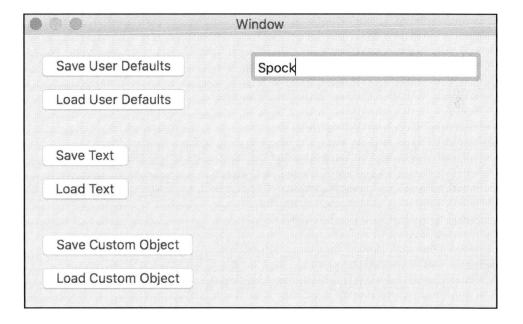

Saving the file produces the following output:

```
Successfully archived Spock to
/Users/stu/Documents/Spock.person
```

Loading the file produces the following output:

```
Successfully retrieved person: Spock
```

5. Now enter another name in the text field and hit **Load Custom Object**, and you'll get something similar to this:

```
Couldn't find person: Guy in the red shirt
```

And that's it; you can store any custom class that you create by simply implementing the two NSCoding protocol methods.

More complex objects

In principal, we can extend the complexity of objects to an arbitrary degree without having to modify these methods. Objects that contain other objects are also no problem, so long as those *contained* objects are also NSCoding--compliant. Such a hierarchy of objects is often referred to as an **object graph**, and the code we have written so far will reconstruct every aspect of such a graph's structure, as well as the data content of its properties.

Once we get into searching for objects, and setting relationships between them (as well as other, more complex, functionality), we'll be glad to have something that does a lot of the arduous repetitive tasks for us. In the next chapter, we'll cover Core Data, Cocoa's framework for handling large numbers of complex objects, which is just the thing we mean.

Presenting open and save dialog boxes

Before we wrap up this chapter, let's look at offering the user a way to choose the location in which a file is to be saved, and to load a file from any location in the file hierarchy.

This goes beyond what is included in the Foundation framework; we need Cocoa, so we need to modify the CustomFileManager import statement as follows:

```
import Cocoa
```

Creating the **Open** dialog box could hardly be easier. Add the following method to the `CustomFileManager` class, using a new extension:

```
extension CustomFileManager
{

  func openFile() -> URL?
  {
    let myFileDialog = NSOpenPanel()
    myFileDialog.runModal()
    return myFileDialog.url
  }

}
```

As you can see, this returns the URL of the file chosen by the user.

The dialog box should look familiar:

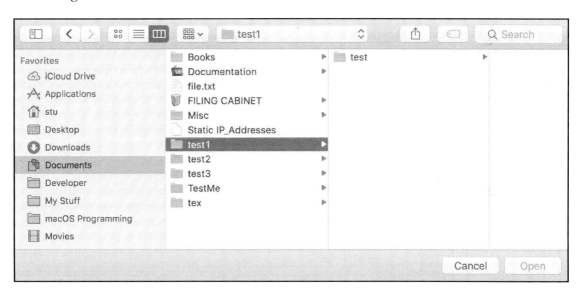

Note that there is no **New Folder** button, because we are searching for a file, not saving one. Also note that the **Open** button is grayed out as long as a directory is selected. This is also because we are searching for a file.

Both of these are default values of the NSOpenPanel object. We must change those if we are to allow the user to specify a location to save a file.

Add the following method to the CustomFileManager class, using the new extension:

```
func listDirectory()
{
   let myOpenDialog = NSOpenPanel()
   myOpenDialog.canChooseDirectories = true
   myOpenDialog.canCreateDirectories = true
   myOpenDialog.runModal()

   let url = myOpenDialog.url
   print("User selected \(url)")
}
```

Now that we have set canChooseDirectories and canCreateDirectories to true, the user is able to create and select folders as she chooses.

Once the file's URL is obtained, we can open or save it with the code we have already looked at.

If we were to need a list of the contents of a directory, we would add the following code to the listDirectory method:

```
if let path = myOpenDialog.url?.path
  {
     print("path = \(path)")

     do {
        let contents
     = try FileManager.default.contentsOfDirectory(
                  atPath: path)
        print(contents)
     } catch {
        print(error)
     }
  }
```

Summary

There are many other ways to save and load files in Cocoa, but once you have mastered the techniques presented in this chapter, you'll find that the others are easy to assimilate.

You have learned the following in this chapter:

- The various methods available for using the `default UserDefaults` object
- Loading objects with default values
- Saving structured data
- The `NSCoding` protocol and `NSKeyedArchiver` methods
- How to create, store, and load `NSCoding`--compliant classes
- Convenience methods for writing some data types to disk
- Special methods for saving and retrieving text
- How to offer the user the standard system open and save dialog boxes

The next chapter, as already mentioned, will cover Cocoa's Core Data framework, with which we will perform more advanced operations around saving, retrieving, and querying data on disk.

14
The Benefits of Core Data

Typically, books and tutorials on Core Data start with an explanation of what Core Data is, and quickly move on to discuss the elements of the Core Data stack, those elements' interactions and interdependencies, and the advanced inner workings that make Core Data such a powerful framework.

And so, before any code is written and any app is working, we are faced with a steep learning curve, and a mountain of new terms and concepts to learn.

This chapter will take quite the opposite approach, and first present a substantial amount of working code that is easy to understand (and thus remember) and is suitable for experimental tweaking, bending, and breaking, which is the basis of mastering any coding topic.

Only when we have seen Core Data in action will we look at the theory behind it, with the aim of turning what you already know into a strong theoretical and practical base upon which you can take your skills to much higher levels, should you decide that Core Data is for you and your projects.

So, the chapter is split broadly into three sections:

- Using Core Data and Cocoa Bindings to quickly produce a functioning app that will persist and present a simple dataset
- Using code to explore Core Data's further organization and manipulation of data
- A look under the hood at what is going on, what else Core Data will be able to do for us, and when we might wish to use it

In this chapter, you will learn about the following:

- Using Core Data with Cocoa Bindings to keep a UI synchronized with its underlying data store
- How to set up a Core Data model, and the roles that its components play
- One-to-one and one-to-many relationships
- Creating objects and specifying their attributes
- Creating relationships between objects
- How to fetch stored data
- Modifying and deleting objects
- A basic outline of the Core Data stack
- When to use Core Data and when not to

What Core Data is, and isn't

For the moment, we'll just talk very briefly about why we'd even need Core Data.

Core Data basically offers you a way to avoid reinventing the wheel every time you need to store, manage, and present data. We're all developers, we all need data management, and to a large extent (and I do mean large), Core Data saves us a ton of code writing, testing, and debugging, by exposing to us ready-rolled solutions for many of the tasks surrounding data.

Core Data is not a database. It contains abstractions of dealing with databases, and very efficient ones at that, but it is not a database as such, and it is much more than a wrapper around SQLite (for example). However, a lot of the concepts and nomenclature around Core Data are borrowed from the database world.

Core Data allows us to quickly, reliably, and efficiently deal with data, in a way that is consistent across apps and platforms. If you ever walk into a job and take over an app on day one, with nothing more than a "There's your desk, we need the app to work better, good luck," you'll be glad to be confronted with a familiar Core Data implementation instead of a custom-built solution, including custom bugs, that will almost certainly be poorly documented, if at all.

Elements of a Core Data model

To make sense of the rest of the chapter, we need to look at three important building blocks of a Core Data model: entities, attributes, and relationships.

Entities

Many apps are mostly data. A To Do app, for example, may be nothing more than a list view that presents a way to read and write object data to and from an array. A single piece of data, or record, is referred to in Core Data as an **entity**.

Think of entities as classes that Core Data creates and manages for you, and you won't be far off the fundamental idea of entities.

Attributes

If entities are like classes, they probably have properties, right? And indeed they do, but they are referred to as **attributes**. They can be strings, dates, integers, or one of many other types, just as we would expect from a class property.

Relationships

When entities maintain references to each other, we talk of **relationships**. A `Taxi` entity may have a `driver` attribute that is a single instance of a `Person` entity. A `Fleet` entity may hold references to any number of `Taxi` instances, and so on.

Anyone with a reasonable degree of familiarity with either object-oriented programming or databases will have little trouble gaining an intuitive grasp of these concepts.

With that said, it's time to turn to Xcode.

Core Data, Cocoa Bindings, and no code

Okay, let's get started with the fastest way to get Core Data up and running. It's also a way that amply demonstrates how well Core Data is designed to integrate seamlessly with Cocoa Bindings, and therefore also with Interface Builder.

It is, in fact, possible to create a simple app that uses Core Data and synchronizes it with its UI, without writing more than one single line of code.

Create the project

Create a new project using the **Cocoa Application** template. The app will list the crew of a Star Trek starship, so you may wish to name the project more imaginatively than the `5623_14_code` name that this book uses.

 If you do choose to use a name that starts with a digit, that starting digit will be replaced by an underscore in one or two places where names must begin with an underscore or letter character. So, the `.xcdatamodedl` file created by Xcode for this chapter's project will be called `_623_14_code.xcdatamodeld`, for example.

Be sure to tick both **Use Storyboards** and **Use Core Data**, as shown in the following screenshot:

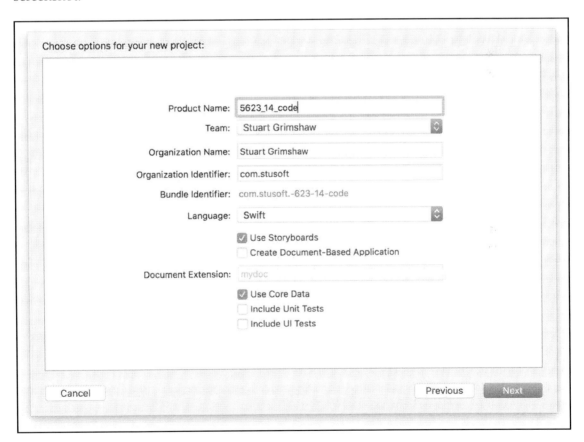

Take a look at the `AppDelegate.swift` file.

That's a *lot* of boilerplate code. In addition to a few functions, we also see four `lazy var` statements that make up the bulk of the code in this class. Once upon a time, in fact, until very recently, it was necessary to absorb all this code before it was possible to do anything of any value with Core Data.

Fortunately for us, we will not only build a simple Core Data app without making any in-depth reference to these variables, we will also be able to replace all of them with just a few lines of code in the second half of this chapter.

For the moment, we need only press the **Don't Panic** button, and move onto creating the UI in Interface Builder.

Create a simple UI in Interface Builder

To keep our focus on the use of Core Data, we will restrict our app to the simplest UI that we can get away with.

Adding the necessary UI objects to the Scene

Build the UI as follows:

1. Add a **Table View** object to the app's **View Controller Scene**.
2. Below that, add two **Text Field** objects.
3. Below them, add two **Gradient Button** objects, and resize them to taste.
4. Set the **Image** of one to **NSAddTemplate**.
5. Set the **Image** of one to **NSRemoveTemplate**.
6. Select the entire **View** and click **Add Missing Constraints** to set up a simple set of default constraints that will serve our purposes adequately.

Your **View Controller Scene** should now look something like this:

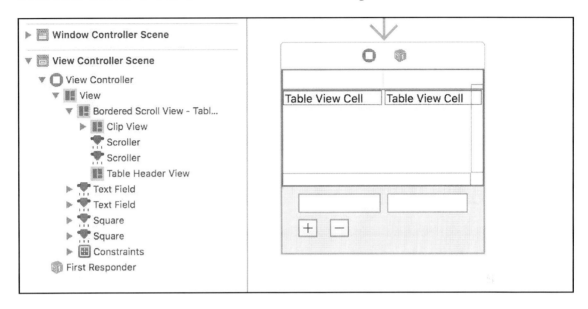

If you run the app now, and there are no issues to be fixed, it should look like this:

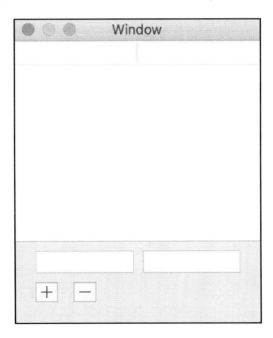

This could be the list view of any number of apps, and we will soon see how easy it is to hook it up to Core Data, and all the goodness that it brings with it.

Add an Array Controller

Add an **Array Controller** object to the **View Controller Scene**. We saw this object previously, as we were dealing with Cocoa Bindings in `Chapter 6`, *Cocoa Frameworks - The Backbone of Your Apps*.

Setting up the data model

Before we can hook up the UI to the **Array Controller** object, we'll need to set up the data model.

So, this is where we finally get our hands on Core Data:

1. Navigate to the *yourAppName.xcdatmodeld* file.
2. Click on **AddEntity** (or use the application menu: **Editor | Add Entity**) and rename the **Entity** object that is created to **Person**.
3. Note that we use uppercase, just as we would for the name of a class.
4. With the **Person** entity selected, click on **Add Attribute** (or select **Editor | Add Attribute**) and call it **name**.
5. Set its attribute **Type** to **String**.
6. Note that we use lowercase here, just as we would with a class variable.
7. Untick the **Optional** box in the Data Model Inspector (*Command-Option-3*).
8. Create a second non-optional string attribute, named **shirtColor** (lower camel case).

And now we have a simple but usable data model.

The app version of `Hello World` is often a To Do app, and this data model would already be sufficient for that, although we'll be jazzing it up a little later on.

Preparing the View Controller

The `ViewController` class doesn't have much to do here, but it does need to expose a reference to the `NSManagedObjectContext` that is maintained by the `AppDelegate` class.

Add the following property to the `ViewController` class:

```
var managedContext = (NSApplication.shared().delegate
    as! AppDelegate).managedObjectContext
```

And believe it or not, that's all we'll be adding to the `ViewController` class. In fact, it's the only code we'll be adding at all in the first half of this chapter.

Connecting up to the storyboard

Now it's time to return to Interface Builder in order to connect up the controls, the array controller, and the Core Data model itself.

Connecting the buttons

Perform the following steps to connect buttons:

1. Control-drag from the add button to the **Array Controller** and set the connection to the **add:** action of the **Array Controller**.
2. Control-drag from the remove button to the **Array Controller** and set the connection to the **remove:** action of the **Array Controller**.
3. A *control* + click on the **Array Controller** should show these new connections, as shown in the following screenshot:

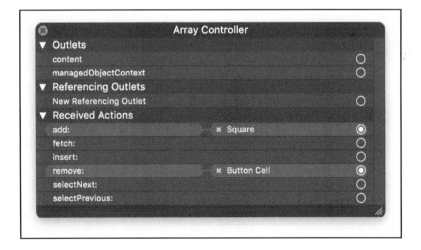

Connecting the Array Controller

Connect the **Array Controller** using the following steps:

1. Select the **Array Controller** and go to the **Attributes Inspector**.
2. Under **Object Controller,** set the **Mode** to **Entity Name**. Set the **Entity Name** to Person.
3. Ensure that **Prepares Content** is checked.

4. The **Object Controller** section in the **Attributes Inspector** should look as follows:

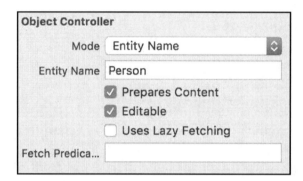

5. Now switch to the **Bindings Inspector** of the **Array Controller**.
6. Under **Parameters**, bind the **Managed Object Context** to the **View Controller** with the **Model Key Path** set to managedContext.

Setting up the table columns

We now turn to the individual table columns:

1. Select the first **Table Column** and go to the **Bindings Inspector**.
2. In the **Value** section, bind the column to the **Array Controller**.
3. Set the **Controller Key** to arrangedObjects.
4. Set the **Model Key Path** property to name. This is the name attribute that we created for the Person entity in the Core Data model.

Now we do the same for the second column:

1. Select the second **Table Column** and go to the **Bindings Inspector**.
2. In the **Value** section, bind the column to the **Array Controller**.
3. Set the **Controller Key** to `arrangedObjects`.
4. Set the **Model Key Path** property to `shirtColor`. This is the `shirtColor` attribute that we created for the `Person` entity in the Core Data model.

Connecting the Table Cell Views

Now we need to connect up the **Table Cell View** (*not* the **Table View Cell**):

1. Select the **Table Cell View** of the first table column, as shown in the following screenshot:

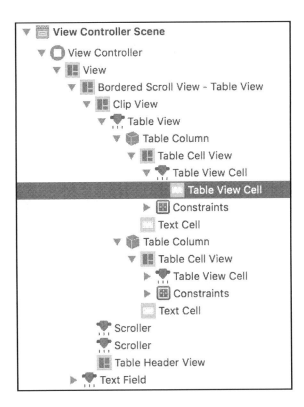

2. In the **Value** section of the **Bindings Inspector**, bind the cell view to **Table Cell View**.

3. Set the **Model Key Path** to `objectValue.name`.

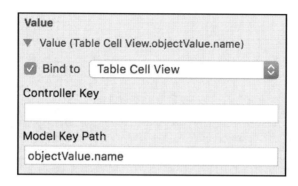

4. Select the **Table Cell View** of the second column and go to the **Bindings Inspector**.
5. In the **Value** section, bind the cell view to **Table Cell View**.
6. Set the **Model Key Path** to `objectValue.shirtColor`.

Connecting the text fields

Finally, we need to hook up the **Text Field** objects to the **Array Controller**:

1. Select the first **Text Field** and go to the **Bindings Inspector**.
2. In the **Value** section, bind the text field to **Array Controller**.
3. Set the **Controller Key** to `selection` and set the **Model Key Path** to `name`.
4. Now select the second **Text Field** and go to the **Bindings Inspector**.
5. In the **Value** section, bind the text field to **Array Controller**.
6. Set the **Controller Key** to `selection` and set the **Model Key Path** to `shirtColor`.

Okay, we're ready to run the app. Once launched, the app should look similar to the following screenshot:

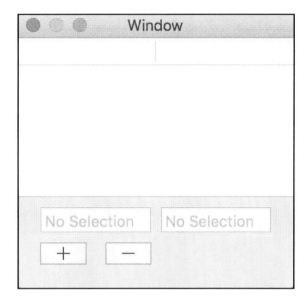

You should now be able to use the add button to create entities, the text fields to set the `name` and `shirtColor` attributes, and the remove button to remove entities.

Furthermore, you should be able to quit the app and relaunch it to find those same entities have been automatically saved and loaded by the Core Data framework.

Pretty good for one line of code, I'd say.

Using our data model

So, now that we have seen our Core Data model persisting data, and our Cocoa Bindings loading and updating the data for us, it's time to go into a little more depth and discover the rich framework of functionality that we have signed up for, by choosing to implement our data model and persistence using Core Data.

Using NSPersistenceContainer

We mentioned previously that most of the `AppDelegate` class's boilerplate code was going to be dispensed with, and we'll do this now.

At the moment, we are looking at a lot of code involved in creating the Core Data stack. Your `AppDelegate.swift` file will look very much like this one at the moment:

We won't need all of that. At least, we won't need all that code; the complete Core Data stack can now be created within an `NSPersistenceContainer`, through which we can access as much of the stack as we require.

To do this, we make three changes to the `AppDelegate` class:

- We initialize (lazily) an instance of `NSPersistentContainer` using our app's name
- We discard the four lazily initiated variables that are now accessible through the `NSPersistentContainer`
- We replace references in the code to `managedObjectContext`

So, let's get cracking.

Adding an NSPersistentContainer instance

Make sure you have the correct name of your app - the name of the `.datamodeld` file is the one you want (the bit preceding the dot):

Next, add the following property to the `AppDelegate` class:

```
lazy var persistentContainer: NSPersistentContainer =
{
  let appName = "YOUR_APP_NAME"

  let container
   = NSPersistentContainer(name: appName)
              container.loadPersistentStores(
          completionHandler:
    {
          (storeDescription, error) in
          if let error = error as? NSError
        {
          print(error)
        }
      })
  return container
}()
```

Using `NSPersistenceContainer`, we are able to reduce nearly a hundred lines of code down to a single call to an `init` method.

Delete the unneeded properties

Delete the following variables, including the closures after the = sign:

```
lazy var applicationDocumentsDirectory: Foundation.URL
lazy var managedObjectModel:
        NSManagedObjectModel
lazy var persistentStoreCoordinator: NSPersistentStoreCoordinator
lazy var managedObjectContext:
        NSManagedObjectContext
```

Replacing references to the context

Now we need to replace the seven occurrences of `managedObjectContext` with references to `persistentContainer.viewContext`, which the compiler will bring to our attention in the following places:

- `saveAction`
- `windowWillReturnUndoManager`
- `applicationShouldTerminate`

We could build and run the app now, but we will have lost any data that we had entered using the old implementation. This is because the persistent container stores the data in a different place, namely here: `User/Library/Application Support/YOUR_APP/`.

Although you may frequently need to access this folder during development and debugging, don't ever write to or read directly from this directory. This is Core Data's business, not ours, and any messing around we do with it will only break the data model. Think of it as comparable to Xcode's *derived data* directories. You may need to delete the content when resetting your app while working on it, but don't do anything else.

Is it an interesting read? Well, it looks like this:

```
%%ÅWtableZ_PRIMARYKEYZ_PRIMARYKEYCREATE TABLE Z_PRIMARYKEY (Z_ENT INTEGER
PRIMARY KEY, Z_NAME VARCHAR, Z_SUPER INTEGER, Z_MAX INTEGER)f;Å
indexZPERSON_ZSUPERIOR_INDEXZPERSON
CREATE ... etc. etc.
```

You decide, but I'd rather be reading P.G. Wodehouse, myself.

Creating a data manager class

For the purposes of demonstration and experimentation, we will create a data manager class into which we can write the code as it is discussed:

1. Create a new Swift file and name it `DataManager.swift`.
2. Add the following code below the `import Foundation` statement in the `DataManager.swift` file:

```
import CoreData

class DataManager
{
    let managedObjectContext: NSManagedObjectContext
```

```
            init(managedObjectContext: NSManagedObjectContext)
            {
                self.managedObjectContext = managedObjectContext
            }
        }
```

We now need to maintain an instance of this class in the `AppDelegate` class.

3. Add the following property to the `AppDelegate` class:

```
var dataManager: DataManager!
```

4. And add the following call to the `applicationDidFinishLaunching` method:

```
func applicationDidFinishLaunching(
                              _ aNotification: Notification)
{
    dataManager = DataManager(
      managedObjectContext: persistentContainer.viewContext)
}
```

Non-string entity attributes

At the moment, we have two attributes for the `Person` entity, `name` and `shirtColor`, and they are both of type **String**. Let's add another attribute, that's an **Integer** type.

1. Select the `.datamodeld` file in the project navigator.
2. Select the `Person` entity.
3. Click on **Add Attribute**, naming the new attribute `rank` (lowercase again), and setting the **Type** to **Integer 16**, as shown in the following screenshot:

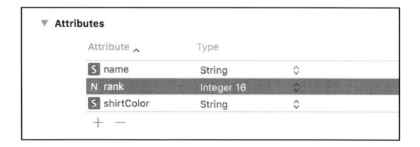

Let's assume that not all **Person**s are members of a starship crew (pretty sure I'm not) and leave the `rank` attribute's **Optional** property ticked.

Creating entity instances

Okay, we're ready to start creating a crew. So far, we've done that by using the UI, but it's very common to create entities in code according to, say, the results of an HTTP request. In our `makeCrew` method, we'll have a look at how to do that.

Add the following method to the `DataManager` class:

```
func makeCrew()
  {
    let captain = Person(context: managedObjectContext)
    captain.name = "Kirk"
    captain.rank = 1
    captain.shirtColor = "Yellow"
  }
```

This code is pretty self-explanatory.

What is a managed object context?

Think of a managed object context as a (potentially) huge dictionary of objects, that contains both the descriptions of object types, and records of object instances (and a lot more besides).

It's an *everything an app needs to know about a data model and its data, in a consistent format* sort of thing.

To fire this method, add the following call to the DataManager class's `init` method:

```
makeCrew()
```

Run the code, and you'll see the following:

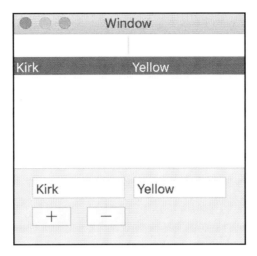

There's nothing stopping you from adding crew members manually--go ahead and type in McCoy (blue shirt, if I remember rightly).

Fetching data

Although our interface is doing a grand job of keeping up with the data, any work we want to do with the data will require us to *fetch* it first.

Add the following method to the DataManager class (and a call to it in the class's init method):

```
func doFetchCrew()
  {
    let fetchRequest: NSFetchRequest =
                         Person.fetchRequest()

    do {
        let result =
          try managedObjectContext.fetch(fetchRequest)

      for person in result
      {
        if let name = person.name
        {
            print("NAME = \(name)")
        }
```

```
            print(person)
        }
    } catch {
        print(error)
    }
}
```

Although this code is new, it needs little explanation:

1. We create a typed `NSFetchRequest`, which means we know the type of the `[Any]` array being returned as a result of the fetch.
2. The request is initiated with the name of the entity we require to have returned in the resulting array.
3. The `fetch` method throws an error, so it needs to be in a `try` block.
4. We then iterate through the resulting array, and for each successful cast to an `NSManagedObject` instance, we check if there is a value for the key that we specify.
5. If there is, we print it.
6. We also print the description of the object. Running the code will produce this output in the debug console:

```
NAME = Kirk
<Person: 0x6000000abe80> (entity: Person; id: 0x600000032780
<x-coredata:///Person/t35A582E7-7E6B-4926-B487-499FD04DF25F2> ;
data: {
    name = Kirk;
    rank = 1;
    shirtColor = Yellow;
})
```

Let's add a few more crew members and add a couple of relationships between them.

Adding relationships between entities

To add relationships between entity instances, we need to return to the data model. There are two types of relationship:

- One-to-one relationships (a ship only belongs to one fleet)
- One-to-many relationships (a fleet may contain many ships)

Furthermore, relationships may be *optional*:

- Optional (a ship may or may not belong to a fleet)
- Non-optional (every fleet has ships)

We will add one of each type to our data model, so navigate back to the .datamodeld file.

One-to-one relationships

With the Person entity selected, follow these steps:

1. Click the + sign in the **Relationships** section.
2. Set the newly created **Relationship** name to superior, lowercase again.
3. Set the **Destination** to **Person**.
4. Leave **Inverse** for the moment.
5. Leave the **Optional** property ticked, since not all crew members will have a superior (nobody tells Kirk what to do).
6. Leave the **Type** property set to **To One**.

In the data model Inspector, the relationship's properties should now look like this:

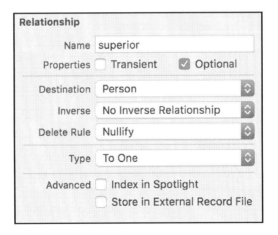

At the moment, the superior relationship has no **Inverse**, but that will change in a moment.

One-to-many relationships

Now let's create a one-to-many relationship:

1. Click the + sign in the **Relationships** section.
2. Set the **Relationship** name to `subordinates`.
3. Set the **Destination** property to `Person`.
4. Set the **Inverse** property to `superior`.

> Note that **superior's Inverse** value is now set automatically to `subordinates`.

5. Leave it set to **Optional**.
6. Set the **Type** to **To Many**.

The relationships between `Person` entity instances should now look like this:

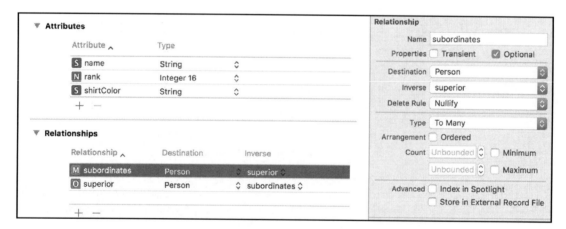

Adding relationships to the crew

We'll now create a few more crew members, setting the `superior/subordinate` relationships between them as we go.

Add the following code to the `makeCrew` method:

```
let cso = Person(context: managedObjectContext)
    cso.name = "Spock"
    cso.rank = 2
    cso.shirtColor = "Blue"
    cso.superior = captain
```

Having added this code, run the app again. The output will look like this:

```
NAME = Kirk
<Person: 0x6080000a9360> (entity: Person; id: 0x608000037c60
<x-coredata:///Person/t1711A77F-FDE6-48AC-8BA3-4DD936485CBD2> ;
data: {
    name = Kirk;
    rank = 1;
    shirtColor = Yellow;
    subordinates = (
        "0x608000038140 <x-coredata:///
    Person/t1711A77F-FDE6-48AC-8BA3-4DD936485CBD3>"
    );
    superior = nil;
})
NAME = Spock
<Person: 0x6080000a9420> (entity: Person; id: 0x608000038140
<x-coredata:///Person/t1711A77F-FDE6-48AC-8BA3-4DD936485CBD3> ;
data: {
    name = Spock;
    rank = 2;
    shirtColor = Blue;
    subordinates = ();
    superior = "0x608000037c60 <x-coredata:/// Person/t1711A77F-
    FDE6-48AC-8BA3-4DD936485CBD2>";
})
```

Do you notice something interesting about Kirk? Although we have not changed our code when creating him, he now gets not only `superior` and `subordinates` arrays; the latter is also populated with a `Person` entity.

Core Data is doing the obvious for us, and this is one of the strengths of using it. We set up the relationships in a declarative fashion, and Core Data does the rest.

We can't see from the log that the subordinate is Spock, unless we look closely at the ID: 0x608000038140. However, this is not really relevant to actually using Core Data; this is simply the default `description` method of the class.

Notice that Kirk's `superior` value is `nil`, and Spock's `subordinates` array is empty.

Same thing, the other way around

Just as we set the value of Kirk's `subordinates` array by setting Spock's `superior` relationship, we can set a member's `superior` relationship by adding him or her to Kirk's array of `subordinates`.

Add the following code to the `makeCrew` method:

```
let uhura = Person(context: managedObjectContext)
uhura.name = "Uhura"
uhura.rank = 3
uhura.shirtColor = "Red"

let kirkSubordinates = captain.mutableSetValue(
  forKey: #keyPath(Person.subordinates))

kirkSubordinates.add(uhura)
```

A glance at the debug console will show that we have added `Uhura` to the crew:

```
NAME = Uhura
<Person: 0x6000000a3e40> (entity: Person; id: 0x600000031d40
<x-coredata:///Person/tB442B7FB-6113-4AB0-8C5E-0FED42486EE64> ;
data: {
    name = Uhura;
    rank = 3;
    shirtColor = Red;
    subordinates = ();
    superior = "0x608000035b60 <x-coredata:///Person
    /tB442B7FB-6113-4AB0-8C5E-0FED42486EE62>";
})
```

And if we check Kirk's ID of 0x608000035b60, we'll see that this is indeed the value of Uhura's `superior`.

We can also add several entities to a one--to--many relationship at the same time by providing an array of those entities to the `addObjects` method.

Add the following code to the `makeCrew` method:

```
let sulu = Person(context: managedObjectContext)
    sulu.name = "Sulu"
    sulu.rank = 3
    sulu.shirtColor = "Yellow"

    kirkSubordinates.add(sulu)

    let doomedSecurityGuy = Person(context:
                               managedObjectContext)
    doomedSecurityGuy.name = "Nameless"
    doomedSecurityGuy.rank = 3
    doomedSecurityGuy.shirtColor = "Red"

    kirkSubordinates.addObjects(
        from: [sulu, doomedSecurityGuy])
```

We won't print the console output here, but it will confirm the addition of the two crew members. And, at last, we have the nameless guy in the red shirt that never makes it back from beaming down to somewhere nasty. We will cover more of him (well, less of him, actually) later on.

Sorted fetches

It would be a weird data management framework that didn't offer us at least some sorting functionality when returning results, and Core Data offers us about as much as we could realistically ask for. We have at our disposal a full suite of sort functions, which offer a high degree of flexibility, are implemented way more efficiently than we are likely to be able to do ourselves, and which are ready right out--of--the--box

Let's have our results returned ready-sorted by `rank` for us. Not only that, let's have crew members of equal `rank` be sorted by `name`. This is where we start to notice the extent to which some investment in time up-front with Core Data starts to pay dividends as we begin to actually work with the data.

Add the following method to the `DataManager` class:

```
func sortedFetchCrew()
  {
    let fetchRequest =
          NSFetchRequest<NSFetchRequestResult>(
          entityName: "Person")

    let rankSortDescriptor = NSSortDescriptor(
```

```
                    key: "rank",
                    ascending: true)

    let nameSortDescriptor = NSSortDescriptor(
                    key: "name",
                    ascending: true)

    fetchRequest.sortDescriptors = [rankSortDescriptor,
                                    nameSortDescriptor]

    do {
        let result
            = try managedObjectContext.fetch(fetchRequest)

      for managedObject in result
      {
        let object = managedObject as! NSManagedObject

        if let rank = object.value(forKey: "rank"),
           let name = object.value(forKey: "name")
        {
          print("rank: \(rank): name = \(name)")
        }
      }
    }
    catch {
        let err = error as NSError
        print(err)
    }
  }
```

Look how easy this is. Just create one or more NSSortDescriptor objects that specify the key by which we want the entities sorted and the sort order, and then put them into the fetch request's sortDescriptors array.

Be sure, however, to put them in the right order. So, we place our rank sort descriptor first in the array, followed by the name sort descriptor. It should be pretty clear what would happen if we reversed the order of those two sort descriptors (give it a go anyway).

Don't forget to call the method in the class's init method.

Run the code. The results in the console should look like this:

```
rank:  1:  name = Kirk
rank:  2:  name = Spock
rank:  3:  name = Sulu
rank:  3:  name = Uhura
rank:  4:  name = Nameless
```

Sorting in the table view

So how about the UI? All this console stuff is no good to the user, who won't have access to error logs (or, indeed, be at all inclined to look at them if they were made available). Fortunately, this is really easy:

1. Go back to the `Main.storyboard` file.

2. Select the first **Table Column** and set its **Title** to `Name` in the attributes inspector.

3. Select the second **Table Column**, and set its **Title** to `Shirt Color` in the attributes inspector.

4. The **Table Column** entries will now be called **Name** and `Shirt Color`:

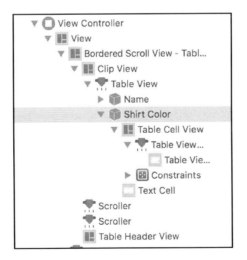

Run the code again and click on the table column titles. They will sort themselves in the table, and a second click will sort them in the reverse order. Think of how much code that would be to write from scratch. That's a lot of code we're not writing here.

The app window should now look something like this:

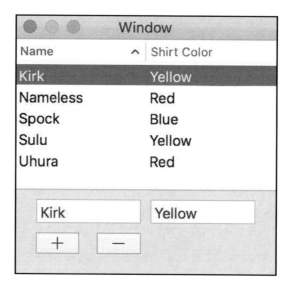

In the preceding screenshot, we see the crew members sorted by (ascending) name attribute.

Predicate fetching

What if we don't need all the crew members, but just a subset of them? This is, in fact, one of the most valuable features of Core Data; we don't have to fetch the whole data array in order to be able to work with it.

For example, what if we're only interested in crew members with a rank value of 1 or 2?

This is very simple using an NSPredicate object, as follows.

 If the result of a question is yes or no (or Boolean, as we'd call it), it's a **predicate**. *The cat is dead* is a predicate. *The cat's favorite food* is not.

Add the following method to the DataManager class, as well as a call to it in the class's init method:

```
func predicateFetchCrew()
{
    let fetchRequest: NSFetchRequest
```

```
                  = Person.fetchRequest()

        let nameSortDescriptor = NSSortDescriptor(
            key: "name",
            ascending: true)
        fetchRequest.sortDescriptors = [nameSortDescriptor]

        let predicate = NSPredicate(format: "%K < %i",
                              "rank", 3)
        fetchRequest.predicate = predicate
```

 %K represents the key path. You may have not seen this before, it's not used a lot outside of Core Data.

```
    do {
        let result
          = try managedObjectContext.fetch(fetchRequest)

        for person in result
        {
          if let name = person.name
            {
              print("NAME = \(name)")
            }
            print(person)
        }
      } catch {
        print(error)
      }
    }
```

We have seen all of this code before, with the exception of the one line in which we initiate an NSPredicate with the format of the predicate we require; in this case, the value of the rank key should be less than 3.

The results look like this:

```
    rank: 1: name = Kirk
    rank: 2: name = Spock
```

Using other predicates

While we're looking at NSPredicate, here are a few more useful format values:

Searching for a string

We can look for a character or string:

```
let predicate = NSPredicate(
   format: "%K CONTAINS %@",
   "name", "r")
```

Searching for a case - insensitive string

We can do this as a case--insensitive search:

```
let predicate = NSPredicate(
   format: "%K CONTAINS[c] %@",
   "name", "K")
```

 Adding the [c] creates a case--insensitive predicate.

Combining predicates

We can combine predicates into a compound format:

```
let predicate = NSPredicate(
   format: "%K CONTAINS[c] %@ AND %K < %i",
   "name", "K", "rank", 2)
```

Relationship predicates

We can use relationships' attributes:

```
let predicate = NSPredicate(
   format: "%K == %@",
           "superior.name", "Kirk")
```

As you can see, a fetch request can be as finely nuanced as we require; the only limit is our specification of the data model itself.

Deleting the red guy

We're nearly done for this section, but we haven't yet deleted an entity in code. And the nameless guy in the red shirt is still there.

We'll assemble all the red-shirted guys on a dangerous planet, but we don't want to delete Uhura, so we'll need to do a little testing too:

```
func deleteDoomedSecurityGuy()
{
    let fetchRequest: NSFetchRequest
        = Person.fetchRequest()

    let nameSortDescriptor = NSSortDescriptor(
        key: "name",
        ascending: true)
    fetchRequest.sortDescriptors = [nameSortDescriptor]

    let predicate = NSPredicate(format: "%K < %i",
        "rank", 3)
    fetchRequest.predicate = predicate

do {
    let result
        = try managedObjectContext.fetch(fetchRequest)

    for person in result
    {
        if let name = person.name
        {
         print("NAME = \(name)")
        }
            print(person)
    }
} catch {
    print(error)
    }
}
```

%K represents the key path. You may have not seen this before; it's not used a lot outside of Core Data.

Basically, if you're wearing red, and you're not `Uhura`, you're done for. Run the preceding code, preceding it and following it with a call to `sortedFetchCrew`, so that we see the results.

Those results will confirm that the nameless guy has ominously been deleted from the crew roster:

```
rank: 1: name = Kirk
rank: 2: name = Spock
rank: 3: name = Sulu
rank: 3: name = Uhura
rank: 4: name = Nameless
Zap!
rank: 1: name = Kirk
rank: 2: name = Spock
rank: 3: name = Sulu
rank: 3: name = Uhura
```

We have broken with tradition here by leaving the disappearance of the nameless guy in the red shirt till the end. But it did seem like a suitable way to round off the section.

More about Core Data

Before we finish with Core Data, we'll take a look at how the different parts of the framework fit together, and then talk about when we might (or might not) want to use it.

The Core Data stack

Although it is encapsulated in the persistent container that we used in our `AppDelegate` class, we still have access to the entire Core Data stack, a collection of objects that create and manage the underlying data store that we don't need to access directly.

In this chapter, we have hardly touched the stack directly either. We have referenced the managed object context, but that is all. Although we cannot delve into great depth here, let's have a high-level look at the various parts of the stack and what they do.

The stack could be visually represented like this:

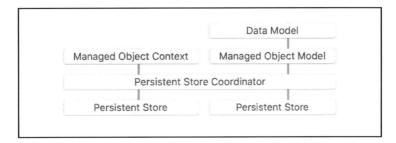

The three big players here are as follows.

NSManagedObjectModel

The `NSManagedObjectModel` contains information about the underlying data model of the application, that is, information about the entities of the object graph, their attributes, and the relationships between them.

NSManagedObjectContext

The `NSManagedObjectContext` object manages a collection of instances of the `NSManagedObject` class. Our app has only used one object context, but it is possible to have more.

NSPersistentStoreCoordinator

The `NSPersistentStoreCoordinator` not only persists data to disk, it also ensures the persistent store (or stores) is compatible with the data mode. It is the bridge between the persistent store (or stores) and the managed object context, and also manages data loading and caching.

Does app X really need Core Data?

Core Data is not a silver bullet for all our data needs. It comes with an initial cost in terms of setup, and is not always easy to debug. In some cases, it is not the right tool, and in others, it is simply overkill.

So, let's weigh up the pros and cons of entrusting our app's date model to Core Data.

The pros

Apple claims that using Core Data typically reduces the amount of code you write by 50-70%. It's always worth taking such claims with a pinch of salt, and it depends very much on the situation at hand, but these numbers appear pretty close to the truth to me.

Core Data offers you a ton of stuff that 90% of developers will need reasonably often. Core Data can (and does) fill whole books, and we can't cover all of those points here, but it is certainly worth knowing that these features are built into Core Data:

- Integration and synchronization with the application's UI.
- Grouping, searching, filtering, and organizing data.
- Archiving and unarchiving data.
- Maintenance of *change propagation* and relationships between objects.
- Validation of property values, both in terms of completion and value ranges.
- **Schema migration**, which means dealing with changing an app's data model without making your users' existing data invalid. This is a really big thing; it needs to done right, and Core Data will really help.
- **Lazy loading** of objects and partial loading (called **faulting**) of data, thus reducing IO operations significantly. Fancy the idea of getting an `array.count` without loading the array? Core Data can do that.
- Automatic data caching.
- Query composition through the use of `NSPredicate`, making complex queries very easy to do.
- Built-in management of undo and redo functionality.

In addition to all this, we should not forget that we are unlikely to be able to beat the reduced memory and CPU usage that Core Data provides us with.

A lot of very smart people have been working for a very long time on Core Data.

The cons

Arguments against using Core Data generally resemble one of the two following points:

- Core Data is another layer of abstraction on top of whichever database is being used. More layers means more potential problems and, often, less clarity.
- Core Data is a generic solution, and generic solutions have to make a lot of compromises.

These are perfectly valid points (which we have massively over-simplified). If you're a database or object graph ninja, you won't need any advice here.

Making that decision

I would like to quote an excellent summary from Apple:

"In general, the richer the model, the better Core Data is able to support your application."

Never a truer word said. If your app's data model is little more than piping HTTP request results into a UI, you are unlikely to save much time by setting up the whole Core Data thing. Core Data doesn't come completely for free, bugs are sometimes hard to find, and the error messages are notoriously difficult to decipher.

But once you need to archive and unarchive data, maintain relationships between data types, present different views of data objects, search the underlying data store, use the Undo Manager, and a host of other things, Core Data quickly starts to pay off.

On the Web, there is much debate over the pros and cons of using Core Data versus raw SQLite and such. It might be prudent to adopt this approach. If you can roll your own solution, you're already completely able to make that call yourself. If you're unsure about dealing with object graphs, schemas, and complex data persistence, you'd be well advised to get across Core Data.

Core Data is sometimes hard to understand, it's not perfect, and there are alternatives. But it's a really valuable, powerful, and feature-rich framework. Not checking it out seems a real shame.

Summary

Core Data is a big topic, but this chapter should have given you a firm basis on which to build your skills.

You have learned the following in this chapter:

- The meaning of entities, attributes, and relationships
- How to set up a Core Data model
- One-to-one and one-to-many relationships
- Using `NSPersistenceContainer` to simplify creating a Core Data stack
- How to fetch stored data, using predicates and sort descriptors, using different predicate types, as well as sorting in an `NSTableView`
- How the various parts of the Core Data stack fit together
- Some considerations as to when to use Core Data in your apps

In the next chapter, we will cover connections to the outside world via HTTP.

15
Connect to the World - Networking

There are still some apps that need no connection to the World Wide Web, though I'm not sure I have used many of them this week. The System Preferences app, that's all I can think of right now.

It's probably fair to say for all of us, that networking is an indispensable part of our toolkit as developers. Doing Mac OS means doing networking. Fortunately, Foundation Kit's **URLSession** framework provides us with a rich set of classes that take us well beyond the basics of Internet connectivity.

The following topics are covered in this chapter:

- URLSession's patterns for asynchronous downloads
- Creating a test server on your machine
- Simple HTTP requests using closures
- Customizing sessions, requests, and download tasks
- Using session delegates to interface with the OS
- Monitoring a download's progress
- Cancelling, suspending, and resuming downloads

This chapter will focus both on downloading data into our apps and downloading files onto disk.

Patterns for downloading data

We have two broad patterns that we can use with the URLSession framework. One is very simple and will suffice for many situations, and the other requires a fair amount of additional coding, but offers us a much greater degree of control and flexibility.

Both patterns deal with asynchronous requests that will not block further execution of your code. Synchronous requests are not covered in this chapter, and you will quite possibly never need them.

Simplicity

The simplest set of calls to URLSession will involve passing a closure to whichever method we are calling. That closure must simply accept the correct arguments from the system when it gets called back. Once the download is complete, this closure will be populated with a response, some data, and an error, any of which may be `nil`. Any code you need to run once the download finishes will go in this closure.

Control

A more complicated pattern, but one which affords us a higher level of control that we are likely to need sooner or later, involves creating a delegate class which will be called by the system at various stages of the download. The delegate protocols, wide range of methods give us ample opportunity to exert a high degree of control throughout the request's life cycle. We will look at the following delegate protocols:

- URLSessionDelegate
- URLSessionTaskDelegate
- URLSessionDownloadDelegate

Downloading using closures

So, let's start with some of the simpler stuff, although we'll be cutting no corners. Firstly, we'll set up a local server onto which we can easily *upload* data, and then we'll go through some examples of using URLSession, starting with the simplest HTTP requests and then progressing to more customized solutions.

Starting a local test server on your machine

Before we write the Swift code to make our HTTP requests, we'll need something to send those requests to. Rather than us putting some example resources somewhere on the Web at which you can point your code, wouldn't it be much more satisfying to be able to quickly and simply start up a local server on your own machine that will host anything and everything you may need to explore the material presented in this chapter? (At least, as long as we need fast access to the data - once we get into the more complicated stuff we'll want to run the code under realistically slow Internet-speed circumstances.)

Starting the server

If you've never done this before, you'll be amazed at how simple it is:

1. Choose or create a folder in which you'll save the Xcode project file a little later on.
2. In the Terminal, navigate to this folder (or simply drag the folder onto the Terminal icon, that's often quicker).
3. At the command--line prompt, enter the following command:

   ```
   python —m SimpleHTTPServer
   ```

4. You should see the following response in the Terminal window:

   ```
   Serving HTTP on 0.0.0.0 port 8000 ...
   ```

   Python? I thought this was about Swift. Where do I get Python, anyway?

So, the truth is, whatever language you're learning, it's likely you're going to need a passing familiarity with at least a few other languages. In this case, we're using Python because Swift doesn't come with such a convenient server just waiting for a single line of code to start it up. If you've got Mac OS - and of course you have - then you've got Python already installed, and the preceding line of code is all you're going to need for the time being.

That's it. I don't imagine Amazon are about to start worrying about the competition you represent right now, but basically your hard drive is now a data center.

As long as you leave that Terminal window open, you can host anything you want in the folder from which you started the Python server.

Creating a JSON file

To give us something to start testing our request code on, we could use any number of files, including HTML or just plain text files, but we're going to create a small JSON file.

In the folder from which you started the Python server, create a plain text file called `test.json`.

If you use `TextEdit` or some other feature-laden word processor, you *must* save the file in plain text format. You can use Xcode, though, which gives you all that fancy syntax coloring and formatting, or your favorite command--line text editor (if you've never used one, check out **nano**, it's pretty simple).

The contents of the `test.json` file should be as follows:

```
{"people":[
    {"firstName":"Polly", "lastName":"Styrene"},
    {"firstName":"Olly", "lastName":"Stone"},
    {"firstName":"Molly", "lastName":"Bloom"}
]}
```

Save the file.

Testing the server

The easiest way to check that all is as it should be is to enter the following URL into any browser (Safari, Chrome, it doesn't matter which): `http://127.0.0.1:8000/test.json`.

Or, you can use this URL, which does exactly the same thing: `localhost:8000/test.json`.

In the browser window, you'll see the JSON data you put into `test.json`, pretty much as it appeared previously.

However, we are coders, are we not? Let's test the server in code, which will allow us to dig a little deeper into what is going on, and catch a first glimpse at Swift 3's new `URLSession` API:

1. Create a new **Cocoa Application** Xcode project.

2. Add a new **Swift** file, and call it `HTTPRequestManager.swift`.

3. Under the `import` statement, add the following code:

```
class HTTPRequestManager
{
    static let sharedInstance = HTTPRequestManager()
    private init() {}
}
```

We create a class, add a `sharedInstance` static constant, with which we ensure that there is only ever one instance of this singleton class. Just to make sure that no other class can inadvertently create a separate instance, we declare the `init` method to be `private`.

4. Now add the following test function to the `HTTPRequestManager` class:

```
func localTest()
{
    let url = URL(string: "http://127.0.0.1:8000/test.json")!
    let session = URLSession(configuration: .default)
    session.dataTask(with: url, completionHandler: {
        data, response, error in
        print(response)
    }).resume()
}
```

Don't worry if you don't get any of this, we will return to each of these method calls shortly and explain them in context. This is just to test the server.

5. Navigate to the `ViewController.swift` file and add the following code to its `viewDidLoad` method:

```
override func viewDidLoad()
{
    super.viewDidLoad()
    let requestManager = HTTPRequestManager.sharedInstance
        requestManager.localTest()
```

```
        }
```

6. Now run the app and you'll see output that looks very similar to this:

```
Optional(<NSHTTPURLResponse: 0x608000038e60> { URL:
http://127.0.0.1:8000/test.json } { status code: 200, headers {
    "Content-Length" = 155;
    "Content-Type" = "application/json";
    Date = "Mon, 12 Sep 2016 02:29:29 GMT";
    "Last-Modified" = "Mon, 12 Sep 2016 00:29:25 GMT";
    Server = "SimpleHTTP/0.6 Python/2.7.10";
} })
```

So, why does it look like this? This isn't the JSON data we stored in `test.json`. Well, if you look back at our `localTest` method, you'll see that we print the `response` object, not the `data`. We'll get to turning the data into something usable in a moment; if you print the unformatted `data` object now, all you'll get is seemingly random text.

But the `response` object is not without interest. You can see the URL that the request went to (and when an app has sent requests to several URLs, you'll be glad of that), as well as a date stamp and a few other bits and pieces.

Perhaps most important of all is the `status code: 200`.

`200` is good. `200` means that everything went okay. We made a request and that request was fulfilled without any problems, the server is happy, the client app is happy, and that usually leads to happy developers too.

But we're getting ahead of ourselves a little. We will now build up a repertoire of HTTP requests, starting with the simplest possible, progressively incorporating more customization as we go.

Implementing an HTTP request manager

If you've used NSURLSession before, much of this will look very familiar, but by the time we're through, you'll hopefully have gained a lot of insight into what you already know, as well as learned a lot of new things.

If you've never used Swift to make HTTP requests, you'll soon be up to speed, and you may well find that the code in this chapter covers everything you will ever need of the URLSession framework.

We will build up an HTTP manager, a singleton that will hide all details of HTTP web requests from the client classes that make use of it. Those clients will not know, or ever need to know, about how the data is being requested, returned, and formatted into Swift objects; the implementation will be completely opaque.

So, the fact that we're accessing local test data from our modest little Python server need not disturb the rest of the app at all. The rest of the app asks for a dictionary of objects in return for a URL string, and the rest of the app gets that dictionary of objects, and that's all it cares about.

None of the client classes should be creating Swift URL objects, those are all taken care of by the HTTP manager class.

The web as an asynchronous entity

The Internet is inherently asynchronous. You fire off a request and it disappears into the ether, where you have no control of it whatsoever. What comes back, and when it comes back, and even if something come back at all, is all at the mercy of a billion tiny switches in somebody else's cellar; your code will get the results of its request when the Internet is good and ready, and not before.

With that in mind, there are three ways your Swift code can deal with the situation:

- It can wait, doing nothing, blocking everything, until the Internet responds
- It can make the request and attach to it a delegate that will be notified when something comes back
- It can give the request a closure that will be executed once the response has arrived

The first way, synchronous HTTP requests, is only very rarely the way to go. In the bad old days of NSURLConnection, it used to be the easiest way, too, which led to a lot of bad HTTP request stuff working its way into otherwise quite reasonable code. And we will studiously ignore it here.

Using delegate callbacks, the second approach, is fine, and we'll look at it later, in contexts in which we have no alternative than to use them.

The third approach is what we'll look at first. We simply write a block of code that takes three arguments, the data, the response, and an error object, and does something with those arguments. The HTTP layer doesn't know or care what. It's not the hardest code in the world, and it will fulfill most of our requirements in many scenarios.

The simplest request possible

Let's start off with a very basic request, using default values wherever we can.

Add the following method to the HTTPRequestManager class:

```
func defaultValuesRequest(urlString: String)
{
    let url = URL(string: urlString)!
    let session = URLSession.shared
    let task = session.dataTask(with: url,
                         completionHandler: {
                             data, response, error in

                             if error != nil
                             {
                                 print(error)
                                 return
                             }

                             print(response)
    })

    task.resume()
}
```

We start off by passing the method's only argument, the urlString, to URL's init method. We can force-unwrap the returned optional value because, well, whatever String object you put in there, you're going to get a URL object back. It might be a completely useless URL, but that's not the URL init problem. The only times you don't get back a URL is when the app crashes (try the empty string, for example), and what's the use in testing an optional once the app is dead?

We then create the instance of URLSession returned by its shared property, which you can't customize very much, but which will often fulfil our requirements.

Then, we use that session to create a `URLSessionTask`, passing in the `url` that we created previously, and the `completionHandler`, a closure to be executed once the request completes.

The completion handler

Once we have a response to our request (whether or not it was successful), we can get to its details through the `completionHandler` that we provided. That handler is called by the system, which passes three arguments: a `Data` object (which you might remember in ancient times used to be called `NSData`), a `URLResponse` object (which you might remember used to be called `NSURLResponse`), and an `Error` object (which, you may remember... okay, you get the picture).

The closure we have passed defines the objects `data`, `response`, and `error`, named that way for obvious reasons, but we can call them anything we want.

So what does our completion handling closure do?

The first thing it does is check that the `error` is nil, meaning that nothing has gone wrong on our side, the client side. This doesn't mean to say that the response doesn't contain an error, but it does mean we successfully sent a request, and we got back a response from the server side.

So, for example, if you make a request using a `URL` object that was initiated with the string `"this is a dud"`, you'll get an error message in the console similar to this:

```
Optional(Error Domain=NSURLErrorDomain Code=-1002 "unsupported URL"
UserInfo={NSUnderlyingError=0x60800004bcd0 {Error
Domain=kCFErrorDomainCFNetwork Code=-1002 "(null)"},
NSErrorFailingURLStringKey=x, NSErrorFailingURLKey=x,
NSLocalizedDescription=unsupported URL})
```

Try it. Call this method from the `viewDidLoad` method of the `ViewController`, using a random string instead of the `localhost` URL.

The error gets printed to the console and the method returns.

If we have no client-side error, then we have a valid `URLResponse` object in response, and at the moment our method simply prints this response to the console. We'll get to the data soon.

Improving the simplest request possible

Now, as simple as this function is, it has a serious problem.

Its handler is full of code. Yes, it is only printing the `response`, but it has no business doing anything at all with the `response`, or the `data`, or the `error`. The HTTP manager's job is to get and pass on data, nothing else. Just doing that can, under some circumstances, require a large amount of code, and the last thing we need is to mix it up with a heap of data handling functionality.

So what we need to do is to add an argument, which will itself be a completion handler, of the same type, namely `(Data?, URLResponse?, Error?) -> Void`.

Replace the implementation of the `defaultValuesRequest` method with the following:

```
func defaultValuesRequest(urlString: String,
  dataHandler: @escaping (Data?, URLResponse?, Error?) -> Void)
  {
    let url = URL(string: urlString)!
    let session = URLSession.shared
    let task = session.dataTask(with: url,
                            completionHandler: dataHandler)
    task.resume()
  }
```

So, we have added a second argument to the function and, to avoid confusion at this early stage, we have named it `dataHandler`, to distinguish it from the `session.dataTask` second argument. However, most people call such a function `completionHandler`, or just `completion`, or just `handler`, so be prepared to see all of those when reading other peoples' code.

 Older Swift veterans beware: The types of three arguments are not prefixed with `NS`, as they once were.

And this is probably how most of your arguments to a `Session` completion handler should look. Handling the data, whether formatting it, or using it directly, or storing it, should be somebody else's business. Even if the only thing you're going to do with the data is parse it for the URLs of a second tier of requests (as we shall see in the next chapter), all that stuff belongs in a dedicated method of its own, which can ask the request manager for the data, supplying its own completion handler. Such a call would look something like this:

```
let requestManager = HTTPRequestManager.sharedInstance
let remoteData = requestManager.defaultValuesRequest(
```

```
            urlString: "someURL",
            dataHandler: {
                    data, response, error in
                    // parse data
                    // use data
    })
```

 Resist the temptation to place subsequent request calls in a request call's completion handler; before long, you end up with nested completion handlers within nested completion handlers that become cumbersome to read, and understand, therefore maintain.

Finally, what's that `@escaping` doing there? This allows the closure to continue to exist after the request function itself has returned. Remember, that closure will be called asynchronously at some unspecified time in the future, long after the request-calling function itself has finished. In that sense, it *escapes* the request function; it lives longer.

And if you forget to add it, Xcode will point this out to you and refuse to compile, which is reassuring.

So far, so good; the URLSession default values enable us to access data stored on a network. However, we have the opportunity to customize a session to our taste by initiating it with a **URLSessionConfiguration**.

Customizing URLSessionConfiguration properties

So far, we have used a preconfigured catch-all URLSession instance, called `shared`. It's great; it not only does a lot of stuff with a single word of code, but it also got us through the first few pages of this chapter without us having to worry about configuring it, so allowing us to focus on URLSession's basic way of working (and a lecture about separation of concerns).

So, what might we wish to change about the session that will require us to configure our own instead of using `shared`?

There are many things, and we won't cover all of them here, but the most common include:

- Adding content type headers
- Adding authorization key headers
- Setting a **cache policy**
- Setting timeout intervals for the request and/or response

We will look more closely into some of these a little later on, so think of this section as being more *how* than *why*. So let's add a new method to our request manager class, after which we'll go through it and talk about what's going on.

In order to create our own custom session, we will need to go through the following steps:

1. Create an instance of one of the NSURLConfiguration types.
2. Set the properties of that configuration to our requirements.
3. Use that configuration object to initiate a URLSession instance.

Add the following code to HTTPRequestManager:

```
func configurationValuesRequest(urlString: String,
  dataHandler: @escaping (Data?, URLResponse?, Error?) -> Void)
  {
    let url = URL(string: urlString)!

    let configuration = URLSessionConfiguration.default

    configuration.httpAdditionalHeaders =
                      ["Accept":"application/json"]
    configuration.requestCachePolicy = .useProtocolCachePolicy
    configuration.timeoutIntervalForRequest = TimeInterval(10.0)

    let session = URLSession(configuration: configuration)
    let task = session.dataTask(with: url,
                        completionHandler: dataHandler)
    task.resume()
  }
```

Having initialized a URL from the passed-in urlString, we initialize a default URLSessionConfiguration.

 Because URLSessionConfiguration is a class, not a struct, we can use the let keyword, because we can *mutate* a class's property values (assuming the properties are themselves mutable). This is not the case with structs.

We have chosen the .default type here; see the following section for a discussion of the .ephemeral type that is also available.

We set the httpAdditionalHeaders property, which is a [String: String] dictionary, to contain an entry for each header we wish to set. In our case, we are telling the server that we are expecting application/json data in the response.

Then, we set the cache policy for the session, although the value we have chosen here is the default value anyway. More about caching later in this chapter.

Finally, we set a `timeoutIntervalForRequest`, which sets a `TimeInterval` (a double, in seconds) on requests going through this session.

Now that the configuration is the way we want it, we use it to initiate a `URLSession`.

> That `URLSessionConfiguration`, along with all its properties, is passed by value to the `Session` initialization; any changes you make afterwards to the configuration will not affect the `Session` object.

So, the code here is similar to what we had when using a URLSession `shared` instance, but now we have tailored the session to our needs. Requests made by this session will use those values, unless they are overridden by the next level of customizability, which is the properties of each individual **URLRequest**.

Customizing URLRequest properties

There are different types of HTTP request, using one of four HTTP methods, and requests can carry a payload of data in their request body. These settings, and others, some of which may override the values set in the `URLSessionConfiguration`, can be set on an individual basis.

```
func requestValuesRequest(urlString: String,
  dataHandler: @escaping (Data?, URLResponse?, Error?) -> Void)
  {
    let url = URL(string: urlString)

    var request = URLRequest(url: url!)

    request.addValue("application/json",
                  forHTTPHeaderField: "Content-Type")
    request.addValue("application/json",
                  forHTTPHeaderField: "Accept")
    request.httpMethod = "PUT"
    request.timeoutInterval = TimeInterval(5.0)
    request.cachePolicy = .returnCacheDataElseLoad

    let bodyParams = ["someKey":"someValue"]
    do
    {
        let data = try JSONSerialization.data(
            withJSONObject: bodyParams,
```

```
            options: [])
        request.httpBody = data
    }
    catch let error
    {
        print(error)
    }

    let session = URLSession.shared
    let task = session.dataTask(with: request,
                                completionHandler: dataHandler)
    task.resume()
}
```

 You may have noticed that we declared `request` with the `var` keyword. In contrast to `URLSessionConfiguration`, `URLRequest` is a `struct`, and so its properties are not mutable unless we declare the whole request to be mutable, using `var`.

We then add a couple of header fields to the request, which may override the configuration's values.

The same goes for the next two lines of code, in which we (rather arbitrarily) override the configuration's **timeoutInterval** and `cachePolicy` values with values for this individual request. We have shortened the timeout for this particular request, and changed the caching policy to allow the `URLSession` to use cached data if it exists, or fetch new data if it doesn't, thus potentially saving HTTP traffic and speeding up data retrieval.

If a request needs to send data (apart from the data set in the headers), it needs to do it by adding data to the HTTP body. We do this by performing the following steps:

1. Create a `Dictionary` object containing the body data (often named `parameters`).
2. Using a `try...catch` statement in a `do` block, we attempt to encode the `Dictionary` as raw `Data`.
3. If the encoding succeeds, we assign its value to the request's `httpBody` property.
4. If the encoding should throw an error, we catch it and print it.
5. We pass the `request`, not the `url`, to the `URLSessionTask`. The method is overloaded to take either a `URL` or a `URLRequest` object.

And again, we use the `dataHandler` closure as the `completionHandler` argument.

Of course, these parameters are all gettable as well as settable, and you may find printing them comes in handy during debugging:

```
print(request.allHTTPHeaderFields)
print(request.value(forHTTPHeaderField: "Content-Type"))
print(request.httpBody)
```

Customizing URLSessionTask properties

Finally, we can get and set various property values of the URLSessionTask (of which URLSessionDataTask is a subclass).

Add the following method to the HTTPRequestManager class:

```
func prioritizedTaskRequest(urlString: String,
  dataHandler: @escaping (Data?, URLResponse?, Error?) -> Void)
  {
    let url = URL(string: urlString)!
    let session = URLSession(configuration: .default)
    let task = session.dataTask(with: url,
                                completionHandler: dataHandler)
    task.priority = 0.5
    task.resume()
  }
```

So, just for the sake of it, because we can, we have set the task's priority property, which takes a Float value between 0.0 and 1.0. Don't imagine this is going to get you faster Google results, though; this is a hint intended for Mac OS, and there are no guarantees that it will be honored.

Of course, you can combine these session, request, and task customization settings; we've separated them here for the sake of clarity.

Downloading using a URLSession delegate

For the many situations in which we need more control over the download as it progresses, we can adopt a different approach to communicating with the OS, one that gives us much greater flexibility as to how and when we use the downloaded data.

To do this, we must create a class that conforms to at least some of the URLSession delegate protocols (of which there are several, but never fear, we'll start off with just a few). We can add various functions that will be called by the system to inform us that a download has finished, or has been cancelled, or how far through the download we are, for example.

Using a session delegate also allows us to use background download configurations.

 Actually, by supplying a closure to the download methods we have used so far, we have made use of a system supplied delegate.

There is no SessionDelegate class to subclass; we need to create a class from scratch, one that adopts the necessary protocols.

The following list summarizes the steps we will follow:

1. Create a singleton HTTP request manager that uses the delegate design pattern (instead of functions that take a closure, as we did previously).
2. Create a delegate class that will implement the necessary delegate callback functions, that will be called by the system as the download progresses through it's life cycle.
3. Make a very simple UI, with which we can start, stop, suspend, and resume downloads.

The files we will download will be provided online. One of them is a tiny PDF, which will download in just a second or so, and the other is much larger, which will give us an opportunity to suspend and resume downloads and generally watch the whole process as it progresses.

The smaller file is at this URL: http://grimshaw.de/Mac OS-book/Small.pdf.

The larger one is here: http://grimshaw.de/Mac OS-book/Haskell.pdf.

 If you do follow the advice offered earlier in the book and spend a weekend learning some functional programming with Haskell, you might be glad of that larger file, though I'd start with the recommended website first.

Adding HTTP compatibility to the app

You may have noticed that both URLs are HTTP and not HTTPS. If you did, well done.

Either way, we're going to need to tell our app that we're happy for it to be involved in non-secure HTTP traffic with the `grimshaw.de` server:

1. Navigate to the `Info.plist` file in the navigator.
2. Right-click on it and select **Open As | Source Code**.
3. Add the following XML anywhere in the top level `<dict>`:

```
<key>NSAppTransportSecurity</key>
 <dict>
    <key>NSExceptionDomains</key>
    <dict>
        <key>grimshaw.de</key>
        <dict>
            <!--Allow subdomains-->
            <key>NSIncludesSubdomains</key>
            <true/>
            <!--Allow HTTP requests-->
            <key>NSTemporaryExceptionAllowsInsecureHTTPLoads</key>
            <true/>
        </dict>
    </dict>
</dict>
```

Now your app can access both `http` and `https` loads coming from the specified `grimshaw.de` domain and its subdomains. Bear in mind that this is only valid on that domain; if you try to access HTTP loads on other domains, you must include those domains in this whitelist.

With that in place, we're ready to start writing the app.

Creating a simple UI

The first thing we'll need is a bunch of buttons to push:

1. Open a new Xcode project and set up the storyboard interface to look the same as the following screenshot:

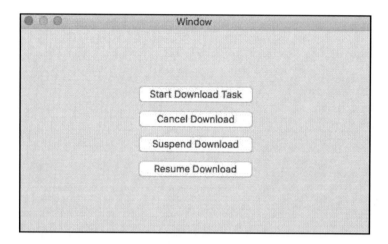

2. Navigate the `ViewController.swift` file and add the following methods:

```
@IBAction func downloadTaskButtonClicked(_ sender: AnyObject)
{
    let requestManager =
                HTTPRequestManager.sharedInstance
    requestManager.downloadRequest(urlString:
                "http://grimshaw.de/Mac OS-book/Small.pdf")
}

@IBAction func cancelButtonClicked(_ sender: AnyObject)
{
    let requestManager =
            HTTPRequestManager.sharedInstance
    requestManager.cancelDownloads()
}

@IBAction func suspendButtonClicked(_ sender: AnyObject)
{
    let requestManager =
            HTTPRequestManager.sharedInstance
    requestManager.suspendDownloads()
}
```

```
@IBAction func resumeButtonClicked(_ sender: AnyObject)
{
    let requestManager =
            HTTPRequestManager.sharedInstance
    requestManager.resumeDownloads()
}
```

Obviously, the compiler will scream at you that it doesn't know what all this means, but we'll get to that in a moment. Notice that we're using the small PDF file in our `downloadRequest` call.

3. Connect up the buttons in the interface with the `IBAction` methods - I trust the names make clear enough which button belongs to which method.

Creating the manager

Now let's implement that HTTP request manager:

1. Create a new Swift file and name it `HTTPRequestManager.swift`.

2. Under the import statement, create the `HTTPRequestManager` class by adding the following code:

```
class HTTPRequestManager
{
    static let sharedInstance = HTTPRequestManager ()
    let session: URLSession
    let sessionDelegate: HTTPRequestDelegate

    private  init()
    {
        let configuration =
URLSessionConfiguration.background(withIdentifier:
                "downloadConfig")
        configuration.httpAdditionalHeaders
                    = ["Accept": "application/pdf"]
        sessionDelegate = HTTPRequestDelegate()
        session = URLSession(configuration: configuration,
                                delegate: sessionDelegate,
                                delegateQueue: nil)
    }
}
```

Once again, the compiler is puzzled by the stuff it doesn't know about: in this case, the `HTTPRequestManager`. Patience, dear compiler.

The first line of code set the manager up to be a singleton, as we have seen before. The second line declares the `session` property of the type URLSession, because we are going to want to keep a reference to the session we create.

Our `sessionDelegate` class will become clear very soon; it's the class that will handle all the system's callbacks to us.

Since the class will only use one URLSession instance, we will initiate it in the `private init` method. The URLConfiguration we create is no longer the `.default` type, but the `.background` type. This will allow us more flexibility later on. The header type is also different to what we have seen before; this time we are specifying that we want a `.pdf` file.

Having initiated the class's `sessionDelegate` property, we use that and the configuration to initiate the class's `session` property. By passing nil as the `delegateQueue` argument, we get a default serial queue, which is fine for our purposes.

Add a `downloadRequest` method to the `HTTPRequestManager` class, using the following code:

```
func downloadRequest(urlString: String)
{
    let url = URL(string: urlString)!
    let task = session.downloadTask(with: url)
    task.taskDescription = "download pdf"
    task.resume()
    sessionDelegate.downLoadTasks.append(task)
}
```

Two things to note here. Firstly, we've taken the opportunity to set the `taskDescription` property of the `URLSessionDownloadTask`, which we won't use functionally but which may come in useful for debugging purposes.

Secondly, we add the `task` to the `downloadTasks` array of the `sessionDelegate`. This small piece of housekeeping will be important in a short while.

Now, before we finally go on to implement the delegate class itself, return to the `ViewController` class and comment out these three lines of code:

```
requestManager.cancelDownloads()
requestManager.suspendDownloads()
requestManager.resumeDownloads()
```

This is because we're going to want to run the code before we get to writing those methods.

Having done that, you should be left with just two compiler alerts, telling you there's no such thing as an `HTTPRequestDelegate`. Of course, the compiler is quite right about this at the moment, so we need to fix that. After we have done so, we'll be able to run the code, and get a real-life, full-on download going.

Creating a session delegate class

Create a new Swift file, and call it `HTTPRequestDelegate.swift`.

Create the `HTTPRequestDelegate` class under the `import` statement:

```
public class HTTPRequestDelegate:NSObject,
    URLSessionDelegate,
    URLSessionTaskDelegate,
    URLSessionDownloadDelegate
{
    var downLoadTasks: [URLSessionDownloadTask] = []
}
```

Now you've got rid of all the compiler alerts you had before, but you have a new one, telling you (quite rightly, once again) that our class does not yet conform to the `URLSessionDownloadDelegate` protocol. This protocol has one obligatory method, which we will add next.

URLSessionDownloadDelegate methods

The `URLSessionDownloadDelegate` protocol has three methods, one of which is not optional, which we will add now. We'll use one of the optional methods later, when everything is running smoothly:

1. Add the following method to the `HTTPRequestDelegate` class:

```
public func urlSession(_ session: URLSession,
                    downloadTask: URLSessionDownloadTask,
```

```
                                    didFinishDownloadingTo location: URL)
    {
        print(#function, downloadTask.taskIdentifier)
    }
```

Notice that the function is declared to be `public`, since the system will need to access it. The Swift compiler won't let you forget it, though.

2. OK, hit the **Run** button in Xcode. Wait a few seconds, and the debug console should show the following:

```
    urlSession(_:downloadTask:didFinishDownloadingTo:)  1
```

Great! The download has succeeded. But where's the file? In your **Downloads** folder perhaps?

Nope. While your method runs, it's in a temporary location, where it's waiting for you to move it to somewhere safe, because that `temp` location will pop out of existence just as soon as the delegate function returns! And then it's gone. 14 KB of the finest PDF data vanished.

So, let's fix that.

Handling the data

What we'll do, once we have the data, is create a folder, called something imaginative like `OurFolder`, and use it to store a file that we will create using that data.

1. Within the `urlSession(_:downloadTask:didFinishDownloadingTo:)` method, immediately after the `print(#function, downloadTask.taskIdentifier)` statement, add the following code:

```
    let fileManager = FileManager.default
    let documentUrls = fileManager.urls(for: .documentDirectory,
                                        in: .userDomainMask)

    guard let firstURL = documentUrls.first  else {return}

    let ourDocsFolderPath =
    firstURL.appendingPathComponent("OurFolder")
    do {
        try FileManager.default.createDirectory(
            at: ourDocsFolderPath as URL,
            withIntermediateDirectories: true,
            attributes: nil)
```

```
    }
    catch let error {
    }
```

This code should be familiar to you from Chapter 13, *Persistent Storage*. Now that we have a location to which we can copy the new file, we can access the method's `downloadTask` argument to get the `temp` location of the downloaded file.

2. Add the following code immediately after the code you just added:

```
let fileName
    = downloadTask.response?.suggestedFilename ?? "untitled.pdf"
let diskLocation =
    ourDocsFolderPath.appendingPathComponent(fileName)

do {
    try FileManager.default.moveItem(at: location,
                                     to: diskLocation)
}
catch let error {
}
```

3. Run the app, and once it has launched, click on the **Start Download** button.

After a few seconds, you will see the following in the debug console:

urlSession(_:downloadTask:didFinishDownloadingTo:) 1

Well, it seems to have worked; check your `Documents` folder for the `OurFolder` folder, in which there'll be a file named `Small.pdf`. If you click on the **Start Download** button again, you'll see this:

urlSession(_:downloadTask:didFinishDownloadingTo:) 2

The session we are using increments the `task.identifier` each time.

Catching errors

At the moment, we are catching any errors that might be thrown by the `try` statements, but we're not yet doing anything with them. To avoid writing the same error handling code over and over again, let's write a class that deals with those errors:

1. Create a new Swift file and name it `HTTPError.swift`.

2. Add the following code after the `import` statement:

```
class HTTPError
{
    static func downloadError(source: String, error: Error?)
    {
        if let err = error
        {
            print(source, err)
        }
    }
}
```

The `HTTPError` class has just one `static` method; the function is called on the class itself, not an instance, as we shall see in a moment. All that this code does is unwrap the `error` argument if it is not nil and print it along with whatever `source` string has been passed along with it. We're going to have a lot of `try... catch` blocks, so this will save us half a dozen lines of code in each call.

And, of course, we may later decide to do something else with those errors, and now we can do that all in one place.

3. Back in the `HTTPRequestDelegate` class, add the following call to both of the `catch` blocks:

```
HTTPError.downloadError(source: #function, error: error)
```

Now, when we run the app, we should see any errors that occur.

4. So, let's do just that; hit **Run**.

> And, hey presto, we have an error!

```
Error Domain=NSCocoaErrorDomain Code=516
""CFNetworkDownload_YcKgF5.tmp" couldn't be moved to "OurFolder"
because an item with the same name already exists."
```

Actually, we had that error the whole time, but of course we couldn't see it. And, as we can now see from the error string, our code is not overwriting the file that exists already. Whether or not this is appropriate for an app depends, of course, on many things, but we will leave the behavior as it is.

Seeing that error means that the download was actually successful, but if it disturbs you because it has the word `error` in it, simply delete the file before re-downloading it.

Getting progress information

Now that the download is running, we'll make use of another `URLSessionDownloadDelegate` method, which will keep us informed of the download's progress in terms of the number of bytes written to disk:

1. Add the following method to the `HTTPRequestDelegate` class:

```
public func urlSession(_ session: URLSession,
                       downloadTask: URLSessionDownloadTask,
                       didWriteData bytesWritten: Int64,
                       totalBytesWritten: Int64,
                       totalBytesExpectedToWrite: Int64)
{
    print(totalBytesWritten, "of", totalBytesExpectedToWrite)
}
```

   It should be pretty clear what's going on here. We are simply printing the values provided by `totalBytesWritten` and `totalBytesExpectedToWrite`. It would be very simple to add a progress bar to the UI to show this data, but we will keep our focus on the download delegate code and be satisfied with the debug console as our progress indicator.

2. Run the app again, and you'll see the progress of the download being printed to the console. Note that, even if the file still exists, that error is being thrown by the file creation code; the download itself finishes without issue:

```
1100 of 14185
4248 of 14185
. . .
14185 of 14185
urlSession(_:downloadTask:didFinishDownloadingTo:) 1
urlSession(_:downloadTask:didFinishDownloadingTo:) Error Domain=
. . .
```

Time to add the ability to stop a download.

Canceling a download

Okay, if we're going to look at cancelling a download, we're going to need a larger file that takes a little longer to find its way into our app. So, switch the URL in the ViewController's downloadTaskButtonClicked to the larger PDF: http://grimshaw.de/Mac OS-book/Haskell.pdf.

Now, we won't have to frantically rush for the **Cancel** button in order to test it. It needs some code:

1. Add a new method to the HTTPRequestManager class:

```
func cancelDownloads()
{
    print(#function)
    for task in sessionDelegate.downLoadTasks
    {
        task.cancel()
    }
}
```

Now we see the reason for adding sessionDelegate.downLoadTasks.append(task) to the HTTPRequestManager's downloadRequest method; we have a reference to every task started by the session.

We will simply iterate through the downloadTasks array and cancel all the tasks in it.

2. Go to the `ViewController` and uncomment the following code from the `cancelButtonClicked` method:

```
requestManager.cancelDownloads()
```

3. Run the app, start a download, and then test that clicking the **Cancel** button does what we expect, which is to stop the (large) download, and log the function name to the debug console.

But we still need to empty the `downloadTasks` array, which is otherwise going to get pretty clogged up with old download tasks that have been cancelled.

URLSessionTaskDelegate methods

Rather than flush the `downloadTasks` array when we call the `cancelDownloads` method and separately remove each task as it finishes in the `urlSession(_:downloadTask:didFinishDownloadingTo:)` method, we can put our clean-up code in one of the methods from the `URLSessionTaskdelegate` protocol. The advantage of doing this is that this method gets called by the system whenever a task finishes, whether or not it completed. So a cancelled `URLSessionDownloadTask` or a finished `URLSessionDownloadTask` both make this same callback:

1. Add the following method to the `HTTPRequestDelegate` class:

```
//MARK:- URLSessionDelegate
public func urlSession(_ session: URLSession,
                       task: URLSessionTask,
                       didCompleteWithError error: Error?)
{
    print(#function)

    for (index, storedTask) in downLoadTasks.enumerated()
    {
        if storedTask == task
        {
            downLoadTasks.remove(at: index)
            print("removed ", task.taskDescription)
        }
    }

    HTTPError.downloadError(source: #function, error: error)
}
```

2. Run the app, and start a download (or a few, if you like - you can download the same file multiple times in parallel).

3. Click the **Cancel Download** button and observe the following log to the debug console:

```
urlSession(_:task:didCompleteWithError:) Error
Domain=NSURLErrorDomain Code=-999 "cancelled" UserInfo={
...
NSLocalizedDescription=cancelled,
NSErrorFailingURLKey=http://grimshaw.de/Mac OS-book/Haskell.pdf}
```

4. So, here we can read the reason for ending the download prematurely. Furthermore, we see that the task has been removed from the downloadTasks array:

```
urlSession(_:task:didCompleteWithError:)
removed  1
```

Remember, that 1 is the identifier, not the number of tasks removed.

Adding suspend and resume

Let's wrap up the download code by adding suspend and resume functionality:

1. Add these two methods to the HTTPRequestManager class:

```
func suspendDownloads()
{
    print(#function)
    for task in sessionDelegate.downLoadTasks
    {
        task.suspend()
    }
}

func resumeDownloads()
{
    print(#function)
    for task in sessionDelegate.downLoadTasks
    {
```

```
                task.resume()
        }
    }
```

2. Return to the `ViewController` class and uncomment the calls to these methods:

```
@IBAction func suspendButtonClicked(_ sender: AnyObject)
{
    let requestManager = HTTPRequestManager.sharedInstance
    requestManager.suspendDownloads()
}

@IBAction func resumeButtonClicked(_ sender: AnyObject)
{
    let requestManager = HTTPRequestManager.sharedInstance
    requestManager.resumeDownloads()
}
```

3. Run the app and check that the download pauses and resumes as you'd expect

No third-party frameworks?

Once upon a time, Cocoa's networking offering wasn't that amazing. It was complicated, it didn't offer a lot of what was needed (without some serious background knowledge), and it even encouraged some poor programming practices by making the *right* way the hard way. Those were the days before NSURLSession.

Into this rather bleak landscape marched a few intrepid developers who released Objective C frameworks that filled this gap. There were several worthy candidates, many of whom built upon experience gained by their predecessors. Most successful was Scott Raymond and Matt Thompson's AFNetworking framework. Almost everybody used it, it became a de facto standard.

The release of NSURLSession made the case for using third-party code like AFNetworking less clear. The new Apple framework had adopted much of what had been developed by third-party developers, and was a better solution in every respect. Certainly, the most common tasks (and not just the simplest) had become much less intimidating to implement using native code, and although the ubiquity of AFN certainly meant it was necessary for most developers to be able to code with it, NSURLSession became more widely accepted, and used, than its predecessor, NSURLConnect, had ever been.

And then came Swift. Swift's easy closure syntax and rigorous type checking has made networking code so much easier than it once was, and it might be suggested that the case for third-party code has all but disappeared.

It is probably good advice to say this: learn the native stuff first. Learn it well, and use it a lot. Then wait and see if there's something still missing that justifies learning to use a third-party framework.

Disclosure:

I say that about most third-party kits that offer to simplify the use of native frameworks. Rolling your own solutions using native code has so many advantages in the long term. I have found it to be a worthy programming philosophy. I strongly encourage you to find somebody online that disagrees with me, to hear their side of the story.

The NS has been dropped, the API has been Swiftified. URLSession is a really good technology.

The URLSession framework

So, let's take a short look at the URLSession framework itself.

Generally, an app will only need to use one session instance, or in the case of tabbed and document-based applications, one session per tab or document window.

All tasks in any given session share configuration settings, some of which may be overridden by the individual request settings.

URLSessionTasks

In this chapter, we have used two different types of URLSessionTask, but there are three in total:

- URLDataTask
- URLDownloadTask
- URLStreamTask

Now that you have a reasonably solid grounding in data and download tasks, you should be able to get to grips with stream tasks without too much of a headache.

Ephemeral sessions

In addition to the `.default` and `.backgroundURLSessionConfiguration` types, we can also declare a session to be of type `.ephemeral`:

```
let ephemeralSession = URLSession(configuration:
                                  URLSessionConfiguration.ephemeral)
```

Such a configuration has no access to cookies, stored credentials, or caches: This is your classic private-browsing setting.

Cache rewards

Sometimes, it has to be fresh, be it bread, fish, or data.

But, sometimes, what you have got is what you need. And you don't need up-to-the-minute refreshes of data that you have already obtained. Cocoa offers much flexibility when it comes to caching request responses, and here's the easiest way to do it:

```
func cacheDataRequest()
{
  let urlString = "http://www.grimshaw.de/Mac OS-book/test.json"
  let url = URL(string: urlString)!
  let request = URLRequest(url: url,
                           cachePolicy: .returnCacheDataElseLoad,
                           timeoutInterval: 20)
  let session = URLSession.shared
  let task = session.dataTask(with: request,
                              completionHandler:
    {
      data, response, error in
      do {
          let jsonData = try JSONSerialization.
                                  jsonObject(with: data!,
                                  options: [.allowFragments])
          print(jsonData)
      }
      catch let error {
          HTTPError.downloadError(source:
                      #function, error: error)
```

```
        }
    })
    task.resume()
}
```

We are using a convenience initializer for `URLRequest` for the first time here. Note that the `cachePolicy` argument has a value of `.returnCacheDataElseLoad`. As the name would suggest, if the requested data has already been downloaded once, it will have been cached (yep, we don't need to write that caching code) and we return that data from the request. If the cache is empty, we load the data from the network.

As far as the rest of the app is concerned, the data just gets returned, whether fetched or retrieved from the cache.

The rest of the code is nothing new, but for the sake of space and simplicity, we have hardcoded the request string into the function itself. Don't do this at home.

When you run this code the first time, there'll be a short delay while the data downloads, and then the debug console will display the results. The second time will be noticeably faster, even with this tiny amount of data. Now disconnect the machine from the Wi-Fi or Ethernet connection, run the code again, and it *still* works.

How about that? Don't forget to turn the network back on, though.

Using different request cache policies

There are a number of different cache policies defined by the `CachePolicy enum` defined by `NSURLRequest`.

 Swift's URLRequest is a `struct` and is not really related to NSURLRequest, but it does have a `CachePolicy` property that is of the type `NSURLRequest.CachePolicy` (which is the previously mentioned enum).

Here is a brief look at each of them:

- `useProtocolCachePolicy`: This is the default policy for URL load requests. This basically means use the default cache behavior, defined elsewhere by Cocoa.

- `reloadIgnoringLocalCacheData`: So, as we might expect from the name, this type ignores any locally cached data. However, any server--side cached data may still be used, at the discretion of the server. If your code asks a server every 5 seconds what the weather in London is like, the server just might decide to risk giving you the same data it gave you 5 seconds ago, instead of going off to get fresh weather data.

- `reloadIgnoringLocalAndRemoteCacheData`: No cached data at all, not local, not server side. Exchange rates aren't noted for their stability, and a client app might well want to insist on the server disregarding its own cached data (assuming you are communicating via a protocol that allows this).

- `returnCacheDataElseLoad`: This is the one we chose for our code. If there's cached data, we'll take it, no matter how old it is. Data that tells us that Andy Warhol's birthday was the 6th of August is unlikely to become invalid. Not so good for news updates.

- `returnCacheDataDontLoad`: This is good for offline mode: If there's cached data, we want it; if there's none, then consider the request as having failed.

- `reloadRevalidatingCacheData`: If the origin source confirms its validity, cached data may be used, otherwise the data is refreshed from the origin. As you might have guessed, there is a *lot* of work being done by Cocoa here. We're just piggy-backing. Once you have indicated to URLSession which caching behavior you require, the cache-flow (geddit?) looks like this:

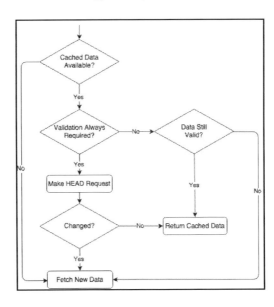

Since you have your own server running on your machine, you should be able to test these various behaviors by changing the request cache policy, and changing the local data, to see what happens.

Do bear in mind that caching is for `URLSessionDataTasks`. There's not much point in caching data when you've downloaded it to disk(!), and streams are by their nature not cacheable.

Summary

In this chapter, you have learned:

- How to launch a test server on your own machine
- How to make HTTP requests using closures
- Customizing sessions, requests, and download tasks
- When to use a session delegate instead of a closure
- How to suspend, resume, and cancel requests

In the next chapter, we will stick with networking as we explore the world of concurrency and asynchronous code, including how best to handle multiple requests that may return data in an unpredictable order.

16
Concurrency and Asynchronous Programming

Any program that you write for Mac OS will need to share the processor's computing power with other programs.

Any program you write for Mac OS will almost certainly run on more than one processor at the same time. That is, even if only one user is using it, it will still be running on more than one processor.

And the majority of programs you will write will sometimes need to ask other programs somewhere, anywhere on the planet, for their help.

Apps, programs, tasks, and processes, call them what you will and draw the dividing lines where you wish, are very sociable entities; working together is the essence of their being.

Welcome to concurrent and asynchronous programming.

As developers, it is our responsibility to ensure that this cooperation between processes runs smoothly, efficiently, and reliably. It is the responsibility of this chapter to ensure that, after working through it, you will have a firm understanding of the concepts involved, the challenges they present, and some of the tools that are at our disposal and with which we will meet those challenges.

The title of this chapter is a little risky, in that it may entrench a common misconception, namely, that concurrency and asynchronicity are sort of the same thing, along with parallel processing and threads and all that other stuff. But they're not. Not even sort of.

So before we look at any frameworks or code, we'll clear up exactly what the relationships between these ideas are. It's not difficult, but it is important; only with a firm grasp of these concepts can we, as developers, hope to make good use of the tools that are available from the Cocoa frameworks.

We'll break it down into the following general points:

- The difference between concurrent and asynchronous processes
- The difference between concurrent processes sharing one processor, and processes using multiple processors
- How we can entrust the most difficult tasks in thread management to native frameworks

Once we have that cleared up, we will move on to look at some concrete examples of how to use those frameworks.

We will also look at some of the frameworks in more detail.

In this chapter you will learn the following:

- The meanings of concurrent and asynchronous programming
- The difference between multithreading and multiprocessing
- Understanding Cocoa's operational framework
- Understanding operations and queues
- Controlling operations with dependencies
- Creating custom operations
- Solving asynchronous challenges with custom operations

Concurrency and asynchronicity

Concurrency and asynchronicity are not the same thing.

If you go back to the first two paragraphs of this chapter, you'll notice that we are talking about conceptually related but nevertheless separate topics:

- One processor must be able to run several programs at the same time
- One program must (or at least should) be able to run on more than one processor at the same time

- A program may need to ask another process for assistance, and continue functioning while waiting for that help to arrive

The first point brings us to *multithreading*, and the second requires us to look at *multiprocessing*, both of which are aspects of *concurrent programming*.

The third point brings us to *asynchronous programming*.

Before we go any further, we will clear up what those terms mean.

Concurrency

When two processes run together, they are said to be running concurrently.

An example of this would be an app that monitors a user's input, say, typing, while at the same time downloading an update in the background. But that's just within one app. Several apps, as well as scores of other system processes, daemons, and whatever, are all running concurrently on any computer running on Mac OS. To get an idea of just how many, we can use the **Activity Monitor** app:

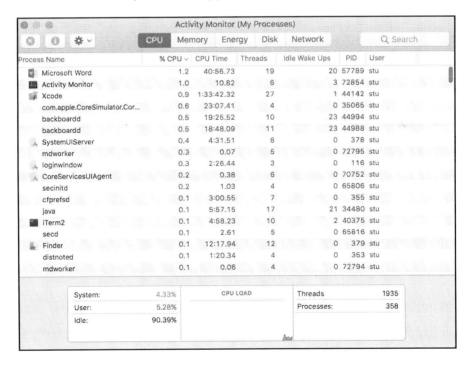

A glance at the scrollbar on the right will give you an idea of how many more processes there are that we can't see.

Some of these processes, indeed most of them, will be inactive, but in the preceding case we can see that over 20 processes, about 10 % of the total, are actively running, which means sharing CPU time.

It's clear then, that a lot of processes need to share CPU time, however many cores a processor chip may have.

Concurrency and parallelism

Concurrency and parallelism are also not the same thing.

The machine on which this screenshot was taken has a dual-core processor. The number of processes would have been the same on a single core machine-we would just have more processes sharing fewer resources.

Processes are distributed across all the available processors; so there are two things here we need to distinguish from each other:

- Two or more processes sharing a single processor are said to be multithreaded
- A system using two or more processors is said to be a multiprocessing system

Let's take a brief look at what that means.

Multithreading

Concurrent processes may be running on separate threads on the same processor, in which case the operating system is alternating which thread is being allocated CPU cycles; as far as the user is concerned, they are running together.

Tasks may be prioritized, and we will see in this chapter that Foundation offers us several tools in this respect, in which case the prioritized task receives an appropriately higher proportion of the available processor time.

But basically, processes running concurrently on a single processor are running one at a time, with some very fast shunting between them being done by the system.

Multiprocessing

When the boffins that were busy doubling the speed of processors every few years finally ran up against some inconvenient physical barriers, such as the speed of light and stuff, they came up with the rather smart alternative of having several processors share the same piece of chip real estate, and share the work too.

The programming implications of this were not their problem.

And so concurrent processes may also be running on separate processors (or cores of processors, we won't get too pedantic here, though), in which case each process is running on a separate CPU.

Tasks can be farmed out to individual processors in a way that keeps computationally expensive tasks from interfering with those that need to be kept responsive at all times, the user interface being the most obvious example. The user doesn't want clicks, drags; and typing to be slowed down by, say, a download that is taking place concurrently.

Tasks can also be balanced between processors, to keep them all busy. While this is to some extent left to the system to manage automatically, when using some frameworks, as we shall see, the practicality and efficiency of this idea also depend on the developer's skill in breaking up large serial processes into a number of smaller, independent tasks that can be distributed across the available processing resources.

Threads, and why you don't need to worry

The down-to-the-metal, low--level technicalities of running separate threads on a single processor, and coordinating processes that are distributed across multiple processors, are real hard-core difficult stuff. Ask anyone who needs to deal with manual thread management, and they'll tell you: threads are really, really hard.

Fortunately, Cocoa offers us several levels of abstraction to make direct thread management unnecessary. Be very glad of this.

One framework that is beautifully simple to use, and which nevertheless meets the vast majority of our concurrent programming needs, is Foundation's operation framework. It provides object--level abstractions of tasks, called **operations**, that are performed on different threads, as well as abstractions of the OperationQueues in which they are placed, to be started and managed by the framework's actual threading mechanism, a mechanism that you never have to see.

It is a really great framework; the `Operation` class and its siblings, `BlockOperation` and `OperationQueue`, transform an area of programming that is difficult, time-consuming, and error-prone, into a simple and elegant workflow, which allows the developer to think in terms of the tasks that need to be performed, and the relationships between them, rather than a minefield of implementation details. And it does this in an efficient and resource-friendly manner.

Asynchronicity

The essence of asynchronous programming is that our code relinquishes control over an asynchronous process until it has completed, failed, or been canceled.

 An asynchronous process can run on the same processor as the process that called it, or it can run on another core or processor, or even on another machine on some other continent (think search engines).

Our code then continues doing whatever it has to do, until that asynchronous process gets back to us, in one of several ways, of which we have used the two most often used by Cocoa itself:

- We may pass a closure to the asynchronous method, to be executed by that process when it deems it to be appropriate (presumably when it has finished running its own code).
- Or we may implement a callback method, which will generally be specified in a delegate protocol to which our code declares itself to conform. That callback method (or methods, there are frequently several) will be called by the asynchronous task as needed, with at least one of them being called on completion of that task.

In `Chapter 14`, *The Benefits of Core Data*, we used both of these patterns extensively. Cocoa's own frameworks also use both of these patterns, and while Swift is certainly moving towards the former pattern, it is still necessary for any Mac OS developer to be comfortable using both approaches, whether designing custom classes and methods, or using those provided by Cocoa.

The challenges of asynchronous programming

Whether passing closures or using the delegate pattern, our program design must take into account a few challenges thrown up by this relinquishing of control:

- The results of asynchronous method calls can be returned in an unpredictable order. HTTP requests are a common case.
- Some tasks may be dependent on the previous completion of other tasks, and so we will need some sort of dependency management strategy.
- An asynchronous task may fail to complete. In addition to the function failing, which affects synchronous code too, we need to take into consideration that a program may be suspended or terminated before the asynchronous code returns any result at all.

Cocoa offers us an advanced and matured toolkit to deal with these challenges.

Dependencies, and why you don't need to worry

What if we need some calls to finish before others begin? Do we have to put the dependent calls in the completion code of the others? And what if there are several dependencies; where do we put the completion code?

As if the `Operation` framework didn't solve enough problems already, we will soon discover that it provides excellent support for operation dependencies. Before adding a task to a group of tasks that will be started at an appropriate time, you simply add others as dependencies that will prevent that task from starting until they are complete.

Operation framework

The `Operation` framework, previously known as `NSOperation` (the name under which you'll find most information on the Web) is an object-orientated solution to the issues raised by concurrent processes, asynchronous programming, and the very concept of a block of code being considered an object in itself.

 Swift's adoption of functions as *first-class* entities that can be passed as arguments, returned from methods, and stored for later use, is part of a wider trend in programming towards code being handled as encapsulated objects per se. An `Operation` even enables us to attach properties to blocks of code. This bodes well for Swift's future as a language rich in features that support experimentation in programming.

In this section, we will cover the following topics:

- How a task can be wrapped in an Operation object
- How to use operations and queues
- How to define custom operations and why we would want to
- How to define custom operations with an asynchronous completion block
- Some general observations concerning operations, queues, and block operations

Understanding operations and queues

An Operation object is a block of code, wrapped up in an object that is equipped with a multitude of properties, methods, and even KVO-compliance. An instance of the Operation class has all it needs, out-of-the-box, to enable it to be easily and efficiently managed by an OperationQueue.

A BlockOperation is a subclass of the Operation class that allows us to manage one or more blocks of code, as if they were one object. Thus several code blocks may be started or canceled as a group. A block operation is not considered complete until all of the code blocks that it encapsulates are themselves complete.

OperationQueue is a class that regulates the operations assigned to it. Those operations remain the responsibility of an operation queue until they have either finished execution or been explicitly canceled, and are organized by priority level and dependencies within that OperationQueue instance.

For more detail on these classes, see *A peek under the hood* of the Operation framework.

But before we get into anything too theoretical, we'll look at some code.

Basic use of an OperationQueue

So let's take a look at how to use the three classes that interest us here:

- OperationQueue
- Operation
- BlockOperation

We'll start with the simplest code possible:

```
func ops1()
{
   let someClosure = {print("someClosure")}
   let opQueue = OperationQueue()

   opQueue.addOperation(someClosure)
}
```

We create a closure, or block, of code, which in this case trivially prints to the debug console.

Creating an `OperationQueue` is even simpler, in that there is only the one initializer, which takes no arguments.

We then call the `addOperation` method on `opQueue`, which takes the block of code, wraps it up in an `Operation` object, and adds it to the queue. Since we did not create the operation explicitly ourselves, we just leave it at that. As Apple's own documentation says:

> *"You should not attempt to get a reference to the newly created operation object or determine its type information."*

As soon as `opQueue` adds an operation that it can execute, it starts; there is no need for an explicit `start` command.

So far so good, but we haven't yet done anything that would be any different from just running the block of code, which we have named `someClosure`, directly. However, we will soon begin to see what Operation and Co can do for us.

Try running the next section of code half a dozen times:

```
func ops2()
{
   let opQueue = OperationQueue()

   for index in0..<3
   {
      opQueue.addOperation({print("index = \(index)")})
   }
}
```

You may get the results in a different order each time; `OperationQueue` makes no guarantees as to the order in which the `Operation` instances are started (let alone in which order they complete).

You may come from a programming background in which the very word *queue* means that things are used in the order in which they are added, first-in-first-out (FIFO) and all that; or maybe you grew up waiting for English buses. Either way, it will seem an abomination that these things are called operation *queues*.

It's true that they are not queues at all. I share your pain.

And that's all part of the beauty and convenience of OperationQueue. Imagine that, rather than printing a snippet of text to a console, your block of code is computationally expensive, and that you are iterating through that loop not three, but 3,000 times. In a world in which even phones have multiple cores, it would be a shame to have the operations standing in line on one processor, executing one at a time. OperationQueue will do all the hard thread management work in the background (and thread management is seriously hard work), assigning each block to a processor as appropriate.

We will see shortly that it is simple to make a queue operate serially when we need to.

There are many more benefits from using operation queues, this is just the start.

Adding dependencies to BlockOperations

One of the most valuable features of using operation blocks is that they can be made to wait until other blocks in the same queue have completed. We do this by adding a **dependency** to an operation.

But how do we do that, if we only pass a block of code to an operation queue? We can't attach anything to a block of code.

This is where the third class, BlockOperation, comes in. We initialize a BlockOperation instance with a block of code (hence the name, one would imagine), after which we can add dependencies as required, not to the code, but to the operation block as an encapsulating object, as the following code illustrates:

```
func ops3()
{
  let opQueue = OperationQueue()
  let cleanUpOp = BlockOperation(block: {print("Cleaning up")})

  for index in0..<3
  {
```

```
    let blockOp = BlockOperation(block: {print("index = \(index)")})

    cleanUpOp.addDependency(blockOp)
    opQueue.addOperation(blockOp)
  }

  opQueue.addOperation(cleanUpOp)
}
```

So we create an `OperationQueue` instance, as before.

We then create a `BlockOperation` instance, named `cleanUpOp` here, initializing it with a block of code.

We enter the loop and again use `BlockOperation` instances to wrap our code blocks (`blockOp`), which we can add as dependencies to `cleanUpOp`. We also add each `blockOp` to the `opQueue`.

Once all the `blockOps` have been added as dependencies, we add the `cleanUpOp` itself to the queue.

 We have to add dependencies *before* we add `blockOp` to the queue.

Run that code, and you will see something similar to this in the debug console:

```
index = 2
index = 0
index = 1
Cleaning up
```

The order in which the `blockOp` blocks complete is to all intents and purposes random, but the `cleanUpOp` is prevented from starting until its dependencies have all completed. We'll be putting this to good use later in this chapter.

More BlockOperation features

A `BlockOperation` can be initiated with a block of code, as we have seen, though it can also be initiated as an empty operation using:

```
let emptyBlock = BlockOperation()
```

We can add more blocks dynamically, as required:

```
let blockOp = BlockOperation()
blockOp.addExecutionBlock({print("We could")})
blockOp.addExecutionBlock({print("also use")})
blockOp.addExecutionBlock {
  print("Trailing closure syntax")
}
```

Thus we can build up a block operation dynamically according to runtime conditions.

 We have to add execution blocks *before* we add a `BlockOperation` instance to an `OperationQueue` instance.

Remember how all bets are off when it comes to the order of execution within a queue? Well the same goes for execution blocks within a `BlockOperation`. Take a look at the following code:

```
func ops4()
{
  let opQueue = OperationQueue()

  for index in0..<3
  {
    let blockOp = BlockOperation()

    blockOp.addExecutionBlock({print("index = \(index)")})
    blockOp.addExecutionBlock {
        Thread.sleep(forTimeInterval: 1.5)
        print("post-snooze Block \(index)")
    }

    opQueue.addOperation(blockOp)
  }
}
```

You might expect that, although the three block operations are started in random order, the blocks inside each block operation would come complete as a group. But running the preceding code produces the following output at the debug console:

```
index = 1
index = 2
index = 0
post-snooze Block 2
post-snooze Block 1
post-snooze Block 0
```

So don't forget: You must add dependencies where you want the different code blocks to run in a specific order.

> You might be surprised to see we are declaring a block operation with `let`, before adding code blocks. This is because, as we are adding blocks to a property of a class, there is no need to use `var`. The properties are declared with `var` within the class definition. `OperationQueue`, `Operation`, and `BlockOperation` are all class types, not structs.

BlockOperation completion blocks

Finally, `BlockOperation` has a `completionBlock` property:

```swift
func ops5()
{
  let opQueue = OperationQueue()

  for index in0..<3
  {
    let blockOp = BlockOperation(block: {print("index = \(index)")})

    blockOp.addExecutionBlock {
          Thread.sleep(forTimeInterval: 1.5)
          print("post-snooze Block \(index)")
    }

    blockOp.completionBlock =
          {print("blockOp \(index) complete")}

    opQueue.addOperation(blockOp)
  }
}
```

The preceding code produces something like the following output:

```
index = 2
index = 1
index = 0
post-snooze Block 0
post-snooze Block 1
post-snooze Block 2
blockOp 0 complete
blockOp 2 complete
blockOp 1 complete
```

As you can see, the `completionBlock` also run asynchronously and may execute in any order.

Defining a custom Operation object

There will be times when the default `Operation` object does not meet our needs completely. In such cases, we subclass it and add whatever is missing. The amount of work that this involves differs markedly between concurrent and non-concurrent operations.

For a concurrent operation, you must replace some of the existing infrastructure with your custom code. The following sections show you how to implement both types of object.

This is where we see the power of the `Operation` framework used more fully.

When we have a number of asynchronous calls being made, and the further execution of a process (in the broader sense) must wait until all those calls have completed, we need a way to keep track of which calls have finished.

It won't work to create a queue of simple blocks containing asynchronous calls, since each block will be complete once it has made its asynchronous call, at which time the calls will probably not yet have returned.

Let's look at a concrete example. We have a file on a server, we'll call it `datamap.json`, which lists the paths to further files that we need to access, which we'll call `data1.json` through to `data3.json`. We wish to assemble a list of one of the data fields in each of those files, in our case, the name of the file's author.

The `datamap.json` file is online here: `http://grimshaw.de/Mac OS-book/api/datamap.json`.

Its contents look like this:

```
{"paths": [
    "data/data1.json",
    "data/data2.json",
    "data/data3.json"
]}
```

The contents of the data files, whose URLs we must parse from the `datamap.json` resource, look like this:

```
{"fileMetadata":
    {"fileName":"data3",
     "author":"toni"}
}
```

For the sake of simplicity, we will simply assemble the `author` strings into an `Array` and print it. Once we have the array finished, we will have achieved our aim; its journey onwards from here need not concern us.

 We will assume you have set up an Xcode project, and that you can decide yourself where to add the code that follows. Let's agree to add a single call to the `ViewController` class's `viewDidLoad` method, `getAuthors()`, to get things started.

So let's get some code written:

1. Add the following code to your project:

```
let baseURL = "http://grimshaw.de/Mac OS-book/api/"
let datamapPath = "datamap.json"

var authorsArray = [String]()
```

Not much to say here; we are given a base URL for an API to the service we are using, and a path to be appended to the base URL to get to a specific resource, the `datamap.json` file. So our entire data structure is an `Array`.

Now we'll add some helper functions that will provide us with the following functionality:

- A simple HTTP request function
- A function to convert JSON data into a Dictionary
- A function to fetch specific files and convert them, using the preceding functions
- A function to parse the resultant Dictionary for the paths to the data files we need from the server

Let's turn that into code:

2. Add the following utilities code:

```
func simpleRequest(urlString: String,
                   dataHandler:
@escaping (Data?, URLResponse?, Error?) ->Void)
{
  let url = URL(string: urlString)!
  let session = URLSession.shared
  let task = session.dataTask(with: url,
              completionHandler: dataHandler)
  task.resume()
}

func parseJSONData(data: Data) -> [String: AnyObject]?
{
do {

    let json = try JSONSerialization.jsonObject(
       with: data,
       options: .allowFragments) as? [String: AnyObject]

    return json

  } catch {print(#function, error)}

return nil
}
```

3. Add the following code to parse our data files, looking for an `author` object:

```
func parseDataFile(data: Data)
{
```

```
if
  let jsonDict = parseJSONData(data: data),
    let fileMetadata
      = jsonDict["fileMetadata"] as? [String: String],
    let author = fileMetadata["author"]
  {
      print(author)
      authorsArray.append(author)
  }
}
```

Now that we have that in place, we can make a first attempt at using an operation queue and block operation dependencies to process the authorsArray once it has been populated:

4. Add the following function:

```
func parseDataMap(data: Data)
{
if
   let jsonDict = parseJSONData(data: data),
    let paths = jsonDict["paths"] as? [String]
  {
    let opsQueue = OperationQueue()
    let processAuthorsArray = BlockOperation(
      block: { print("authorsArray", authorsArray)
} )

for path in paths
    {
        let op = BlockOperation(
          block:{
            simpleRequest(urlString: baseURL+ path,
            dataHandler: {data, response, error in
                      if
                        let data = data
                      {
                          parseDataFile(data: data)
                      }
            })
        })

    processAuthorsArray.addDependency(op)
    opsQueue.addOperation(op)
  }
  opsQueue.addOperation(processAuthorsArray)
```

```
        }
    }
```

This is similar to what we have seen before; we are simply adding the individual data-fetching ops as dependencies to our `processAuthorsArrayop`.

5. So now add the following code to get the show rolling:

```
func getAuthors()
{
    let dataMapUrlString = baseURL+datamapPath

    simpleRequest(urlString: dataMapUrlString,
                dataHandler: {data, response, error in
    if let data = data {
        parseDataMap(data: data)
                }
    })
}
```

This is the function that we call from the `ViewControllerviewDidLoad` method.

Before you hit the **Run** button, remember you'll need to add `grimshaw.de` to your whitelisted HTTP servers in your `Info.plist` files, as described in `Chapter 14`, *The Benefits of Core Data*.

6. Run the code, and you should see the following log in the debug console:

```
authorsArray: []
chris
alex
toni
```

So we have our `author` names, but look what has happened. The block operations have all fired off their HTTP requests, and now consider their work done; so then the `processAuthorsList` operation is executed, as we have specified with the dependencies.

All this takes place long before the HTTP request responses come back with their data.

It is the `parseDataFile` method that is printing the name to the debug console. Once those calls have all returned, we have our populated `authorsArray` that we can then process. But not before. At the moment, the array is being processed too early.

So we need a way to ensure that we know when all the requests have returned data.

This is where things could start to get messy. We can't simply assume that each operation will be executed; a cancellation could take place. So we can't just keep a count of the number of operations and the number of times `parseDataFile` has been called. And even if we could be certain that an operation won't be canceled (and we can't), we'd still have some very untidy and fragile code.

Wouldn't it be great to have an `Operation` object that didn't report itself as complete until it had a response from its HTTP request? Well, of course, this is feasible. What sort of book would lead you this far and then leave you standing?

Concurrent and non-concurrent operations

Operations come in two flavors, concurrent and non-concurrent. A concurrent operation is, as the name might suggest, inherently asynchronous, and a non-concurrent operation is synchronous.

Since operation queues create threads for all of their operations, whether concurrent or non-concurrent, it is quite usual to fill a queue with non-concurrent operations, since the extra work involved in creating concurrent subclasses of operations is significant, and in this case superfluous. Operation queues turn everything into asynchronous code, to the extent allowed by their dependencies.

The take-home of this is as follows. If you are using queues to execute your operations, you can create non-concurrent operation classes, and they will still be executed by the queue asynchronously.

So, to return to our current conundrum concerning the `authorsArray`, we will create a custom *non-concurrent* subclass of `Operation`.

Defining non-concurrent custom operations

Creating your own non-concurrent (that is synchronous) operation is pretty simple. All you need to do is code your `main` method and respond to cancellation events by reading the `isCancelled` property; the class itself does the rest of the work for you.

Creating one that will wait for the completion of a block of code is only slightly more work. We just leave the code in a `while` loop that checks whether or not the completion block has run:

1. Add the following `SynchronousDataLoadOperation` class to the code:

```
class SynchronousDataLoadOperation: Operation
{
    let urlString: String
    let onLoaded: (Data) -> ()

    init(urlString: String,
        onLoaded:@escaping (Data) -> ())
    {
        self.urlString = urlString
        self.onLoaded = onLoaded
        super.init()
    }

    overridefunc main()
    {
      var isDone = false

      simpleRequest(urlString: urlString,
                dataHandler: {
                    data, response, error in

                    if let data = data
                      {
                         self.onLoaded(data)
                         isDone = true
                      }
                      // else handle error
       })
       while isDone ==false{}
    }
}
```

What we have done here is create a subclass of `Operation` that is initialized with a URL string and a completion block; the overridden `main` method (a quaintly archaic name, don't you think?) makes an HTTP request, using that completion block.

2. Now all we need to do is change our `parseDataMap` method:

```
func parseDataMap(data: Data)
{
 if
    let jsonDict = parseJSONData(data: data),
     let paths = jsonDict["paths"] as? [String]
     {
       let opsQueue = OperationQueue()
       let processAuthorsArray = BlockOperation(
        block: { print(authorsArray)} )

       for path in paths
       {
        let op = SynchronousDataLoadOperation(
           urlString: baseURL+ path,
           onLoaded: parseDataFile)

        processAuthorsArray.addDependency(op)
        opsQueue.addOperation(op)
      }
      opsQueue.addOperation(processAuthorsArray)
   }
}
```

As you can see, the responsibility for dealing with the request's response is now encapsulated in the `SynchronousDataLoadOperation` class itself.

That's the only function that needs changing; everything else stays the same.

3. Run your code. Now the debug console shows us that the `processAuthorsArray` method is not called until the array has finished being populated:

```
alex
chris
toni
["alex", "chris", "toni"]
```

Defining concurrent custom operations

You may find there are occasions in which you want to manage the running of an operation yourself, which will mean not adding it to an operation queue. If that operation is to be synchronous, then there are no problems with that.

But if you want the code to run asynchronously, you have a bit more work to do, in that you must create a concurrent operation.

When doing this, we need to make sure we have a few things covered:

- We need a custom `init` method to set the operation in a known state
- We need to override the main method with our custom code
- We need to ensure that the class complies with KVO, on which the operation framework depends

A concurrent operation will not complete until it issues its `isFinished` notification, thereby allowing it to permit any of its asynchronous tasks to finish.

The system knows that it is a concurrent operation by polling its `isAsynchronous` property, which any custom class must override with `true`.

There are a number of methods and properties that must be overridden, as we will see in a moment. Don't be put off by the amount of code that you need; it's mostly boilerplate, really. We won't put all of this code into one class, as that would lead to an unnecessarily complicated and bloated class:

Let's define first an all-purpose concurrent operation, which we will subclass later, adding the custom `init` and `main` code.

Here is the code for our custom `ConcurrentOperation` class:

```
class ConcurrentOperation: Operation
{
  enum State: String {
   case Ready, Executing, Finished
    var keyPath: String {
     return"is"+rawValue
    }
  }

 var state = State.Ready {
   willSet {
        willChangeValue(forKey: newValue.keyPath)
        willChangeValue(forKey: state.keyPath)
```

```
        }
    didSet {
            didChangeValue(forKey: oldValue.keyPath)
            didChangeValue(forKey: state.keyPath)
        }
    }

    override var isReady: Bool {
        return super.isReady&&state == .Ready
    }
    override var isExecuting: Bool {
        return state == .Executing
    }
    override var isFinished: Bool {
        return state == .Finished
    }
    override var isAsynchronous: Bool {
        return true
    }

    override func start()
    {
            if isCancelled {
            state = .Finished
            return
        }
     main()
     state = .Executing
    }

     override func cancel() {
     state = .Finished
    }
}
```

This class doesn't actually do anything except keep tabs on its own state, make that state available to KVO, and override the start and cancel methods, which up till now have not been visible to us when using the Operation class directly.

The most important thing to notice here is that the main method is overridden, but does nothing except set its state to Executing. When we subclass ConcurrentOperation, we will add the program-specific code here.

We'll do that next, by defining a `JSONDataLoadOperation` that will not mark itself as finished until the results of its HTTP request have been received:

```
class JSONDataLoadOperation: ConcurrentOperation
{
    private var urlString: String
    var onLoaded: (Data) -> ()

    init(urlString: String,
        onLoaded:@escaping (Data) -> ())
    {
        self.urlString = urlString
        self.onLoaded = onLoaded
        super.init()
    }

    overridefunc main()
    {
        simpleRequest(urlString: urlString,
                    dataHandler: {
                    data, response, error in

                    if let data = data
                    {
                        self.onLoaded(data)
                        self.state = .Finished
                    }
                    // else handle error
    })
    }
}
```

All we have done here is to add a `String` property for the URL, and an `onLoaded` closure property of type `(Data) -> ()` that will be called by the `simpleRequest` method, passing its returned data as the single argument.

For the sake of brevity, we have left out the error-handling code, which we wouldn't do in real code.

We can see, then, that although the `ConcurrentOperation` class looks a little complicated, subclassing it for use in our code is actually very simple.

To execute this operation directly, instead of adding it to an operation queue, we call its `start` method. However, it can also be added to a queue, just as we did with the non-concurrent custom operation.

So, for example, to use this code to assemble our `authorsArray`, we can slightly simplify our `parseDataMap` method, as follows:

```
func parseDataMap(data: Data)
{
  if
      let jsonDict = parseJSONData(data: data),
        let paths = jsonDict["paths"] as? [String]
      {
        let opsQueue = OperationQueue()
        let processAuthorsArray = BlockOperation(
        block: { print(authorsArray)} )

      for path in paths
      {
          let op = JSONDataLoadOperation(
            urlString: baseURL+ path,
            onLoaded: parseDataFile)

          processAuthorsArray.addDependency(op)
          opsQueue.addOperation(op)
      }
      opsQueue.addOperation(processAuthorsArray)
    }
}
```

Now that the completion handling code is encapsulated in the operation itself, the `datamap` parsing code is a lot cleaner.

The extent to which it is worth encapsulating code within a custom operation will differ according to the circumstances, of course.

Summary

We have covered some pretty advanced material here, on topics that are widely regarded as considerably more complex than most. Hopefully you are convinced that the `Operation` framework is a powerful yet reasonably straightforward tool to use. The recent changes to Swift serve to underpin the philosophy behind encapsulating thread-based code in objects that can be manipulated in an intuitive and consistent way.

In this chapter, you have learned the following:

- How to use the `Operation` framework to simplify concurrent programming
- How to use the `Operation` framework to manage asynchronous programming tasks
- How to create your own solutions by subclassing the `Operation` class
- The differences between multithreading and multiprocessing
- The relationships between operations, code blocks, and operation queues

In the next chapter, we will demystify debugging, and look at some advance debugging techniques and tools that are at our disposal, making coding a considerably more pleasant activity than it might otherwise have been.

17
Understanding Xcodes Debugging Tools

Debugging your code is a fact of life. No matter how good we get, how experienced we are, how closely we have followed best practices, stuck to the spec, and thoroughly planned our code, we still frequently come up against occasions when the app just isn't doing what it should.

And at first glance, we don't know why.

Code shouldn't get messy, but it often does. Classes shouldn't become bloated, but some of them inevitably do. And the big picture should always be clear and illuminated by divine light, but sometimes it's just not. And so we have to find a way to move through the maze without getting lost and disheartened, while tracking down that errant, explicitly unwrapped optional.

Now, one chapter in one book (not even this one) is not going to be able to provide a magical spell to make clarity wash over you, leaving you enlightened and emboldened, ready to type in the solution to any and all bugs in your code. What this chapter does set out to do is to provide you with a guide to some of the more important of the many tools that Xcode provides, to make searching for bugs easier and quicker. Much of what we will look at here is how to help ourselves understand what our code is doing, when it's not doing what we want it to do. Everything we cover in this chapter will provide a huge amount of return on the time you invest in it. Debugging well will save you heaps of time, and spare you a lot of frustration.

In this chapter you will learn about the following:

- The debugging tools that Xcode provides
- Differentiating Target and Debugger output
- The different breakpoint types and their capabilities
- Customizing breakpoint behavior
- Launching scripts with a breakpoint
- Line-by-line debugging and stepping through code

Checking out Xcode's debugging tools

Xcode has come a long way since its modest beginnings, and offers us a comprehensive suite of features and applications designed to make debugging code as painless as possible. All of the tools and techniques we will cover in this chapter are available without leaving Xcode, although some of the tools we will discuss are also available on the command--line, but we'll cover that in a later chapter.

We will also leave utility applications such as Instruments for later.

For now, it's Xcode all the way.

Debug area

Let's start with using the so-called debug area to the fullest.

This is the area of the Xcode window that consists of the **debug console**, and the **variables view**. We have used the console extensively throughout this book, but there are many tricks left that we have not yet uncovered. However, we will start with the variables view, which offers us a lot more help in debugging our code than you might be aware of.

To show and hide the debug area, type *Command + Shift + Y*.

Variables view

There is no keyboard shortcut to show and hide the variables view within the debug area (as there is for the console), so if it's not showing, click on the left disclosure button in the bottom--right corner of the window, next to the trash icon:

First we're going to need an app to test. We will create a command--line tool (meaning simply a program that has no UI), that will allow us to focus on the features we are looking at, without having to whip up a full app.

Yes, a full app doesn't take much work, we can use the Xcode template and that will be fine. In fact, later in this chapter, we will. But it's a good idea first to become comfortable with the idea of prototyping some app classes and methods by using the command--line tool template.

This is also an excellent but gentle introduction to the command--line.

1. To begin with, create a command--line tool project (*Command + Shift + N* | **Mac OS Command Line Tool**).

2. Add the following code after the `import` statement:

```
var varString = "Here we go"

class MyClass
{
    var integerProperty = 777
}

var myClass = MyClass()

print ("Bye")
```

At the moment, we are just creating a class with a property, and adding a `print` statement where we can pause the program by setting a breakpoint, thus setting the debug machinery in motion.

3. Set a breakpoint on the last line of the code.
4. Now hit **Run.** Xcode will launch the program and pause the code at the last line, as we would expect, as in the following screenshot:

Hmm, not much to see. We would expect the console to be empty (apart from the **(lldb)** prompt, more of which later), but you might be surprised to see nothing at all in the variables view. This is because the variables view defaults to showing only the variables that are in scope at the point at which the code is suspended.

Select **All** instead of **Auto** from the menu at the bottom of the variables view, and now you can see all variables in the app, including global variables such as varString, in the following example:

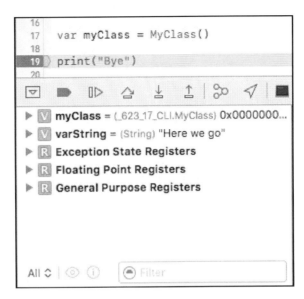

However, as our example program gets larger, this list will quickly get unwieldy. This was just to demonstrate the view's scoping settings, so set the scope back to **Auto**, and set a breakpoint within the MyClass brackets, at the integerProperty variable. If you run the code again, you'll now see self listed in the variables view.

Select self in the variables view.

Hit the right-arrow (or click the disclosure triangle if you prefer) to reveal the variables that are in scope. Later on, when we have more to see in the variables view, you'll find that navigating it with the arrow keys, combined with a couple of other tricks, makes getting the information you need from this view very fast.

If you right-click on anything listed in the variables view, you'll see a contextual menu containing a shortcut to many of the techniques we will discuss throughout this chapter and the next.

Also, note that the list comes with a **Filter** field that will save you a ton of work, once this view starts to fill up with scores of variables. True, it's not much use at the moment, since we only have one variable.

Don't underestimate how helpful these filters can be. They reduce brain-clutter, which is a valuable aid in itself, and that in turn also encourages more frequent use of these tools, leading to a reduction in adding `print` statements, rerunning your code, and so on.

Clicking on the info icon to the right of the scope menu (which should now be set back to **Auto**) prints details of the selection to the console without having to disclose all of its contents in the menu itself, which is another feature we will be glad of as the view becomes more heavily populated. This is a good way to quickly print the contents of an `Array` object, for example, to the console.

With `self` selected in the variables view, clicking on the info icon prints something like this to the console:

```
Printing description of self:
<MyClass: 0x100a027b0>
```

Not the most informative description we could wish for.

If our class is a subclass of `NSObject`, we can add more info to it. To do this with our class, we need to make two changes:

- Declare our class to be a subclass of `NSObject`
- Override the `NSObject debugDescription` variable

Replace the `MyClass` implementation with the following code:

```
class MyClass: NSObject
{
  var integerProperty = 777

  overridevar debugDescription: String {
      return "This is the class debugDescription"
  }
}
```

Now, when you run the program again and select `myClass` in the variables view, pressing the info button will print the following to the console:

```
Printing description of myClass:
This is the class debugDescription
(lldb)
```

There is also another way to make information about your classes available to the debugger; using the Quicklook feature.

Using Quicklook

With `self` selected, click on the little eye icon to the left of the info icon, or hit the spacebar, to see more information about the selection, as illustrated in the following screenshot:

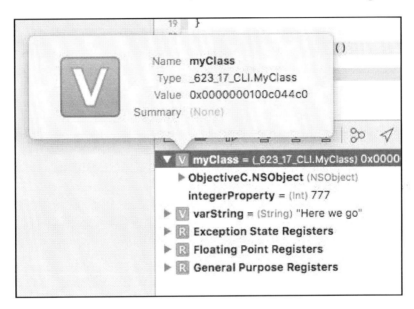

We'll now add a method to our class that will enable us to present a string of any data we wish when Quicklook is activated.

Add the following method to the `MyClass` class:

```
func debugQuickLookObject() -> AnyObject
  {
    let info =  "This is my class, its intProp value is
               \(integerProperty)"asAnyObject
    return info
  }
```

This produces a differently formatted description:

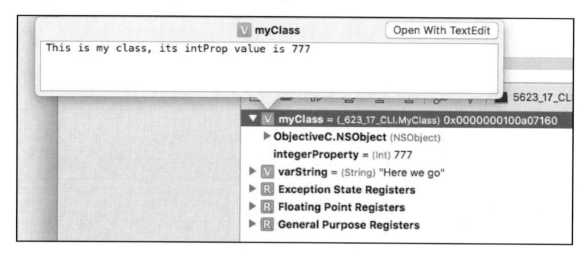

This is good to know when our class is an NSObject subclass. What about our classes which do not subclass NSObject?

If we remove :NSObject from our class declaration (and the debugDescription method), and run the program again, we get the standard Quicklook summary:

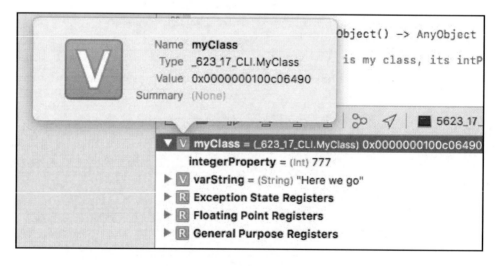

Most Cocoa classes produce this kind of summary. Later on, we will see how to make printing a description of a class to the console much more informative.

Console view

We're going to be doing a lot of work in the console in this chapter, so let's see what it offers us in terms of workflow.

If it is not visible, you can show the console within the debug area with the *Command + Shift + C* shortcut.

Firstly, it has the same **Filter** as the variable view. There is simply no better way to sift through hundreds of lines of debug output than to use this filter to get to what you need.

You can clear the console by clicking on the dustbin icon, or by typing *Command + K*.

By default, the console shows **All Output**, but you can select either **Debugger Output** or **Target Output** to restrict what is shown. Let's see this in action:

1. Remove or disable any breakpoints that you have set.
2. Add the following print statement to the code, and set a breakpoint at that line:

```
28   var myClass = MyClass()
29   print("This is Target Output")
30   |
31   print("Bye")
32
```

3. Right-click on the breakpoint, and select **Edit Breakpoint...**.
4. Tick the **Automatically continue after evaluating actions** box.
5. Select **Log Message** from the **Action** menu, and enter `"This is Debugger Output"`.
6. Run the program.

This produces console output similar to the following:

```
This is Debugger Output
This is Target Output
(lldb) |
```

Now select **Target Output** or **Debugger Output** from the output menu, and you'll see the appropriate line disappear.

Do you notice the difference in font and color between the two lines of output?

 You can change the font for the debugger output (and any other output) by selecting **Preferences | Fonts & Colors**, and selecting the **Console** tab from that screen. Change **Debugger Console Output**. This is a really helpful feature, allowing you to see at a glance the source of a given line of console output.

Debugging in the navigator area

You are already familiar with most of the tabs of the navigation area, and in this chapter we will concentrate on the three that are of use to us when debugging our code. These are:

- The debug navigator (type *Command + 6*)
- The breakpoint navigator (type *Command + 7*)
- The report navigator (type *Command + 8*)

We will take a brief tour of the navigator panes before we get to some serious breakpoint customization and other topics, starting with the tab that you have probably experienced the most, the debug navigator.

Debug navigator

By default, Xcode shows you the debug navigator when your programs crash. This probably isn't your favorite screen, am I right?

So let's see how we can make the best use of this screen and turn it into one of our strongest assets, instead of being merely a bringer of bad news. There is a lot of helpful information available from this tab, beyond a long list of seemingly arcane thread information.

To see this, set a breakpoint at some point in the code, it doesn't matter much where at this point, and run the program until it halts. The navigator pane will look like this:

We're not going to delve into threads here. That is most certainly useful information, and we will get to it in time, but at the moment we will look around at what else this pane provides.

The project I created to run this code was called rather unimaginatively 5623_16_CLI, and that is the name displayed at the top of the tab. To the right of that are two circular icons, which we will investigate next.

Hiding and showing additional information

On the left is the **Hide Debug Gauges** button, which explains the otherwise completely unrecognizable icon. By default, it is turned on, showing you the additional information that is available from this pane (**CPU**, **Memory**, and the rest), as can be seen in the preceding screenshot.

Let's look more closely at the **Network** entry as an example.

Add the following code to main.swift:

```
func googleRequest() ->URLSessionDataTask
{
  let mySession = URLSession.shared
  let request = URL(string: "http://google.com")!
  let task = mySession.dataTask(with: request,
  completionHandler:
  {
```

```
      data, response, error in
      print(response)
   })
   return task
}

googleRequest().resume()

while true {

}
```

This code is easy enough to understand; it will simply give us something to see on the **Network** screen. However, we also need to include the `while true` loop, to keep the program ticking over, waiting for the response from the HTTP request, instead of exiting (remember, this is a command--line program).

Now run the program and select the **Network** screen, to see the following:

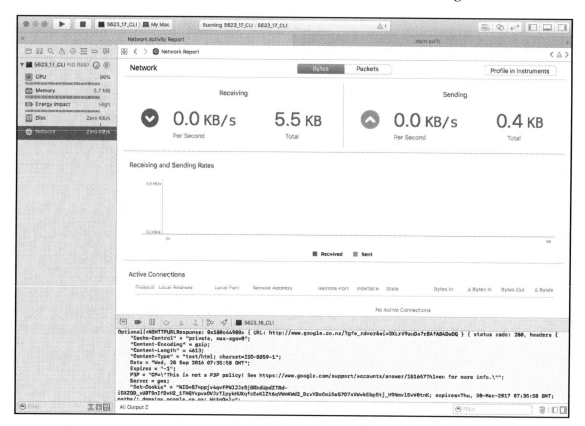

You may notice that the **CPU** and other screens are also vying for your attention with their animated blue mini bar charts, so check those out while you're here.

Note the **Profile in Instruments** button; we'll meet the Instruments app in a later chapter.

Delete the HTTP code you added previously, including the `while` loop.

Changing the process view

To the right of the gauge button is the drop-down menu that will allow you to access different views of the running processes:

 In a Mac OS app, you will also be able to select a hierarchical view of the UI elements of your app from this list.

Breakpoint navigator

The breakpoint navigator is something you're also doubtlessly familiar with, so here again we are just taking a look over what it offers us before we delve into how we best put it to effective use.

The breakpoint navigator has its own **Filter** field, which is a great aid for enabling or disabling a large group of breakpoints. Don't miss the small ticked breakpoint icon at the right-hand end of the field, which will hide all disabled breakpoints with one mouse click.

In this navigation pane, you can right-click any breakpoint to access a contextual menu with the following features:

- You can choose **Enable Breakpoint**, **Disable Breakpoint**, or **DeleteBreakpoint**, which need no further explanation here
- You can choose **Move Breakpoint To...**, with which you can move a breakpoint into the **User** group of breakpoints, which is available from all of your Xcode projects (see the *Symbolic breakpoints* section for suitable candidates), or out of that group and back into the project's own breakpoint group.

- You can choose **Share Breakpoint**, which will add the breakpoint to version control, and will be committed along with other code changes; in this way, other developers working on the same branch of the repository will see that breakpoint.
- You can choose **Edit Breakpoint...**, which is covered in detail later.

Once we have looked into just how powerful, flexible, and time-saving breakpoints can be, you'll want to have a good grasp of everything in this navigation pane.

Report navigator

The report navigator generally receives very little attention, and yet it is an invaluable tool in comparing console logs from different builds (that is run sessions) of the program.

There are two types of entry in the list that it displays:

- Select **Debug** to see logged console entries from every build of the program since the Xcode app was launched.
- Select **Build** to see a list of warnings and errors produced by any particular build. Here you can save a warnings and errors report to disk as an `.rtf` file. Build issues can be filtered.

Leveraging breakpoints

Breakpoints are a lot more powerful than one may suspect. Breakpoints don't need to even interrupt the execution of the program (or brake it, but then they'd be called brake-points).

Rather, they are instructions to Xcode (and the OS beyond) as to what to do when the program's execution reaches a certain point; these are instructions that can be a simple as pausing the program, right up to executing bash and Python scripts and whatever other actions we may choose to attach to them.

One great advantage of breakpoints in Xcode is that they are local to the user; they can do many things that code can do, without being part of the program, and thus they are suitable for all manner of tasks that don't need to ship with an app, or be included for other developers working on the same code.

Logging, for example, can be a real pain when it's somebody else's mountain of console logs you are looking at, sometimes stuff that was added in a debug session and never removed, and the like. By using breakpoints to log to the console, we keep it free from our own personal clutter, and other devs are free to add *their* own logs and so on.

Different types of breakpoint

There are, in fact, several different types of breakpoint, in addition to the type that is created by clicking in the breakpoint gutter on the left of the code editor window. We will spend most of our time in this chapter with those standard breakpoints, as we discover just how powerful they are, but before we do let's take a look at those other specialized breakpoint types.

Click the + button in the bottom left corner of the breakpoints navigator to see a list of possible breakpoint types you can create.

Swift error breakpoints

We can create and customize a breakpoint that will trigger when any or all `Error` types are thrown in the code. Let's use this in our project:

1. Select **Swift Error Breakpoint** from that list.
2. Right-click on the new symbolic breakpoint in the breakpoint navigator, and select **Edit Breakpoint...**.
3. Set **Type** to **MyError**.
4. Set **Action** to **Log Message**, using the text `MyError.general was thrown`.
5. Add the following code to `main.swift`:

```
enum MyError: Error {
case general
  case other
}
enum MyOtherError: Error {
    case other
}
func throwAnError() throws ->Bool {
    throw(MyError.general)
}
func throwAnotherError() throws ->Bool {
    throw(MyOtherError.other)
}
```

```
let a = try? throwAnError()
let b = try? throwAnotherError()
```

Having declared two error types, and two functions, each of which throws one of those error types, we call both functions, using `try?` so that we don't need to add any `catch` code, just for the sake of brevity.

6. Run the code again.

You'll see that only the `MyError` type has been logged, as we specified in the breakpoint edit window.

Symbolic breakpoints

The next type of breakpoint, symbolic breakpoints, is triggered wherever the symbol specified in the breakpoint is detected in the code. Some caution is advised here, since some symbols are found all over the place. View, for example, occurs so often in both our own code and in the framework code that it is of very limited value as the symbol for a symbolic breakpoint.

To illustrate what symbolic breakpoints can do for us, we will leave our command--line tool and create a new project targeted at Mac OS, where we can access the many Cocoa frameworks typical of a Mac OS app, without needing to write much code.

 Don't trash the command--line program we've been using until now, as we'll be returning to it in the next chapter.

Let's get it going:

1. Create a new **Mac OS** project.
2. Go to the breakpoint navigation pane (*Command + 7*, in case it slipped your mind).
3. Click on **+** to get the contextual list of possible breakpoint types, and select **Symbolic Breakpoint**.
4. Right-click the breakpoint and choose **Edit Breakpoint....**
5. Set the **Symbol** to **viewDidLoad**.

6. Set the **Action** to **Log Message**, with the following text:

```
viewDidLoad was executed
```

7. You might as well tick **Automatically continue...**, since we won't need to examine the code that hits the breakpoint.
8. Run the code.

And now a couple of unusual things occur:

Firstly, the console shows us that three methods that include `viewDidLoad` in their names have been triggered. Yep, it's not just your code that's running, but a whole load of framework stuff too.

Secondly, the breakpoint in the breakpoint navigator has expanded to a whole list of breakpoints, as can be seen here:

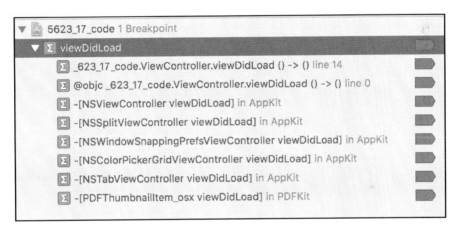

And now you can see why the following text appeared multiple times in the console:

```
viewDidLoad was executed
```

There are many methods that also include that symbol, dotted around the frameworks. This alone is a great way to work out what methods are present in frameworks and libraries to which you don't have access. If you look again, you'll see that each breakpoint from a framework *has been listed with the name of the framework it has been found in*, in this case `AppKit` and `PDFKit`.

Moreover, you can now enable and disable, on an individual basis, the various breakpoints that share the `viewDidLoad` symbol.

Symbolic links are an essential part of your logging and trouble shooting kit. It is difficult to read more than a dozen answers on Stack Overflow without coming across at least one recommendation to employ symbolic breakpoints (exceeded only by advice to delete the Derived Data folder).

Try it again, this time using *view* as the specified symbol. Long list, huh?

Other breakpoint types

Open GL, Exception, and Test Failure breakpoints are not covered here, but the reader is encouraged to remember that they are there (once this book has been read, absorbed, and hopefully lent to the next guy).

Adding and removing breakpoints

You already know that you can add and delete standard breakpoints in the gutter.

You can also add or remove breakpoints at whichever line the cursor is on in the code editor window, by typing *Command* + \. Backslash, not forward slash.

All these actions can also be performed with a right-click on the breakpoint in the breakpoint navigator. One other useful thing you can do here is select **Move Breakpoint To...**, which will allow you to move the breakpoint to the User group (or back out of it).

Editing breakpoints

Okay, we've kept you waiting long enough. This is where breakpoints get really interesting. If you want something with which to impress the other geeks at the next *Mac OSDev Meetup Group*, there's a ton of it coming up. Never yet received an e-mail from your own code? The wait is nearly over.

When first editing the breakpoint with a right-click, we are presented with a modest looking window, with four fields:

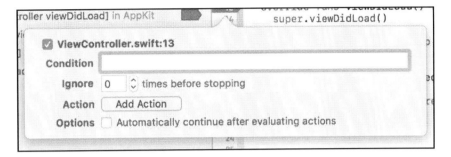

Those four fields are as follows:

- **Condition**: Any Boolean expression
- **Ignore**: The number of times to hit a breakpoint before triggering it
- **Action**: One or more of a huge range of actions that are available
- **Options**: This should be labeled **Option**, there being only one

We will take a look at each one in more detail, adding some code to check it out with.

Conditions

We will write a small loop to test setting a breakpoint condition:

1. Add the following code to the new project's `ViewController` class:

```
func testBreakpoints()
    {
var total = 0

for i in 0..<5
    {
        total += 1
    }
    }
```

2. Call that method from the `viewDidLoad` method:

```
override func viewDidLoad()
  {
      super.viewDidLoad()

      testBreakpoints()
  }
```

3. Now place a breakpoint at this line:

```
total += 1
```

4. In the breakpoint edit window, set the **Condition** to:

```
total < 3
```

5. Set the **Action** to **Log Message**, something like:

```
Incrementing total, %H
```

6. Set it to automatically continue after evaluation.

Now when you run the code, you'll get this:

```
Incrementing total, 1
Incrementing total, 2
Incrementing total, 3
```

Any Boolean expression in the **Condition** field will do. Given that logs in the console quickly become so numerous that finding anything becomes a challenge, it is often worth reserving the breakpoint's logging activity for occasions when you actually need to know what's in the log.

When we get to the **Action** field, we'll see that there are many more interesting things we can do in addition to logging to the console.

Ignore

We can also set the breakpoint to trigger only after it has been hit a specified number of times. This is useful when you have code that should only run once, for example, but that you suspect may be being called more than that.

Set the previous breakpoint **Ignore** value to **2**, and run the code again:

```
Incrementing total, 3
```

We see here that the breakpoint still records the correct number of hits, even though it has been instructed to ignore the first two.

Adding an action to a breakpoint

Now that we can control when a breakpoint does or does not trigger an action, and whether code execution should continue after the breakpoint has evaluated its actions, it's time to put those actions to the test.

Log message

This is the action probably used most of all, since it provides a lightweight and unobtrusive alternative to `print` statements and the like. Lightweight because we don't need to recompile the code to reflect any changes that we make whilst running the program, as we would with `print`, and unobtrusive because only we will see that message; other devs will not (unless we specifically want them to).

And don't forget the font trick. These messages will be easier to trace through a barrage of console logs if they are in a different color and/or font.

Adding **%B** will add the function name to the message, and **%H**, as we have seen already, will add the hit count, which may be crucial to some debug sessions.

Any valid expression may be entered between two @ characters.

Change the breakpoint to read as follows:

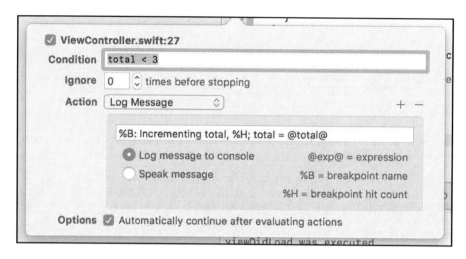

Note that we have set **Ignore** back to **0**.

Run the code again, and the results will look like this:

```
testBreakpoints(): Incrementing total, 1; total = 0
testBreakpoints(): Incrementing total, 2; total = 1
testBreakpoints(): Incrementing total, 3; total = 2
```

So, with very little effort, we can now record the following information in the console:

- The function in which the breakpoint has been hit
- A custom string message
- The total number of hits for that breakpoint
- A custom expression result

All of which constitutes pretty thorough logging, and it can be changed with no recompilation.

Speech!

Just for the sake of it, select the **Speak Message** option, instead of **Log Message to Console**.

Yes, your favorite Mac OS voice can interpret those % signs too! If that seems a bit gimmicky, consider how well it has caught your attention. If your network connection is a bit dodgy, wouldn't you like it to be drawn to your attention whenever it's down? I find this sort of warning well suited to those *should-never-happen* situations.

Debugger Command

The **Debugger Command** option in the **Action** menu adds any command to the breakpoint that you could type into the LLDB debug console (see the following chapter).

Here's an example:

1. Firstly, add the following code to the `testBreakpoints` method:

```
let s = "Doug"
let i = 42
let b = true

var option = "Debugger Command"
```

2. Now set a breakpoint at the line `var option = "Debugger Command"`.

3. Set the values as follows:

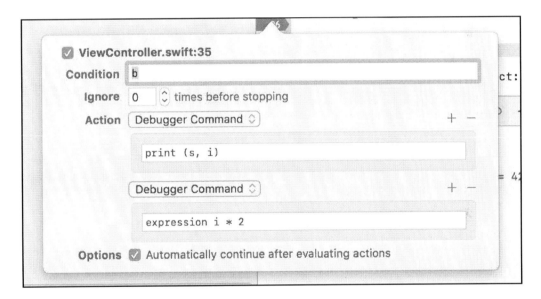

So there are a few points here worthy of note:

We have used the expression b as the **Condition** property of the breakpoint. Since b implies the compiler is of type `Bool`, it is a valid expression for this field.

We have used brackets to make two variables, s and i, into a tuple, which `print` will accept as an argument.

Remember, this is a debugger command, and so it is LLDB's `print` command, not a Swift `print` function.

For the sake of demonstration, we have chosen a simple debugger command, `print`. After we have covered LLDB in more detail in the next chapter, you'll find plenty more to be cooking up here.

The output to the console will look as follows:

```
(String, Int) $R0 = (0 = "Doug", 1 = 42)
(Int) $R1 = 84
```

Even this simple debugger command can prove enormously useful when tracking down bugs.

Shell Command

The **Shell Command** action will, as the name implies, run a command just as if you had entered it into the command--line, using the Terminal.

Add the following code to the `testBreakpoints` method:

```
option = "Shell Command"
```

Set a new breakpoint at that line and select **Shell Command** from its **Action** menu.

You can either choose a script from disk, or enter the command directly. In either case, the arguments to the command are entered separately on the second line. Try this command:

```
whoami
```

This will print your Mac OS user name to the console. And anything that works in a shell script is valid here.

This feature is perhaps of more use when building projects and such, rather than as an aid in debugging, but if you're comfortable with bash scripting, you may find this a convenient way to deal with error occurrences.

AppleScript

The same can be said for the **Action** menu option: **AppleScript**.

Despite the long--predicted demise of AppleScript, it is still alive and kicking. And despite its somewhat ungeeky syntax, we should remember that AppleScript reaches deep into the Mac OS events frameworks and is a perfectly good way to extend Xcode instructions beyond the app itself.

1. Add the following line of code to the project:

```
option = "AppleScript alert"
```

2. Set a new breakpoint at that line and select **AppleScript** from its **Action** menu.

3. Add the script into the text field provided as follows:

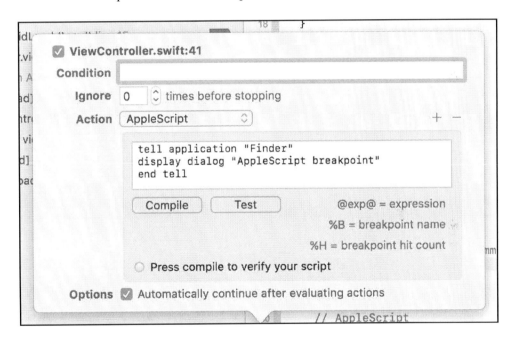

Very conveniently, we have two buttons to check the code syntax and test the script itself.

4. Run the program and you will be presented with a **Finder** dialog box:

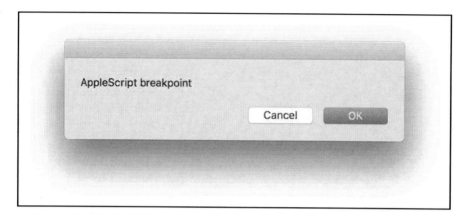

You may find this useful, because it not only draws your attention to whatever the breakpoint has been set to trigger on, but it also blocks subsequent code from executing until you have hit the **OK** button.

We can also get a little more ambitious with these actions

Add the following line of code to the `testBreakpoints` method:

```
option = "AppleScript mail"
```

Set a new breakpoint at that line and select **AppleScript** from its **Action** menu.

Now add the following AppleScript:

```
set recipientName to "Your Name"
set recipientAddress to "you@yourMailAddress.com"
set theSubject to "AppleScript Automated Email"
set theContent to "This email was created and sent using AppleScript!"

tell application "Mail"
set theMessage to make new outgoing message with properties
{subject:theSubject, content:theContent, visible:true}

tell theMessage
make new to recipient with properties {name:recipientName,
```

```
address:recipientAddress}

send

end tell
end tell
```

 Don't forget to make it your e-mail address, or you won't notice very much happening.

Run the program again, and there you have it: Your first mail from your own code.

This rather extreme example illustrates just how far you can go with **Shell Command** and **AppleScript** actions.

Sounds

We covered the use of sounds back in Chapter 3, *Checking Out the Power of Xcode*.

Multiple actions

Any breakpoint can be allocated any mix of actions that you desire. There's probably some practical limit (if you find it, do let me know) but to all practical intents and purposes, you can do whatever you want here.

Breakpoint control flow

Once we have hit a breakpoint and halted on it, we have a fine-tuned control above how we proceed through the code's execution from that point on, on a line-by-line basis.

We have already seen a couple of ways to specify what happens when a breakpoint has been hit:

- Setting the **Ignore** value
- Ticking the **Automatically continue** box

We will now look closely at the control provided to us by the compiler.

Debugger control

We can use the buttons illustrated here:

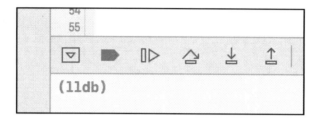

Alternatively, we can enter commands directly into the console, which we will cover in the next chapter.

From left to right, the controls do the following:

Close

The shortcut for this is *Control + shift + Y*.

This just hides the debug area (but does not clear the console).

Enable

The shortcut for this is *Control + Y*.

This applies to all active breakpoints. Toggling it on and off does not enable any previously disabled breakpoints.

Continue

Use this command to continue execution of the code, effectively ending the debug session (until a new breakpoint is reached).

Step over

This will advance execution of the code by one line, unless used at a function call, in which case it will execute that function as an opaque box and halt at the line after that function returns. So basically, if you are moving through code line-by-line, you'll use this to avoid stepping through the function code, treating functions as if they were single lines of code.

> The term *step over* may seem to imply that the line of code is not executed, so just to be explicit: the line of code, or the function, *does* get executed.

Step into

This will advance execution of the code by one line and, when used at a function call, it will step *into* that function.

> Step over and step into are only different at a function call, otherwise they behave the same.

Step out

If you step into a function, but then decide that you would like to leave that function, as if you had used the step-over command, then this is the command you need.

Again, it doesn't prevent that function from being executed, it just takes you to the line of code after which the function returns.

Trying them out

We will now add a function to the `ViewController` class, which we can use to very easily follow what the various step functions actually do:

1. Add the following code to `ViewController`:

```
func testStepCommands()
  {
  func printObservation()
    {
      print("Today you are you!")
```

```
        print("That is truer than true!")
        print("There is no one alive who is you-er than you!")
    }

    func printPrediction()
    {
        print("And will you succeed?")
        print("Yes you will indeed!")
        print("98 and 3/4 percent guaranteed.")
    }

    printObservation()
    printPrediction()
    }
```

2. Now add the following line to the `viewDidLoad` method:

```
override func viewDidLoad()
    {
        super.viewDidLoad()

//      testBreakpoints()
        testStepCommands()
    }
```

   Just to clear things up, we have commented out the `testBreakpoints` method. This stuff can make you a little crazy after a while.

3. Now set a breakpoint at each of the `printObservation` and `printPrediction` function calls, and set breakpoints in the first line of code of each of those two functions, as illustrated in the following screenshot:

```
46
47    func testStepCommands()
48    {
49      func printObservation()
50      {
51        print("Today you are you!")
52        print("That is truer than true!")
53        print("There is no one alive who is you-er than you!")
54      }
55
56      func printPrediction()
57      {
58        print("And will you succeed?")
59        print("Yes you will indeed!")
60        print("98 and 3/4 percent guaranteed.")
61      }
62
63      printObservation()
64      printPrediction()
65    }
66
```

Have a good play around with this setup, and get a good feel for what the various buttons do.

One thing that you may not expect is that `step-over` will only step over a function that contains no breakpoints. But that's the way it is.

Summary

Once these debugging tools have become familiar to you, you'll find that debugging becomes progressively a less arduous and unwelcome part of programming, and instead starts to feel as productive and creative as the rest of the development process.

And that has to be good news, because one thing will never change: We will always need to debug our code. Embrace debugging, we're stuck with it.

In this chapter, you learned the following:

- Xcode's debugging features
- Inspecting variable properties
- The tools in the debug navigator panes
- Using the right type of breakpoint
- Customized breakpoints
- Using breakpoints with shell scripts and AppleScript
- Control flow in the debugger

In the next chapter, we will build on this knowledge as we go more deeply into the LLDB console, and then move from the Xcode app itself into the command--line, where we will use both LLDB and other tools.

18
LLDB and the Command Line

In this chapter, we're going to shift up a gear and reach deep into the LLDB environment, the debugging tool integrated into Xcode, both in Xcode itself and as a standalone process. Some of this stuff may look a little esoteric at first glance, but rest assured, it is anything but.

 LLDB stands for Low Level Debugger

Working professionally as a developer means being comfortable with the command line, being aware of what is available in LLDB, and having at least a working knowledge of the scripting languages that are a part of developing software on almost all platforms.

It's also really, really cool. Once you have a bit of momentum behind you, you'll wonder how you ever lived without these tools, which allow you to automate, customize, and get right into the inner workings of your code.

In this chapter, you will learn about the following:

- What LLDB does
- Running code from within LLDB
- Creating and manipulating breakpoints and watchpoints
- How to customize LLDB to your requirements
- How to run the Swift REPL from within LLDB
- How to run a Python REPL within LLDB

Perhaps more than any other chapter, this one will require a lot of hands-on experimentation to familiarize yourself with what is presented here. So, take this one slowly, and try out as much as you can.

Once you have absorbed this stuff, you'll never be the same developer again.

LLDB

So, what is this LLDB? Why do we see it at the console whenever we hit a breakpoint (or a bug)? This is the LLDB prompt:

```
(lldb)
```

Well, **LLDB** stands for **low level debugger**, and it does what it says it does. It actually does a bit more than that, which we'll get to very soon. LLDB makes use of several components from the LLVM project, which is basically a compiler, parser, and loads of other stuff that we need (or Xcode needs) to build a program. However, as interesting as that is to explore it is beyond the scope of this book, and we will focus entirely on the debugger in this chapter.

LLDB is not only available in the debug area console of Xcode, where we have made frequent use of it already, it can also be used at the command line, which we will also cover in this chapter.

The LLDB interface is a very powerful tool; you can print to it from your code, you can interact with it, configure it to your requirements, change settings on--the--fly, and access both the Swift REPL and the Unix system that underlies macOS, without having to terminate a session.

Using LLDB

Returning to the code we wrote in the last chapter, set a breakpoint at this line of code:

```
printObservation()
```

Once execution has stopped at that breakpoint, type the following into the console:

```
(lldb) bt
```

This will produce a list of all the stack frames on the current thread that lead up to the line of code where execution was halted by the breakpoint: bt stands for backtrace. The output will look like this:

```
(lldb) bt
* thread #1: tid = 0x105a7d, 0x000000010000177c
5623_18_code`ViewController.testStepCommands(self=0x00006080000c2220) -
> () + 12 at ViewController.swift:62, queue = 'com.apple.main-thread', stop
reason = breakpoint 3.1
```

```
    * frame #0: 0x000000010000177c
5623_18_code`ViewController.testStepCommands(self=0x00006080000c2220) -
> () + 12 at ViewController.swift:62
    frame #1: 0x00000001000014b2
5623_18_code`ViewController.viewDidLoad(self=0x00006080000c2220) -
> () + 98 at ViewController.swift:17

... lots more edited out

    frame #16: 0x00007fffbfafc255 libdyld.dylib`start + 1
(lldb)
```

There is no need to understand all of this immediately, but looking through it you will probably recognize the symbols at the top of the stack, since they are the methods that you have coded yourself. Everything leading up to that is provided by the frameworks you use. In this case, we see that most of the work is being done by AppKit, with a modest contribution from our own code (sorry, the truth can hurt at times).

Frame0 is the last frame that was put on the stack. Above that, we see some information about the current thread, its number and thread ID (tid), and so on, as well as the line of code at which execution has been halted, and even the reason for doing so. In this case, we have hit breakpoint 3.1. Remember when the viewDidLoad symbolic breakpoint produced several breakpoints? That's what the number behind the decimal point means, and breakpoint 3 only occurs once, hence there can only be a 3.1.

In large projects, this is an excellent way to answer the perennial question, *how did the code get here?*

Debugging line-by-line

Once we have halted the program at a breakpoint, we can take over control of its further execution:

Continue

The following commands are available to continue execution of the code (up until any subsequent breakpoints):

```
(lldb) continue
(lldb) c
(lldb) thread continue
```

They are all equivalents.

Step over

The following commands are equivalent to clicking on the step-over button:

```
(lldb) next
(lldb) n
(lldb) thread step-over
```

Step into

The following commands are equivalent to clicking on the step-into button:

```
(lldb) step
(lldb) s
(lldb) thread step-in
```

This will advance execution of the code by one line; when used at a function call, it will step into the function.

> The step-over and step-in commands are only different at a function call, otherwise they behave the same.

Step out

The following commands are equivalent to clicking on the step-out button:

```
(lldb) finish
(lldb) f
(lldb) thread step-out
```

Trying it out

Just as you did with the graphical UI in the last chapter, spend some time getting used to stepping through the code using these commands. You'll find that, very quickly, your muscle memory starts to do most of the work for you, freeing up some mental capacity for actually handling whatever bugs you may be dealing with.

If you use one of the `step-over` or `step-into` commands (`n` and `s` are the most convenient), you can hit *return* again to repeat that command, which is a more comfortable way of repeatedly stepping through a debug session.

Enable

The following commands are available for enabling and disabling breakpoints:

```
br disable
br enable
```

As was the case with the graphic controls we looked at in the last chapter, enabling breakpoints *all at once* does not re-enable those that were disabled individually.

Printing in LLDB

LLDB provides three convenient commands to print details of an object to the console:

- The `p` or `print` command gives us a standard description of the object
- The `po` command (meaning print object) gives us either a standard description, or a custom description if we have implemented one
- The `frame variable` command prints the same as `print`, but does so without executing any code, thus avoiding the danger of side--effects

Preparing classes for LLDB descriptions

We can provide custom classes with any description we wish, and have it print with the `po` command, by declaring the class to conform to the `CustomDebugStringConvertible` protocol and then implementing its required variable `debugDescription`.

1. Let's create a Report class, which has a few properties of mixed types, and a `debugDescription` variable:

```
class Report: CustomDebugStringConvertible
{
   var title:    String?
   var date:     Date?
   var approved: Bool?
```

```
    var debugDescription: String {
      return "("Report")n(title)n(date)n(approved)"
    }
  }
```

2. Now create an instance of the class, and one by one populate the optional properties:

```
let report = Report()

report.title = "Weekly Summary"
report.date = Date()
report.approved = true
```

3. Set a breakpoint at the first of those lines, where the report instance is declared.

4. Now type po into the LLDB console. You'll get <uninitialized> in the console.

5. Type s into the console, to step through the code. Keep your eye on the green tinted position pointer in the breakpoint gutter, as it will show you which lines of code are being executed during the initialization of a Report instance.

6. Type s (or *return*) another five times until the initialization is complete, and then type po again. At this point we have the report variable initialized, with its properties still set to nil.

```
(lldb) po report
<uninitialized>
(lldb) s
(lldb) s
(lldb) s
(lldb) s
(lldb) s
(lldb) po report
 <uninitialized>
(lldb) s
(lldb) po report
Report

nil
nil
nil
```

7. Continue stepping through the code, following this session:

```
(lldb) s
(lldb) s
(lldb) s
(lldb) po report
Report
Optional("Weekly Summary")
nil
nil
etc...
```

As you step through the code, you can see the `report` variable being populated with data.

Stop hooks

But what about having an update of an object's state automatically logged to the console every time the code is stopped? Then we wouldn't need to go through all this typing, and as we continue debugging, we only need to worry about where to set breakpoints.

To do that, we can add a so-called **one-liner** to a breakpoint that is then attached to a **stop hook**.

Run the code again, and this time when the code halts, enter the following into the LLDB console:

```
(lldb) b logReport
(lldb) target stop-hook add --one-liner "po report"
```

The first line creates a breakpoint and names it `logReport`.

The second line attaches a command to that breakpoint, equivalent to selecting the Debugger command from the **Edit Breakpoint...** menu as we did in the previous chapter, which does the same as if we had typed `po report` ourselves.

Now add breakpoints to the next three lines of code, so that the code stops at each:

```
28
29  let report = Report()
30
31  report.title = "Weekly Summary"
32  report.date = Date()
33  report.approved = true
34
```

Use the `continue` command (or just c) to move from one breakpoint to the next, and you'll see that, each time, we get a description of the `report` current state.

 Later on, we'll see that there is a way to log an object's state every time it changes, without it being dependent on halting the code and without our having to specify where the changes take place.

Printing formatted numbers

LLDB contains its own formatting functionality, so when necessary we can format integers before they are printed to the console.

We can print an integer as is, using the p command:

```
(lldb) p 111
(Int) $R10 = 111
```

We can print its binary representation using the p/t command (the t stands for two):

```
(lldb) p/t 111
(Int) $R11 = 0b0000...lots of zeroes...001101111
```

A hexadecimal representation is also available, using the p/x command:

```
(lldb) p/x 111
(Int) $R12 = 0x000000000000006f
```

An octal representation is available with the p/o command:

```
(lldb) p/o 111
(Int) $R13 = 0157
```

Executing code from LLDB

One of LLDB's great strengths is its ability to reach into the current state of the program and alter it.

So, for example, we could change the title property of our report object while the code is halted on a later breakpoint, with this code:

```
expr report.title = "Monthly Summary"
```

After this, the code runs as if `"Monthly Summary"` had been entered all along.

This is an essential tool to master when debugging; the ability to change values on the fly can save you hundreds of program relaunches in a single day's debugging or prototyping.

Type lookups

This one is short, but sweet. Using the `type lookup` command, we get a summary of whatever type we may be interested in.

Taking a very small class, our own `Report` class, as an example, type the following into LLDB:

```
(lldb) type lookup Report
```

This will produce output to the console like the following:

```
class Report : CustomDebugStringConvertible {
var title: Swift.String?
var date: Foundation.Date?
var approved: Swift.Bool?
var debugDescription: Swift.String {
  get {}
}
@objc deinit
init()
}
```

Now try it again with a few other types. Try this:

```
(lldb) type lookup Array
```

We won't reproduce the output here (it's quite extensive), but it will give you an idea of just how much information is only an LLDB command away.

Breakpoints in LLDB

We can add breakpoints of all types, and configure them to our requirements, from within LLDB, and with a little practice you'll find this is a whole lot quicker (as well as being more flexible) than clicking in the breakpoint gutter, right-clicking the breakpoint, and wading through the breakpoint edit window (which rather bizarrely is extremely easy to dismiss accidentally).

It might take a while before you're convinced of this, but try to remember the time that you quit Macintosh or OS X apps using the menus.

Adding a breakpoint

To set a breakpoint that is in the current scope, use this command:

```
(lldb) breakpoint set --line 56
```

This can be abbreviated to:

```
(lldb) b 56
```

To set a breakpoint somewhere else, add the name of the file after the `--file` option:

```
(lldb) breakpoint set --file AppDelegate.swift --line 17
```

You can also set a breakpoint by specifying a method name:

```
(lldb) breakpoint set --method testBreakpoints
```

Imagine setting two dozen breakpoints, across a number of files, some by name, some by line number, and doing it all with the mouse. This console business is seriously faster.

Breakpoint list

We can inspect a detailed list of all the breakpoints, of whatever type, and whether they are user or project--bound breakpoints, with the following command:

```
(lldb) breakpoint list
```

Or its shorter version:

```
(lldb) br li
```

Attaching commands to breakpoints

Using the breakpoint list, take note of one of the breakpoints (set an extra one if you have to), which you will alter once you have hit the first breakpoint set in your code.

With the program execution halted on that first breakpoint, type the following into the LLDB console (using a breakpoint number from your own breakpoint list):

```
(lldb) breakpoint command add 4.1
```

You will be prompted to add the command:

```
Enter your debugger command(s).  Type 'DONE' to end.
>
```

So, do as it says:

```
Enter your debugger command(s).  Type 'DONE' to end.
> bt
> DONE
```

We have chosen bt here--as it's a nice big dump of data onto the console, we won't miss it.

Now type:

```
(lldb) c
```

to continue execution, and the program will continue, until it halts at breakpoint 4.1 (or whichever breakpoint you added the command to), and prints the backtrace to the console.

Creating a Swift Error breakpoint

We saw in the last chapter that we can select **Swift Error** from the breakpoint types list at the bottom of the breakpoint navigator pane (using the + button), and this can also be done (substantially more quickly) directly in LLDB.

```
(lldb) breakpoint set -E swift
```

Or we can abbreviate this to one of the following:

```
(lldb) br s -E swift
(lldb) b -E swift
```

We can also restrict the breakpoint to a specific error type:

```
(lldb) b -E swift -O myError
```

For a further discussion of error breakpoints, see the previous chapter's Different types of breakpoint section.

Naming breakpoints

You can create *de facto* groups of breakpoints by naming them. Multiple breakpoints can share a name, and by referring to that name you can enable, disable, and delete all those breakpoints with a single command:

```
(lldb) br set -n testStepCommands -N group1
Breakpoint 3: 2 locations.
(lldb) br set -n testBreakpoints -N group1
Breakpoint 4: 2 locations.
(lldb) breakpoint disable group1
2 breakpoints disabled.
```

Having created two breakpoints that share the name `group1`, we then disable them by passing the `breakpointdisable` command the name of the group.

Watchpoints

We mentioned earlier that we were going to explore a way to log any changes to variables without having to stop the code. This is where we do that.

 We could, of course, use the variable's setter and getter methods to do this, but the point here is that we don't need to change the program's code, recompile, and so on; all of this can be done without restarting the app.

The syntax and console output of watchpoints is generally similar to that of breakpoints, as is made clear from the following input (and console output):

```
(lldb) watchpoint set variable x
```

LLDB confirms `watchpoint` creation with the details of the `watchpoint`:

```
Watchpoint created: Watchpoint 1: addr = 0x7fff5fbfec48 size = 8 state =
enabled type = w
 declare @ '/Users/stu/Documents/Books/myBooks/Packt/macOS
Programming/Content/ch17 LLDB
CLI/5623_18_code/5623_18_code/ViewController.swift:93'
watchpoint spec = 'x'
```

When you run code containing a `watchpoint`, you are basically creating a breakpoint that is attached to a variable rather than a line of code.

Adding conditions and commands

You can also attach conditions to `watchpoint`, just as you can to a breakpoint:

```
(lldb) watchpoint modify -c (x==2)
```

And similarly, `command add` works just as you would expect it to:

```
(lldb) watchpoint command add 1
Enter your debugger command(s).  Type 'DONE' to end.
> print x
> DONE
```

So now you can monitor the progress and state of a variable without disturbing the code at all.

In the preceding code, we simply assign a debugger command to `watchpoint 1`; but how did we get the number of the `watchpoint`? By checking the `watchpoint` list.

Watchpoint lists

Just as for breakpoints, we can get a list of watchpoints, using the following command:

```
(lldb) watchpoint list
```

This gives us a detailed list of all watchpoints, similar to the list below:

```
Number of supported hardware watchpoints: 4
Current watchpoint:
Watchpoint 1: addr = 0x7fff5fbfec48 size = 8 state = enabled type = w
declare @ '/Users/stu/Documents/Books/myBooks/Packt/macOS
Programming/Content/ch17 LLDB
CLI/5623_18_code/5623_18_code/ViewController.swift:93'
watchpoint spec = 'x'
```

 Watchpoints must be small. An `Int` of `Bool` is okay, a `String` object will be too large.

Enabling, disabling, and deleting watchpoints

The syntax for disabling, enabling, and deleting `watchpoints` is the same as for breakpoints:

```
(lldb) watchpoint disable
All watchpoints disabled. (1 watchpoints)
```

This disables `watchpoints` only, not breakpoints

```
(lldb) watchpoint delete
About to delete all watchpoints, do you want to do that?: [Y/n]
y
All watchpoints removed. (1 watchpoints)
```

Persistent customization

If you want LLDB to run commands as it starts up, such as defining a list of watchpoints, breakpoints (and a whole ton of other stuff), you can place them in the `.lldbinit` file, at these paths:

- `~.lldbinit-Xcode` for LLDB within the Xcode debug console
- `~/.lldbinit` for LLDB in the command line

My `.initlldb` file contains a group of named symbolic breakpoints, for things such as `viewDidLoad`, which are of use in most projects but are also disabled by the same file:

```
breakpoint set -n viewDidLoad -N vdl
```

```
breakpoint disable vdl
```

When I need them for debugging I just need to enable them by name, as opposed to defining them from scratch. This is particularly appropriate when breakpoints and watchpoints are a complicated combination of conditions, commands, and so on.

Getting help in LLBD

The following command will provide you with the online docs regarding breakpoints and watchpoints:

```
(lldb) help breakpoint
(lldb) help watchpoint
```

Of course, you can access the complete help pages with the following:

```
(lldb) help
```

Try to get accustomed to using the help pages; they contain a lot of information that is otherwise difficult (or tedious) to find, and overcoming any (understandable) reticence to dive into them is better done sooner rather than later.

Using shell commands in LLDB

You can send shell commands to the system without leaving LLDB by using the `platform shell` command:

```
(lldb) platform shell pwd
/path/to/current/directory...
```

Often, being able to type in these one liners will save you breaking the flow while opening up a Terminal window, navigating to the current directory and so on. Given that shell commands can achieve almost anything on Unix-based machines, you might be tempted to spend a fair amount of time getting used to doing this. Forgot to launch your local server? No problem, just drop into the shell and fire up the server, and then return to the debug session.

REPL in LLDB

The Swift REPL also runs in LLDB.

Actually, whenever you use the Swift REPL, it is running in LLDB. The next time you're running the REPL in a terminal window, try typing a colon, and you'll suddenly discover you were running LLDB all along.

To run the Swift REPL from the LLDB console, type `repl`:

```
(lldb) repl
1>
```

Now the REPL prompt is awaiting input. A session might look something like this:

```
(lldb) repl
1> var a = [1,2]
a: [Int] = 2 values {
```

```
  [0] = 1
  [1] = 2
}
2> a.append(3)
3> a
$R0: [Int] = 3 values {
  [0] = 1
  [1] = 2
  [2] = 3
}
4>
```

This comes in really handy when you need to check an idea in Swift while you are, for example, in the middle of an LLDB session.

Switching between LLDB and Swift REPL

While in the REPL, you can still punch through to <indexentry state="new" content="Swift REPL:LLDBthe underlying LLDB session by prepending a command with a colon:

```
2> :type lookup Report
class Report : CustomDebugStringConvertible {
var title: Swift.String?
var date: Foundation.Date?
var approved: Swift.Bool?
var debugDescription: Swift.String {
  get {}
}
@objc deinit
init()
    }
```

In this example, we've printed a summary of our `Report` class (from a REPL session that knows nothing of that class) by using LLDB's `type lookup` command preceded by the colon.

Leaving a REPL session

To leave the REPL and return to LLDB, type just a colon on its own:

```
(lldb) repl
4> print("repl says hi")
 repl says hi
5> :
 (lldb)
```

The REPL session has not ended, however. If you re-enter it with the `repl` command, the variables you defined previously are still in scope. As long as you don't terminate the LLDB session, you can switch between the two as necessary.

Using Python in LLDB

LLDB has full, built-in `Python support`. If you type `script` into the LLDB console, it will open a Python REPL:

```
(lldb) script
Python Interactive Interpreter. To exit, type 'quit()', 'exit()'.
>>>
```

This is about as powerful a scripting language as you are likely to come across, and now it's just waiting there for you to use it. We'll see an example of what it can do shortly, once we have seen how to reach into the debug session from within the Python REPL.

Accessing program variables from Python

The Python REPL has a number of tools with which you can reach into your program's session:

```
>>> mynumber = lldb.frame.FindVariable("i")
>>> mynumber.GetValue()
'42'
```

So, we have the entire Python scripting language at our disposal, with access to the running program's variables. We saw in the last chapter how we can attach Python scripts to a breakpoint; now we can run spontaneous ad hoc Python sessions as well. Pretty amazing stuff!

Switching between LLDB and Python REPL

Enter `quit` to leave the Python REPL.

However, just as we saw with the Swift REPL, the Python REPL session is not killed as long as the LLDB session is not terminated:

```
(lldb) script
Python Interactive Interpreter. To exit, type 'quit()', 'exit()'.
>>> a = 1
>>> quit
```

```
(lldb) script
Python Interactive Interpreter. To exit, type 'quit()', 'exit()'.
>>> a
1
>>>
```

This ability to switch seamlessly between the two without interrupting either LLDB or the REPL makes this a killer feature of LLDB.

One liners from LLDB to Python

You can also pass a line of Python to the script command and have it executed without entering the REPL:

```
(lldb) script import os
(lldb) script os.system("open http://www.apple.com")
```

Once again, we see an enormous amount of scripting power at our disposal.

Getting help in Python

There is a pretty huge help document available with the following command from within LLDB:

```
(lldb) script help(lldb)
```

Or use the following command for a smaller, more manageable doc set:

```
(lldb) script help(lldb.process)
```

From these documents you have access to more specific topics about Python in LLDB.

 It has to be said that these docs are going to be of more use to an experienced Python programmer who is integrating Python into his or her workflow. To learn Python from scratch (and you should, it's easy), you're better off checking out more tutorial-orientated resources.

Altogether now

Looking over the last few sections, you can see that, from the debug console, you can run LLDB, shell commands, the Swift REPL, and a Python REPL, all without having to kill the running debug session or fire up the Terminal. Once you get comfortable with making use of this, it becomes an indispensable part of the development process.

Standalone LLDB

Starting with Xcode 8, LLDB can run in a standalone Terminal session. To launch it, type the `lldb` command:

```
~ lldb
(lldb)
```

This is great for exploring LLDB, but prototyping and debugging an Xcode project is what we are here for, so let's do that next.

Running Xcode projects in a standalone LLDB session

To debug an Xcode project, we first need the path of the debug build, which we can get by right-clicking on the `Products` folder in the Project Navigator, and selecting **Show in Finder**:

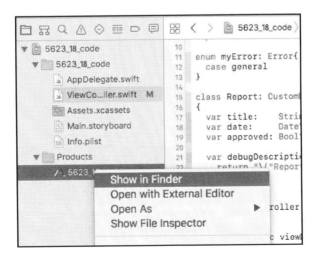

Now add that path as the argument to the `lldb` command (dragging the build from the Finder into the Terminal window is a pretty quick way to do that):

```
~ lldb /Users/.../Build/Products/Debug/5623_18_code.app
```

Hit *return*. This will produce something similar to the following output:

```
(lldb) target create
"/Users/.../Build/Products/Debug/5623_18_code.app"
Current executable set to
'/Users/.../Build/Products/Debug/5623_18_code.app' (x86_64).
```

We haven't got the code running yet, and we'll set a breakpoint before we do:

```
(lldb) breakpoint set --file ViewController.swift --line 31
Breakpoint 2: where = 5623_18_code`_623_18_code.ViewController.viewDidLoad
() -> () + 12 at ViewController.swift:31, address = 0x0000000100001bdc
```

Now run the code:

```
(lldb) run
```

Once we hit that breakpoint, something resembling the following output will be generated:

```
Process 32522 launched:
'/Users/.../Build/Products/Debug/5623_18_code.app/Contents/macOS/5623_18_co
de' (x86_64)
Process 32522 stopped
* thread #1: tid = 0x2039e3, 0x0000000100001bdc
5623_18_code`ViewController.viewDidLoad(self=0x0000000100a69620) -> () + 12
at ViewController.swift:31,
queue = 'com.apple.main-thread',
stop reason = breakpoint 2.1
frame #0: 0x0000000100001bdc
5623_18_code`ViewController.viewDidLoad(self=0x0000000100a69620) ->
() + 12 at ViewController.swift:31
     28
     29          override func viewDidLoad()
     30          {
 -> 31            super.viewDidLoad()
     32
     33            let report = Report()
     34            report.title = "Weekly Summary"
(lldb)
```

As we can see (there's even a little arrow and a code excerpt), the code has been stopped at line 31, as required.

Let's print details of the View Controller's `view` property while we're here:

```
(lldb) p self.view
(NSView) $R0 = 0x0000000100d18070 {
AppKit.NSResponder = {
baseNSObject@0 = {
  isa = NSView
}
_nextResponder = 0x0000000100d324f0
}
}
(lldb)
```

Now we can type `c` to continue the program's execution; but what happens then is that the terminal's input no longer goes to LLDB, which you will notice by the absence of the `(lldb)` prompt. It is going to the running program.

You need to type *control + C* to get back to LLDB.

To return to using the terminal for input to the program, type `c` to continue. Using these two commands, you can toggle between LLDB and the running process, should you need to.

Differences between standalone and Xcode LLDB

There are a few important things to note about running standalone LLDB sessions:

- An LLDB session that is running in a Terminal window ignores all Xcode breakpoints (and other sessions).
- A command line session is available all of the time, without necessarily having to halt the program's execution.
- We can have two (or more) open processes at the same time by launching from different terminal sessions (that is, Terminal app windows). This means we can try variations in our code at the same time:
  - We can use different variable values
  - We can set different breakpoints and watchpoints

Some of these differences make clear the advantages that a standalone session offers over LLDB running in Xcode. We won't necessarily need these features all the time, but it's a good idea to get comfortable with debugging in a separate app. When you do need those features, you'll be glad you did.

Summary

In this chapter, we have had more than a superficial glimpse of Xcode and LLDB's advanced features, though there is more to discover here than we could fit into a couple of chapters.

You have learned the following in this chapter:

- Using LLDB's advanced debugging features
- Making your custom classes debug-printable
- Running your projects in standalone LLDB sessions
- Using stop hooks and watchpoints in addition to breakpoints
- Using shell, Swift, and Python commands in an LLDB session in addition to LLDB's own command set

The next chapter will present the integration and use of third-party frameworks and SDKs in your projects, which will also involve some work on the command line.

19
Deploying Third - Party Code

Whatever it does, your app almost certainly does a lot of stuff that other apps do. This is the whole reason why frameworks exist, and Cocoa's frameworks supply you with a huge number of classes and structs that save you writing all that code again. A framework is, in the end, nothing more than some lines of finished code, possibly accompanied by resources such as images or localized strings, which is made available to your project.

There are likely to be times when the functionality you need to write is not available from any Cocoa framework, or is not in a form that suits your requirements. And on many of these occasions, you'll find that someone else has faced the same situation, and has made their solution available to other developers, often for free.

So this chapter deals with the reasons for and against using other people's code, and covers some of the ways that we can integrate that code into our own projects.

We will be covering the following topics:

- The uses, pros, and cons of integrating third-party code
- Third-party code distribution methods
- Manual installation of third-party code
- Native installation using the Swift Package Manager
- Third-party alternatives that are available

We'll begin by answering the question: Why would I need third-party code?

Common use cases

Sometimes it's great to re-invent the wheel. And sometimes it's just not.

A developer may release a framework in some specialized area. She may have spent months, or even years, working on it, and you have insufficient time or expertise to develop a custom solution of your own.

Often, a client will see some fancy UI feature in another app, and add it to the requirements for the app that you are being paid to build.

Some functionality cannot be built by yourself, however skilled you are. Analytics frameworks, for example, are full of proprietary code that is deliberately encapsulated in a framework, and thus hidden from view. Google is happy for you to use their engines, but they don't necessarily want you rewriting their code.

Distribution methods

This section offers some very general information on the different ways in which third-party code can be shared.

Third - party source code

This is the simplest way to make use of code that somebody else has made available. You just need to get the source code file, import it into your projects, and you're ready to go. Assuming, that is, that the source code doesn't need other third-party code itself, which you'll need to find, and add, if it does.

Third - party libraries

Libraries are basically collections of source code files. There are no other resources; it's all code, usually with some theme or functionality that binds them together.

You are already using libraries all the time. From your very first line of Swift, you have been using the Swift Standard Library, for example, which defines much of the most basic layer of Swift functionality, including:

- Fundamental data types, such as `Int` and `String`
- Data structures, such as `Array` and `Dictionary`
- Protocols, such as `Comparable` and `Error`

There are many, many more libraries out there that offer things that Cocoa doesn't.

Third-party frameworks

Frameworks may include source code files, but are not limited to them. A framework can also contain assets, such as images and other resources; for example, XML data. It may also contain libraries, and possibly different versions of those libraries.

In fact the term `framework` is rather fuzzily defined, and may contain anything that a developer wishes to make available to a project.

One buzzword that is very popular in the blogosphere at the moment is *Inversion of Control*, meaning that our app supplies details for use by the code that is contained within the framework, but that the framework itself takes over the running of the app, calling on our code when necessary, that is "Don't call us, we'll call you" (also referred to as the *Hollywood Principle*).

However, the term *framework*, as used in this book, and by Apple themselves, does not necessarily imply such an inversion. A framework may very well offer no more than prefabricated, passive classes and methods that are then at our disposal.

But the Internet says...

There are a lot of varying opinions out there as to what exactly separates libraries and frameworks. The meaning of libraries is pretty much universally agreed on, but frameworks are more difficult to define (or at least, more difficult to agree on). Add to that the fact that Apple also has its own idea of what frameworks are, and you could be forgiven for finding it very hard to see the wood for the trees.

At the moment, it's not that important to get deeply into the semantics. The fact is, any third-party code you'll use will come in whatever form it comes. It may give you a few options, which we'll look at shortly, but you'll probably find some installation documentation along with the source code. Whether the vendor of the code calls it a framework, or a library, or an SDK (software development kit) will have very little effect on anything.

Pros and cons

Using third-party code is not always the best way to go (that is, assuming that you have found third-party code that meets your requirements), but rejecting it outright is similarly unwise.

The decision ultimately rests with whatever combination of requirements, timelines, developers, managers, and clients is involved in a project (as well as all of those who have been involved on the project in the past, if that's the case).

But let's take a look at both sides of the scales.

The case for third - party code

There are very good reasons to use third-party code. Some very good developers do it all the time, and most do it often. So here are some reasons to resist the temptation to announce proudly *I don't use third-party code on principle*:

- Time. Very often, you'll save yourself hours, days, or even weeks of coding, by using code that someone else has written already. Before you decide that rewriting a ton of source code will be a great learning experience, it's worth considering how much time that learning experience is really worth. And your client might have an opinion here, too.
- Using popular, well established libraries and frameworks means that you are adding peer-reviewed, well tested code to your project. The time you spend in writing the code yourself may fade into insignificance next to the time you'll spend discovering, tracking down, and fixing bugs in your brand new, custom code.

- Using popular, well-established libraries makes life way easier for other developers who are working with you, or taking over a project after you have finished. Many libraries have become *de facto* standards, familiar to a large proportion of developers.
- Third-party code may well have been written and refined by someone with skills that you don't possess. That may be because you don't have decades of professional experience, or because the code is in an area in which you don't work all day, every day.
- Often, a client will see something shiny in an app somewhere, and say "I want that." It won't always be necessary, or tasteful, or easy to integrate, but some customers are always right. And if it's open source, why make your life difficult?

These considerations all assume you have a choice, of course. If you need to add digital rights management libraries to your video-on-demand player, for example, the question becomes moot; there is no alternative to integrating external code.

These aren't the only pros, but they do cover the most significant use-cases.

The case against

Why wouldn't we save ourselves a load of work, and integrate something off the shelf into our projects?

- Generic code is fat; it will inevitably contain more code than you need, and the methods used will need to cover more use cases than yours, and may not be the best possible solution for your requirements.
- The afore mentioned inversion of control will not always be ideal; you must do it the framework's way, and that might not be the best way for your project.
- You don't know code like you know your own code. Anything you have written yourself, you're likely to know more intimately than any code you download from the Web, and that knowledge may become crucial as a project grows in size and complexity. Increased complexity always comes at a cost.
- Third-party code is updated according to someone else's schedule, not yours. When the platform changes, or frameworks upon which that third-party code itself relies change, you'll just have to wait it out, until everything gets fixed. And one day, it won't be fixed at all.
- Keeping all the external code you use up--to--date introduces management issues of its own. Increased complexity always comes at a cost. Again.

The take-away

The upshot of all this is that you'll most likely need to use third-party code sooner or later, but don't consider it a silver bullet for all your needs. Nor is the situation set in stone; the need for such code may come and go, and Cocoa may well have developed its own solution after a particular framework gains widespread adoption, thus reducing the rationale for using that framework.

A case study

A few years ago, it was fair to say that Cocoa's native code for dealing with HTTP connections and requests left something to be desired. The Objective C `NSURLConnection` framework, as it was called then, was clunky, a lot of work, and presented a steep learning curve to anyone not already acquainted with what can be a most confusing topic anyway.

Into the breach stepped several developers, offering libraries that significantly simplified and streamlined the process of communicating with the Internet. The most widely used was `AFNetworking`, by Mattt Thomson (yep, three T's). It made life so much easier, and was so successful, that it seemed that more projects used it than didn't.

Fast-forward a few years, and we now have Swift and the `URLSession` framework, which learned a lot from third-party solutions, and is generally as easy to use as the `AFNetworking` Swift successor, `Alamofire`.

It is certainly worth resisting the knee-jerk reaction to include a framework just because we always did so in the past. And if you are new to networking anyway, it is essential to learn the Cocoa native code upon which a framework such as `Alamofire` is built.

However great a debt we owe to Mattt for his excellent contribution to the community (and it is a huge debt, it must be said), we still need to focus first and foremost on the needs of the project at hand, and there are many occasions on which native code will be more appropriate.

Leaving it till later

Be sure to do this now; because now you have the time. You don't want to be learning the ins and outs of third-party code integration in the middle of some time--critical project.

While it is possible and very satisfying, to create our own frameworks, we won't be covering this here.

Different installation methods

There are several ways to both download and install third-party code, whether it be a single source code file, or an entire framework (including any other frameworks it depends on):

- Downloading, installing, and updating source code files manually
- Using the Swift Package Manager
- Using third-party package managers, such as Cocoapods or Carthage

We will focus on the first two of these methods. The first is probably the simplest under many circumstances, and the second probably has the brightest future.

We'll use Ruoyu Fu and Pinglin Tang's **SwiftyJSON** framework, for a number of reasons that pertain to this chapter:

- It's easy to install and test
- It can be installed by any of the aforementioned methods
- You might like it and find a use for it

The GitHub repo, including all the docs, can be found here:
`https://github.com/SwiftyJSON/SwiftyJSON.`

This is not to say that I think you need this library, just that it works, simply and reliably, which makes it pretty suitable for our purposes.

Manual source code integration

To install the source code, which in this case, by the way, is a single Swift file, we need to do the following:

1. Get the source code.
2. Add it to the project.

This is not very complicated at all. The code is located at GitHub:
`https://github.com/SwiftyJSON/SwiftyJSON`.

There are two approaches to downloading the source code:

- Download the ZIP file from the GitHub repo
- Clone

Either way, you need to click the **Clone or download** button:

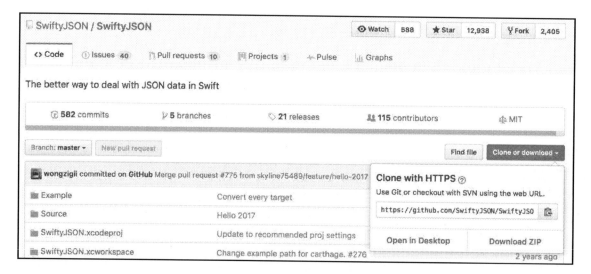

Downloading the ZIP

This is as easy as it sounds. Download the file to somewhere convenient, and when you unpack it you'll see, among many other things, a file named `SwiftyJSON.swift`.

Cloning the repo

If you have never cloned a repository before, you may have to use the command line to install a couple of other programs first. Don't let this put you off; it's something you need to have done anyway, and takes just a few commands in the Terminal app.

Preparing to clone

This is more work at first, but it only needs doing once, and it's unavoidable in the long run. There is no way to skirt around Git (and indeed no need to) when doing any sort of non-trivial development work.

If you already have Homebrew and Git installed on your system, skip to the section entitled *Cloning the repo.*

Installing Homebrew

To install Git, we'll need Homebrew, which is a package manager. A package manger manages packages on Unix, and packages on Unix usually means programs. So it's like a command line App Store, where everything's free. To download it, we need to use **Ruby** in the command line, which is installed by default on macOS.

Open up a Terminal window and enter the following all on one line: `/usr/bin/ruby -e` `"$(curl -fsSL` `https://raw.githubusercontent.com/Homebrew/install/master/install)"`.

Hit *return* and, in a few moments, Homebrew will be installed and available to you on the command line.

Further info about Homebrew is available at: `http://brew.sh`.

Installing Git

Now that we have Homebrew, we can use it to install Git.

Enter the following into the command line (without the $ sign):

```
$ brew install git
```

When installation is done, you'll see something similar to the following output in the Terminal window:

```
/usr/local/Cellar/git/2.9.0: 1,424 files, 31.3M, built in 1 minute 7
seconds
```

A full set of setup instruction for Git is beyond our scope here, but at a minimum you'll need to enter the two following lines into the Terminal:

```
$ git config --global user.name "YOUR_NAME_HERE"
$ git config --global user.email "yourmail@yourserver.com"
```

More information (much, much more) is available at: `https://git-scm.com`.

Once you have Git installed and configured, you can clone the repo.

Cloning the repository

The reason that we'd want to go to the trouble of cloning the repo, rather than just downloading it, is that with a cloned repository you have a directory that is a direct copy of the online repo, which you can update any time (with the command `git pull`) to update the source code (and any other resources contained in the repo). Cloning gives you a lot more than that, but that is our main reason here. And I never met a dev who didn't like playing around on the command line.

1. Decide where you want to store the cloned repo. It will create a directory of its own, so there is no need to create a directory called `SwiftyJSON_Repo` or some such.
2. Drag the directory onto the Terminal icon in the Dock, so that the Terminal opens a window with that directory as its current working directory.
3. Go to the printed SwiftyJSON page, click on the **Clone or download** button, and copy the URL that is shown.
4. Type the following line into the Terminal window (which uses that URL, but do check that it is still correct):

```
$ git clone https://github.com/SwiftyJSON/SwiftyJSON.git
```

After a few seconds the Terminal window will show something like this:

```
Cloning into 'SwiftyJSON'...
remote: Counting objects: 2534, done.
remote: Compressing objects: 100% (20/20), done.
remote: Total 2534 (delta 7), reused 0 (delta 0), pack-reused 2513
Receiving objects: 100% (2534/2534), 835.55 KiB | 138.00 KiB/s,
done.
Resolving deltas: 100% (1476/1476), done.
Checking connectivity... done.
$
```

Use the **Finder** to check that the directory really is there (it will be).

Importing the source code

The file we need can be found at: `SwiftyJSON/Source/SwiftyJSON.swift`.

1. Type *command + option + A* to **Add Files...** to the project, and navigate to the file.
2. Click **Options**, and ensure that **Copy Items if Needed** is ticked.
3. Click **Add**.
4. Select `main.swift` in the project navigator.
5. Contrary to what it might (still) say on the GitHub repo, do *not* add an import statement to the `main.swift` file, but leave the one that is already there.
6. Delete the `"Hello World"` line, if you want.
7. Add the following code to `main.swift`:

```
let json = JSON(["hello", "manual", "installation"])
for str in json
{
  print(str.1)
}
```

8. Run the app, and you should see this output in the debug console:

```
hello
manual
installation
Program ended with exit code: 0
```

And that's it, we're done. The full functionality of SwiftyJSON is now at your disposal.

Swift Package Manager

Now, SwiftyJSON is a simple utility that doesn't depend on any other non-native components to function. But that is by no means always the case, and in larger projects, keeping the third-party frameworks up--to--date, with the necessary (perhaps new) versions of whichever other frameworks they depend on, can become arduous and, worse, error-prone.

Fortunately, there are solutions to this problem. One of them is an integral part of the Swift ecosystem, named the **Swift Package Manager**.

To quote the Swift homepage at `swift.org`:

> *"The Swift Package Manager is a tool for managing the distribution of Swift code. It's integrated with the Swift build system to automate the process of downloading, compiling, and linking dependencies."*

This is just what we need. If a framework, or **package** as we will now call it, requires another package, the Swift Package Manager (SPM, for short) will take care of it, including the downloading, linking, and updating of any necessary files. All we need to do is a little setup, no more than we did for Git, and SPM will take all that error-prone management off our hands.

 The Swift Package Manager is in its infancy. Even officially, SPM is a work in progress. But it is already an excellent tool for our purposes, and I have found it to be both simple and reliable to use. For this reason, it is included here, even though Cocoapods, and to a lesser degree, Carthage, have been around longer.

SPM products

I'd like to quote `swift.org` again:

> *"A target may build either a library or an executable as its product. A library contains a module that can be imported by other Swift code. An executable is a program that can be run by the operating system."*

We see here a loose interpretation of the word `library`.

So, SPM will build an app, which we won't be doing here, or it can build a library package, which we also won't be doing, strictly speaking (the package is built already). We will simply use SPM to download and manage SwiftyJSON, but this time in the form of a package, instead of the source code directly.

 The code in a package may require modules from other packages. These are its **dependencies**. A dependency consists of a relative or absolute URL to the source of the package, as well a set of requirements for the version of the package that is required. SPM's management of all this is recursive. A dependency can have its own dependencies, each of which can also have dependencies, forming a **dependency graph**. It is SPM's job to take care of that dependency graph.

Adding the package to an Xcode project

Most of this is done with just a few commands on the command line:

1. Create a new Xcode project, selecting the **Command Line Tool** template.
2. Use the Terminal to cd into the project directory:

    ```
    $ cd /path/to/project/directory
    ```

    (Or just drag the folder onto the Terminal icon.)

    Now we need to create a Package.swift file.

3. Enter the following into the command line:

    ```
    $ touch Package.swift
    ```

    We'll use Nano to edit the Package.swift file directly in the Terminal.

4. Enter the following into the command line:

    ```
    $ nano Package.swift
    ```

5. Type the following into the opened file:

    ```
    import PackageDescription

    let package = Package(
        name: "YOUR_APP_NAME_HERE",
        dependencies: [
            .Package(url:
                    "https://github.com/SwiftyJSON/SwiftyJSON.git",
                    majorVersion: 3, minor: 1)
        ]
    )
    ```

    Make sure in the name: field that you enter the name of your .xcodeproj file (not including .xcodeproj).

6. Press control + O to write to the file, return to confirm the name and location, and control + X to exit the Nano application.

That's all we need with Nano. It is perfectly acceptable to edit the file in Text Edit, by the way.

7. To download the package, enter the following:

```
$ swift package fetch
```

Within a few seconds, you'll have the package in your project's top directory:

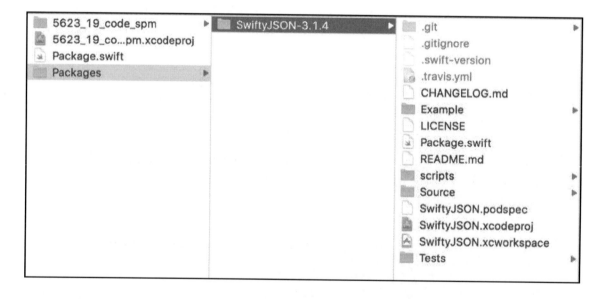

So far, we have the package in the right folder, but Xcode doesn't know anything about it yet.

8. Type the following into the Terminal:

```
$ swift package generate-xcodeproj
```

Swift will have claimed in the Terminal window to have created a `.xcodeproj` file, but for all intents and purposes, it has modified the one we had in there already, to include the contents of the package(s) we have specified in the `Package.swift` file. A look at the project navigator will show that the structure of the project has been altered to conform to the structure required by SPM:

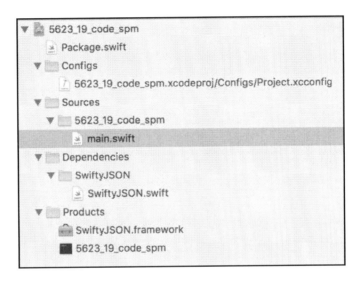

The whole console input (preceded by $) and output will look similar to this:

```
$ touch Package.swift
$ nano Package.swift
$ swift package fetch
Cloning https://github.com/SwiftyJSON/SwiftyJSON.git
HEAD is now at b85a064 Merge pull request #764 from lbrndnr/master
Resolved version: 3.1.4
$ swift package generate-xcodeproj
generated: ./5623_19_code_spm.xcodeproj
$
```

Now we head over to Xcode for the rest. Since we're in the Terminal app, let's use a command to switch to it:

```
$ open 5623_19_code_spm.xcodeproj/
```

This will open our project, just as if we had double-clicked it in the **Finder**.

Over to Xcode

We're almost there.

1. In Xcode, select main.swift in the project navigator, and add the following code:

    ```
    import SwiftyJSON

    let json = JSON(["hello", "swift", "project", "manager"])
    for str in json
    {
      print(str.1)
    }
    ```

     Note that we *do* need to explicitly import the SwiftyJSON package this time.

2. Run the code, and you should get the following output at the debug console:

    ```
    hello
    swift
    project
    manager
    Program ended with exit code: 0
    ```

We're finished. You're now able to use the Swift Package Manager in the command line to add packages and their dependencies to a pre-existing Xcode project.

And at the time of writing, that puts you way ahead of the curve, though it is unlikely to be long before the rest of the field catches you up.

Package baggage

Look in the **Finder** folder, in which the package was downloaded:

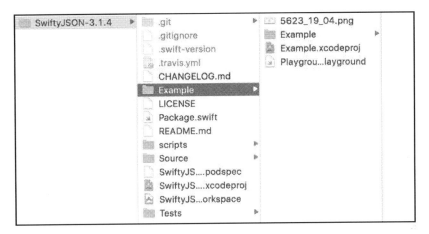

There is a lot there that we don't need, including a whole Xcode project and playground! And this is one drawback of using package managers of any description, whether SPM or one of the others. It's generally a good idea to leave those folders alone, bloated though they are, unless you're sure of what you're doing. But in this case, we can quite safely remove the `Example` directory. It's full of useful information, but it doesn't belong in our project folder.

Other package managers

The Swift Package Manager is the newest of the package managers that are usable with Swift, but there are a couple of others that are certainly worth a mention:

Cocoapods

Cocoapods has been for some years now the de facto standard package and dependency manager for Xcode projects. At the time of writing, Cocoapods has recently changed to version 1.1 from its previous (and long-standing) beta status, and there are a few issues around using it with Swift 3 projects. For this reason, the reader is encouraged to visit the website at: `https://cocoapods.org`.

Installing and using Cocoapods has up till now been reasonably easy, and one assumes that this will soon be the case again.

One thing to note about Cocoapods is that it is fairly intrusive (which, to be fair, is also the case for the Swift Package Manager), creating an `.xcworkspace` file that you will open in place of the `.xcodeproj` file that you usually use. Also, if one library fails to build, all hell breaks loose, and fixing the problem is sometimes something of a test of patience.

But Cocoapods is well supported by most developers that make their Swift code available, including many of the proprietary big players, and that's a huge bonus in favor of pods.

Carthage

SPM and Cocoapods share a couple of characteristics:

- You use their own infrastructure to obtain the libraries you need
- They need to change your Xcode project's structure, in order to integrate those libraries

Carthage takes a different approach, in both these respects. Firstly, it doesn't have its own repositories; you need to find them yourself and add a reference to them in Carthage's configuration file (named `Cartfile`). This usually means simply adding the name of a GitHub repo.

Secondly, once frameworks, and any dependencies, have been downloaded, you perform the steps for integration yourself. On the downside, this is work you do yourself, but on the upside, this is work you do yourself, if you see what I mean.

Many developers prefer this "no smoke and mirrors" approach, and it does offer a significant alternative to SPM and Cocoapods. Ultimately, these things depend on your taste, and your circumstances, and perhaps just as much on what your colleagues are using.

I'll mention here that Carthage is written in Swift, for what it's worth, because everyone always mentions it.

More information can be found at Carthage's own GitHub repo at: `https://github.com/Carthage/Carthage`.

The price of complexity

As with all the shiny toys that are available to developers, package management begs the question: is it worth it? Adding package management in any form undeniably adds another layer of complexity to a project, and as we all know, complexity is the enemy. So it's worth thinking good and hard about whether a project really needs any of the tools covered in this chapter.

If you work alone, and your project only uses a handful of libraries, ones that don't have a complex dependency graph of their own, then there's a good argument for keeping things manual. Changes in the tools won't affect your project, changes in the libraries can be updated manually, and you know exactly what's going on all the time.

If you work in a team, or a large project, that already uses some form of package management, then you have no choice, you need to follow the pack. If you need a proprietary framework that is only available through a package manager, the same holds true.

And between those two extremes is a whole spectrum of cases, some of which will inevitably make package management look very attractive. The reader would certainly be well advised to have at least a passing familiarity with some of these tools. SPM and Carthage are new, and have yet to prove their long-term worth, Cocoa is well established, and has a huge range of packages, but now and again the wheels drop off, and a project grinds to a halt.

Get a feel for these tools and after that, you'll be the one living with whatever decisions you make around package management.

Summary

Third-party code and package management are probably not the sexiest topic in this book, or programming in general. But it's one of those things that you'll run up against sooner or later, and you'll be glad of any exploratory work you do now, particularly if you find yourself in a team environment, where you'll be expected to just run with it.

You have learned about the following topics in this chapter:

- The advantages, and disadvantages, of using third-party code
- The various ways code libraries can be distributed
- The advantages, and disadvantages, of using package management
- Manual installation without any management tools at all
- Native installation using the Swift Package Manager
- Third-party tools: Cocoapods and Carthage
- Homebrew and Git installation and their use in package management

The next chapter wraps up the book with a look at where to go from here.

20
Wrapping It Up

Now that you have an app ready to release to the world, or perhaps to a cohort of app-testers first, you need to wrap up your code and resources in a bundle that is suitable for distribution.

Releasing Apple programs, particularly through the Mac App Store, comes with a lot of hoops to jump through. macOS users benefit from a high level of security and control when it comes to app distribution, a fact that undoubtedly adds to the attraction of the platform. But as developers, we are the ones that need to invest just a little more work in readying our software for release.

In this chapter, which takes you through the whole release and app submission process, you will learn about the following:

- Using suitable settings during project creation and setup
- The requirements of iTunes Connect
- Archiving the app
- Uploading the archive to the App Store
- Exporting the archive for other channels of distribution

App distribution

The process of building and submitting an app to either of the Apple App Stores has become the stuff of legend. In the past, it really hasn't been easy. It seemed to change regularly, was documented poorly, and generally seemed to be absurdly difficult.

Fortunately, things became a lot easier with the release of Xcode 8, which offered what it calls ad hoc code-signing, meaning that in most cases, Xcode will know which certificates and profiles you need, and will talk to the Apple developer portal any time something is missing.

The old way, the hard way, is still available, if you or your organization needs it, but this chapter will make full use of the new ad hoc signing. It's not only easier, it also happens to just work, as they say.

 You may well have already successfully submitted an app to the Mac App Store in the past, and if you have, go with whatever setup you have working for you. The same goes if you have submitted iOS or tvOS apps; there is very little difference. This chapter assumes you have a developer account with Apple, but nothing else.

If you have never done this before, it might be a very good idea to practice first with a dummy app. You can go through the whole process without actually releasing anything into the wild, and doing it now, separately from some brilliant piece of work that you're just dying to get out there, is likely to be a more relaxed, and therefore more productive, experience.

To get an app built and distributed (whether via the App Store or not), we'll need to make sure that we get the following steps covered:

1. Use suitable project settings when creating and setting up a new project.
2. Create an Apple developer account.
3. Add icons to the project and any other iTunes Connect requirements.
4. Archive the source code.
5. Validate the archive.
6. Upload the archive to the App Store.
7. Alternatively, export the archive to create an `.app` or `.pkg` file on disk.

The right settings on project creation

So let's get set up with a dummy app that will do nothing at all. You can simply select the **Cocoa Application** template, bearing a couple of points in mind.

The product name

This is the name of your app as it will appear in the store. It is also the name that will appear in the Finder and Launcher when the app is installed on the machine. If you can, pick something now that you will stick with-it can be changed, but getting it right now saves you changing it in several places later on.

The **Product Name** must be no longer than 255 bytes and be no fewer than two characters. And anyway, if you wanted the name X for your app, it would have been long gone by now.

Team

This will be prepopulated for you if you are a sole developer, and thus a member of only your own team. Otherwise, make sure to pick the right team.

The Organization Identifier

The **Product Name** and **Organization Identifier** are concatenated to create the default **Bundle Identifier** using the reverse domain name service (reverse DNS) notation. This ID needs to be unique to your app, so it's important to set the organization identifier to a string that nobody else will use; the reverse DNS convention assumes that you and only you will use the name of your own domain. So your organization name should resemble this: `com.yourDomain`.

If you don't have a domain, be sure to pick something that will be unique to yourself.

Bundle ID

Using the reverse DNS convention for your organization name will produce a **Bundle Identifier** like this: com.yourDomain.yourApp.

This is done automatically for you in Xcode 8.

Setting up the project

Drag a label into the **View Controller Scene**, so that we can see that the app is indeed running when we hit **Run**.

Before we do anything further, here is something not to do. Don't change this setting:

 Don't click on **Enable Development Signing**. If you do, you'll be handed full control of (and responsibility for) certificate and profile management, and we are going to be avoiding that here.

If you really do need to enable development signing, then there will be aspects of your project and/or team structure that we cannot guess at here and you'll be unlikely to be reading this at all.

Setting the Application Category

Select the app in the project navigator.

In the **General** tab, you must choose an **Application Category** if you choose to submit the app to the Mac App Store:

Enabling sandboxing

Also for the App Store, you'll need to enable the **App Sandbox** in the **Capabilities** tab:

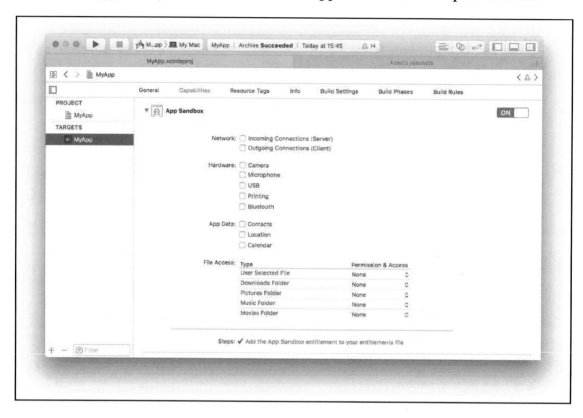

For the purposes of this chapter, we won't activate any of the access parameters listed in the **App Sandbox** section.

 The sandbox restricts the areas of the file system that can be accessed by an app, which provides both security and stability, since one app cannot use or corrupt another's data. Sandboxing is a *Really Good Thing*.

Your developer account

If you haven't created an Apple developer account, you'll need to do so. You'll also need to pay some money for the honor, so keep your credit card handy. The developer portal is here: `https://developer.apple.com`.

We assume here that you have created and configured your account.

You'll want to create a team if you have testers that will test your app on registered development machines other than your own (which we will not cover in depth here, beyond exporting `.app` files that are suitable for such testing).

With your account set up and paid for, you're ready to go.

Registering an app ID

Return to the **Account** window of the developer portal.

Click on **Certificates, Identifiers & Profiles**, and in the following window click on **App IDs** in the **Identifiers** section.

Click on the + button to create a new app ID, and enter the required information. It is essential that the **Bundle ID** field is correctly filled out, so copy it from the project's **Bundle Identifier** field of the **General** tab.

Leave the **App Services** unticked for this app, and click on **Continue**. Confirm the details are correct, then click on **Register**.

You can now leave the developer portal.

Providing the required icons

The built archive, which we will produce shortly, will not pass any of the validation tests or be unloadable to iTunes Connect (that is the App Store) unless we have provided a full set of icons. Creating the icon image assets themselves is beyond the scope of this book, but once you have them, they are a breeze to add to the project.

If you don't have a full set of correctly sized icons lying around, you can download one at: `http://grimshaw.de/macOS-book/macOS_icon_set.zip`.

There are many utility apps out there that will create all these files from a single image. I use **iConeer**, available in the App Store, though there are many others.

In the project navigator, select the `Assets.xcassets` file. Select **AppIcon** in the document organizer, and simple drag the requisite image file from the **Finder** onto the right-hand pane:

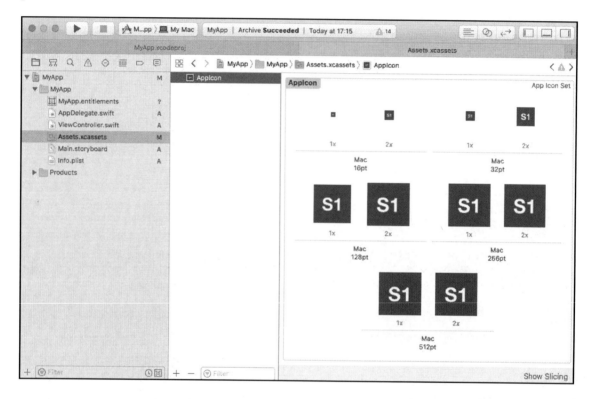

The images will be automatically copied to your project directory:

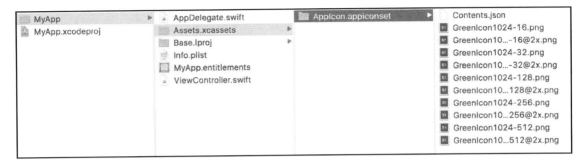

Archiving the app

We now need to produce a `macOS App Archive`.

In the main Xcode menu, select **Product | Archive**.

Archiving generally takes a few seconds, assuming a small app like ours. When it has completed, it will open the **Organizer** window with the new archive selected.

Validating the archive

We can now save ourselves some trouble and frustration further down the line by validating the archive. This validation is done (behind the scenes) by iTunes Connect, and ensures that the archive contains all the necessary resources (for example, the icons), and that the settings are all valid (for example, the **Application Category**).

These tests are repeated later during uploading, but it's better to do them now, while things are still easy to fix.

Hit the **Validate** button:

Choose which validation you need, according to which method of distribution you intend to use: either through the App Store, or directly, by download.

Select your development team in the next dialog box, and click on **Choose**.

The validation process starts by code-signing the app (with Xcode doing all that work for you, ad hoc), and then waits for confirmation that you wish to validate:

Click on **Validate** and wait (for several minutes, it's not terribly quick) for the confirmation that all went well:

Hit **Done**.

You're now ready to either start the process of app submission to the Mac App Store, or export the archive for either testing or distribution.

Uploading to the App Store

To upload the app for submission to the App Store, we first need to prepare an **App Record** in iTunes Connect.

Creating app records in iTunes Connect

Our journey through iTunes Connect starts here: `https://itunesconnect.apple.com`.

Sign in, and click on the **My Apps** button.

On the following page, click the **+** button to add a new app record, selecting **New Mac App**:

1. On the following page, enter the **Name** of the app as you want it to appear in the App Store.

2. Select whatever **Primary Language** is appropriate.
3. Copy the **Bundle Identifier** from the project's **General** tab and paste it into the **Bundle ID** field. Once again, it is imperative that there are no mistakes here.
4. The **SKU** field is a unique ID for your app, in a format of your choice that is not visible on the App Store.
5. Click on **Create**.

iTunes Connect will create the new app record, and take you to the **App Information** page for that app. The **Mac App** status will now read **Prepare for Submission**, meaning two things:

- You're good to go with uploading the archive to the App Store
- You have a whole bunch of info and images to add to the iTunes Connect app record, that we need not cover here; only you have that information

Uploading from Xcode to the App Store

Return to Xcode, and hit **Upload to App Store...**.

Xcode will validate and code-sign the app, build the `.pkg` file, and then upload it to the App Store, confirming that everything went okay with this very welcome dialog box:

Hit **Done**, with a deservedly emphatic flourish.

All that's left to do is complete the iTunes Connect paperwork, and hit **Submit for Review** in the **Mac App** pane on the website.

Oh, and then tap your fingers on the desk for a few days while you wait to hear whether your app has been accepted. If you submitted a dummy app, it won't be, I assure you, so don't do that.

Exporting the app for distribution

Now, what about that **Export...** button?

There are several purposes for which you may wish to export the archive, either as a .pkg or .app file:

- Exporting a finished .pkg file for somebody else to upload to the App Store (unlikely if you're not working in a reasonably large organization)
- Exporting a finished .pkg file to test the Installer package
- Exporting an .app file for ID-signed distribution
- Exporting an .app file for unsigned distribution

Whichever option you choose, exporting creates a date-stamped folder (if you accept the default name before saving it) containing the package.

Preparing an archive for export can take ages, as many files get code-signed, so don't be surprised if you're sitting there for several minutes before anything happens. You might need to allow Keychain Access at some point in the process.

When you click on **Export**, you'll be asked to select the development team, and once you've clicked on the **Choose** button to enter that choice, you'll need to select one of these options:

- **Save for Mac App Store Deployment**
- **Export a Developer ID-signed Application**
- **Export a Development-signed Application**
- **Export as a macOS App**

Let's take a look at what each of these means.

Save for Mac App Store Deployment

Selecting this option will create a .pkg file, which is an Installer package file.

Bear in mind that the **Sandboxing** capability must be set to **On** in the **Capabilities** tab for Mac App Store deployment.

This file can be provided to someone else who may be responsible for uploading the app to the App Store. This is frequently the case in teams that are large enough to separate the responsibilities of development from those of distribution. That person may use Xcode, but is more likely to use the **Application Loader** app from Apple, which facilitates uploading without the whole Xcode show.

Secondly, this file allows you to test the Installer package.

Testing the Installer package

To test the package, don't double-click on the .pkg file, as you would when installing software normally. Instead, use the command line.

Type the following command, substituting your own path and app name:

```
$ sudo installer -store -pkg /path/to/MyApp.pkg  -target /
```

You'll need to enter your user password (the one you log in to your computer with), since we're using sudo.

The output will look something like this:

```
installer: Note: running installer as an admin user (instead of
root) gives better Mac App Store fidelity
```

```
installer: MyApp.pkg has valid signature for submission: 3rd Party Mac
Developer Installer: Your Name (xxxxxx)
installer: Installation Check: Passed
installer: Volume Check: Passed
installer: Bundle com.yourDomain.MyApp will be installed to
/Applications/MyApp.app
installer: Starting install
installer: Install 0.0% complete
installer: Install 100.0% complete
installer: Finished install
```

The installer tells us that everything has a valid signature, as well as what it is installing where. In our very simple case, the only file written was to the user's Applications folder, namely the MyApp.app file.

Export a Developer ID-signed Application

If you intend to intend to distribute your app through media other than the Mac App Store, you can produce a code-signed .app file with this option. This allows your users to run the app without having to disable the Gatekeeper security feature of macOS.

Export a Development-signed Application

This option provides you with an .app file that will only run on machines that have been registered as development devices for your developer account. This means that you, and any testers you may have at your disposal, can run the app on these machines without having to worry about unauthorized copies making it out into the wild. Anyone trying to run a copy of this file without an authorized machine is going to be out of luck.

Export as a macOS App

This option creates an unprotected .app file that can be used by anyone, as long as they are willing to temporarily disable Gatekeeper when running the app for the first time. Files like this may have unfettered access to the user's filesystem and present a serious security risk.

Summary

And those are the basics of package distribution. As the projects grow larger, and as the size of the development team increases, the process can become more complex. It is worth consulting the Apple documentation on a regular basis, as the process continues to evolve.

You have learned the following in this chapter:

- Preparing the project for release
- Fulfilling the requirements of iTunes Connect app record creation
- Adding icons to the project
- Archiving, validating, and uploading an archive to the App Store via iTunes Connect
- Exporting the archive for the purposes of testing and distribution
- Testing the Installer package

And finally

Any book, however large, can only cover a small subset of the vast collection of topics that comprise macOS development. With the material in this book under your belt, you should be well placed to make best use of the huge pool of resources out there, although it is often hard to know where to start (and what to skip).

The book website

Accompanying this book is the following website: `http://grimshaw.de/macOS-book`.

This includes a (very subjective) list of resources for further reading and study, one that I hope will grow with time.

It covers several topics that would have been great to include in the book, but which didn't make it for reasons of space.

It will also record any errata and clarifications, as well updates to the code that become necessary as Swift develops, and there'll be a link through which you can submit feedback on the book, and any suggestions for inclusion on the site itself.

I hope that reading, and working though, this book has been both enjoyable and rewarding. And I hope that it is part of a long journey. There is a lot still to be discovered; Office and Facebook are not the end of the story. The role you play may turn out to be revolutionary or incremental, but either way, software development has much to offer both the developer and the world at large; we are at the very beginning of a digital age that is just a few decades rather than centuries old.

Index

Made in the USA
San Bernardino, CA
23 February 2019